THE TRAVAIL OF NATURE

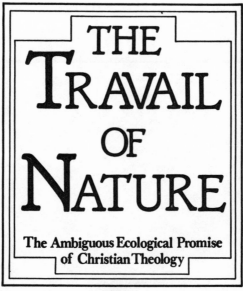

THE TRAVAIL OF NATURE

The Ambiguous Ecological Promise of Christian Theology

H. Paul Santmire

FORTRESS PRESS   **PHILADELPHIA**

Biblical quotations, unless otherwise noted, are from the Revised Standard Version of the Bible, copyright 1946, 1952, © 1971, 1973 by the Division of Christian Education of the National Council of the Churches of Christ in the U.S.A. and are used by permission.

Library of Congress Cataloging in Publication Data

Santmire, H. Paul.
  The travail of nature.

  Includes index.
  1. Nature—Religious aspects—Christianity—History of doctrines. I. Title
BT695.5.S255 1985   261.8'362   84–47934
ISBN 0–8006–1806–8 (pbk.)

K978F84   Printed in the United States of America   1–1806

TO
JOSEPH SITTLER
Pioneering Theologian of Nature

CONTENTS

ACKNOWLEDGMENTS

Selections are reprinted from Augustine *City of God*, in *A Select Library of Nicene and Post-Nicene Fathers*, Series II, Volume II, ed. Philip Schaff (Grand Rapids: Wm. B. Eerdmans, 1955–56). Reprinted by permission of the publisher.

The selection from Edwin A. Burtt, *The Metaphysical Foundations of Modern Physical Science*, rev. ed. (London: Kegan, Paul, Trubner, 1932), is reprinted by permission of Routledge & Kegan Paul, Ltd.

The selection from Albert Camus, *The Rebel*, trans. Anthony Bower (New York: Alfred A. Knopf, Inc., 1954). Copyright © Alfred A. Knopf, Inc. Reprinted by permission of the publisher.

Quotations are reprinted from Mircea Eliade, *The Sacred and the Profane* (New York: Harper & Row, 1957).

Selections are reprinted from Allen D. Galloway, *The Cosmic Christ* (London: James Nisbet & Co., 1951). Used by permission of James Nisbet & Co.

The selection from Zachary Hayes, *The Hidden Center: Spirituality and Speculative Christology in St. Bonaventure* (New York: Paulist Press, 1981). Copyright © Paulist Press. Used by permission of the publisher.

The quotation from HOW GREAT THOU ART by Stuart K. Hine. © Copyright 1953, Renewed 1981 by Manna Music, Inc., 2111 Kenmere Ave., Burbank, CA 91504. International Copyright Secured. All Rights Reserved. Used by Permission.

Quotations are reprinted from G. W. H. Lampe, "The New Testament Doctrine of *ktisis*," *Scottish Journal of Theology* 17:4 (December 1964).

The selection from George F. Whicher: THE GOLIARD POETS. Copyright 1949 by George F. Whicher. Reprinted by permission of New Directions Publishing Corporation.

The selection from Charles T. Wood, *The Age of Chivalry: Manners and Morals 1000–1450* (New York: Universe Books, 1970). Copyright © 1970 by Charles T. Wood. Reprinted by permission of the author.

PREFACE

This study is written with two sometimes overlapping groups of people in mind: first, environmentalists, students of ecology, humanists, and all others who are concerned about our attitudes toward the natural world; second, those who have self-consciously identified themselves with the Christian faith, and who are concerned to become better acquainted with the teachings of their own tradition concerning the meaning and value of the natural world.

To the first group, I address this invitation. I encourage you to approach the Christian tradition with an open mind, to assess both its strengths and its weaknesses, as far as our attitudes toward nature are concerned. Although I am a believer and take my own tradition with utmost seriousness, I can well imagine that people who stand in other religious traditions or who espouse no religion at all might well benefit from a study such as this one, since the Christian tradition is indeed a spiritual force to be reckoned with today, as in earlier years, for better or for worse. In a day when the Christian tradition has received a lot of bad press from environmentalists and others with reference to its alleged failure to take nature seriously, I hope that this study will correct some uncritical judgments, while it attempts to assess some liabilities as well in a critical fashion.

To the second group, to those who self-consciously identify themselves with the Christian faith, I address a similar word. Some of you are suspicious of any kind of interest in the theology of nature. Be assured that I am aware of many, if not all, of the reasons for your suspicion. I hope to show you that the theology of nature need not be a theologically questionable area of interest, indeed that it can be richly rewarding. On the other hand, to others who, perhaps in light of selected biblical passages—from the Psalms to the saying of Jesus about the lilies of the field—assume that the Christian theological tradition as a matter of course affirms nature and prompts us to cherish good stewardship of the environment, I say, look with me at the evidence. Our tradition *is* promising, as far as the development of new and positive attitudes toward nature is concerned. But it is also ambiguous in many respects, sometimes profoundly ambiguous. I invite you to be both affirmative and critical of the tradition.

The reader will soon see that this study covers a vast amount of territory. From a scholarly point of view, it is perhaps more than ambitious. But I would like to think that this book can be of service to those who wish to go no further at this point, who are seeking a generally accurate and instructive introduction to Christian thought about nature. For others, who wish to pursue the subject in greater detail, I hope that this study can be a good beginning: that it has explored what has hitherto been a mostly obscure area in the history of Christian thought with a point of view and sufficient thoroughness that will encourage further research and discussion.

Throughout I have obviously had to depend heavily on the work of many others. At times, to be sure, in the absence of available studies or when recognized historians or theologians in a given context were evidently concerned with other questions, I have had to look at the data afresh and draw my own conclusions. Although I have made every effort to present those data fairly and clearly, and my thesis judiciously, I have no illusions about anyone being able to explore some three millennia of a religious tradition in ten chapters in a way that will measure up to everyone's canons of historical research or meet everyone's expectations about the proper course of a theological argument. I hope then that this study will be judged finally in terms of the adequacy of its approach and the suggestiveness of its thesis.

The book is dedicated to Joseph Sittler, a pioneering theologian of nature in our time, with the hope that it may lend some modest support to his own elegant theological program. I have learned a great deal from him over the years.

I also want to mention the names of three colleagues, each of whom read part or all of my manuscript at various points in its history: Professor Richard Baer, Jr., Cornell University; Professor Clifford Green, Hartford Seminary; and Professor Mark U. Edwards, Purdue University. I want to thank them publicly for their helpfulness, but assure them too that I take full responsibility for the argument which follows.

In addition, I want to thank the members of Grace Lutheran Church, Hartford, Connecticut, for their constant support and affection. Without that community of Christian friends, I would never have had the spiritual energy I needed to complete this project.

Most of all, however, I want to thank my wife and children for their love and their patience while I was working on this study for long periods and at many odd hours during the past several years. Now I hope to be able to take a few more walks over to the park with them, as I feel less called to sequester myself in the thicket of papers around my desk.

Note: Regarding Classroom Use

The argument of this book unfolds sequentially. Its force is cumulative. Its whole shape cannot be fully seen in any one of its parts, especially since it traces the story of a sometimes subtle ambiguity and an occasionally elusive promise. The reader will benefit most fully from an encounter with the claims of this book if he or she walks with me, so to speak, each step of the way.

At the same time, I am aware from thirteen years of college teaching that not every volume employed in a course can be assigned to students to read from cover to cover, however desirable that prospect might be from a pedagogical point of view. I have kept this in mind in writing the book.

Most of the historical-descriptive chapters can be read as units in themselves (chapters 3 through 8 especially). If one or more of these chapters is assigned, however, the student should also be asked to read the Introduction (chapter 1) carefully, in particular the brief discussion of the ecological and spiritual motifs (pp. 9–10). It would be wise, in addition, for the student to read two other sections in chapter 2 (pp. 17–29), which also focus on those motifs; and chapter 3, especially the discussion of "the great chain of being" (pp. 45–47).

Hartford, Connecticut   H.P.S.

1

INTRODUCTION

The Travail of Nature

THE CONTEMPORARY ECOLOGICAL CRITIQUE
OF CHRISTIAN THEOLOGY

It has been alleged that the Western theological tradition is ecologically bankrupt. That is the largely unexamined position espoused by scores of ecologists, historians, philosophers, poets, nature writers, political activists, and even some theologians who have identified themselves with the ecology movement. The Christian tradition, they have asserted, has little or nothing to offer to those who are reflecting about new ways of approaching the natural environment in this time of global ecological crisis. The Christian tradition, in their view, can only stand mute before that crisis, which so pervasively threatens human life today. This critique of the Western theological tradition has appeared in many forms. We may appropriately refer to it as "the critical ecological wisdom."

As a result of this popular reading of Western Christian thought, many who have been concerned with environmental issues have turned to other traditions, such as Eastern religions[1] or native American religions,[2] in order to find theological or metaphysical resources for the new kind of inclusive thinking that the emerging ecological consciousness seems to require — to view humanity as part of nature, not as a species above or against nature, to understand God as immanent in the vast expanses and diversities of cosmic history, as well as immanent in the unfolding dramas of human history.

The famous landscape architect Ian McHarg summarizes the popular point of view typically when he asserts that "historic Western anthropocentric-anthropomorphic tradition" reduces nature to inconsequence. "Judaism and Christianity have long been concerned with justice and compassion for the acts of man to man," McHarg explains, "but [they] have traditionally assumed nature to be a mere backdrop for the human play."[3] The critical ecological wisdom was given its most sophisticated historical articulation in 1967 by Lynn White, Jr., in his enormously influential essay in *Science*, "The Historical Roots of our Ecologic Crisis,"[4] reprinted in many scholarly and popular volumes and ubiquitously referred to by those who write about the environmental crisis.

1

White maintains that, due to what he calls "orthodox Christian arrogance toward nature," Christianity "bears a huge burden of guilt" for the contemporary environmental crisis.[5] To be sure, White does see a few gold particles hidden in the vast dross of the Western theological tradition, namely, the life and teaching of St. Francis. Others, similarly, find some elements of ecological value in the Western tradition. Thus, McHarg identifies a minority tradition in the West "which has a close correspondence to the Oriental attitude of an aspiration to harmony of man in nature, a sense of a unitary and encompassing natural order within which man exists."[6] Yet even when such fragments of value are identified, the underlying point of view remains the same: overall, the Western theological tradition is ecologically bankrupt.[7]

Another expression of the critical ecological wisdom is the attack on the biblical-classical theological tradition mounted by the feminist critic and philosopher of religion Rosemary Radford Ruether. She holds that Christianity was the heir of both classical Neoplatonism and apocalyptic Judaism, both of which, she maintains, presuppose a thoroughgoing estrangement from nature. "The classical doctrine of Christ," she writes, "which fused the vision of the heavenly messianic king [Jewish apocalypticism] and the transcendent *logos* of immutable Being [Neoplatonism], was a synthesis of the religious impulses of the late antique religious consciousness, but precisely in their alienated state of development."[8] One of the results of this "alienated" world view of the early Christian centuries, she notes, was "the domination or rejection of nature by spirit." Other results, she states, include the alienation of the mind from the body, the alienation of the subjective self from the objective world, and the subjective retreat of the individual, who was alienated from the social community.[9] Ruether further traces this pervasive phenomenon of cultural alienation to what she considers to be its most fundamental expression, sexual dualism: "the alienation of the masculine from the feminine is the primary sexual symbolism and sums up all these alienations."[10]

This means, in Ruether's view that, although "recent proponents of ecology" have rightly pointed the finger at Christianity as the carrier of "this debased view of nature, as the religious sanction for modern technological exploitation of the earth," Christianity did not originate this view. "Rather," she argues, "it appears to correspond to a stage of development of human consciousness that coincided with ripening classical civilization."[11] Christianity merely took over the alienated world view of late classical civilization. Whether Ruether's analysis can be justified or not, her critique has in fact lent further credence to the critical ecological wisdom.

The critical ecological wisdom has also drawn support from some of the traditions of European humanism. A hundred years ago Ludwig Feuerbach had contended: "Nature, the world, has no value, no interest for Christians. The Christian thinks of himself and the salvation of his soul."[12] In our own century, the same theme has been expressed poignantly by Albert Camus in his novel *The Rebel*, with reference to the tumultuous events of European history in the first half of the twentieth century. Here the villain, so to speak, is not late antique culture, as it is for Ruether, but the "Gothic" culture of northern Europe:

> The profound conflict in this century is perhaps not so much between the German ideologies of history and Christian political concepts, which in a certain way are accomplices, as between German dreams and Mediterranean traditions . . . in other words between history and nature.
>
> Christianity, no doubt, was only able to conquer its catholicity by assimilating as much as it could of Greek thought. But when the Church dissipated its Mediterranean heritage, it placed the emphasis on history to the detriment of nature, caused the Gothic to triumph over the romance, and, destroying a limit in itself, has made increasing claims to temporal power and historical dynamism. When nature ceases to be an object of contemplation and admiration, it can be nothing more than material for an action that aims at transforming it. These tendencies . . . are triumphing in modern times, to the detriment of Christianity itself, by an inevitable turn of events.

These words are quoted approvingly by Vine Deloria, Jr., in his book *God Is Red*, with the purpose of helping to undergird his own far-reaching attack on the Christian tradition.[13] Christianity has forsaken nature, he argues passionately; and therefore, in this ecological era, it can no longer have any real meaning for us. We are better advised to turn to native American traditions for the spiritual underpinnings we need to allow us to define a new, more ecological world view.

THE UNCERTAIN VOICE OF CONTEMPORARY
CHRISTIAN THEOLOGY

Since the 1960s, when these issues began to gain public prominence, numerous Christian theologians—although not all, by any means—have more or less accepted that critical ecological wisdom as their own, either self-consciously or by default. White's attempt to excoriate Christian theology for causing the contemporary environmental crisis has drawn some sharp criticism.[14] According to a large number of contemporary theological writers, however, Christian theology never has had, nor should it have, a substantive ecological dimension. These writers are convinced that Christian theology must focus primarily—even exclusively—on human history, not on the history of nature. A substantive Christian theology of nature, in their view, is a contradiction in terms.

Thomas Derr's 1973 study *Ecology and Human Need* is a good illustration of this widely presupposed theological perspective.[15] In contrast to some theologians, who refuse to see the contemporary environmental crisis as a challenge to the human species that is worth taking seriously, much less a challenge to Christian theology, Derr does take the environmental crisis seriously. Still, his dominating interest is to undergird the biblical image of God as the Lord of righteousness who seeks justice for the oppressed in human history. His interest in environmental issues is, in this sense, self-consciously anthropocentric.

Derr argues that the Bible focuses on human history or, more specifically, on God's history with humanity. He denies that the Bible—and by implication the classical theological tradition that stems from the Bible—shows any substantive concern for the world of nature. "The Biblical view of man's relation to nature," he explains, "is . . . definitely anthropocentric, but devoid of false confidence in the results of man's mastery."[16]

Within this anthropocentric framework, Derr seeks to develop what has come to be called—in scores of sophisticated and popular theological essays and articles—a theology of "responsible stewardship" of the earth.[17] He explains:

> Man lives in the context of history and community and his decisions regarding nature must be responsible to that setting. He does not enjoy absolute right of disposition over natural resources, but is their steward, the caretaker of the Divine owner, using them and preserving their usefulness to future ages.[18]

Since God takes human history seriously, in other words, we must now take environmental issues seriously, insofar as they can be a matter of life and death for human history, especially for the poor.

But our primary theological interest will continue to focus, properly in Derr's view, on the anguish and the promise of God's history with humanity. "Nature," Derr tells us, "is a complement to the primary drama of redemption which takes place in history."[19] To think otherwise, he believes, is to begin to undercut the foundations of biblical faith. It is to allow the ancient repudiated nature-gods of Canaan, and their sanctification of the status quo in human society, to gain a new kind of foothold beside the throne of the one God, who is the righteous Lord of history and whose will is the liberation of the oppressed.

Derr's argument is not only sharply construed, it is representative of a widely held set of theological assumptions in our century. These can be summarized in one generalization: *Christian theology has to do primarily with human history*—with the unfolding providential story of God and humanity, with God and the people of God, or with God and the believing human soul— *not with nature*. Derr's attempt to develop an ethic of responsible stewardship represents, accordingly, the most typical ethical response—among those theologians who have chosen to respond—to the environmental crisis today. It is not the only response, as we will see presently, but it is a highly visible way of thinking that is shared within the ranks of several otherwise opposing schools of thought and by many church leaders and popular theological essayists.[20]

Derr's theology of God and humanity has a certain underlying affinity with the aforementioned critical ecological wisdom. Derr more or less takes for granted the kind of historical reading of the Christian theological tradition presupposed by many environmentalists and other critics today. Although Derr has pointedly contested some of Lynn White's claims,[21] and although he would not wish to say baldly that the classical Western theological tradition is ecologically bankrupt, his self-consciously anthropocentric theological response to the environmental crisis illustrates, and therefore confirms de facto, the assumptions held by those who espouse the critical ecological wisdom about Western theology: that orthodox Christian thought always construes God and humanity apart from, or over against, the world of nature.

The kind of argument that Derr develops, with both systematic and ethical concerns, has also been projected by Gordon Kaufman, from the vantage point of fundamental theology.[22] Kaufman takes it for granted that the biblical-classical theological tradition has been overwhelmingly anthropocentric in its approach to nature. What the tradition *has in fact been*, Kaufman then suggests, is probably what it always *must be*, if it is to be true to its own originating intuitions.

Kaufman points out that the great words of the Christian vocabulary—sin, salvation, forgiveness, repentance, hope, faith, love, righteousness—have to do primarily with humanity and with relationships between humans. The rest of the creation, he observes, with the exception of the angels, though always recognized and sometimes acknowledged, "never became the subject of any technical theological vocabulary or doctrines."[23]

Further, Kaufman points to the fundamental affinity of God and humanity in Christian thought: humanity was created by God "in the image of God." Ultimate reality then was appropriately thought of in anthropomorphic terms; and nature was seen appropriately for many centuries as having significance chiefly insofar as it mirrored aspects of the human predicament or the human relationship with God.

Then Kaufman arrives at his most fundamental point: "An inner logic or consistency in Western religious traditions was being worked out here."[24] The ultimate reality with which humanity had to do was understood primarily as "a personal and moral agent who required of his devotees not only absolute devotion but also moral rectitude."[25] Accordingly, the moral side of human existence—willing and doing—was given the profoundest kind of metaphysical sanction possible. "Thus," Kaufman explains, "both man and that which was taken to be ultimately real were understood in terms of those features of man's being which most sharply distinguish us from other creatures, namely, the abilities to act, to decide, to order behavior by reference to preconceived and deliberately chosen ends, to devote ourselves to such values as righteousness, mercy, and love."[26] Along with this, Kaufman points out, it is not surprising that the terms that were used to depict the context of human life were political—such as the "kingdom of God"—rather than organic or material.

It follows from this inner logic of the Christian faith, Kaufman concludes, that the natural world is of "an ontologically different order from man." Human creatures are "lifted far above the rest of nature" by their moral and personal character. Therefore: "nature is not conceived primarily as man's proper home and the very source of his being, but rather as the context of and material for teleological activity by the (non-natural) wills working upon it."[27]

Kaufman allows that the picture of Christian belief he presents here is overdrawn. Still, he emphasizes that "the theological problem of nature is not simply one of rearranging emphases or details, lifting up certain motifs in the tradition that may have been neglected. It goes far deeper than that, into the logic of the central concepts of our religious tradition." Thus, he notes, the very concept of God itself, as it has been developed in the West, "has built into it a depreciation of the metaphysical, and certainly the religious, significance of nature." Any theological reconstruction, therefore, will have to go down "to the deepest roots of Western religious sensibility and vocabulary."[28] Whether such a reconstruction is possible is a question Kaufman leaves very much in doubt.

In contrast to Derr, Kaufman, and many others, a few theologians have been willing to undertake the task of theological reconstruction, to seek to develop "a new theology of nature" which is less anthropocentric than the traditional and contemporary theologies with which they are familiar and which is more explicitly ecological in scope. Among these theologians, those who have been influenced by the process metaphysics of Alfred North Whitehead are perhaps the most noteworthy. But their enterprise, particularly as we see it unfolding in the works of John Cobb and Charles Birch,[29] tends to beg the historical question.

Since process theologians have been so thoroughly committed to the fundamental rebuilding of the received tradition, on the basis of Whiteheadian metaphysics, they have tended to push historical concerns to the periphery of their argumentation. Notwithstanding many references to the Bible and to some classical theologians in their works, in other words, these process thinkers have not been primarily concerned to identify the substantive continuity of their argumentation with the received theological tradition. Their "new theology of nature" is structured on never fully identified historical foundations.

This is why their approach to the theology of nature sometimes appears to be so strikingly *new*, even at those points where it is in fact not new at all. The work of the process theologians, therefore, by default, although generally not by conscious intention, tends to lend further credence to the judgment of the critics who hold that the biblical-classical theological tradition in the West, at its deepest levels, is ecologically bankrupt.

Contemporary theologians have thus tended to reenforce the widespread critical reading of the biblical-classical tradition, either directly (Derr, Kaufman) or indirectly (Cobb, Birch): that the normative theological tradition in the West has serious deficiencies, ecologically speaking, if it is not totally bankrupt, because it is so thoroughly anthropocentric. This is the uncertain voice of contemporary Christian theology as it addresses itself to ecological issues.

THE NEED FOR HISTORICAL STUDY

Is traditional Christian thought about nature ecologically bankrupt? It is the contention of this study that that kind of historical verdict has been too hastily and too simplistically rendered. Few writers have taken the time to explore the rich intricacies and the subtle complexities of the theology of nature which is actually given in the biblical-classical Christian tradition.[30] This, then, is the place of embarkation for this study: the recognition that both the critics and the protagonists of Christian thought about nature need a much more adequate account of biblical and classical Christian thought about nature than is currently at their disposal.

A second, more particular point of departure for this study has to do with the possibility of constructing a "new theology of nature" in our time. This study is predicated on the assumption that the theology of nature *is* worth pursuing. It is worth pursuing for both extramural and intramural theological reasons. To begin with, the environmental crisis is real and, notwithstanding exaggerated claims by some environmentalists, it is deep-seated.[31] It seems clear that Christian theologians have a public responsibility to respond to that crisis in terms of both a critical appropriation of their own tradition and a constructive exploration of the possibility of new ways of valuing nature, along with new ways of affirming the values of human history.[32]

Further, it is becoming increasingly apparent that a new kind of crisis related to nature is emerging in our time in the affluent West, if nowhere else, an existential crisis. There is evidence—in literature, films, television, and other expressions of the popular mind—that a profound alienation from the natural environment is surfacing in our time. This burgeoning trend of alienated attitudes can be called the rise of the gnostic spirit, with reference to that starkly anticosmic religious world view which flourished in the early Christian centuries.[33] If this is indeed a current cultural trend of increasing magnitude, as it appears to be, then Christian theology must surely be prepared once again to become an advocate of the goodness of the material order, as it was in the early Christian era when Gnosticism was on the rise. These are some of the extramural reasons why the theology of nature is very much worth pursuing in our time.

Within the life of the church parallel reasons can be identified which affect the church's faith, its hope, and its love.[34] For example, what becomes of the church's sacramental life if it accepts an alienated view of nature as its own? What becomes of essential teachings such as the resurrection of the body and the renewal of the cosmos in the last times? What becomes of the church's commitment to ministry in this concrete biophysical world? If its members are alienated from nature will they not be tempted to seek some kind of "angelic" escape from the challenges posed by our existence in nature today, to shy away from their obligations to tend to the health and feeding of all, globally as well as locally? These questions point to some of the intramural reasons why a new theology of nature is worth pursuing in our time.

Both extramurally and intramurally, Christian theologians today must attend to the theology of nature with a new vigor. But that theological undertaking must presuppose a critical appropriation of the received tradition. Otherwise we will doubtless continue to encounter a succession of new books, as we have in the last two decades, each of whose authors has freshly discovered the need for a new theology of nature but most of whose authors then proceed to devote themselves to that task generally unaware of either the strengths or weaknesses of more than two millennia of theological reflection about nature.[35]

The work of both the critics and the theologians, therefore, requires a new historical understanding of biblical-classical theological reflection about nature.

THE AMBIGUOUS ECOLOGICAL PROMISE
OF CHRISTIAN THEOLOGY

This study will attempt to show, when all has been said, that the theological tradition in the West is neither ecologically bankrupt, as some of its popular and scholarly critics have maintained and as numbers of its own theologians have assumed, nor replete with immediately accessible, albeit long-forgotten, ecological riches hidden everywhere in its deeper vaults, as some contemporary Christians, who are profoundly troubled by the environmental crisis and other related concerns, might wistfully hope to find.

In traditional Christian thought, in other words, the rudiments for a rich theology of nature are not lacking. Indeed, at points, the tradition is dramatically suggestive, for those who have eyes to see. But such rudiments must be carefully and cautiously identified, and then separated from numerous less promising or even antithetical elements which also permeate the same tradition. This is why it is appropriate to speak of the ambiguous ecological promise of Christian theology. As a whole, Christian thought is both promising and not promising for those who are seeking to find solid traditional foundations for a new theology of nature. Which historical tendencies within the tradition are promising and which are not, moreover, is by no means self-evident.

To highlight this ambiguity and its complexities, as we proceed, we will be able to identify two fundamental ways of thinking in Western theology, *two theological motifs*, that are relevant to our concerns. What a "theological motif" is will be more precisely defined in the next chapter. Here it will suffice to note that each of these ways of thinking is in evidence at various points in the tradition—sometimes in the works of a single theologian—and that they stand in a pronounced tension with each other.

The first is predicated on a vision of the human spirit rising above nature in order to ascend to a supramundane communion with God and thenceforth to obey the will of that God in the midst of the ambiguities of mundane history. This can be called, without further explanation at this point, the *spiritual motif*. The fundamental data of theological reflection, in this case, are God and the soul, God and "the elect," or God and the whole of humankind (perhaps also the angels): those beings which have a certain spiritual, personal, or rational affinity. A paradigmatic expression of this motif is the famous utterance of the young Augustine in his *Soliloquies*: "I desire to have knowledge of God and the soul. Of nothing else? No, of nothing else whatsoever."[36] In theologies shaped mainly by this spiritual motif, nature tends always to be interpreted or validated (if it is validated) finally in terms of spirit.

The second way of thinking which we will have occasion to notice in several contexts is predicated on a vision of the human spirit's rootedness in the world of nature and on the desire of self-consciously embodied selves to celebrate God's presence in, with, and under the whole biophysical order, as the context in which the life of obedience to God is to be pursued. This can be called the *ecological motif* of theological reflection. "Ecological" is understood here as pertaining to a system of interrelationships between God, humanity, and nature. The word is used theologically, therefore, akin to the way the word "economy" is employed in the expression "the economy of salvation." "Ecological" is also purposely used here in order to draw on more general nuances of the word, so as to highlight the inclusion of *nature* in the originating moments of theological reflection. This way of thinking, then, has to do with a dialectical interrelationship of three, not two, fundamental data of theological reflection: God, humankind (perhaps also the angels), *and* the world of nature. A paradigmatic expression of this motif, indirect but powerful, is the picture given to us in the narratives about St. Francis's death: how at this moment of his most intimate communion with God he kept reciting his elegant Canticle to the Sun, thus placing himself in solidarity with the birds, the insects, the sun and the moon, and indeed the whole world of nature. In theologies shaped by this ecological motif, nature is not an ideational epiphenomenon, which gains its theological valence only because it participates in the dynamics of what is thought to be the primary relationship between God and humanity. Nature, rather, like God and humanity, is a theological *fundamentum,* given in the original moment of theological reflection.

The proponents of the critical ecological wisdom generally have grasped a truth about Christian attitudes toward nature, therefore, notwithstanding their tendency to depend on forcefully stated generalizations rather than on careful historical study. They have seen signs of the history of the spiritual motif in Western Christian thought about nature. But, as a general rule, they have not noticed that there is a second mode of thought about nature in Western theology. This is the ecological motif. The proponents of the critical ecological wisdom should not be faulted too much for this oversight, however, since the contemporary exponents of the Christian tradition—historians, theologians, and others—have not betrayed too much familiarity with the ecological motif themselves, so much has the modern theological mind in the West been shaped by the spiritual motif.

One of the assumptions of this study is that theologies shaped by the ecological motif are more promising, as far as the theology of nature is concerned, than theologies shaped by the spiritual motif. But it is one thing to articulate this relatively self-evident assumption. It is another thing to explore and then to display the particular tendencies wherein the two motifs have in fact existed side by side or have been interwoven with one another. That is the challenge before us in this study: to identify and to highlight that ambiguity and its complexities, in concrete historical terms.

The lead word in the title of this book, accordingly, is intentionally ambiguous—"travail." This is a familiar biblical image that points to a complex, primordial human experience. "We know," St. Paul wrote to the church at Rome, "that the whole creation has been groaning in travail until now" (Rom. 8:22). Thus the apostle invoked the ambiguity of the birth experience in order to illuminate the existential coherence of distress and hope. The experience of giving birth is both pain and promise. The same ambiguity also captivated the mind of St. John: "when a woman is in travail she has sorrow, because her hour has come, but when she is delivered of the child, she no longer remembers the anguish, for joy that a child is born into the world" (John 16:21).

As a theological construct, nature has been in travail throughout most of Western history. At times it has appeared as if the theology of nature has been at the point of joyful birthing. At other times the theology of nature has never really emerged in its own right. On some occasions, indeed, it would appear that that theology was stillborn. This is the ambiguous ecological promise of Christian theology. It is a story that must be told if there is to be a viable Christian theology of nature in our time, if Christian reflection about nature is to stand on its own, with historical integrity and critical authenticity.

Whereas the first word in the title, "travail," is chosen because its ambiguity reflects the complex data of the Western theological tradition, the last word in the title, "nature," is chosen primarily because of its commonplace familiarity and its general intellectual accessibility. It is also chosen with the hope that its well-known terminological ambiguities can be set aside or at least set in clear relief, so that they might be bracketed, at the outset.

The term "nature" is notoriously difficult to define. Arthur Lovejoy has identified dozens of definitions[37] and undoubtedly there are more.[38] The task of defining the word "nature" calls to mind the comment of St. Augustine about time: that he knew what it was until someone asked him about it. Nature is one of those terms deeply rooted in the precognitive depths of a culture. It resists simple definition.

We will be considering "nature" here, in a variety of historical settings, *as a theological construct*. We will take "nature" as a synonym for a more concrete theological term, rooted in biblical parlance, "the earth":[39] "In the beginning God created the heavens and the earth" (Gen. 1:1). All other related concepts —such as "ecology," "environment," and "cosmos"—will be understood in terms of this fundamental theological construct.[40] The earth, we can say, is the material-vital aspect of God's creation. Thomas Aquinas, for one, thinks of nature or the earth in this sense as "the realm of irrational things."[41] Nature, in this context, is thus the first portion of what the Nicene Creed refers to as "all things visible and invisible."

The human creature, seen in this perspective, is surely "natural" or "terrological," if that neologistic expression be permitted (from the Latin, *terra,* meaning earth). The human creature is essentially "of the earth" (as in the Hebrew "Adam" and "soil," *adam* and *adamah*). At the same time, as creatures who enter into personal communion with God who alone are created in "the image of God," and as creatures whose being is essentially constituted not only through their relationship to all visible creatures but also by the intangible, interpersonal dynamics of human community and faith in God, human creatures also transcend the earth. Traditionally this was expressed, for example, in Thomistic parlance, by thinking of the human creature as the "rational animal." Often, throughout the centuries, various theologians employed the biblical teaching about "the image of God" to define and express this dimension of human self-transcendence. The human creature is thoroughly natural, in other words, thoroughly of the earth, yet the human creature is the one visible creature of the earth that is more than the earth also.

This is the theological construct we will have in view as we proceed: nature understood as "the earth." To be sure, we will have to make every effort to have this terminological preunderstanding facilitate and not block our grasp of particular theological constructions along the way. Likewise, we shall have to be aware that this way of asking the question sets the terminological assumptions of this study apart from those of numerous theologians throughout Christian history, who used the word "nature" in a variety of differing ways. "Nature," for example, has often been taken to refer to the whole creation, to "all things visible and invisible," to the earth *and* to the heavens, in order to comprehend all things, not just the material-vital aspect of the creation, as we are employing the term here. But whether or not they may or may not have used the word "nature" in this sense, all Christian theologians of note do have a doctrine of creation, and that means that they at least have an implicit conception of "the earth" or "nature" as we will be using the term: that realm created, sustained, and consummated by God, and constituted by creatures such as the stars, the land, the waters, vegetation, the swarms of living things; and human beings, insofar as they are bodily creatures, along with the material and vital products of human creativity, such as gardens or buildings.[42] Every Christian theologian worthy of the name has a construct for what the Bible means when it says "the earth is the Lord's and the fulness thereof" (Ps. 24:1). It is this construct that we shall be examining in many historical contexts, as we explore our theme, the travail of nature.[43]

2
THE APPROACH

Discerning the Roots of Classical Christian Thought
About Nature

Is it true that nature has been of no interest for Christians? Is it true that they have been such a people, wandering as strangers and pilgrims through this world, that they have never had the time, nor the occasion, nor the will, nor the rudimentary spiritual experience to respond to nature with the kind of theological intensity they have always devoted to God and humanity? Is it true that nature does not belong to the inner logic of the Christian faith as we have known it for the last two thousand years?

How can we begin to answer such questions? How are we to look down into "the deepest roots of Western religious sensibility and vocabulary" (Kaufman) to determine whether nature has had any formative meaning for the Christian mind and heart throughout the centuries?

The obvious place to begin our investigation would seem to be with the Scriptures. In a fundamental sense, much if not everything depends on the witness of the prophetic and apostolic writings of the Old and New Testaments concerning nature. That task of biblical interpretation must surely be pursued. We will turn to it, in a schematic way, at the end of this study.

But we will focus our attention primarily on the postbiblical theological tradition. We will undertake some selective explorations of classical Christian thought about nature, akin to the work of the archaeologist who sinks trenches here and there, at what will hopefully be judiciously chosen places, in order to determine what evidence is to be found at particular locations and levels that could cast light on the whole.

This is surely an undertaking that is worthwhile in its own right. We do need to know what the classical theological tradition has said about nature, since we are its heirs, for better or for worse. At the same time, we also need to know what that tradition has said about nature, since, as the archaeological image suggests, this kind of study of the tradition can in principle help us to locate the still more deeply embedded structures of biblical thought about nature as well. This is one important way—not the only way by any means—to "get at" the theology of the Bible, by going through the tradition, rather than around it.[1]

So, with proper caution, we may undertake some probes at what seem to be strategic points in the history of Christian theology in order to take a reading by inference on the tradition as a whole, and beyond that to set some guidelines for further exploration of biblical theology itself. It will then be up to other students of the biblical-classical tradition to determine whether our findings are sufficiently self-authenticating to allow and to encourage a more complete excavation of the whole site, and whether the guidelines we identify for approaching the Scriptures merit further explication and application.[2]

AIDS FOR THE INVESTIGATION: METAPHORS AND MOTIFS

If we are "to look down into the deepest roots of Western religious sensibility and vocabulary" concerning nature, we will need some appropriate instruments. We will as a matter of course be concerned with people's articulated *ideas* about their relationship to God and nature, but we must probe more deeply than those ideas themselves. We will need to investigate fundamental apperceptions of human identity in the world of nature as that identity is shaped by faith in God. We will have to probe, as best we can, the complex and nuanced depth and breadth of *lived human experience,* intuitive as well as cognitive, subliminal as well as self-conscious, tacit as well as articulated, archaic in form as well as contemporary in content, as that experience gives testimony about human identity in relationship to God and nature.

To this end, as a way of uncovering some of the more fundamental nuances of the various theological constructions we will be encountering, we can helpfully prepare ourselves to look for the influence of certain "root metaphors" which have allowed people to give expression to their lived relationship with God and nature.[3] "Root metaphor" is a technical term which was given a specific currency by Stephen Pepper.[4] It will be employed in the ensuing discussion, however, in a more general sense which we can briefly specify here, building on some constructs of Alfred North Whitehead and Langdon Gilkey.

"Every philosophy," Whitehead once observed, "is tinged with the coloring of some secret imaginative background, which never emerges explicitly into its traces of reasoning."[5] In a similar way, theology is rooted, Gilkey maintains, "in deep prereflective levels of awareness, 'prehensions' of the sacral forces on which man depends, combined with man's own deepest subjective responses to his world. . . . "[6] This immediate, affective experiential flow of awareness, replete with powerful, formative images and evocative metaphors, is later —through the mediation of cultic action and communal experience generally—gathered and shaped into myths. Myths function to organize this "world" of human experience, Gilkey argues, by giving it its first reflective articulation.[7] Theology, when it arises still later, then serves as a discursive-rational explication of a religion's mythological expressions.

If this kind of interpretation of the experiential roots of theological reflection is sound, and there is every reason to think that as a phenomenological generalization it may readily be taken to be so, then it also seems possible to identify an *interface* between the most original experiential moments of the religious life and the secondary levels of mythological-theological reflection and speculation. This interface we may call the dimension of root metaphors. Such metaphors, we can say for our purposes here, are coordinating analogies, which gather and begin to organize the fluid, momentary images of immediate religious experience, as that experience is in the process of taking on reflective mythological-theological form. The native home of root metaphors, then, is not the world of theological discourse as such, not the conceptual foreground, but the communal, mythopoeic background: the cult, the life of prayer, and the concrete social matrix of moral interaction and exhortation.

On the other hand, root metaphors bridge the distance between the prereflective and the reflective elements in religious experience. They therefore find a home also, sometimes visibly, sometimes only implicitly, in the most rigorously conceptual forms of theological discourse. As integrating elements given in the primary world of religious experience, they are continually taken for granted, and never left behind, even at the most universal levels of abstract thought.[8] Root metaphors arise from the hidden imaginative background of all theological thinking and then remain influential at the discursive level of analysis and self-conscious argument.

When certain root metaphors cluster together and shape a tradition of theological reflection, or when a single root metaphor exercises a formative influence on a tradition over a period of many years, that cluster of metaphors or that single metaphor can be called a "theological motif."[9] As a mode of thinking that persists in a given tradition of reflection, a theological motif is the name we can give to a habitual employment of one or more root metaphors. A theological motif, in other words, is not yet a "theological model" in the contemporary sense of the latter expression because it is not self-consciously chosen, as a model is, as a formative principle for theological reflection.[10] Theological motifs, rather, are presupposed, taken for granted, and employed as a matter of course. They are not self-consciously constructed. Theological motifs function in self-conscious theological reflection as "ways of thinking that seem so natural and inevitable that they are not scrutinized with the eye of logical self-consciousness."[11]

As we survey the long history of Christian thought regarding nature, we can see three major root metaphors exercising a formative influence and two dominant theological motifs. We will refer to these imaginative elements on numerous occasions in the following exposition, where in the midst of the concrete details of historical study their meanings will be much more readily apparent than they can be at this preliminary juncture in the discussion. Still, some description of these metaphors and motifs is essential at the outset.

Two of these metaphors appear to be dependent on a single, almost universal experience in human history, which we will call the experience of the overwhelming mountain. These are the metaphor of ascent and the metaphor of fecundity. A third root metaphor is dependent on a different kind of experience which apparently is not nearly so universal as the first; indeed it seems to have found its chief if not its only cultural expression in the history of Hebraic and post-Hebraic peoples. This is the experience of the promising journey. The metaphor to which it gives birth is the metaphor of migration to a good land.

One of these metaphors, the metaphor of ascent, through persistent employment, becomes the "spiritual motif" in Western theology. The other two, the metaphor of fecundity and the metaphor of migration to a good land, tend to cluster—when they are given in the same imaginative environment. When they do cluster, through time, they become the "ecological motif" in Western theology.

Understanding the imaginative process whereby the three root metaphors become the two theological motifs is complicated by the fact that two of the metaphors come from the same originating experiential matrix—the overwhelming mountain—even though they stand in pronounced tension with each other. One of the two, the metaphor of ascent, becomes the spiritual motif. The other, the metaphor of fecundity, tends to coalesce with the metaphor of migration to a good land, and the two then become the ecological motif. The inner dynamics of this imaginative process can be diagrammed as in Figure 1.

FIGURE 1

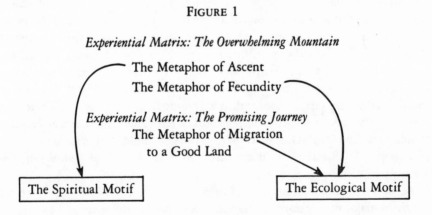

Experiential Matrix: The Overwhelming Mountain
The Metaphor of Ascent
The Metaphor of Fecundity

Experiential Matrix: The Promising Journey
The Metaphor of Migration
to a Good Land

The Spiritual Motif   The Ecological Motif

The identification of these metaphors and these motifs, however, and their imaginative dynamics, cannot be justified in advance. Here we can only describe them. Their value as instruments of interpretation can only be demonstrated in terms of their helpfulness in the discussion that is to follow.

THE EXPERIENCE OF THE OVERWHELMING MOUNTAIN:
THE METAPHORS OF ASCENT AND FECUNDITY

In his "Hymn Before Sunrise," Samuel Taylor Coleridge presents this image of Mount Blanc in the Alps, and its impact on his own religious consciousness:

> . . . thou, most awful Form!
> Risest from forth thy silent sea of pines,
> How silently! Around thee and above
> Deep is the air and dark, substantial, black,
> An ebon mass: methinks thou piercest it,
> As with a wedge! But when I look again,
> It is thine own calm home, thy crystal shrine,
> Thy habitation from eternity!
> O dread and silent Mount! I gazed upon thee,
> Till thou, still present to the bodily sense,
> Didst vanish from my thought: entranced in prayer
> I worshipped the Invisible alone.[12]

Coleridge is here giving expression to a certain romantic sensibility, which blossomed in his era, after many centuries of apparent disregard of mountains themselves as edifying objects for religious contemplation.[13] But at this point, he also stands in continuity with a much more universal experience, more archaic in form and more variegated in its historical manifestations, evident in many cultures at many times, which we can conveniently call the experience of the overwhelming mountain. "In the ancient civilizations from Egypt to India and beyond," one student of the subject tells us, "the mountain can be a center of fertility, the primal hillock of creation, the meeting place of the gods, the dwelling place of the high god, the meeting place of heaven and earth, the monument effectively upholding the order of creation, the place where god meets man, a place of theophany."[14] It is this archaic and classical experience that will concern us here, not, as such, the romantic expression of it in the modern West. It is an experience whose image is given in the originating moments of the biblical-classical theological tradition in the West, as we know those moments from the Scriptures, and which has constantly been presupposed and reappropriated throughout the various epochs of that tradition.

The image of the overwhelming mountain is rich, but ambiguous, as far as its assumptions about human identity and nature are concerned. It brings with it powerful but complex nuances that combine the dimensions of both height and breadth. Edwyn Bevan has alluded to this ambiguity in his discussion of the image of "the heights" in his book *Symbolism and Belief.*[15] "To climb a mountain," he explains, "is a continued achievement of will, against gravity; and at the same time the range of vision increases with the altitude." But it is the overwhelming character of the experience, rather than the ambiguous and mingling nuances of height and breadth, that most interests Bevan. This is his description of the experience:

> There is something in intellectual, artistic, moral and spiritual achievement which gives a feeling that man instinctively recognizes as analogous. The higher summits of a mountain were for primitive man, if not utterly inaccessible as the sky was, at any rate very difficult of access and those upper mountain regions were, if not quite unknown, at any rate a world very rarely seen, very little known, a world apart from the familiar places through which primitive man roamed.[16]

But we should not lose sight of the ambiguities of the experience either.

The Metaphors of Ascent and Fecundity

I can seek to ascend the overwhelming mountain with my sights fixed firmly on the ethereal reaches above. The way up the mountain is then my way to seek transcendence, far removed from the mundane things of the earth below. I constantly look up to the infinite reaches of the sky above. I am shaken by the brilliance of the awesome cloud formations. At midday especially, I lift up my eyes to the blinding mystery of sunlight. I find moments when I feel carried away from every earthly constraint, dizzy with the uncharted heights above, spiritually transfixed by the limitless glories of the light flooding around me. This is one form of the experience of the overwhelming mountain. This is the aspect of the experience which gives birth to *the metaphor of ascent.*

Alternatively, I can seek to climb the mountain with my eyes fixed not so much on the ethereal regions above as on the vistas of the surrounding valleys which are mine as I slowly ascend to the peak of the mountain. My goal, then, is to ascend to the heights in order to gain a new perspective of the whole earth, everything that I can see from horizon to horizon, forward and back, left and right, and around again. In this case I am not seeking to take myself beyond the mundane things of this earth, but to rise to a vantage point where I can begin to apprehend the earth's vastness and mystery and beauty. Up at the heights I look back to behold the lavish greens of the forests below and I hear in my soul the washing of myriad streams of cold, fresh water cascading down the mountain. My imagination is taken likewise with the knowledge of the thousands of species of animals and plants that inhabit those descending slopes. The eyes of my soul also look out to the lush green valleys below, fed by the mountain springs from above. And I see a vision of an enormous diversity of living forms and material shapes charged with wonder and awe. This, then, is the second form of the experience of the overwhelming mountain. This is the aspect of the experience that gives birth to *the metaphor of fecundity*.

For a less impressionistic and more categorical presentation of these phenomena, we can turn to the historical investigations of Mircea Eliade.[17] Eliade observes that people in ancient and archaic societies often experienced themselves as being driven to relate themselves to "the Center of the World" (*axis mundi*). It was at this sacral Center that they encountered the Real in the midst of a world of constant and often threatening change. "The man of traditional societies could only live in a space pointing upward," Elaide explains, "where the break in plane was symbolically assured and hence communication with the *other world*, the transcendental world, was ritually possible."[18] As a matter of course, moreover, the cosmic mountain was a central and virtually omnipresent theme in this kind of symbolism, according to Eliade.[19] To this central symbol others were assimilated, such as the symbolism of the elevated city or the elevated temple. In every such case, the image of the heights was of utmost importance. "Since the sacred mountain is an *axis mundi* connecting earth with heaven," Eliade observes, "it in a sense touches heaven and hence marks the highest point in the world; consequently the territory that surrounds it, and that constitutes 'our world,' is held to be the highest among countries."[20]

So the dimension of height is of crucial importance for this symbolism. But the dimension of breadth is also vividly attested in the materials Eliade adduces. In this context, with the addition of charged symbolical nuances from the imagery of birth, the mountain can be seen as the creative center of the world, from which all things are given life. Eliade writes:

> A universe comes to birth from its center; it spreads out from a central point that is, as it were, its navel. It is in this way that, according to the *Rig Veda* (X, 149), the universe was born and developed—from a core, a central point. Hebrew tradition is still more explicit: "The Most Holy One created the world like an embryo. As the embryo grows from the navel, so God began to create the world by the navel and from there it spread out in all directions." And since the "navel of the earth," the Center of the World is the Holy Land, the *Yoma* affirms that "the world was created beginning with Zion." Rabbi ben Gorion said of the rock of Jerusalem: "it is called the Foundation Stone of the Earth, because it is from there that the whole Earth unfolded."[21]

This Elaide calls a hierophany. Under the aegis of the overwhelming heights, the sky and all its powers of transcendence, the whole earth can take on the transfixing luminescence of the Divine. Eliade comments:

The world stands displayed in such a manner that, in contemplating it, religious man discovers many modalities of the sacred, and hence of being. Above all, the world exists, it is there, and it has a structure; it is not a chaos but a cosmos, hence it presents itself as creation, as work of the gods. This divine work always preserves its quality of transparency, that is, spontaneously reveals the many aspects of the sacred. The sky directly, "naturally," reveals the infinite distance, the transcendence of the deity. The earth too is transparent; it presents itself as universal mother and nurse. The cosmic rhythms manifest order, harmony, permanence, fecundity. The cosmos as a whole is an organism at once *real, living,* and *sacred*; it simultaneously reveals the modalities of being and of sacrality. Ontophany and hierophany meet.[22]

Such charged nuances, archaic and classical, hover around the primary image now before us, the overwhelming mountain, and its two derivative imaginative forms, the metaphor of ascent and the metaphor of fecundity. We will have occasion to view both these derivative forms in a number of contexts as we explore various Christian attitudes toward the life of the human creature in nature and in relation to God.

Some Exemplars of the Metaphor of Ascent

A paradigmatic biblical instance of the first metaphor, the metaphor of ascent, is the account of Moses at Sinai:

Then Moses went up to the mountain, and the cloud covered the mountain. The glory of the Lord settled on Mount Sinai, and the cloud covered it six days; and on the seventh day he called to Moses out of the midst of the cloud. Now the appearance of the Lord was like a devouring fire on top of the mountain in the sight of the people of Israel. And Moses entered the cloud, and went up on the mountain. And Moses was on the mountain forty days and forty nights. (Exod. 24:15–18)

We can imagine the people below, transfixed in wonder, looking up to the Divine Fire, to the place where Moses had ascended to be with Yahweh.

Perhaps the most sublime postbiblical accent on the metaphor of ascent, we will observe, appears in the *Divine Comedy* of Dante. Here the poet rises to the heights of ecstatic contemplation of God, the exalted, all-transcending Trinity, the Light of lights, through a long spiritual ascent that finally takes him above, far beyond the cosmic hierarchy of this material world. His poem tells passionately of the experience depicted more conventionally by Milton in *Paradise Lost*:

In contemplation of created things
By steps we may ascend to God.[23]

It should be clear, furthermore, that the metaphor of ascent brings with it implicitly or explicitly, as we will observe in a number of contexts, the nuances of not merely rising toward God above, but specifically rising above and beyond the world of nature, in order to enter into communion or union with God who is thought of as pure spirit. This is evident, to draw on one of many examples which could have been cited here, in the following words of Coleridge. This is his image of the archangel Raphael sent to instruct Adam. The poem begins with a glimpse of the divine fecundity (with reference to the "one Almighty . . . from whom all things proceed"), but then quickly shifts so that the mind is taken on an itinerary which leads from the rudimentary levels of matter to the most exalted heights of pure spirit.

> O Adam, one Almighty is, from whom
> All things proceed, and up to him return,
> If not depraved from good, created all
> Such to perfection; one first matter all
> Endued with various forms, various degrees
> Of substance, and, in all things that live of life;
> But more refined, more spirituous and pure,
> As nearer to him placed or nearer tending
> Each in their several active spheres assigned,
> Till body up to spirit works in bounds
> Proportioned to each kind.[24]

Coleridge's words here also tell another related story. They clearly presuppose the long metaphysical history in the West which focuses on reflection about the "Great Chain of Being." This story has been impressively traced by Arthur Lovejoy in his monograph which has that title.[25] We will consider this metaphysical theme at some length, particularly in our discussion of Origen's thought. But that metaphysical articulation of the metaphor is not our concern here. Rather, our purpose is to highlight the metaphorical roots of that metaphysical conceptuality.

Some Exemplars of the Metaphor of Fecundity

A paradigmatic biblical instance of the metaphor of fecundity is not given explicitly with the picture of the mountain which is presented in the accounts we have of the Sinai event. To find an explicit example, we must look elsewhere, to a point later in the biblical tradition. Here, however, the concrete image of the overwhelming mountain is not specifically mentioned, although the complementary dimensions of height and breadth, characteristic of the metaphor of fecundity, are dramatically in evidence: this is the poetic commentary on the fullness of the creation and God's universal creative activity which we encounter in Psalm 104. Here the poet places himself at the vantage point of the heights and then surveys the fecundity of the whole earth, celebrating the Divine creativity at every level. He begins with the vision of the Creator above, praising the One who dwells in inaccessible glory, yet who works his way majestically with all things (vv. 1–4). Then the poet's eyes shift to the whole earth, to its wondrous divinely bestowed order and stability (vv. 5–9). From this panoramic angle of vision, he turns to celebrate the springs gushing forth in the valleys and the rains renewing the whole earth (vv. 10–13). Next, his vision focuses more particularly on a variety of individual living creatures, first of all the human creature, fed by the rich green growth of this world and made happy by its effusive wine, also the birds nesting in the trees and the wild goats finding their home in the mountain crags. The poet even peers into the night hours, when the many other beasts of the forest come forth, and he celebrates their life also (vv. 14–23). Then, once more, he steps back and surveys the whole earth, as from on high, and praises yet again the Creator's providential governance:

> O Lord, how manifold are thy works!
> In wisdom hast though made them all;
> the earth is full of thy creatures. (v. 24)

Toward the end of his paean of praise for the universal divine creativity, the poet prays that this vast and variegated glory of God in nature might endure forever, and that God might rejoice in all of his works (v. 31).

Probably the best postbiblical example of the vision of the divine fecundity is the parabolic life story of St. Francis who, as we will see, climbed the holy mountain of God and then turned back to embrace in joy and love the whole material world below. Francis's life demonstrates profoundly the experience illustrated with a more mundane tonality, yet powerfully in its own way, by the beloved twentieth-century folk hymn—translated from the original Swedish into many languages—"How Great Thou Art":

> When through the woods and forest glades I wander,
> I hear the birds sing sweetly in the trees;
> When I look down from lofty mountain grandeur
> And hear the brook and feel the gentle breeze;
> Then sings my soul, my Savior God, to thee,
> How great thou art! How great thou art![26]

The metaphor of fecundity has not only shaped such songs in the West, but, like the metaphor of ascent, it has also helped to shape the tradition of metaphysical reflection about the "great chain of being," to which we have already alluded. In that metaphysical context, as we will see in detail in later chapters, the metaphor becomes the self-consciously articulated theme of "overflowing goodness." But, as before, our concern here is not with that metaphysical doctrine as such. We are interested in the metaphorical context.

THE EXPERIENCE OF THE PROMISING JOURNEY: THE METAPHOR OF MIGRATION TO A GOOD LAND

The experience of the promising journey brings with it a multiplicity of nuances. It is portrayed in the Bible above all in the Book of Deuteronomy, where we see the people of Israel being led by Moses toward the promised land. This is the biblical statement of that promise:

> For the Lord your God is bringing you into a good land, a land of brooks and water, of fountains and springs, flowing forth in valleys and hills, a land of wheat and barley, of vines and fig trees and pomegranates, a land of olive trees and honey, a land in which you will eat bread without scarcity, in which you will lack nothing, a land whose stones are iron, and out of whose hills you can dig copper. (Deut. 8:8, 9)

Later, the very journeying to the good land is itself interpreted in terms of what is to come. The first exodus, according to Deuteronomy, is surely blessed from on high, with manna, for example; nevertheless it clearly unfolds in two stages, the time of wandering and the time of fulfillment in the land of Canaan. The return from the exile to the land, however, as we see it depicted as a promise of God by 2 Isaiah, is a return wherein the very way to the good land is interpreted in terms of what is to come. The overflowing blessedness of the promised land is depicted as shaping the people's experience as they move toward the promised land as well:

> Behold, I am doing a new thing; now it springs forth, do you not perceive it? I will make a way in the wilderness and rivers in the desert. The wild beasts will honor me, the jackals and the ostriches; for I give water in the wilderness, rivers in the desert, to give drink to my chosen people, the people whom I formed for myself that they might declare my praise. (Isa. 43:19–21)

I can imagine myself, accordingly, with the people of ancient Israel wandering in the wilderness with the exodus and Sinai behind me. I can imagine being threatened by hunger, thirst, wild beasts, and hostile peoples. I can imagine my life being shaken by the loss of loved ones in the struggle for survival, and by the possible loss of my whole people. I can imagine myself wandering into despair, rootless and with little hope for tomorrow.

Likewise, with ancient Israel, I can imagine hearing promises of a land flowing with milk and honey, promises spoken by some charismatic leaders, compelling in their own right, but doubly so in view of the precariousness of the people's predicament. So I can see myself, with the whole people, with any belongings I might have packed, undertaking one last pilgrimage of faith and hope toward that promised land beyond the Jordan. My identity in the present, insofar as I can sustain my sanity and not give in to despair altogether, is profoundly rooted in the image I have of myself and my family and my entire community as living and prospering one day in the good and fecund land ahead. My very being is determined, in this respect, not by the violence all around me—the loss of life through hunger and thirst, wild animals attacking, the warfare of the peoples—but by the peace of that new land, where the lamb will lie down with the lion and the streams will flow with honey and all swords will be beaten into plowshares. That day, to be given to me freely at the end of my pilgrimage, as I follow the Lord of Hosts who goes before me, will be a day of peace and light, ending, once and for all, the strife and darkness of this wilderness world.

Some Exemplars of the Metaphor of Migration to a Good Land

The third-century Christian humanist Lactantius (ca. 260–317) presents us with a picture of the end of the world that well exemplifies some of the nuances of the metaphor of migration to the good land. This world, he stresses in his *Institutes*, is a world yet to come, akin to what the classical poets said about the remote past, the "golden times when Saturn was reigning." But it is not a world of the past. It is a world of the future.

> Then, there will be taken away from the world those darknesses with which the sky is obscured and blocked from sight, and the moon will receive the brightness of the sun, nor will it be diminished anymore. The sun, however, will become seven times brighter than it now is. The earth, in truth, will disclose its fecundity and will produce the richest crops of its own accord. Mountain rocks will ooze with honey, wines will flow down through the streams, and rivers will overflow with milk. The world itself will rejoice and the nature of all things will be glad, since the dominion of evil and impiety and crime will have been broken and cut off from it. Beasts will not feed on blood during this time nor birds on prey, but all things will be quiet and at rest. Lions and calves will stand together at the manger to feed; the wolf will not steal the sheep; the dog will not hunt; hawks and eagles will not do harm; a child will play with snakes.[27]

Similar sensibilities, although not so exuberant given their thisworldly object, shaped the minds and hearts of the first Puritans in New England, and they have shaped the American consciousness to one degree or another ever since. Thus, in his *Wonder-Working Providence of Sions Savior in New England*

(1654) Edward Johnson imagined himself addressing the Pilgrim saints as they were about to embark for America: "for your full satisfaction, know this is the place where the Lord will create a New Heaven and a New Earth in, new Churches, and a new Commonwealth together . . . you shall be fed in this Wilderness, whither you are to go, with the flower of Wheate, and Wine shall be plentiful among you. . . ."[28] The decadence and the oppression of Europe—so this image helped many Americans to believe—were to be left behind. A new beginning for a new Adam in a new Garden was being established by God. Likewise, a later generation looked to the great American frontier as that good land, the place of innocence and material abundance.[29]

DISJUNCTION AND THE CONJUNCTION:
THE THREE METAPHORS AND THE FORMATION OF THE
SPIRITUAL AND ECOLOGICAL MOTIFS

It should be apparent by now that these root metaphors have different valences as far as human life in nature is concerned.

The primary image of the overwhelming mountain is essentially ambiguous, as we have seen. We can say that it is *ontically* ambiguous. One's identity as a human being may be essentially rooted in the world of nature (the metaphor of fecundity) or it may not be (the metaphor of ascent). Within the imaginative horizon of the overwhelming mountain, one's being may be a being-in-the-earth, essentially, or a being-beyond-the-earth. If the one who rises to the heights continually looks back, then the glorious vistas of the earth will be of great moment in his or her religious consciousness. If, however, the goal is to keep looking upward to the ethereal, supramundane reaches on high, as it sometimes can be, then the ascent to the heights may in fact represent an attempt to separate oneself from the earth, in order to enter into a totally landless ethereal glory.

The congenital ambiguity of the primary image of the overwhelming mountain is sometimes obscured by the fact that both derivative metaphors, the one accenting height, the other accenting breadth, contain within them the nuance of climbing to the top of the mountain. This similarity can bring both metaphors, on occasion, into close proximity in the imagination. But that proximity will always be unstable, given the inner dynamic of each derivative metaphor. The movement toward the heights in the one case is a movement aimed at rising above and leaving the world behind. The movement toward the heights in the other case is a movement aimed at seeing one's solidarity with the whole world, and in that sense it is a movement whose end is a certain poetic and affective embrace of the world.

In contrast to the primary image of the overwhelming mountain, the image of a life-and-death migration to a good land is not ontically ambiguous, whatsoever, by definition. One never leaves the land behind. One's identity is always given with a "land experience."

However much I might be alienated from the land now, I am always moving toward yet another "good land" experience. That future prospect therefore qualifies the present: as an essentially and blessedly landed creature in the future—that is my destiny—I must, in some fundamental sense, be essentially and blessedly a landed creature now. Otherwise, I would have no fixed identity, no commonality with my future being. So the nuances of escaping from or rising above the entanglements of material-vital reality in order to flee to some higher identity with God will be minor if not altogether absent in theological systems, where this metaphor is dominant. In this context, indeed, to be removed from the land is finally to have no identity whatsoever: to be no one. In a similar vein one cannot readily imagine a final destruction of one's present earthly milieu, that is, apart from a succeeding act that rehabilitates the earth in which one lives and moves and has one's being, for that also would entail a destruction of one's present identity. In the thought world of the metaphor of migration to a good land, one can never lose one's rootedness in the world of nature.

Under the aegis of this root metaphor, indeed, the most intense of spiritual experiences will always be located not apart from nature, but in the midst of nature, surrounded by the creatures of the earth. A paradigmatic case of this would be Noah who, although he was to be rescued from the chaos on the earth, nevertheless took all the animals with him. He was, after all, destined to return to the land, with the promise of the rainbow, after the flood. It would be difficult, in comparison, to imagine Dante contemplating the luminescent Trinity on high, in the *Paradiso,* surrounded by giraffes and monkeys and pigeons, which he had taken up there two by two with him on his pilgrimage.

The metaphor of migration to a good land, to be sure, is not without its own ambiguities. But, at most, there are *ethical* ambiguities alone, in contrast to the image of the overwhelming mountain, whose ambiguities are both ontic and ethical. In the case of the mountain imagery, one's identity can be essentially nature-related or not essentially related to nature. Ethically, that ontic ambiguity may lead to profound tensions between a thisworldly ethos and an otherworldly ethos.

In the case of the metaphor of migration, however, the question can only be *how* one relates to the land—as suzerain, as servant, as friend, or in some other way—not *whether* one is essentially and positively related to the land at all. Ethical tensions may surely emerge in this context—for example, should one dominate the land or preserve it or contemplate it or perhaps relate to it in some other way?—but such tensions will always be variations on a theme, engagement with the land, wherein one's identity is rooted.

The metaphor of ascent and the metaphor of fecundity thus stand essentially in a relationship of tension with each other, notwithstanding the fact that, existentially, both are derivative forms of a more primary experience, the overwhelming mountain. The metaphor of fecundity and the metaphor of migration, in contrast, although of different existential lineages, will as a matter of course tend to cluster with each other, if they are given together in the same imaginative environment, since both lead the mind into an experience of solidarity with the earth and both envision that solidarity, when all has been said, in terms of goodness. Both are nature-affirming metaphors, in contrast to the metaphor of ascent which, in the end, is a nature-denying metaphor.

The clustering of the metaphors of fecundity and migration can be seen in the following verses by the eighteenth-century poet Thomas Olivers, from his hymn—still in many hymnals—"The God of Abraham Praise," which celebrates both a renewed land and the sacred heights overflowing with fecundity.

> Though nature's strength decay,
> and earth and hell withstand,
> To Canaan's bounds I urge my way
> At his command.
> The watery deep I pass,
> With Jesus in my view,
> And through the howling wilderness
> My way pursue.
>
> The goodly land I see,
> With peace and plenty blest;
> A land of sacred liberty,
> And endless rest.
> There milk and honey flow,
> And oil and wine abound,
> And trees of life forever grow
> With mercy crowned.
>
> There dwells the Lord our king,
> The Lord our righteousness,
> Triumphant o'er the world and sin,
> The Prince of Peace.
> On Zion's sacred height,
> His kingdom he maintains,
> And glorious with his saints in light
> forever reigns. [30]

We will encounter evidence of the mingling of the two metaphors, fecundity and migration to a good land, above all in the works of Augustine, and in the life of Francis.

In a like manner, akin to the tension that exists between the metaphors of ascent and fecundity, the metaphors of ascent and migration to a good land also stand in a thoroughgoing tension with each other. They cannot exist together in the imagination in any permanently complementary way. Here even the element of similarity which sometimes links the metaphors of ascent and fecundity—climbing to the top of the mountain—is missing. These two metaphors differ both essentially and by existential context. The one is essentially and visibly land-transcending. The other is essentially and visibly land-affirming. If these two metaphors are found together in the same imaginative context, therefore, it will always be the case that one or the other will finally emerge as the dominant or concrete metaphor, while the other will become recessive or ornamental. Origen, for example, can invoke the biblical metaphor of the good land as the goal of this earthly pilgrimage; but for him the metaphor of ascent is so dominant that "the land" he has in mind is spiritualized to the point where it has lost all of its tangibility. Land, for Origen in this respect, is merely an ethereal image, abstracted from its concrete setting in Hebraic thought, and used to give one more expression to a spiritualizing vision of reality informed predominantly by the metaphor of ascent.

We see two imaginative tendencies emerging here. The first is the tendency of the metaphor of ascent to repel the other two metaphors, and vice versa. The second is the tendency of the latter two, the metaphors of fecundity and migration to a good land, to attract each other—when they are given together existentially—since both are essentially nature-affirming metaphors.

These two imaginative tendencies, we may now observe, lie behind the two theological motifs that we have previously identified, the spiritual and the ecological motifs. The one is a habit of thought predicated, simply, on the dominance, through time, of the metaphor of ascent. The second is a habit of thinking predicated, more complexly, on the tendency of the metaphor of fecundity and the metaphor of migration to a good land to coalesce, that is, if both metaphors are given in the same imaginative environment. These dynamics of the imagination can be schematized in Figure 2.

We turn now to the beginning of classical Christian thought about nature, to two thinkers, Irenaeus and Origen, in whose theologies the influence of two of these root metaphors—migration to a good land and ascent—is, respectively, well attested. In Irenaeus's thought, moreover, the metaphor of fecundity is also influential. Hence in these two early Christian theologies we can see the initial stages of an imaginative history which we will be tracing from that early

FIGURE 2

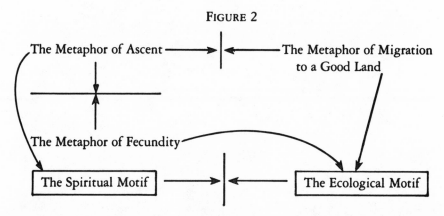

Christian era to our own century, the trajectories of the spiritual motif (the metaphor of ascent influential through time) and the ecological motif (the metaphor of migration to a good land and the metaphor of fecundity, influential through time).

Aristole
Aquanas
Teilhard
Origen
Barth

Irenaous
augustine
Luther
Bonaventure

3

THE HISTORICAL BEGINNINGS

Irenaeus and Origen

St. Paul was called by God, he believed, to be the Apostle to the Gentiles. By the time of Irenaeus of Lyons (ca. 130–200) and Origen (ca. 185–254), gentile Christianity had become a reality around the Mediterranean basin. But the Christian church was far from established. Living as it did in an often hostile cultural and political environment, it faced uncertainties on every side, sometimes threats to its very existence. Within the church, moreover, the theological norms which modern Christians take for granted, especially the great christological and trinitarian dogmas, had not yet been defined and adopted. It was an era, nevertheless, of rich theological creativity.[1] Yet the theological diversity within the church sometimes brought with it destructive elements too. In this time of external challenge and threat to the church, and internal richness yet turmoil within the church, each of the thinkers whom we will be considering found himself called to an apostolate of his own.

Irenaeus was a bishop. He wrote to defend the church against what he considered to be the radical distortions of faith and life perpetrated by Gnostic sectarians and their fellow travelers. He also wrote—and this is not always immediately apparent, given the polemical cast of his major work, *Against the Heresies*—to interpret and to celebrate the essentials of the Christian gospel on behalf of the whole church of his day.

Irenaeus's stature as a theologian has sometimes been underestimated, due to his strong emphasis on presenting what he saw to be the essentials of biblical theology, and not his own speculative constructions. Thus, Allan Galloway often refers to Irenaeus's biblical "conservatism," as if this church leader of the second century had no mind of his own but was merely repeating biblical teachings.[2] In this respect, Galloway compares Irenaeus unfavorably to both the Gnostics and Origen who, he holds, notwithstanding the several shortcomings of their respective theologies, at least made the attempt to interpret the Bible in terms of the thought patterns of their day. But this is only to encounter Irenaeus's thought at the edges. At the center, behind Irenaeus's evident "biblicism," lies a creative theological mind. In the same vein, Irenaeus was not merely an "anti-gnostic father." He fought the mythological speculations and

31

the anticosmic dualism of the Gnostics and of others, such as Marcion, with great energy. But he did so on the basis of a consistently integrated and passionately argued theology of his own. It is perhaps best, if we are to characterize his thought, to speak of him as a confessional theologian. His theology consists in "telling the mighty works of God," in an integrated, comprehensive way. It is a reflective exposition—often thoroughly shaped by polemical interests—of the symbolic and parabolic narratives of biblical faith; and it remains within that narrative setting bequeathed to it by the Scriptures. Among those theologians who worked within that kind of confessional framework at that time, Irenaeus is equaled by few others in theological power and symbolic coherence.[4]

Origen was a teacher. Serving in a catechetical school in the cosmopolitan environment of Alexandria, he sought to interpret the faith to the educated circles of his time. In preparation for this teaching, he undertook a course of studies in the best learning of the day. Later, when he became head of the school, he reorganized it into "a kind of university" which was "for the use of cultivated laymen," including subjects taught in Hellenistic schools, such as philosophy.[5] In this milieu, Origen made what can only be thought of as a heroic effort to interpret the substance of biblical faith as he understood it—its apocalyptic framework was not readily intelligible in a Hellenistic setting—in terms of the most sophisticated forms of metaphysical discussion of his day. He was a devoted student of the Scriptures at the same time, and a spiritual guide whose gifts were widely recognized.[6]

Each of these thinkers must be understood, of course, in terms of his own historical context. To this end, we will explore the thought-world of Gnosticism as a prelude to our study of Irenaeus's theology, and the cultural world of Hellenism generally, as an introduction to our consideration of Origen's teachings.

THE CHALLENGE OF GNOSTICISM:
THE MESSAGE OF AN ALIEN GOD AND
AN EVIL EARTH

Gnosticism, which Irenaeus opposed so relentlessly, is an extremely complex historical phenomenon.[7] It would take us too far afield to attempt to identify the specific forms of Gnosticism which Irenaeus himself was opposing. But it is the main features of the Gnostic world view, in any case, which are of interest here, so it will suffice to highlight those characteristics, with specific attention, to be sure, to the Gnostic understanding of the biophysical world. For the most part we will be following the still valuable treatment of the Gnostic world view by Hans Jonas.[8]

The rise of Gnosticism as a religious movement is roughly contemporary with the rise of Christianity. It became a religious force to be reckoned with during the first two centuries of the Christian era.[9] It reached its apex in the teaching of the third-century prophet Mani, whose doctrine Jonas calls "the most monumental single embodiment of the Gnostic principle."[10] Various forms of Gnosticism were contested by Christians from the earliest times, beginning already with the New Testament. Augustine, who first became a disciple of Mani and then attacked the religion of the Manichees, is just one in a line of eminent Christian thinkers who felt called upon to reject and refute the Gnostic approach to reality.[11]

The thought of Gnosticism has been instructively expounded by Jonas under the rubric, "the message of the alien God."[12] The alien God is the key to Gnostic thinking. With regard to the world or what Christians have called the creation, the Gnostic deity is absolutely transcendent. The life of this God is utterly removed and disconnected from mundane reality, which the Divine neither created nor governs. Compared to the light of the Divine, the material world, for the Gnostic mind, is a self-contained and distant realm of darkness. Thus, the relation of God to the world is conceived of in a radically dualistic way.

The Earthly Prison and the Salvation of the Divine Spark

A fundamental conviction of Gnosticism, accordingly, is that the earth and everything contained in it is evil.[13] "The universe, the domain of the Archons," Jonas explains, "is like a vast prison whose innermost dungeon is the earth, the scene of man's life." The archons, the gods of this world, collectively rule over the world. "Their tyrannical world-rule is called *heimarmene*," Jonas tells us, "universal fate, a concept taken over from astrology but now tinged with the Gnostic anti-cosmic spirit." This rule, or Fate, has two aspects, on the one hand psychic, which in some schemas includes the Law of Moses and which aims at the moral enslavement of humans, on the other hand natural, which is the rule of nature's law and which aims accordingly at the bodily enslavement of humans.[14]

This is not the last word about human beings, however, for Gnostics believed that a segment of the Divine, which has fallen into the world, is enclosed within the human soul. This is the spirit or the divine spark. The idea here is that the archons created human beings for the express purpose of imprisoning the pieces of substance from the transcendent beyond.[15] From this perspective, then, humans are radically distinguished from the earth, as God is. Insofar as humans are carriers of the divine spark, the world is also an evil and hostile reality for them.[16] The point here is summarized by Jonas as follows:

> Gnosticism . . . removes man, in virtue of his essential belonging to another realm, from all sameness with the world, which now is nothing but bare "world," and confronts him with its totality as the absolutely different. Apart from his accessory outer layers contributed by the world, man by his inner nature is acosmic;

to such a one, all the world is indifferently alien. Where there is ultimate otherness of origin, there can be kinship, neither with the whole nor with any part of
the universe. The self is kindred only to other human selves in the world—and to
the transmundane God, with whom the non-mundane center of the self can enter
into communication. [17]

This picture sets the stage for the Gnostic doctrine of salvation. Through a
mission of a savior who descends from the transcendent realm—a savior who is
often associated in some way with the Jesus of orthodox Christianity—humans
are supplied with saving knowledge, *gnosis*. Thus equipped, each individual
soul then travels upward after death, leaving behind it all its vestments received
from the several spheres of the various archons. At last, stripped of all foreign
accretions, the spirit or the divine spark reaches the alien God, its true home,
and is reunited with the divine substance. [18]

In this way, the evil of the earth and the other lower regions of the Gnostic
universe are left behind, the body being abandoned in the dungeonlike earth
and the soul finally being abandoned after passing through the spheres of the
world in which it first took shape when sparks of the divine fell from the divine
substance. Jonas suggests, moreover, that "on the scale of the total divine
drama, this process is part of the restoration of the deity's own wholeness,
which in pre-cosmic times had become impaired by the loss of portions of the
divine substance." The last act of the Gnostic universal drama, according to
some systems, is the abolition of the cosmos. Deprived of its elements of light,
it logically has no reason for continued existence. [19]

Assessment: The Metaphor of Ascent Out of Control

The Gnostic approach to nature thus has three main characteristics. First,
God utterly transcends, and is of a character different from, the world of nature.
The one is light, the other is darkness and evil. Second, insofar as humans are
identified with the light, as carriers of the divine spark, they are lost travelers
imprisoned in the darkest part of the universe, the darkest part of the earth or
nature. Third, nature in itself is a prison; it is ruled by capricious powers that
ever enslave humans, especially through the human body. Nature belongs altogether to the sphere of darkness and evil. It is worthy only of final destruction.

Gnosticism is perhaps the most extreme example in Western history of a
world view shaped by the metaphor of ascent—by that metaphor, indeed, and
by no other. In the Gnostic schema any influence from either the metaphor of
fecundity or the metaphor of migration to a good land has been totally eclipsed.
We see here the effect of the metaphor of ascent in its radical singularity—left
to itself, as it were, gone out of control. Salvation for this esoteric faith is understood entirely in terms of rising above and beyond the world of nature, which is

itself envisioned as a prison. Moreover, the aim of salvation is that the scattered divine sparks might return to their true home above, in order to be reunited with an essentially anticosmic deity. The world of nature in turn is left behind, befitting its evil character, to perish.

IRENAEUS: THE DYNAMICS OF CREATION HISTORY
AND THE AFFIRMATION OF NATURE

Irenaeus took issue with Gnosticism for many reasons. Some of these reasons have become much more evident in recent years, given the discovery of hitherto unknown Gnostic writings. But, notwithstanding a number of varying interpretations of Irenaeus's motives, this much remains clear and well-established.[20] As a defender of the faith and a witness to its promise, Irenaeus could not countenance the Gnostics' rejection of the Creator God of the Old Testament, nor their postulate of an entirely alien, passive deity who was utterly removed from the material order of everyday experience, nor their scorn and rejection of that material order. Rather he saw nature, as he perceived the Scriptures to see it, as humanity's God-given home—blessed, embraced, and cared for by the very God who took on flesh in order to redeem a fallen humanity and thereby also to initiate a final renewal of the whole creation.

Irenaeus's theology, at its deepest levels, is an exposition of what can be called creation history. His thought begins with a picture of God's act of bringing the whole creation into being, to the end that God might bring all he has created to final fulfillment, through an all-encompassing history. In the middle of this comprehensive creation history, Irenaeus then sees the figure of the Incarnate Word who—as the eternal Logos, together with the Spirit of God—is the ever-present life-giving principle of creation history and who—as the Logos become flesh—moves the whole creation decisively toward the goal of fulfilling the original divine intention for the creation.

To understand this fundamental framework of Irenaeus's theology, it is probably necessary for the modern reader to make a distinction explicitly, which Irenaeus seems to take for granted. This has to do with the scope and meaning of the final fulfillment of the creation history. God's original intention in creating the world, according to Irenaeus's way of thinking, is to bring all things to that final fulfillment or consummation. Hence, so to speak, there would have been a final fulfillment even had Adam not sinned. That is the inner, although mostly implicit, logic of this creation-history framework. This theme is most visible in Irenaeus's thought in the context of his anthropology. He pictures Adam as being created by God as a child, destined for growth.[21] So the whole creation would have had a history of growth and consummation, apart from any disruption wrought by human sinfulness. Further, Irenaeus seems to stand in the tradition of those who later would explicitly affirm that the incarnation was destined by God to happen also, even if Adam had not sinned (among others, Maximus the Confessor and Duns Scotus held this view). Now Adam did in fact sin, and his heirs remain in bondage to the devil, in Irenaeus's view. Hence Christ has a twofold vocation, according to this way of thinking: to fulfill the creation on the one hand, and to redeem humanity on the other. It is perhaps permissible then if for the sake of clarity in this chapter we can reserve the term "salvation" for the first universal-eschatological aspect of Christ's vocation and the term "redemption" for the second particular-anthropological aspect. This will help us to understand how, for example, Irenaeus not only can affirm, as we shall see, that the cosmos has not fallen, but also maintain resolutely that it will be renewed in the end times. That was its destiny from the beginning.

But such thoughts must remain at the margins of our interpretation of Irenaeus's thought. Characteristically Irenaeus is not interested in them as such. He is self-consciously opposed to anything that appears to be "speculation." He is a concrete thinker who chooses, as we have already noted, to expound his theology in the narrative terms which he inherited from first-century biblical Christianity.

Creation History: The One Work of God

Interpreters often observe that Irenaeus is opposed to theological speculation, because he does not want to open the door to an incursion of the kind of emanations-speculation which so preoccupied the Gnostics, and to which he was so unalterably opposed. This reading of Irenaeus's mind is surely correct, as far as it goes. But there is also a deeper tendency operative in his thought. He is self-consciously not interested in the world of God's eternity before the creation—not only because he wants to avoid speculation but also because he *is* so interested in affirming and focusing attention instead on the creation and God's history with the creation. His is a theology of unity of all things (*ta panta*) under the creative providence of God. Like other early Christian thinkers Irenaeus adapts the schema of the "seven days" of creation to the history of the whole creation. This is the universal "economy" (*oikonomia*) of God. "Creation, the incarnation of Christ, redemption, and resurrection," Aloys Grillmeier explains, "belong together as different parts of the one all-embracing saving work of God."[22]

Grillmeier's use of the expression "saving work of God" here is appropriate and illuminating, because this creation history or divine economy has a pronounced eschatological character, as Irenaeus sees it, as well as a christological center. All things are moving toward, are destined for, a final day of salvation or consummation. In this sense, for Irenaeus, the whole of creation history is a saving history. Everything will be saved. Nothing of the good creation will be lost.

If it is a *saving* history, for Irenaeus, it is also a saving *history*. Creation has a beginning and an ending. It moves temporally through seven epochs or "days." When it comes to the ending, that fulfillment will be a new thing, Irenaeus holds, not merely a return to the beginning.

Even Christ, who is of such central importance in Irenaeus's thought, as far as human redemption is concerned, is understood also in terms of that larger creation history of God as we already have had occasion to observe. As the Incarnate Word or Logos of the Creator, Christ *recapitulates* what has gone before in the history of the creation, particularly in human history.[23] In so doing, he both overcomes the distortions of sin, which entered through Adam, *and* he carries the whole history of creation one final step further into the era of its last days, thus serving as the inaugurator of the final consummation, through his resurrection. As Irenaeus writes:

> The Word, being made man, summing up all things in Himself, so that as in the super-celestial, spiritual and invisible things the Word of God is supreme, so also in things visible and corporeal He might possess supremacy, and taking to Himself the pre-eminence, as well as constituting himself Lord of the Church, He might draw all things to Himself at the proper time.[24]

Hence the vocation of Jesus Christ, in Irenaeus's view, is as we have seen, to serve the whole divine history of creation, not just fallen and redeemed humans—until the very end, when he will deliver his rule over to the Father, who will then be all in all.[25]

The Importance of "Last Things"

Irenaeus's realistic vision of the end of creation-history—"end" in the sense of ending (*finis*) and fulfillment (*telos*)—has been something of an embarrassment to many of his intepreters. There is a tendency to laud his Christology, for example, but to decry his eschatology. Galloway is typical in this respect when he writes: ". . . the fathers of the West, typified for us by Irenaeus, were sufficiently conservative in their outlook to retain the Jewish, physical reference of the symbol [of the end times]; but this conservatism was so extreme that they scarcely attempted any reinterpretation at all, but simply reasserted the Biblical symbols with a literalism which was no longer possible in their cultural environment."[26] But Irenaeus's eschatology is not simply a repristination of the biblical narratives for the sake of remaining faithful to the Bible. It is consistent with, and indeed the capstone of, his vision of creation history. That Irenaeus's thought still moves within the "unbroken myth" (Tillich) of the narratives of the New Testament at this point—as did the mind of the entire Western church through the end of the third century—should not be held against him, as it were, any more than when, for example, we attempt to expound his Christology. "Demythologization" and then "symbolization" (Sittler) as a theological program may have the highest priority for those who would appropriate Irenaeus's theology today. But selective demythologizing, even by implication, at the level of historical exposition, must be avoided, on the ground of the truncated or fragmented historical interpretation that can result.[27]

So the failure to give Irenaeus's eschatology its full due leads to some one-sided interpretations of his thought as a whole. Galloway avers, for example, that Irenaeus did not wrestle as profoundly with the problem of evil as Origen and the Gnostics did. We cannot attempt to resolve that question here. But it does seem clear that Irenaeus approached the problem of evil eschatologically, with reference to his several images of the final triumph of God. If, then, one sees Irenaeus's eschatology as a mere carry-over from the New Testament, and not as an essential building block of his thought, his handling of the problem of evil would perforce have to be seen as less than satisfactory as well. And this in turn would represent a distortion of what he is attempting to say.

Irenaeus believed that he was living in the last times. He thought that the last of the six days of creation was in progress. The beast of the apocalypse will soon come, or already has come, he believed, along with the dawning of the general resurrection and the last judgment. Then the whole creation will be richly renewed, not abrogated: "Neither the substance nor the essence of the creation will be annihilated . . . but 'the fashion' of the world passes away."[28] In this context, Irenaeus reaffirms the New Testament image of a messianic banquet for the righteous.[29] Moreover, for a thousand years they will reign on earth, growing stronger, more accustomed to "partake in the glory of the Father," and enjoying communion with all spiritual beings as well.[30] Then finally the seventh day of creation history will come, the ultimate Sabbath rest of God,[31] when, following the Pauline proclamation, Irenaeus expects the Son to conclude his work and the Father to be all in all.[32]

Accenting the Divine and Human Immanence in an Unfallen Earth

It will be evident, as we now proceed to examine Irenaeus's theology of creation history in detail, particularly his theology of nature, that the major operative and integrating root metaphor influential in his thought—although mainly unspoken, except in the context of his eschatological affirmations—is migration to a good land. The influence of this metaphor is given with his particular eschatological consciousness—especially with his "chiliasm," the idea of the saints reigning on earth for a thousand years—and from there it permeates all his thinking.

And more. Since, for Irenaeus, that good land of the final fulfillment is so vividly the renewed good earth *of the Creator* of all things, and since the same Creator is perceived by Irenaeus as governing immediately now throughout the whole creation, that profound sense of ultimate material-vital-spiritual goodness flows back, as it were, and qualifies Irenaeus's vision of the present life. As a result, the way is opened in Irenaeus's thought for influence also from the side of the metaphor of fecundity. The God who pours down infinite blessings at the very end, in other words, who will be all, who will one day renew all things, also takes on the role of the God who *now* blesses all things, who is *now* immediately present to them, who *now* constantly renews them in their courses in this world—a set of images which, taken together, is reminiscent of the celebration of the divine creativity and care for the whole creation which we encountered earlier in Psalm 104. For Irenaeus, the God who will be all in all, who will permeate all things with his glory on the seventh day, is already in some vital, although not fully realized sense, the God who is all in all now.

God, says Irenaeus, is the one "who containing all things, alone is uncontained."[33] God is by no means alien to the world of matter and life. On the contrary, we almost see a picture here of God embracing the whole creation with his hands, as a parent reaches out to a child. "Hands" is Irenaeus's characteristic way of referring to the work of the uncreated Word and the eternal Spirit of God. Irenaeus is very much concerned with the so-called economic Trinity, that is, with God in three persons ruling as providential Lord of the creation. Irenaeus presents us with this image of the Trinity as the living God, who is constantly involved with his creation: ". . . the Father planning everything well and giving His commands, the Son carrying them into execution and performing the work of creating, and the Spirit nourishing and increasing."[34]

Irenaeus rejects speculation about the world emerging from God through a hierarchy of emanations. This is not just because he is opposed to philosophical speculation, as we have seen, but because he wishes to affirm the nearness of the hands of the Creator to all things. He insists that angels—the idea of angels as mediating agents of the divine emanations was common at the time—had nothing, and will have nothing, to do with the works of the Creator. That would mean that God is far removed, which for Irenaeus would be a distortion. The nuance here, if anything, is not that God is wholly other, exalted in the spiritual heights above this material world, but rather that God tenderly touches this creation through his "hands":

> It was not the angels therefore, who made us, nor who formed us. . . . For God did not stand in any need of these, in order to accomplish what He had Himself determined beforehand should be done, as if he did not possess his own hands. For with him were always present the Word and Wisdom, the Son and the Spirit, by whom and in whom, freely and spontaneously, he made all things.[35]

Likewise, Irenaeus can say that the eternal Logos "in an invisible manner contains all things created, and is inherent in the entire creation, since the Word of God governs and arranges all things. . . ."[36] This very creative Word "brings an infant which has been conceived in the womb into the light of the sun, and lays up wheat in the barn after he has given its full strength on the stalk."[37] In the same vein, Irenaeus can envision the Creator bestowing a blessed and richly diversified harmony on the whole creation through the works of his hands:

> He himself, after a fashion which we can neither describe nor conceive, predestinating all things, formed them as He pleased, bestowing harmony on all things, and assigning them their own place, at the beginning of their creation. In this way he confirmed on spiritual things an invisible nature, on supercelestial things a supercelestial, on angels an angelical, on animals an animal, on beings that swim a nature suited to water, and on those that live on the land one fitted for the land—on all, them—while he formed all things that were made by His Word that never wearies.[38]

Furthermore, although Irenaeus repeats the Genesis theme that the earth is cursed because of Adam's sin, he does not accept the idea of a cosmic fall. The great majority of creatures, he says "persevered, and still do persevere, in subjection to Him who formed them."[39] So, nature in general retains its created goodness, in Irenaeus's eyes. This view stands in sharpest contrast to the teachings of his gnostic opponents.

More particularly, as far as human life in nature is concerned, we can appropriately say that for Irenaeus humanity is "at home" in the midst of the whole creation of God, at home in the body and at home in nature more generally. At the beginning, Irenaeus tells us, human flesh "received the skillful touches of God." "Numbers would fail to express the multiplicity of parts in the human frame, which was made in no other way than by the great Wisdom of God."[40] Flesh is in no sense alien to essential human life for Irenaeus; this is the legacy of his strong emphasis on the resurrection of the flesh (he does not use the more elusive term "body") in the end time, and his view of that time as being a world of material, as well as spiritual, blessings.

As humans are at home in the body, furthermore, so are they at home in the physical world generally. They live in a world in which they may know vividly that they are constantly being blessed, from every side, by the Creator, both in earthly and spiritual experience; indeed, in the closest unity of the two, body and soul, especially the body:

> And as we are His members, we are also nourished by means of the creation (and He Himself grants the creation to us, for He causes His sun to rise, and sends rain when He wills). He has acknowledged the cup (which is part of his creation) as His

own blood, from which He renews our blood; and the bread (also part of the creation) He has established as his own body, from which He gives increase to our bodies.[41]

A Qualified Anthropocentrism

So much does Irenaeus depict the human creature at home in nature, indeed, that a question arises about his anthropocentrism. Does Irenaeus teach that the whole purpose of the creation history is to provide a place for human life and to bless human life? More particularly, does the whole raison d'être of creation hinge, in his view, on God's saving purposes with humankind?

That the human story of creation, fall, and redemption is central in Irenaeus's vision of creation history there can be little doubt. Irenaeus is preoccupied with the narrative that runs from Adam to Christ and then to the church. The question, however, is whether this is a central *accent* in his thought, whether it is *prima inter pares*; or whether it forms the essential *core* of his thinking, to which every other idea is subordinate, whether it is, simply, *prima*. It seems clear, notwithstanding some statements which seem to point in the opposite direction, that the former interpretation rather than the latter (which is so dear to modern theology, as we will see), more nearly portrays Irenaeus's intentions.

Irenaeus does want to maintain that human beings are not only at home in the whole creation and in their bodies, in particular, but that the whole creation was made *for the sake of* human beings. "Man was not made for its sake [the creation's]," he says in a characteristic utterance, "but creation for the sake of man" (*non enim homo propter illam, sed conditio facta est propter hominem*).[42] Some interpreters have assumed, without further investigation, that Irenaeus means here that *the sole purpose* of the creation is to provide a stage, as it were, for human salvation.[43] There is a certain a priori attractiveness to this interpretation; and it is easy to attribute the idea to Irenaeus, since it is found elsewhere in the period, for example, in Origen's theology, as we will see presently. But Irenaeus does not assume a dialectic of human salvation and the whole creation, as Origen and many later theologians were to do. He does not envision any kind of pretemporal drama in eternity, where the elect are chosen (thesis); next a scene in time, the creation of the whole world for the sake of providing a place wherein the human creatures or rational spirits already chosen might be saved (antithesis); and then, finally a scene of reconciliation, where the human creatures or rational spirits are enabled to return to God again (synthesis). Rather, Irenaeus begins with the temporal beginning of the creation, as we have seen, and envisions *one act* of God, one divine economy, aimed at bringing the entire creation of a new status to a final fulfillment through the Word and the Spirit.[44]

To be sure, in this one stream of creation history the human creature in Irenaeus's schema occupies a central place. One might readily call the human creature the most favored creature of God, as far as Irenaeus is concerned. But Irenaeus's nuance is not that the world was created by God for the *sole* purpose of blessing humanity and offering humanity redemption, but rather that *when* it was created it was *arranged* or shaped so as to offer humanity blessings and to communicate salvation to humanity. Thus when he remarks, as we have heard him say, that "man was not made for its sake, but creation for the sake of man," he means as he says in the same place: "all such [creatures] have been created *for the benefit* of that human nature which is saved."[45] Or he means, at greater length:

> God *arranged everything* from the first with a view to the perfection of man, in order to deify him and reveal His own dispensations, so that goodness may be made manifest, justice made perfect, and the Church may be fashioned after the image of His Son. Thus man may eventually reach maturity, and, being ripened by such privileges, may see and comprehend God.[46]

In this sense Irenaeus's view of human life in nature is self-consciously anthropocentric. But this is an administrative anthropocentrism, as it were, not an ontological anthropocentrism. Creation's arrangement is for the sake of human life. But humanity is not its sole purpose. Indeed, that sole purpose for Irenaeus is theocentric, not anthropocentric: that the Creator might begin, nourish, and fulfill the whole creation and then be all in all. In this connection it is important to recall that Christ, for Irenaeus, is more than the one who provides the remedy, or the redemption, for human sin. His coming signals the coming of the Perfecter of creation, the one who carries the whole creation forward into its last days, which was the Creator's intention from the very beginning.[47]

Moreover, this limited kind of administrative anthropocentrism does not stand alone. It is set in the overall context of a vision of theocentric purpose being realized in this present world, as well as in the world to come. Irenaeus always strikes a balance: the Creator who cares so intimately for his most favored human creatures also favors and cares for all his other creatures. Irenaeus goes out of his way to show not only that God made the world but that it is a worthy, even beautiful product of his hands. He likens it to a beautiful work of music.[48] To this degree, for God, all the creatures of nature are not only arranged to benefit human destiny, they are also arranged for the sake of God himself, who is bringing them also to their final day of rest. Irenaeus constantly sees the whole picture, the providential activity of God throughout the fullness of the creation. This is the God who is near to the human creature:

> He it is who fills the heavens, and views the abysses, who is also present with every one of us. For he says, "Am I a God at hand, and not a God afar off? If any man is hid in secret places, shall I not see him?" For His hand lays hold of all things, and

that it is which illumines the heavens, and lightens also the things which are under the heavens, and trieth the reins and the hearts, is also present in the hidden
things, and in our secret thoughts, and does openly nourish and preserve us.[49]

Likewise, at the end. Here again the human creature is the most favored creature of God. Set in the center of things, the human creature is blessed with the
abundant richness of the creation now renewed. But again there is the balance:
the whole creation is to be renewed also. Irenaeus writes:

> If, then, God promised him [Abraham] the inheritance of the land, yet he did not
> receive it during all the time of his sojourn there, it must be, that together with
> his seed, that is, those who fear God and believe in Him, he shall receive at the
> resurrection of the just. . . . For God is true and faithful; and on this account he
> said, "Blessed are the meek, for they shall inherit the earth."[50]

Irenaeus thus concludes:

> The predicted blessing, therefore, belongs unquestionably to the times of the
> Kingdom, when the righteous shall bear rule upon rising from the dead, when also
> the creation, having been renovated and set free, shall fructify with an abundance
> of all kinds of food, from the dew of heaven, and from the fertility of the earth.[51]

The animals will once again be subjected to humans in the peace that reigned
before the Fall, he tells us, and they will revert to their original foods, that is,
no longer will they prey upon each other.[52] Finally, this new creation will be
permanent. It will abide, while humans always continue "fresh converse with
God": "these things shall ever continue without end, as Isaiah declares. . . ."[53]

Assessment: The Emergence of the Ecological Motif

Such are the fruits of one theologian's energetic and consistent envisioning of
reality in terms of the metaphor of migration to a good land, and then, in the
context of that vision, also in terms of the metaphor of fecundity. Since God is
the God who pours out blessings in the "landedness" of the end times, flooding
his whole creation with new life, Irenaeus's mind as a matter of course finds it
congenial to think of God also in terms of fecundity, not only then but now. In
Irenaeus's vision the whole creation is full of goodness, harmony, beauty, and
life at all times, all continually pouring forth from the hands of God. God is not
some distant ruler, far removed in the heavens, sending out his commands
through intermediaries.[54] Rather God is one who contains all things, works
richly in them, gives them their individual places within the whole, and thus
bestows harmony on all things. The human creature likewise is at home in the
creation, not a stranger and pilgrim in an alien world. Humanity is constantly
blessed by the fruits of the earth in general, and by the sacraments in particular.
The human creature, moreover, is at home in the body, which Irenaeus cele-

brates as a special gift from God and which he depicts as gloriously resurrected and participating in the messianic banquet in the times to come."

Faced with a system of thought that enshrined the most radical extrapolations from the metaphor of ascent (Gnosticism), Irenaeus thus countered with a diametrically opposite kind of thinking. In place of thought shaped by the metaphor of ascent, he drew on the metaphor of migration to a good land and the metaphor of fecundity. We see in his thought then the emergence of what we have called the ecological motif, that is, the coalescence of the influence of those two metaphors.

We can also see that Gordon Kaufman's analysis of the "inner logic" of Christian thought with regard to nature does not readily apply to Irenaeus's thought. Irenaeus's theology does not focus as singularly on the doctrine and the vocabulary of sin and grace, as later Western theology was wont to do. Rather he presents us with a unified, universalized theology of creation history, from alpha to omega. The universal divine economy is the energizing theological dynamic of Irenaeus's theological vision of reality, not chiefly the drama of the human fall and human redemption, although the latter surely is his central concern. For Irenaeus, God and humans are not ontologically set apart from nature, in the radical way Kaufman portrays this relationship in general terms, by virtue of their personal, moral character. Nor is Irenaeus's concept of God so defined as to depreciate nature. On the contrary, both God and humans are viewed by Irenaeus as being at home in the world of the flesh and in the material-vital creation generally. The divine governance, moreover, has a certain nurturant, embracing character in Irenaeus's view; God surely does not dominate the earth as some alien, despotic other. Accordingly, human dominion over nature is a muted, not to say scarcely visible, theme for Irenaeus. The accent is not on teleological activity, but on *communion*—eating in the midst of the overflowing blessings that God gives in nature. For Irenaeus, this is true in this life; but it will be all the more true of the times of the coming new heavens and new earth, when the righteous will gather for the glorious messianic banquet, when the lamb will lie down with the lion, when God will be all in all.

ORIGEN'S CULTURAL ENVIRONMENT: ALIENATION FROM NATURE IN AN AGE OF ANXIETY

We have already noted that Origen placed himself self-consciously in the midst of the most sophisticated intellectual currents of his time. He was first and foremost a philosophical theologian. This is not to suggest, either directly or by implication, that such a stance is somehow problematic in itself or that it is to be considered the preferred theological position. The question before us in this study, in this respect, is not whether it is better to be a philosophical theologian, as Origen was, or a confessional theologian, as Irenaeus was. The question rather, in Origen's case, is *what kind* of philosophy did he employ, and in *what context.*

The Great Chain of Being

Origen's intellectual context has been treated materially by patristic scholars, with great clarity and with much attention to detail, in terms of the trends of "Middle Platonism," in the midst of which Origen found himself and to which he contributed.[56] Here, however, our discussion requires a more formal kind of analysis. To this end, it will suffice to highlight a conceptuality to which we have already alluded — the metaphysical schema of the great chain of being — and to see that conceptuality in the context of Origen's cultural world. Reality, according to this way of thinking, is a universal hierarchical structure. At its peak is "the One" or God, dwelling in world-transcending ineffability or mystery. Along its descending levels are found many gradations of being, "the many" or, in Christian parlance, the creation. The philosophical mind ranges up and down these gradations, seeking understanding.

This "world construct" has been carefully studied by Arthur Lovejoy, to whom we have already referred in this connection. Although much of his attention focuses on the philosopher Plotinus (ca. 205–70), Origen's great contemporary, his analysis offers important insights into the themes we are pursuing here as well.

The gradations of the hierarchy of being define an ontology of the spiritual and the material. At the constituting and dominating apex of this ontological structure we see the ineffable divine principle, variously called the One, the Good, or God, the perfect and most spiritual of all realities. The chain then extends down toward a primordial flux and nonbeing at the nadir. From the apex to the nadir, the spiritual gradually gives way to the material. Nearest to God are the purely angelic creatures; next the human creatures, who are embodied spirits; then the animals, plants, and material elements; finally the flux and nonbeing.

Lovejoy identified three major characteristics of this ideational framework, which he calls principles: *plenitude,* or universal fullness; *continuity,* an idea which is derived from the first (all gaps will be filled); and *gradation,* the notion of a hierarchy of perfection extending from the apex to the nadir of the chain, from the One to the many, until the lowest level of being. Creatures closer to the One, especially intellectual creatures, more nearly approximate the purely spiritual reality of the One, and in this sense are more perfect, than do creatures that occupy lower positions in the hierarchy, especially visible animate or inanimate creatures.

The inner dynamic of the traditional great chain of being conceptuality,

Lovejoy points out, is the logic of "goodness."[57] By its very nature, so this reasoning proceeds, the One is pure perfection; therefore it cannot be jealous. Hence it overflows. Thus emerges, through a process of emanation from the One to the many, a universal, infinitely variegated and indeed timeless pyramid of being. In most Neoplatonic systems, this emanation is seen as the very overflowing of the One itself, which is understood to take different forms at different levels. In Christianized versions of the schema, the hierarchy is looked at as a world of creatures, fashioned by God out of nothing (ex nihilo).

Lovejoy also notes, and this observation is of great importance for our concerns here, that the vision of this hierarchy of being contains within itself a certain structural tension, indeed, in Lovejoy's estimate, a contradiction. This is as we might expect, since the great chain of being conceptuality appears to bring together the influence of two countervailing imaginative energies: the metaphor of ascent and the metaphor of fecundity. The great chain of being conceptuality, furthermore, seems to be in fact a categorical expression of the existential encounter with "the overwhelming mountain," which we considered earlier. As such it embodies the opposing imaginative forces given with that image, the tension between the metaphor of ascent and the metaphor of fecundity.

If one is proceeding up the mountain with one's eyes on the heights, we can recall, then the experience suggests a certain disengagement from, or even hostility toward, the whole visible world below. But if one keeps looking back as one ascends, particularly if one is at the peak looking back, then one has in principle a global vision of solidarity with the whole biophysical world on every side.

The great chain of being conceptuality brings with it that kind of tension. Looking up, one sees "the Good," the world-transcending spiritual ground of all material and biological things. From the apex, looking down, one sees "Goodness," the overflowing abundance of that divine principle.

Without considering this metaphorical background, Lovejoy is nevertheless prompted to speak of "the One" not as one, in fact, but as two Gods: "He was the idea of the Good, but he was also the idea of Goodness; and though the second attribute was nominally deduced from the first, no two notions could be more antithetic. The one was an apotheosis of unity, self-sufficiency, and quietude, the other of diversity, self-transcendence, and fecundity."[58] The one God was, in effect, the God of world-denial (the Good); the other was the God of world-affirmation (Goodness). Lovejoy observes that historically speaking there were, in fact, two ideas of God behind this contradiction, the purely contemplative, all-transcending Deity of Aristotle's Metaphysics, the Unmoved Mover (the Good); and the active, immanent God of Plato's Timaeus (Goodness). Plotinus's thought can be viewed as an effort to combine the two.[59]

Within the tradition of Platonism, according to Lovejoy, the balance between the two approaches to God shifted more often than not in the direction of the otherworldly, anticosmic implications of this grand ontological vision. This was in large measure due to the Platonic and Neoplatonic division of the hierarchy of being into two major levels, the intelligible and the sensible. The great gulf in the order of emanation then, according to this sophisticated construction of the hierarchy, was not between the Creator and the creature, as in the Old Testament for example, but between spirit and matter. The Neoplatonic logic, therefore, was clear: "God and the soul, being intelligibles and not sensibles, were species of the same genus, and if the latter is found to be entangled in the sensible world to which the body belongs, it has fallen from its proper place and must attempt to free itself from the one so as to return to the other, that is to say, it must abandon the body."[60]

Such was the shape of this world construct of Hellenistic thought, in its Neoplatonic variations. This was the ideational framework that was readily and understandably appropriated by the church's theologians during the earliest Christian centuries, as they sought to articulate their faith in the most attractive and universally applicable philosophical categories of their time. They eschewed Stoicism—except at times, when they drew on its naturalism as an aid in combatting gnostic dualism—because of what they saw as its pantheistic characteristics: God seemed to be swallowed up by Nature. They likewise rejected a variety of other philosophical or mythological alternatives that were either implicitly or explicitly atheistic or polytheistic. So it happened that the vision of the great chain of being became the cognitive matrix for Christian theology during its formative, postbiblical centuries. The kind of narrative theology represented by Irenaeus faded from the mainstage of theological reflection as Christian thought, by a certain historical necessity, became "Hellenized."[61]

An Ethos of Alienation

Fatefully, however, and here the plot thickens, the vision of the great chain of being was appropriated by Christian theologians in a time when the sense of cosmic affirmation implicit in the idea of goodness was on the wane, culturally speaking. Classical Platonism and Stoicism had articulated what has been called a "cosmic optimism." They viewed the universe as beautiful, as a mirror of ultimate goodness. Yet for most of its formative years, Christianity found itself taking shape and growing as part of what E. R. Dodds has called, borrowing W. H. Auden's phrase, an Age of Anxiety.[62] It was an era of marked sociopolitical uncertainty, not to say pronounced pessimism. One of the expressions of this general cultural malaise was a sometimes thoroughgoing alienation from the biophysical world generally, and from the human body in particular.

The most extreme expression of these anticosmic tendencies was undoubtedly the various expressions of Gnosticism, which we have already considered. But Gnosticism did not stand alone in this era. Much less exaggerated but not altogether dissimilar sentiments were shared by many during this period, as Dodds has shown. It was widely believed, for example, that the earth was the lowest part of the universe, the center where the mere dregs and sediments of the cosmos had come to rest, due to their excessive weight.[63] Some singled out the human body and human sexuality as especially loathsome. Thus, although Plotinus self-consciously rejected gnostic dualism and, in particular, the view that the body is evil, he appeared nevertheless to be ashamed of having a body at all.[64]

Hence, given what might be called the anticosmic ethos of the times, Christian thinkers, in adopting the schema of the great chain of being as their world construct, were culturally predisposed to accent the otherworldly, world-denying possibilities latent in that schema, as were many others in that era, especially those who identified themselves with the Platonic tradition.

Creation as a Secondary Theological Concern

But there are more substantive, inner-theological reasons for some of these trends as well. We may say that Christianity, as it spread throughout the Hellenistic world after the first century, was fundamentally a new religion of human salvation that tended to take creation for granted. In this respect, Irenaeus's thought—and the deliberations of some of the "Apostolic Fathers"—was a marked divergence from what came to be the most widely articulated theological trends of the times. The Bible of Christianity was the Old Testament, to be sure, but the message that the early church first proclaimed to the world—and, therefore, the message that most captivated many Christian thinkers—was the gospel of human salvation through Jesus Christ, the Son of God. Many Christian thinkers were preoccupied, accordingly, with christological, soteriological, or Trinitarian issues, rather than with issues related to the doctrine of creation. Once the church had successfully warded off the anticosmic dualism of gnostic thought, with the help of writers such as Irenaeus, and also the related attempt by Marcion to excise the Old Testament and with it the idea of God the Creator, it turned its attention with a passion to other doctrinal and practical matters, most of them pertaining to human salvation.[65] There was, indeed, much work to be done. The great chain of being conceptuality did not readily lend itself to giving expression to the new confessions of the incarnation of the eternal Word and the unity of the godhead. Fatefully, however, it was generally assumed that those alone were the chief pressure points that needed attention, not issues related to the theology of the whole creation (with the exception of the ideas of creation *ex nihilo* and the commitment to refute gnostic dualism).

The Tendency to Envision a Nature-Denying Salvation

Taken together, all these trends lent force to a certain disinterest in, even at times an alienation from, nature in the mind of patristic theologians. As they sought to reflect about the salvation they believed the church was called upon to proclaim to the world, which was often their chief concern, their impulse was to accent an otherworldly and, finally, a nature-denying salvation, since that was not only suggested by the temper of the times, but it was also intrinsically, if implicitly, commended by the very Hellenistic conceptuality that they were employing.[66] In this respect, as in others, Irenaeus obviously stood apart. Origen, however, did not. This was the metaphysical environment in which he worked and with which he struggled.

ORIGEN: THE DYNAMICS OF THE HIERARCHY OF BEING AND THE DEGRADATION OF NATURE

Origen's thought is predicated on a vision of the unchanging One, God, dwelling above in eternity, surrounded by a world of rational spirits (*logikoi*), whom God creates eternally to live in perfect communion with God. As free spirits, however, some of them become "sated," according to Origen, and turn from God. They fall away from God, toward nonbeing. This act of spiritual rebellion establishes the condition for God's creation of the world.

The Material World as a Gracious but Punitive Afterthought of God

Origen depicts God as creating the material-vital world as a kind of gracious act, to stop the fall of the rational spirits toward ultimate nonbeing. They then become encased, as it were, in matter. God creates the world, from its highest reaches to its lowest, from its spiritual heights to its material depths, as an ordered hierarchy of being.[67] The fallen rational spirits are embodied in the upper echelons of the hierarchy in gradated positions, from the highest heavens to the human level. Thus encased in matter, as Origen suggests in his commentary on Romans, all the rational spirits—the substance of the human soul, the spirits that animate sun, moon, and stars above, even the angels and archangels above them—groan for their own liberation.[68]

The material world thus comes into being as a result of divine benevolence in a sense, but its more fundamental raison d'être is the fall. Essentially the material world is created to be a kind of purgatory, in that sense a punishment, as far as Origen is concerned.[69] It is not evil, as he sees it. Against the pagan philosopher Celsus, Origen argues that evil does not reside in matter. Rather, matter is created by the goodness of God. Still, matter is created, according to Origen, only for the purpose of educating humanity, through trials and tribulations, to return to a higher incorporeal, spiritual destiny.

Of the material world itself, Origen has a consistently low opinion, whether it be the human body in particular, which he approaches with a radical kind of asceticism, or the world of irrational and inanimate things, more generally. The world of the flesh is the realm of the demons.[70] Gross matter, indeed, is the domain of Satan, one of the rational spirits who fell so far that his glory "was turned into dust."[71] The stars and the planets, to be sure, are rational creatures (as was generally believed in Origen's time). The *logikoi* in these creatures did not fall as far as the others; so they are less embedded in materiality. The further they fall, however, the less brightly they shine.[72]

Below humans in the hierarchy Origen depicts a world that resembles a pernicious wilderness, much more than a life-sustaining home. The animals apparently, for him, are not bearers of the fallen spirits, as humans are; the animals exist solely as agents of purgation for the moral education of humanity.[73] Indeed, they and other irrational creatures seem to have a certain nauseating quality, as far as Origen is concerned. At one point, for example, he likens the creation of humanity to the birth of a child, and the world of irrational and inanimate things to "the afterbirth which is created with the child."[74]

Correspondingly, since humanity is the only embodiment of the fallen rational spirits in the biophysical world, Origen holds that the whole of sensible reality, contrary to Celsus's view, was made not for the sake of the whole, and each creature for its own sake as part of the whole, but that all was made for the edification of the human creature: "The Creator, then, has made everything to serve the rational being and his natural intelligence."[75]

The logic of descending goodness is thus radically qualified by Origen: through his emphatic hierarchically ordered spirit-matter dualism. The creatures of the visible world, for him, have no other value than the service they render to humanity and to the human quest for salvation beyond the material world. Origen's anthropocentrism at this point thus does not strike the balance which Irenaeus's does. It is ontological, not just administrative. For Origen, it would be a disgrace to God to think of him as embracing and nurturing the whole world of nature, as well as caring for human life. The kind of divine caring for nature that we see in Irenaeus's thought is totally missing in Origen's constructions.

The Final Negation of Matter

The ultimate goal of divine providence, according to Origen's schema, will be the return of all the rational creatures to their original state in eternity.[76] Unlike Irenaeus, he holds that the end *is* like the beginning.[77] This ending

Origen depicts in highly spiritualistic terms, as we might expect, since the creation of matter was only, for him, an instrumental expression of the divine will,
undertaken in order to make it possible for God to restore the rational spirits to
their original immaterial unity with God. The material world will presumably
fall back into nothingness, from whence it came, at the very end.[78]

In this context, Origen makes an effort to affirm the church's teaching about
the resurrection of the body, but that effort, at best, is less than convincing. He
maintains that the substance of the resurrected body "will be like ether, of a celestial purity and clearness."[79] He finds the idea of a "spiritual body" in Paul;
but in Origen's thought the "spiritual" is so emphasized that one can legitimately wonder if any substantive meaning really remains for the "body." Our
resurrection bodies will be so refined physically, he says, that they will have lost
their corporeality.[80]

The contrast between Origen and Irenaeus at this point could not be starker.
The latter envisions salvation in terms of a messianic banquet in the renewed
heaven and earth, depicted in the most sensual and corporeal of terms. Origen
can only see God far above and removed, utterly transcending the biophysical
world of ordinary human experience. That realm above for him is the locus of
human fulfillment. Origen then has to shape the biblical belief in the resurrection of the body to fit into that hierarchical, spiritualizing conceptuality. It
would seem that he so radically shapes the idea, in the process, that it is bent
out of shape altogether, even shattered.

The Ascent of the Soul Above the Earth

All this is graphically illustrated by the recommendations Origen gives as a
spiritual director who is interpreting the Scriptures. He consistently subsumes
the metaphor of migration to a good land under the metaphor of ascent, with
the result that the former loses all its dynamism and tangibility. He interprets
the narrative of biblical wandering to the promised land, for example, "in a
spiritual sense," in terms of his reading of Eph. 4:10, "He who also descended is
also he who ascended."[81] He asserts that the forty-two stages of pilgrimage
which, in his view, the people of Israel experienced according to Numbers 23
correspond to the forty-two generations depicted in Matthew 1, through which
the Word of God descended in order to be born of a virgin. He descended in
this way, Origen suggests, so that we might ascend or return to God, in the
same way. "In descending to the Egypt of this world," Origen explains, "Christ
passed those forty-two generations as stages; and those who ascend from Egypt
pass by the same number, forty-two stages."[82]

So Origen traces "the stages of that journey and ascent of the soul" from "the
Egypt of this world to the Promised Land" above.[83] There the soul will have

"returned to its rest," he says, that is, "to the fatherland in paradise."[84] This, then, is his advice to the aspiring Christian soul. He speaks about a radical rising above the biophysical world as we might have expected him to say, in view of his underlying dependence on the metaphor of ascent. He writes:

> If you do not wish to fall in the wilderness, but to have attained the promised land of the fathers, you should have no portion in the land nor should you have anything in common with the earth. Let your portion be only with the Lord, and you will never fail. Therefore, the ascent from Egypt to the promised land is something by which, as I have said, we are taught in mysterious descriptions the ascent of the soul to heaven and the mystery of the Resurrection from the dead.[85]

Assessment: The Triumph of the Spiritual Motif

We witness in Origen's thought, then, the thoroughgoing triumph of the idea of the good over the idea of goodness, and the underlying triumph of the metaphor of ascent over the metaphor of migration to a good land. This, then, is the dominance of what we have called the spiritual motif in Origen's thought. Matter, for Origen, has no divinely bestowed integrity of its own. It is entirely subordinated to a rational-spiritual teleology. Nature is sheerly a structure put in place by God to provide the place for the process of human salvation. Or to use Origen's striking metaphor, nature is the afterbirth of the human birth. It has at best the value of punishment, purgation, and education; but ultimately it has no value before God whatsoever. It would have been better, from Origen's point of view, if the material world had never existed. Such is his degradation of nature.

Origen's thought, to be sure, is not explicitly Gnostic. For him, matter is not created by some evil power. The metaphor of fecundity is, in this respect, marginally influential in Origen's thought. He affirms the idea of "the goodness of creation" in a formal, limited way. He does not teach, as the Gnostics did, that matter has nothing to do with the God who is good. Still, his view of the material order, in its cumulative existential force, comes strikingly close to the apperceptions and the sensibilities of Gnosticism. Human identity, for Origen, is essentially spiritual.[86] Human life in nature, accordingly, is something alien, something to be overcome, something to be left behind, in order to be united with the immutable, immaterial One, who dwells in majestic, unchanging, and tranquil splendor far above in eternity.

This is the legacy of the root metaphor of ascent, when it alone is the dominating metaphor: the degradation of nature. If this metaphor alone is the formative principle of one's thought—that is, if one's thinking is shaped by the spiritual motif only—the result can only be, however many qualifications may be added along the way, an otherworldly view of salvation and a radical depreciation of the world of nature.

In the case of Origen, therefore, Kaufman's estimate of the inner logic of Christian theology regarding nature seems to be perfectly justified. Nature is not made the subject of any technical vocabulary or doctrines for Origen, since the focus of his thought is so closely fixed on the redemption of the fallen spiritual world. Likewise, there is a radical ontological dissimilarity between God and humans, on the one hand, and nature, on the other. Further, the very way Origen's concept of God is designed implies, by definition, the depreciation of nature. For Origen, God is defined by his nature-transcending qualities.

Long after Origen died, the church condemned his theology. He had been a passionately committed theologian of the church, given to vigorous discipline and to the life of prayer and contemplation. He had been an intellectual par excellence in his time—when there were few, if any, dogmatic guidelines. He had sought to interpret the Scriptures faithfully, in light of the best and most appropriate metaphysical categories of the day. But certain portions of his theology—specifically his Christology and his (reputed) doctrine of the transmigration of souls—were condemned, and he was thereby publicly discredited.

Still, he remained enormously influential—especially with respect to those areas of his thought that had not been condemned. His theology of nature, in particular, would remain a theological position that tended to be taken for granted, particularly regarding the way he employed the conceptuality of the hierarchy of being. In ensuing centuries the position he espoused, in this regard, became part of the assumed data of the tradition, even though it did not often bear his name. We shall hear echoes of Origen's thought more than once in the following chapters, nowhere more poignantly than in the early works of the great doctor of the Western church Augustine. To his theology of nature we must turn as we continue to pursue the story of the ambiguous ecological promise of classical Christian theology.

4

THE FLOWERING OF THE PROMISE

Augustine

If, as Whitehead has suggested, the history of Western philosophy is but commentary on Plato, one might be bold enough to make a similar claim for Augustine (354–430) in the history of Western theology. "In Latin Christendom," Frederick Copelston has written, "the name of Augustine stands out as that of the greatest of the Fathers both from a literary and a theological standpoint, a name that dominated Western thought until the thirteenth century and which can never lose its lustre. . . ."[1] We focus our attention on the great African doctor, then, for self-evident reasons. But we also consider his thought in the midst of these particular explorations, because here we will be able to see some foundations for the theology of nature, and evidence of other less-enduring constructions, that illuminate the vectors of the whole Christian tradition's approach to nature in a way that is perhaps unsurpassed by any other single Christian theologian.

Augustine was thoroughly influenced by his metaphysical environment, as was Origen. That environment, indeed, was strikingly similar to Origen's three centuries earlier. Augustine's spiritual quest, well known from his own accounts of it in his *Confessions,* was in a certain sense a metaphysical pilgrimage. He moved from one school of philosophy to another, finally coming to rest within the tradition of Neoplatonism, in which context his mature theological work emerged. Like Origen and unlike Irenaeus, Augustine was at home in the world of categorical thought. In this sense, throughout his life he was like Origen a philosophical theologian.

At the same time, in his middle and later years, Augustine was able to sense the textures and the resonances of biblical faith, above all the biblical concern for history, far more adequately than Origen was able to do. In this respect Augustine was much closer to Irenaeus than to Origen, and for this reason he may also be thought of as a confessional theologian.[2]

We shall see, indeed, a kind of creative synthesis emerging in his thought. It recapitulates some of the major moments in the story of ambiguity and promise which we have begun to follow in these historical explorations. We see him first as an exponent of the most radical kind of anticosmic fascination with the transcendent good, standing within the tradition of Gnosticism. Then we see him occupying various positions within the broad flow of the Platonic tradition, at times appearing very much like Origen. Finally, he moves to a way of thinking that is still indebted to the tradition of Platonism but that is fundamentally shaped by the theme of creation history, akin to the theological framework of Irenaeus.

To do this, Augustine shifted from one root metaphor to others and, accordingly, from one motif to another. At first, as a Manichee, his mind was totally dominated by the metaphor of ascent, that is, by the spiritual motif. Later, he left that motif behind for the most part as he became more and more positively disposed toward the created order. He thought increasingly in patterns shaped by the metaphor of fecundity. Categorically, his thought moved in the milieu of the great chain of being conceptuality, as Origen's did. However, unlike Origen he was fascinated not with the world-transcending good as such but more with the thought of God's overflowing goodness. At the same time, the metaphor of migration to a good land shaped his thinking more and more; his thought accordingly became more "historical," above all in the *City of God*. Under the aegis of the metaphor of migration to a good land, we can say, Augustine historicized the overflowing goodness of God. As a result, he developed a theology of creation history reminiscent of Irenaeus's thought, but portrayed much more vividly, elaborately, and self-consciously than Irenaeus had done. Notwithstanding some other, countervailing factors in his thought, we can say, then, that the ecological motif of Western theology comes to its full flowering in the theology of Augustine.

AUGUSTINE'S DEVELOPMENT:
BEYOND THE LEGACY OF THE MANICHEES

Augustine's intellectual and spiritual pilgrimage began auspiciously for him when as a young man who had been raised by a Christian mother he allied himself with some disciples of Mani.[3] Mani took for granted the existence of two coeternal, opposite principles, good and evil. He depicts the good as an eternal center of light that is attacked by the principle of evil and then scattered and exiled—passively, helplessly—in the material world, which is a prison fashioned by the evil principle. Salvation, then, is a return of the scattered sparks of the divine light to unity with the good, the process of extricating them from the alien world of matter and reuniting them with the One which dwells in the ineffable brilliance of eternity. As part of this overall schema, Mani and his disciples developed a strikingly hostile attitude toward the human body, viewing it not only as an alien reality to be overcome but also as an actively evil power in devilish design. Humanity, according to Mani, is begotten bodily, in a most repulsive way, by demons.[4]

The Influence of Plotinus

As Augustine left Manicheism behind, the influence of Plotinus made itself felt in a thoroughgoing way. In Plotinus's schema, the power of goodness always maintains the initiative, as Peter Brown comments: "The One flowed out, touching everything, molding and giving meaning to passive matter, without itself being in any way violated or diminished." In contrast, "the darkest strand of the Manichean view of the world, the conviction that the power of the Good was essentially passive, that could only suffer the violent impingement of an active and polluting force of evil, was eloquently denied by Plotinus." The latter's universe was a "continuous, active whole, which could admit no brutal cleavages, and no violent interruptions."[5]

Augustine's acceptance of Plotinus's vision had a twofold effect on his thinking. On the one hand, it allowed him to see God as utterly transcendent, as the good; and it helped him to see himself as totally a creature (not carrying a fragment of the divine substance within him). On the other hand, it allowed him to acknowledge God as the ultimate mystery of goodness which embraces all things, even the "lowest" material things, even—presumably—his own sexuality. "I no longer desired a better world," he wrote poignantly in his *Confessions* as he looked back on the radical, otherworldly quest championed by Mani.[6] Within the school of Plotinus, he had learned how to understand the world, still hierarchically construed, as an expression of the overflowing goodness of the transcending good.

The "Six Days of Creation" as an Integrating Construct

If Plotinus's thought was a decisive resting place along the way in his spiritual pilgrimage, Augustine's mature thought about the biophysical world generally and the human body in particular was substantially forged, within that resting place we might say, through his long and intense engagement with the Book of Genesis 1 and 2. No less than five times, spanning a period of some thirty years, did he struggle to interpret these creation narratives.[7] The importance of this encounter with the world-affirming vision of Hebraism, in this respect, should not be underestimated.[8]

The shift in his thinking that resulted was subtle, but real. It was a kind of figure-ground reversal. In Paul Tillich's terms, Augustine's work with the Genesis creation narratives—and with the faith of the biblical writers more generally—helped him to reshape his thought so that it was no longer defined primarily by the spatial categories of Plotinus, but more and more by the temporal categories of biblical history.[9]

The theme of world history having six days or periods, which we have already encountered in the thought of Irenaeus, was commonplace in patristic literature prior to Augustine.[10] The temporal character of the creation narrative in Genesis 1 as a matter of course lent itself to such historical extrapolations. In his early writings, however, Augustine tended to represent that schema not in world-historical terms, but rather as a Platonic ascent of the soul, through various stages of growth to full human maturity.[11] He traced the journey of the soul from the lower to the higher realities, from the material to the spiritual. It was in this period of his life that he uttered the oft-quoted words, which we have already cited: "I desire to have knowledge of God and the soul. Of nothing else? No, of nothing else whatsoever."[12]

Later, however, he refocused his attention, as he reread Genesis, and perhaps as he reflected more on the patristic theme of a world history with six "days." He saw the temporal character of the creation much more vividly in any case: the theme that the created world had a beginning, since it was given reality *ex nihilo* by God; the theme that it will have an ending, the kind promised by biblical proclamation of the new creation; and perhaps most important of all, the theme that the created order has a once-and-for-all middle point, the incarnation of the Word.[13]

Accordingly, in his theological maturity Augustine would seek and be able to know much more than God and the soul. He would attempt to contemplate *the whole of reality as a universal, richly endowed history, guided and blessed by God throughout.* "Plotinus, when he wrote on 'Providence,'" Brown explains, "had already presented the natural world as a harmony of minutely articulated parts. The same sense of wonder which is so marked a feature of the way in which Plotinus speaks of the Universe—the Cosmos—will flood into the language of Augustine as he speaks of the marvelous and perfectly ordered distribution of the ages."[14] Brown illustrates this point with the following quotation:

> God is the unchanging conductor as well as the unchanged Creator of all things that change. When he adds, abolishes, controls, increases or diminishes the rites of any age, He is ordering all events according to his providence, until the beauty of the completed course of time, whose parts are the dispensations suitable to each different period, shall have played itself out, like the great melody of some ineffable composer.[15]

For Augustine, "the epochs of the world are linked together in a wonderful way" by the gradual development of the divine plan in history.[16] In this sense, the "temporalizing of the Great Chain of Being," which Arthur Lovejoy identified with developments in the eighteenth century,[17] was well underway in Augustine's mature thought.[18]

But we must be specific about our characterization at this point. It is of great import for us to notice which aspect of the great chain of being conceptuality was temporalized. It was not the world-transcending logic of the good that was temporalized. It was the world-affirming logic of goodness. So it followed for Augustine, as a matter of course, that he should take up and reaffirm a biblical motif that was earlier of little significance for him—although it had been of decisive import for thinkers such as Irenaeus in the second century—the idea of a new creation, the vision of world renewal following the final eschatological conflagration of all things.

Christopher Dawson has observed in this respect that Augustine's own milieu —North Africa, and Carthage in particular—became in earlier decades "the antithesis of Alexandria," where Origen had first flourished, in the development of Christian thought. "It remained a stronghold of the old realistic eschatology and of millennialist ideas," Dawson writes, "which were held not only by Tertullian, but by Arnobius and Lactantius and Commodian." Dawson traces direct influence on Augustine, in this regard, by the fourth-century Donatist writer Tyconius, who "represents the African tradition in its purest and most uncontaminated form. He owes nothing to classical culture or to philosophic ideas; his inspiration is entirely Biblical and Hebraic." Dawson says that Augustine "was deeply influenced by Tyconius, not only in his interpretation of scripture, but also in his theology and in his attitude toward history; above all in his central doctrine of the two cities."[19] It is not too much to imagine, then, that there was a kind of subterranean, but real influence on Augustine from the side of the thought world of Irenaeus, as far as Augustine's increased interest in history and eschatology in his later years was concerned.

So for Augustine, in sharp contrast to Origen, the omega of the created order, like the alpha, is to be determined and blessed by the overflowing goodness of God. There will be a new heaven and a new earth; things will not come full circle to the state of affairs where they began, with God in eternity. In this way, by historicizing goodness, by viewing it as forming and integrating a finite process that has a beginning and an ending, Augustine was able to break decisively with the inner contradictions of the great chain of being conceptuality that had allowed it to function as the ideational framework for both world affirmation and world denial.[20]

It would be fascinating to inquire further which came first in Augustine's development or which was the more fundamental—his increasing preoccupation with historical categories, shaped as that evidently was by the metaphor of migration to a good land (the North African tradition, mediated through Tyconius); or his shift from the all-dominating influence of the metaphor of ascent (Mani) to the encompassing influence of the metaphor of fecundity (Plotinus). But it is sufficient for our purposes here to notice that Augustine's development can be schematized as a movement from a radical dominance of his thought by the metaphor of ascent to a mutually reenforcing formation of his thought by the metaphors of fecundity and migration to a good land.

In Augustine's theology, then, we witness a metaphorical metamorphosis of profound scope, which saw him move from a radical adherence to the spiritual motif on the one hand, to a thoroughgoing adherence to the ecological motif on the other hand.[21]

AUGUSTINE'S MATURE THOUGHT: CREATION HISTORY AND THE OVERFLOWING GOODNESS OF GOD

Augustine's thought in his later years is shaped, perhaps it would be better to say overwhelmed, by his comprehensive—both world-historical and existential —vision of God. For Augustine, God is the timeless, unchanging One, who dwells in unapproachable mystery. To this extent, Augustine still finds the Plotinian notion of God as the exalted good useful; it helps him to articulate the ultimate mystery of the God who is overflowing goodness. But it is the latter idea—which he also found in Plotinus—that more often than not seems to fascinate Augustine. Again and again he emphasizes that the God he is addressing and confessing is no idle deity, no *Deus otiosus*, like the unmoved mover of Aristotle. The God that Augustine points to is one whom, as we already have had occasion to see, he can liken to an ineffable composer of a universal symphony. This is a deity who is ever active, as well as quiet (*semper agens, semper quietus*); immutable, yet changing all things; and close at hand. So Augustine prays:

> O thou supreme, most excellent, most mighty, most omnipotent, most merciful and most just; most secret and most present; most beautiful and most strong; constant and incomprehensible; immutable, yet changing all things; never new, and never old; renewing all things, and insensibly bringing proud men into decay; ever active, and ever quiet; gathering together, yet never wanting; upholding, filling, protecting; creating, nourishing and perfecting all things; still seeking, although thou standest in need of nothing. Thou lovest, yet are not transported; art jealous, but without fear; thou dost repent, but not grieve; art angry, but cool still. Thy works thou changest, but not thy counsel.[22]

For Augustine then God's immutability is not some abstract, eternal sameness, wholly other, totally removed from all things, but much more a concrete relational constancy toward all things, reflecting the theme of goodness now temporalized and akin to biblical images of the Living God.[23]

This deity is addressed and confessed by Augustine, in his mature thought, first and foremost as what might be called creative providence. The latter, in turn, Augustine understands as having two aspects, which are distinguishable, although not separable, which we can call (using Paul Tillich's language) God's "originating creativity" and God's "sustaining creativity."

God's Originating Creativity: The Divine Goodness and the Beauties of Nature

Augustine depicts God as bringing angels and the visible world into being, out of nothing,[24] directly and immediately, without the help of either the angels or the world.[25] This, as Augustine sees it, is the first moment of God's originating creativity. Augustine takes it for granted in his exegesis of Genesis that "the heavens" and "the light" refer to the spiritual world, the realm of the angels, while "the earth" and "the darkness" refer to the primordial matter of things, which is to receive form in the ensuing creative acts of God.[26] It is noteworthy, notwithstanding his identification of primordial matter with the night, that he conceives the primary stuff out of which the universe is constructed not as something alien or threatening but as something essentially receptive to creative formation, as having an "ability to receive form."[27] At the same time, it is clear that for Augustine the spiritual aspect of the creation, the realm of the heavens, is nearer to God, more akin to God, and therefore much more beautiful than the visible aspects of the world; and that primordial matter is a much lesser thing, indeed, near to nothing, lower than any other creature.[28] This is one place, among others, where we can detect the continuing influence of the spatial categories of Plotinus, and behind them the metaphor of ascent.

The creative will of God, as Augustine envisions it, thenceforth brings forth a vast and beautiful hierarchy of being, with each being allotted its own rank of perfection.[29] Although Augustine believes that all things, all visible creatures in particular, are created as a blessing for humanity, this by no means exhausts their raison d'être, as far as he is concerned. Human utility is not the sole reason for the existence of all visible things in the hierarchy. Rather, for Augustine, the most fundamental *telos* of the whole creation is beauty, and the glorification of the God who wills such a magnificent community of being, every part of which has its own divinely validated integrity.

Hence, Augustine writes: when "the heretics" (presumably the Manichees) berate the creation by inquiring about the utility of fire, frost, wild beasts, frogs, and so on, they first of all miss the beauty of the whole, as well as the beauty and harmony of its individual parts; and, second, they rule out the possible discovery of some utility that might be hidden from us:

> They do not consider how admirable these things are in their own places, how excellent in their own natures, how beautifully adjusted to the rest of creation, and how much grace they contribute to the universe by their own contributions, as to a

commonwealth; and how serviceable they are even to ourselves, if we use them
with a knowledge of their fit adaptations . . . and thus divine providence admon-
ishes us not foolishly to vituperate things, but to investigate their utility with
care, and where our mental capacity or infirmity is at fault, to believe that there is
a utility though hidden. . . ."[30]

Even more, Augustine believes, some things, such as certain parts of the human
body, were not created by God with any utility in view whatsoever, but solely
for the sake of their beauty.[31] Every creature, even the lowest, has an "existence
fitting it." We may not realize this, Augustine observes, since from our limited
perspective we cannot see the whole, "in which the fragments that offend us are
harmonized with the most accurate fitness and beauty."[32] Even more:

> If we attentively consider even those faults of earthly things, which are neither vol-
> untary nor penal, they seem to illustrate the excellence of the natures themselves,
> which are all originated and created by God.[33]

Hence, Augustine concludes, "it is not with respect to their convenience or dis-
comfort, but with respect to their own nature, that creatures are glorifying to
their Artificer."[34] In this case, Augustine believes, all things, individually and
considered as a whole, are said by Genesis to be "very good."[35]

As such, the created order is complete, as far as Augustine is concerned. This
is the conclusion of God's originating creativity, at the very beginning of time.
The goodness of the Creator is thus manifest. This is part of the meaning that
Augustine attributes to the "Divine Rest" on the seventh day of creation. But,
again, Augustine's deity is no *Deus otiosus*. Rather, this God is one who is universally immanent and comprehensively active in the providential processes of
sustaining creativity.

God's Sustaining Creativity: The History of Nature

God governs and moves all things from within, in such a way that the whole
creation remains "entirely natural, since all things are from Him, through
Him, and in Him."[36] This Augustinian deity is thus no "oriental despot," as
some have implied, in their analysis of classical Christian thought.[37] God is
omnipotent, for Augustine, not by arbitrary power (*potentia temeraria*) but by
the power of wisdom (*sapientiae virtute*).[38] God's governance of the world, as
Augustine sees it, is not by domination, not by the exercise of heteronomous
might, but by "concursus" (to use a term that gained currency in later dogmatic
theology): "He governs all the things in such a way that he allows them to function and behave in ways proper to them."[39] Augustine often uses the images of
the shepherd and the husbandman to depict God's providential creativity. He
likewise envisions God as "brooding" over the creation in a nurturing way, with

the warmth of the Holy Spirit, like a mother bird resting on her nest.[40] Indeed, he can imagine the Spirit brooding with the sensitivity and power of a
creative artist: "As the creative will of a sculptor hovers over a piece of wood, or
as the spiritual soul spreads through all the limbs of the body; thus it is with the
Holy Ghost; it hovers over all things with a creative and formative power."[41]
Augustine specifically warns against the idea, moreover, that God rules only in
the upper—spiritual—ranks of the creation. No, he maintains, God governs
the whole creation, including the most scorned and common creatures.[42]

God's governance of the creation, to be sure, is mediated, as Augustine sees
it. It has a hierarchical character—again we see the influence of Plotinus and
the metaphor of ascent, in this subordinate mode—which is ordered by God so
that the divine governance works *through* the governance of other creatures,
above all the spiritual creatures.[43] But even at this point where, if anywhere,
one might expect to see the reemergence of the world-transcending deity of
Aristotle in some way, we are presented with a picture of the rich immediacy of
the divine rule: God is distant, yet near. Augustine maintains that God is dif-
fused, as it were, through the universe, ruling and containing all things, effort-
lessly, without labor (. . . *sine labore regans et sine onere continens mundum*).[44]

Given this rich and pervasive vision of the gentle but powerful divine governance of all things, and Augustine's understanding of the universal beauty and
goodness of all things, it comes as no surprise to notice that he portrays what
might be called an omnimiraculous apperception of the whole of natural and
human history. For Augustine, as Margaret Miles has observed, miracles press
on our senses from every side: "For who is there," Augustine declares, "that considers the works of God, whereby this whole world is governed and regulated,
who is not overwhelmed with miracles? If he considers the vigorous power of a
single grain of any seed whatever, it is a mighty thing, it inspires him with
awe."[45] According to Augustine, Miles points out, nothing prevents us from
experiencing this universally miraculous character of the creation, except our
failure to order our affections rightly and to use our senses.[46] Augustine understands the eternal Word of God to be working wonders throughout the whole
creation, which is an idea, he suggests, Christians often neglect as they see the
miracles wrought by the same Word, incarnate in Jesus.[47] Thus, for Augustine, through the "brooding" of the Spirit over all things and the wonders
worked by the Word in all things, the effectual power of God's creative providence is immediately present everywhere.[48] The world for Augustine, in this
sense, is transparent to the goodness and the wisdom of God's sustaining creativity, for all those who have eyes to see.

Along with this vast and all-encompassing vision of the wonders of the divine
causality, Augustine introduces a concept that pertains to the life of the bio-

physical world, within itself. This is his much-discussed idea of the "seminal reasons" of the created order. By this construct he attempts to account for the providentially ordered emergence of novelty within cosmic history, since he has otherwise taken pains to establish the idea that the whole creation was established, once and for all, in its goodness, in a complete form, at the very beginning. He holds that these "seminal reasons" are the seeds of new developments, which lie hidden in the creation, waiting to spring into life in their own time. As he explains:

> All these things indeed have originally and primarily already been created in a kind of web of the elements; but they make their appearance when they get the opportunity. For just as mothers are pregnant with their young, so the world itself is pregnant with things that are to come into being, things that are not created in it. . . .[49]

At one point, in a striking manner, Augustine contemplates a tree and wonders at its growth from seed to maturity. Yes, he says, the whole world grows like that.[50] This image is a fitting complement for his idea of the brooding, nurturing providence of the Spirit of God and his notion of the miraculous workings of the eternal Word of God throughout the whole creation. We see here, therefore, that Augustine has indeed a rich sense for the history of natural being as well as for the more particular history of human being—although the latter is much more familiar to many interpreters, who tend to read the *City of God,* for example, as if Augustine were interested only in the history of human life.[51]

The Importance of "Last Things"

The capstone of Augustine's vision of a universal history of all things is his doctrine, which we have already had occasion to note, of the final renewal of all things.[52] He envisions the whole history of creation as coming to an ultimate rest, totally renewed in eternity with God, following a universal conflagration of all things. Here he returns to reaffirm expectations that shaped the consciousness of the early church, and that were affirmed forcefully by early theologians such as Irenaeus, conjoining and integrating the ideas of cosmic renewal and the resurrection of the body.[53]

When he does this, he does it in his own cautious terms. He is too widely traveled in the world of philosophy and systematic reflection about the faith of the church to be satisfied with a simple narration of the events of the end time. He knows that he sees through a glass darkly (as when he talked about the mystery of the Trinity, he remarked that his intention was to say something so as not to have to say nothing). The contrast with Irenaeus at this point is apparent. Irenaeus, it appears, was still living within the framework of an "unbroken myth," as we suggested earlier. For Irenaeus, the thousand-year reign of Christ could be imagined as beginning tomorrow, as it were, in the Mediterranean world. Augustine was much more self-conscious about the symbolic character of religious language than Irenaeus was. Also, Augustine, for his own historical reasons, was highly suspicious of the political implications of chiliasm, that is, the doctrine of the thousand-year reign of Christ with the saints. He wanted to avoid all implications of any kind of political enthusiasm. But the remarkable thing is then that notwithstanding his theological sophistication and notwithstanding his compelling pragmatic reasons for rejecting chiliasm, he *still* affirmed the coming renewal of the whole world. He still looked forward *to the future* for that final world consummation.[54]

In that future moment, Augustine says, the faithful will see God's creative governance throughout the whole world, not as they do now, through a glass darkly, but *visibly, with bodily eyes.* Here he in effect reaffirms the confessions of Irenaeus, we may say, but in a symbolically self-conscious way. "Wherefore it may very well be, and it is thoroughly credible," he assures us, "that we shall in the future world see the material forms of the new heavens and the new earth in such a way that we shall most distinctly recognize God everywhere and governing all things, material as well as spiritual. . . ."[55] With the coming of the mysterious end time of God, the whole biophysical world will be glorified. It will be visibly transparent to the luminescent presence of God. God will be all in all, not just in the spiritual creation, but throughout the whole world of nature as well.

An Unfallen Earth

The rich valency of Augustine's view of the biophysical world as a beautifully and appropriately ordered historical process, moving toward its own final fulfillment, with its own integrity in the greater scheme of things, is further strengthened by his articulate treatment of the question of the cosmos and sin.[56] The idea that the cosmos as we now know it is a fallen cosmos, or the distorted act of some evil power, was well known to Augustine. He had presumably held the idea himself, when he was a Manichee. Further, there are themes in the biblical writings that he might readily have drawn on to affirm the idea of a fallen cosmos, above all the idea of God cursing the world of nature in the wake of the sin of Adam and Eve; or Paul's image in Romans 8 of the whole creation, having been subjected to futility by God, now groaning in travail as it awaits the liberation of the children of God. Also, Augustine was aware that other doctors of the church, among them Origen, had adhered to the idea that the cosmos as we presently know it is the result of some pretemporal fall. But he passionately denies the idea. "This heaven, I mean, which I see," he writes emphatically, "and this earth which I walk on, from which comes this earth [my body], which I carry. You have made it."[57]

Augustine makes a radical departure, in this respect, when he is discussing Paul's image of the whole creation groaning in travail.[58] He adamantly maintains that the creature (*ktisis*) which Paul is referring to is the human creature alone, not the whole cosmos. No patristic exegete that we know of, prior to Augustine, had interpreted the passage that way. Augustine thus will not even allow any hint that the cosmos has fallen. Correspondingly, Augustine maintains that the curse referred to in Gen. 3:17 touches human life alone; it does not disrupt the cosmos.[59] Similarly, he holds that Satan is not the lord of the physical world or any part of it, but only of the "world" which is made up of sinful and unbelieving humanity.[60]

Augustine teaches, accordingly, that even in the face of human sin, those who have eyes to see can contemplate in the cosmos a world of radiant beauty which everywhere portrays the transcendent and fecund beauty of God:

> How can I tell you of the rest of creation, with all its beauty and utility, which the divine goodness has given to man to please his eyes and serve his purposes, condemned though he is, and hurled into these labors and miseries? Shall I speak of the manifold and various loveliness of sky, and earth, and sea; of the plentiful supply and wonderful qualities of the light; of sun, moon, and stars; of the shade of trees; of the colors and perfume of flowers; of the multitude of birds, all differing in plumage and in song; of the variety of animals, of which the smallest in size are often the most wonderful; of the works of ants and bees astonishing us more than the huge bodies of whales? Shall I speak of the sea, which itself is so grand a spectacle, when it arrays itself as it were in vestures of various colors, now running through every shade of green, and again becoming purple or blue? Is it not delightful to look at in the storm, and experience the soothing complacency which it inspires, by suggesting that we ourselves are not tossed and shipwrecked? What shall I say of the numberless kinds of food to alleviate hunger, and the variety of seasonings to stimulate the appetite which are scattered everywhere by nature, and for which we are not indebted to the art of cookery? How many natural appliances are there for preserving and restoring health? How graceful is the alteration of day and night! How pleasant the breezes that cool the air! How abundant the supply of clothing furnished us by trees and animals! Can we enumerate all these blessings we enjoy?[61]

Again:

> Ask the loveliness of the earth, ask the loveliness of the sea, ask the loveliness of the wide airy spaces, ask the loveliness of the sky, ask the order of the stars, ask the sun, making the daylight with its beams, ask the moon tempering the darkness of the night that follows, ask the living things which move in the waters, which tarry on the land, which fly in the air; ask the souls that are hidden, the bodies that are

perceptive; the visible things which must be governed, the invisible things that govern—ask these things, and they will all answer you, Yes, see we are lovely. Their loveliness is their confession. And all these lovely but mutable things, who has made them, but Beauty immutable?[62]

This resplendent world of nature, as Augustine sees it, is so transparent to the magnificently nurturing and upbuilding providence of God that it can instruct those who survey it concerning God's providential care of human life as well. Augustine here recapitulates a motif from the teaching of Jesus— "Consider the lilies of the field. . . ."—with a compelling, universal tonality. God: "supreme and true, Word and Holy Spirit (which are one) and one God omnipotent, creator and maker of every soul and every body . . .

> from whom is every mode, every species, every order; from whom are measure, number, weight; from whom is everything which has an existence in nature, of whatever kind it be, and of whatever value: from whom are the seeds of forms and the forms of seeds, and the motion of seeds and of forms; who gave also to flesh its origin, beauty, health, reproductive fecundity, disposition of members, and the salutary concord of its parts; who also to the irrational soul has given memory, sense, appetite, but to the rational soul, in addition to these, has given intelligence and will; who has not left, not to speak of heaven and earth, angels and men, but not even the entrails of the smallest and most contemptible animal, or the feather of a bird, or the little flower of a plant, or the leaf of a tree, without a harmony, and, as it were, a mutual peace among all its parts;—that God can never be believed to have left the kingdoms of men, their dominations and servitudes, outside of the laws of his providence.[63]

The Human Body as Spouse

Augustine's attitude toward the human body, that "earth we carry," is concordant with his general approach to the biophysical world, as we have seen it thus far. His thought about the body, as Miles has shown, "moves from the tendency to view the body as the ground of existential alienation to affirmation of the whole person."[64]

In this mature thought, to begin with, in clearest contrast to his Manichean period, and also in contrast to the time when he was most under the influence of the Platonic tradition, he maintains that sin is rooted in the will, not in the body.[65] Likewise, he eschews the idea of a pretemporal fall, as we have already seen, and with it the suggestion by some of the Greek fathers that sexuality was created by God after the fall, with a view to procreation. He argues that there would have been a begetting of children in paradise, before the fall.[66] Accordingly, Augustine understands Adam to have been created with a material body in paradise, not with a spiritual body.[67]

Behind all this, the metaphor that characterizes his mature thought about the body, as Miles has emphasized, is the image of the body as the "spouse" of the soul, in contrast to his early—familiarly Hellenistic—metaphors of the body as "snare" or a "cage."[68] Likewise, as he thinks of matter generally as predisposed to receive form, not as something alien that needs to be dominated, so he thinks of the body as having a kind of passion for the soul, and the separation of the two therefore, as being unnatural, in pronounced contrast to Platonic thinking.[69]

Augustine's thought about the resurrection of the body seems to be the keystone of all these attitudes toward the body (itself intimately related, evidently, to his ongoing reflection about the incarnation and the resurrection of Christ). Having begun his priestly life holding to an idea of immortality of the soul that excluded the resurrection of the body, in familiar Platonic fashion, he not only arrived later at the position where he was affirming that normative Christian doctrine but celebrating it and integrating it as a central theme in his theology.

While he discusses the differences between the body as we know it and the resurrection body, his emphasis is on their identity.[70] In this respect, his treatment of the Pauline notion that the resurrected body will be a spiritual body is far more convincing than Origen's. For Augustine, the identity of this flesh, this earth that we carry, with the transfigured body we will wear in the new creation, is of the utmost importance. Furthermore, he depicts the resurrection body, consistent with his treatment of the temporal body, as having a great beauty, with all members, even those that will have no function in eternity, such as the sex organs, preserved and glorified. Seen in this eschatological light, the body is now a home, a friend, a spouse. "I wanted to be healed completely," he says vividly in a sermon, "for I am a complete whole."[71] Similarly: "Take away death, the last enemy, and my own flesh shall be my dear friend throughout eternity."[72]

Some Isolated Countervailing Themes

On the other hand, Augustine seems never to have emerged from what Miles calls a "psychological dualism," a certain existential alienation from the body —particularly from sexuality.[73] This psychological dualism with regard to the body seems to be paralleled by a certain dualism of piety, a contemplative dualism, with regard to the soul. He tends, at times, to turn away from the manifestations of God in the world around him to the self-disclosure of God in his inner self. In one of his earlier writings, he could say, "We must flee from every corporeal object." At the end of his life he qualifies this remark in his *Retractions*,[74] but the emphasis on turning away from this exterior world to the interior world was a characteristic of his piety that never totally left him. Thus he concludes his major commentary on Genesis with a treatise dealing with the way in which St. Paul was taken up into a mystical vision of the third heaven (the connection with Genesis here being the idea of paradise). To conclude his Genesis commentary, Augustine could conceivably have written a description of the resurrection life of the redeemed in the transformed new heavens and the new earth, in the world to come. But his mind gravitated rather to a discussion of the ascent of the individual soul to God through three types of visions: corporeal, spiritual, and intellectual.[75] Perhaps, he suggests, the apostle Paul was indeed taken out of the body when he saw what he recounts as the third heaven in his mystical union.[76] In these two respects, the metaphor of ascent seems to have exercised a continuing influence on his teaching.

But these dualisms, psychological with regard to the body, and contemplative with regard to the soul, do not seem to have played a major formative role in the explicit theological constructions of his mature thought regarding the biophysical world as a whole. Taken by themselves, they are reminiscent of Origen; but set in the context of Augustine's mature thought they are singular, not systematic elements. The influence of the metaphor of the body as spouse, and his effusive apperceptions of the compelling and universal beauty of the cosmos generally, seeing all things as being virtually transparent to the providential presence of God, along with his vision of a glorious renewed earth in the end times, seem to have been the formative themes that prevailed in the articulated theology of his later years.[77]

A Contemplative Dominion Over the Earth

In the overall context of his theology of nature, we now turn to a theme which a modern interpreter might well have wanted to assess at the outset, human dominion over nature. This, it turns out, is a relatively minor motif in his thinking, as it was in Irenaeus's thought. When that motif does appear, moreover, its nuance is this: it points to a life of peace with nature, in a commonwealth of being blessed by God, in the midst of which human life is situated with its own excellence. That is the accent, rather than any suggestion that God places humanity over a lesser or valueless thing, in order to dominate it. "God . . . made man in his own image," Augustine observes, "for he created for him a soul endowed with reason and intelligence so that he might excel all the creatures of the earth, air, and sea which were not so gifted."[78] Here "dominion over" is, at most, a muted theme. Augustine's interest is chiefly theocentric. It focuses on humanity's excellence with regard to knowing the ways and the will of God, rather than on humanity's operational status and power over other creatures. Augustine does not seem to have much interest at all in the idea that humanity has a "God-given right to reshape the earth" or any other similar idea. So he asks at one point in the *Confessions*: What does having dominion over the fish and the birds and the cattle and wild beasts and the creeping things mean? It means, he responds, that the human creature "judges all things." Humans exercise dominion "by the understanding of the mind, by which [they] perceive the things of the Spirit of God" (*hoc enim agit per mentis intellectum, per quem percipit quae sunt spiritus dei*).[79]

These nuances stand in sharp contrast to some other readings of the Genesis text in the same era, by Gregory of Nyssa, for example, in his treatise "On the Making of Man." Gregory depicts the cosmos as a "royal lodging" created by God for the sake of its human king, to whom God gives "all kinds of wealth . . . stored in this palace." "For this reason," Gregory comments, "man was brought into the world last after the creation, not being rejected to the last as worthless, but as one whom it behooved to be king over his subjects at his very birth."[80]

Augustine, in contrast, seems to envision a much more contemplative and communal relationship between humanity and the world of nature before the fall. His attention is not fixed on the lordly role of the human creature, nor on the resources of the world of nature. This is as we might expect it to be if humanity, created in the image of God, is created to imitate the governance of God. For that governance, as we have seen, is for Augustine a rule not of arbitrary power but of wisdom and propriety, a dominion that allows all things to be and to function in ways appropriate to their natures. The divine governance is one of concursus, and so, *mutatis mutandi*, is the human relationship with nature, as Augustine depicts it.

Domination, or ruling over, as a matter of fact, is a theme that Augustine highlights with regard to the *fallen* life of humanity. The "lust to dominate" (*libido dominandi*) is the characteristic mode of life he sees both in sinful individuals and in sinful human communities.[81] The earthly city, Augustine stresses, in contrast to the City of God, was founded on fratricide, an act of lustful power.[82] Even the beasts, he notes, creatures devoid of rational will, "live more securely and peaceably with their kind than men, who had been propagated from one individual for the very purpose of commending concord."[83] The rightful relationship of humanity with nature, he suggests at many points, is a relationship of solidarity and peace, rather than disjunction and domination.[84]

The Ultimate Rationale for Nature's Being and Becoming:
The Goodness of God

Most of the significant elements of Augustine's mature thought about the biophysical world have now passed before us: the vision of God as the mysterious but overflowing reality of Goodness, from alpha to omega; the theme that the originating and sustaining creativity of God is the immediate source and goal of the whole creation; the attestation of the beauty and goodness and fullness of the creation, each rank of which has its own integrity; the confession of the omni-miraculous character of the whole of nature; the dynamic idea of the "seminal reasons" which are inherent in the biophysical world; the concept of the unfallen character of that world; the witness to the beauty of nature even to sinful human eyes; the remarkable idea—given his Manichean and Neoplatonic background—that the body is the spouse of the soul; the emphasis on the identity of the resurrected body with this earthly body; the contrasting but singular motifs of psychological and contemplative dualism; and the suggestion that human dominion over nature is a kind of solidarity with nature, exemplified by the divine *concursus*. Now it remains to consider a structural element that is missing from Augustine's thought, as it was missing from Irenaeus's thought—missing, that is, as we look back and compare it with the schema of Origen.

Augustine, like Irenaeus, does not coordinate the key theological ideas of world creation and human redemption in any systematic way. Origen had maintained that the material order is created by God in order to provide the ground for salvation of the rational spirits. Like Irenaeus, Augustine simply tells the story of human salvation as part of the story of creation history.[85] From his point of view, the history of most of the invisible and all of the visible creatures—except for humanity—is a straightforward and glorious narrative of uninterrupted responsiveness to the creativity of divine providence, from the very beginning to the very end of God's universal history with all things. *Human redemption history, for Augustine, happens within the broader milieu of the all-comprehending framework of creation history.*

The story of humanity, of course, has its special pathos. In this particular case, for Augustine, God's creative purposes are interrupted (although with divine foreknowledge). Augustine depicts some of the angels falling into sin. Then he envisions God choosing to save numbers of the likewise fallen human race, in order to fill the places lost by the angels. "For this is the promise of the saints at the resurrection," he explains, "that they shall be equal to the angels of God." The elected ones, moreover, are elected in Christ, as their head. He is the "Saint of saints."[86] This election motif then unfolds for Augustine as he pursues his central preoccupation with the history of the two cities, the one heavenly, the other of this sinful world.

Augustine appears to have mainly existential and practical reasons for projecting his doctrine of election as rigorously as he does.[87] It is not a matter of theological speculation for him. We would not expect him to develop a parallel doctrine of election for the whole creation, moreover, since he holds that most creatures—excepting humankind and some angels—have not fallen. The world of nature, therefore, can have its own proper history with God as part of the larger milieu of creation history, without reference to election and the redemption history of the City of God, which is the realization of that election.

For Origen, in contrast, creation served as a kind of stage that was posited by God to catch the fallen rational spirits, in order that by purgation and education they might be saved. According to Origen's thinking, therefore, the purpose of the biophysical order is completed when the redemption of the fallen spirits is completed. The biophysical world then has no further reason for being. It can lapse back into nothingness whence it came. Origen's systematic coordination of world creation with human redemption, then, is the final seal of disapproval, the last word of devaluation, which he pronounces over the biophysical world.[88]

Such a divine dialectic, significantly, never emerges in Augustine's mature thought, as it likewise never emerged for Irenaeus. When all has been said, Augustine rests his case with the theology of goodness. This for him is the all-embracing divine logic for the whole creation's history. He accepts Plato's idea —which he suspects Plato may have learned from Genesis—that the "most sufficient reason for the creation of the world" was that "good works might be made by a good God."[89]

Assessment: The Triumph of the Ecological Motif

We witness a pattern emerging here. In the case of Irenaeus we saw that Kaufman's judgments about the language of Western theology, the inner logic of Western theology, and the Western doctrine of God did not readily apply. In Origen's case they did, almost as if Kaufman wrote them after a close reading of De Principiis. With regard to Augustine now, we can say, as in the case of Irenaeus, only all the more so, that Kaufman's claims have virtually no applicability.

Yes, Augustine is the doctor gratiae, and his writings are as a matter of course full of technical discourse about sin and grace. But that does not prohibit him from developing a rich vocabulary and thoroughly developed doctrines about the world of nature also. Nor is there any inner logic in his thought that prompts him to devalue nature systematically. Likewise, notwithstanding the fact that he is deeply steeped in Platonism, his doctrine of God is not developed in such a way that God is essentially defined as being over against the world of nature. For the mature Augustine, the theology of goodness, not the theology of the good, shapes the Christian doctrine of God.

What does this pattern mean? The answer to this question seems clear, at least on the basis of the three theologians whom we have thus far considered. Theologies that are thoroughly shaped by the root metaphor of migration to a good land and by the root metaphor of fecundity are theologies which can and do, in fact, present us with a rich vision of nature. On the other hand, theologies that are thoroughly shaped by the root metaphor of ascent are theologies that can and do, in fact, present us with an impoverished vision of nature.

With Irenaeus and Origen the debate might center around the question about the merits of confessional theology over against philosophical theology and vice versa. It might be said, for example, that Irenaeus's "biblicism" keeps him closer to the Hebraic appreciation for the goodness of creation, whereas Origen's thought is "Hellenized," and hence he is led to degrade nature. Therefore, so this line of thought could proceed, confessional theology is better equipped to present us with an adequate theology of nature than philosophical theology is. But that would be a superficial reading of the history we are tracing in this study, as the example of Augustine shows. He was at home with philosophy. He thought in the publicly respected intellectual categories of his day. And he presented us with a theology of nature which is day compared to night, when set beside Origen's. So it is not the question whether one writes philosophical or confession theology that is the key issue with regard to the theology of nature, in this respect. Rather, this is the question: If metaphysical categories are self-consciously—or unconsciously—employed, what kind of categories are they and how are they employed? More particularly, how does that philosophy enable any particular theologian to give expression to the vectors of imaginative energy flowing from the metaphor of migration to a good land and the metaphor of fecundity?

That is the pattern which has emerged here. The root metaphor of ascent, by itself, is not suitable for a viable theology of nature. The root metaphor of migration to a good land, held together with the root metaphor of fecundity—the ecological motif—allows theology, whether it be philosophical or confessional in methodology, to move with a self-authenticating sense of direction toward a viable theology of nature. Because this underlying metaphorical dynamic is so visible in the case of Augustine, we can indeed appropriately say that his thought represents the flowering of the ecological promise of classical Christian theology.

5

THE HEIGHTENING OF THE AMBIGUITY

The Renaissance of the Twelfth Century and the Theology of Thomas Aquinas

As we continue our explorations of classical Christian thought about nature, we now arrive at a region in this vast site that, on the surface at least, seems likely to allow us to make further positive discoveries. In the foreground we can see the justly celebrated figure of St. Francis, and we can recall the lyrical paeans of his Canticle to the Sun. Before him we can see developments during what has been called the Renaissance of the twelfth century, especially that era's fascination with, and celebration of, the world of nature. Still, we must reserve judgment about these highly visible phenomena, until we have considered some of the deeper theological dynamics of medieval life and thought, particularly the way in which the three root metaphors, whose formative influence we have been charting, were employed.

We will find that, with the dramatic exception of Francis himself, the flowering of the ecological promise that we saw in Augustine's thought did not fully survive. Rather, we will witness the heightening of the ambiguity in Christian thought about nature. Earlier we encountered this ambiguity when we compared and contrasted the theologies of Irenaeus and Origen. The one affirmed nature. The other degraded nature. Then we saw the same ambiguity taking shape in the developing thought of one theologian, Augustine, as his theology was first shaped by the spiritual motif and then, finally, by the ecological motif. In the Middle Ages we will see the same kind of ambiguity, but now not in terms of two thinkers in the same period holding different positions or one thinker taking different positions at two times in his life, but rather, structurally: both sides of the ambiguity appearing in the work of individual thinkers at the same time.

Augustine's thought presupposed, as we saw, a shift from the spiritual motif to the ecological motif. He turned away from the legacy of Origen—and Gnosticism—to a way of thinking most influenced by the legacies of Irenaeus and Plotinus. Although the thinkers of the Middle Ages, by and large, considered themselves to be disciples of Augustine, they showed little commitment to the ecological motif that shaped Augustine's mature thought. Perhaps they never understood it as such. With few exceptions, Francis again being the most notable, they tended to turn away from the metaphor of migration to a good land altogether. This was evident, correspondingly, in the general waning of historical categories of medieval theology. The kind of thinking evident in Irenaeus and Augustine, with their comprehensive temporal vision of "the six days" of creation history, faded into the background, if not out of the picture altogether. What was left was largely the spatial categories given with the great chain of being conceptuality, and behind that the influence of only two of the root metaphors that we have been considering, the metaphor of ascent and the metaphor of fecundity.

For the most part, we will see, medieval thought about nature, apart from Francis himself, gave primacy to the metaphor of ascent, while it subordinated the influence of the metaphor of fecundity to the former, and either spiritualized the biblical imagery of the promised land or neglected it altogether. This is the ambiguity of medieval thought about nature, generally. It is an internalized ambiguity. On the one hand, we can see the sometimes striking influence of the metaphor of fecundity and the category of goodness. On the other hand, we can see the finally dominating influence of the metaphor of ascent and the category of the good. What M. D. Chenu says in his monograph *Nature and Man—the Renaissance of the Twelfth Century* is applicable to the thought and ethos of much of the Middle Ages: "The Christian contemplating the world is torn by a double attraction: to attain God through the world, the order of which reveals its Creator, or to renounce the world, from which God is radically distinct."[1]

Categorically, this delimitation of medieval thought about nature generally to the field of imaginative energies defined by the metaphors of fecundity and ascent meant that the tensions inherent in the great chain of being conceptuality would now come to the fore and have to be resolved. To recall Lovejoy's judgment, this conceptuality is defined by two "Gods," a world-affirming, overflowing God of goodness (the legacy of Plato's *Timaeus*) and a world-transcending, self-sufficient God who is thought of as the good (the legacy of Aristotle's *Metaphysics*). This conceptual ambiguity, we will observe, for the most part determines the theology of nature in the Middle Ages.

To set these developments in clear relief, we will first consider the pervasive alienation from nature that characterized the early Middle Ages, and then the remarkable rebirth of interest in, and appreciation for, nature in the twelfth century. Next we will witness that theological naturalism finding one resting place, in the thought of Thomas Aquinas (1225–74), who worked with the newly emerged philosophical categories of Aristotle.

In the following chapter we will continue to consider the ambiguity in medieval thought concerning nature. Indeed we will see it in a more pronounced form, as we identify yet another milieu where the influence of twelfth-century theological naturalism is apparent, in the more Platonic thought of Bonaventure and Dante. This will allow us, finally, to assess the concrete theological meaning of Francis of Assisi and to identify the ecological promise of the theology which he so compellingly embodied.

ALIENATION FROM NATURE IN THE
EARLY MIDDLE AGES

Life for many in the early Middle Ages in the West was stark. It was an "Age of Anxiety" that afflicted both body and soul. Political instability and violence were an ever-present threat, and life-sustaining natural resources, particularly through the long winters, were generally scarce. Regarding attitudes toward nature, one historian has written: "With low population, scattered settlements, and impenetrable forests, Europe was not a place which easily gave rise to the notion that man was the master of his environment. On the contrary, the immensity of an untamed nature made it appear that people, far from controlling the world around them, were in fact held in thrall by it."[2] A ninth-century writer, a certain Sedilius Scotus, gives us this bleak picture:

> White squals from the north, amazing to behold,
> Scare us with sudden gusts and threats of cold.
> Earth itself shakes, fearing to be so blown,
> Old ocean mutters, and the hard rocks groan.
> The unruly north wind hollows the vast air,
> Its hoarse voice whines here, now bellows there,
> Stray milk white fleeces thicken into cloud,
> The faded earth puts on a snow shroud.[3]

Hence it comes as no surprise to notice that the praises for nature's beauty and divine glory, which came so readily to the lips of the mature Augustine, are scarcely to be heard in these centuries. Instead we meet the moralizing bestiaries, herbals, and lapidaries, handbooks for the interpretation of a natural world now conceived, sometimes bizarrely, chiefly as a world of symbols that point toward human virtues or to the otherworldly, heavenly mysteries of human salvation.[4]

At a more esoteric level, the anticosmic theological schema of Origen was essentially reproduced by John the Scot (ca. 810–77), who also translated the spiritualizing Neoplatonic works of Dionysius the Areopagite (ca. 500).[5] John taught, in the spirit of Origen, that God had not originally intended his creative power to descend down the hierarchy of being as far as corruptible matter.

The human creatures had been originally intended by God to have a spiritual body only, without animal needs. The subsequent descent of God's creative power followed only after a defeat or a fall.[6] John envisioned redemption, accordingly, as entailing the final abolition of corruptible matter altogether. Matter would perish. It would return to its original nothingness. More particularly, John viewed the resurrection of the body, again akin to Origen, so acosmically that he held that at the end the body would be reconstituted in a wholly spiritual, sexless state.[7]

The Countervailing Influences of Western Monasticism

Almost imperceptibly during these centuries of social strife, economic turmoil, and spiritual alienation from nature, however, new trends were emerging that were profoundly to alter the dominant alienated perceptions of nature. Two in particular merit some attention here, the influence of Benedictine monasticism, generally, and the impact of Irish monasticism, in particular. In the context of these trends we can see nature slowly being transformed, in the mind's eye, from wasteland to garden.

Benedict himself (ca. 480–550) had been disillusioned with the mostly solitary and frequently severe asceticism which had flowed into Western spirituality from the monasticism of the Christian East. With a certain pragmatic, even militarized, Roman spirit, he founded a communal monasticism whose ascetic discipline was to be relatively modest, but highly structured. It was to be predicated on *work,* that is, on action more than contemplation, both in the form of communal worship and—what had hitherto been widely scorned in the Roman world—manual labor. This was the Benedictine vision—*ora et labora.* And in due course, prompted by an evangelical sense of mission, communities of Benedictines did go out into the wilderness areas of Europe and work to tame nature, sometimes with dramatic results, for the purpose of their own survival and as a praise-offering to God.

Benedictine monasticism has been celebrated by scholars such as Lewis Mumford and René Dubos on the basis that it offers a model for ecological responsibility.[8] The Benedictine movement, they tell us, neither turned away from nature as an alien reality, nor did it ruthlessly exploit nature; rather it exercised a "creative stewardship of the earth" (Dubos). Lynn White, in an essay on Henry Adams's famous romanticizing study *The Virgin and the Dynamo,* has also stressed how the celebrated naturalism and Mariology of the twelfth century, to which we will turn presently, was only made possible by the technological advances associated with this spirit of monasticism. Of society in this period, he writes: "it was the building for the first time in history of a complex civilization which was upheld not on the sinews of sweating slaves and coolies, but primarily by non-human power. The century which achieved the highest expression of the cult of the Virgin Mary likewise first envisioned the concept of a labor-saving power technology which has played so large a part in the formation of the modern world."[9]

One can see in the Benedictine spirit, therefore, a certain high confidence in the potential of human mastery over nature, along with a practical befriending of nature, and a will to work with nature for the sake of human betterment within a divinely ordered cosmos. The wasteland of the early Middle Ages in this sense, in the Benedictine mind, had become a garden. This was an ethos, we may say, of *cooperative mastery* over nature—neither passive contemplation, nor yet, as far as we can see, thoughtless exploitation. It was an ethos that was to be of profound significance in ensuing centuries, in theology as elsewhere. It helped to make possible a radical, consciously articulated change in perspective in attitudes toward nature by the time of the end of the twelfth century. It helped to overcome both the practical alienation from nature evident in the early Middle Ages and its sophisticated anticosmic articulation, as in the works of John the Scot. It also enabled—along with some of the economic trends that it helped to set in motion—a new kind of contemplative relationship with nature. It created the existential space, we may say, in which nature could now be seen in more positive terms. In place of the song of winter characteristic of the early Middle Ages, twelfth-century poets now typically began to sing:

Spring returns, the long awaited,
    Laugh, be glad!
Spring, with blossoms decorated,
    Purple clad:
Birds prolong their accords of song there,
    How sweetly!
Trees renew their youth now,
Song brings joy in truth now,
    O completely.[10]

Vivid expressions of a new friendship with nature also emerged during the early Middle Ages in the populace's experience with traveling Celtic monks. Monasticism in Ireland had kept alive the Eastern Christian vision of the saint in the wilderness reestablishing Adam's and Eve's original rapport with the animals, by virtue of his or her sanctity.[11] Irish monks carried this ideal to the continent. A whole literature is in evidence, indeed, depicting the power of saints over animals, both domesticated and wild.[12] One could think of this Irish-ascetic motif as the rise of a certain *contemplative mastery* of nature. This readily went hand in hand with the Benedictine ethos of cooperative mastery.

The saint was the one who was seen to be in perfect control of the world of nature, of birds, wolves, cattle, and many other creatures, real and imagined. The saint was one who lived in the reconstituted spiritual splendor of Adam and Eve in the Garden, before the fall, when Adam had named the animals and they had obeyed him, when humans and animals had lived in peace with one another.

THE REBIRTH OF NATURE IN THE TWELFTH CENTURY

The twelfth century was a watershed in the Middle Ages, in many ways. The confidence in human mastery over the earth, which we have been observing in the spirit of Benedictine and Celtic monasticism, was now bolstered by a number of social, economic, and cultural developments that were to reshape the whole society. The feudal monopoly of the soil began to break up, and with that the static character of social organization began to change. Cities emerged in their own right, and with them cathedral schools, such as the famous center at Chartres. Urban artisans began to organize into guilds. New techniques of production—many of them long established in the monasteries—and new extensions of commerce emerged. The century also saw some of the first sustained stirrings of scientific curiosity—searching out the causes of things, as well as acknowledging the divine cause. This was reflected in the art of the era. Gothic architecture not only signaled soaring human aspirations and a new technological confidence; it also concretely gave expression to a new human encounter with nature, especially in the Gothic capitals, which changed from the most minimal representation of empirical nature in Romanesque art to a much more vivid kind of natural, even erotic realism. This was also the century of the flowering of Mariology, as we have seen, and—not unrelated to the latter—the celebration of the "Goddess Natura" in poetry, as well as the exaltation of courtly love. Intellectually, the century witnessed the revival of classical learning, particularly a renewal of interest in Platonism, fostered by the school at Chartres.

The Timeless Dynamism of the Great Chain of Being and the Mastery of Nature

The guiding vision of much of this century—Chenu has likened it to the public dynamism of the idea of evolution in the late nineteenth century—was the conceptuality of the hierarchy of being. Here the influence of Dionysius and John the Scot was decisive.[13] The imagination of the twelfth century readily approached the world in terms of a spiritual emanation from the One, to the spiritual, and finally to the material, many. There was, to be sure, considerable popular support for the anticosmic themes which earlier had accompanied that schema. Thus the gnosticizing Catharii were a major force during these decades. But that phenomenon can perhaps be viewed as an afterglow of the culture of earlier centuries. Hierarchical thinking in this century, as it was developed by leading theologians, did not give expression to an anticosmic spirit, as a general rule.

Influenced thoroughly by the Plato of the *Timaeus*, and its vision of divine creativity, many intellectuals of this era saw the One as overflowing goodness, from the apex of the chain of being, to the nadir, including all material creatures. The notion of the biophysical world as an essentially fallen or evil world faded from sight. In the same spirit, for much of this century Plato's theory of a "world soul" enjoyed considerable currency.[14] This was the notion that there is an animating spirit, a universal force of vitality, within the whole of nature. Although the idea was condemned by the church during this century, it shows nevertheless the kind of thinking about nature that was developing. The human spirit was coming to rest, as it were, in a more contemplative vision of nature. What it saw, surely, was not a wilderness. Perhaps it was something surpassing even a garden: something akin to the detailed but structured picture of creation in Genesis 1, a multifaceted, yet harmonious architectural creation, speaking of God at every level. Nature was becoming a kind of living cathedral filled with song. Earlier perceptions of a hostility between spirit and nature were still in evidence, but they were on the wane. So, for example, Honorius of Autun writes:

> The supreme artisan made the universe like a great zither upon which he placed strings to yield a variety of sounds, for he divided his work in two—into two parts antithetical to each other. Spirit and matter, antithetical in nature yet consonant in existence, resemble a choir of men and boys blending their bass and treble voices. . . . Material things similarly imitate the distinction of choral parts, divided as things are into genera, species, individuals, forms, and numbers; all of these blend harmoniously as they observe with due measure the law implanted within them and so as it were, emit their proper sound. A harmonious chord is sounded by spirit and body, angel and devil, heaven and hell, fire and water, air and earth, sweet and bitter, soft and hard, and so are all things harmonized.[15]

The link between the growing confidence in human mastery and the image of nature as a kind of ordered structure at human disposal, on the one hand, and the grand ontological vision of the hierarchy of being, on the other, was undoubtedly the idea of the human creature as microcosm. This idea, bequeathed to the century by John the Scot, suddenly "caught on fire" in the final decades of the century.[16] As one created in the image of God, it was now enthusiastically believed, the human creature was also created as an image of the cosmos, as a "world in miniature." This motif, Chenu has commented, "afforded a vision of man's place in the world capable of giving birth alike to science and contemplation. Henceforth Christians would direct interested attention upon the world; they would judge that in exercising such an attention they were fulfilling at least some part of their destiny, on the supposition that man is a being consecrated to the world and that in coming to know the world he comes to know himself as well."[17] As an ordered structure, nature was thus seen as a reflection of the human self, and vice versa.

We are in a position, then, to underline some central motifs in the theological approach of the twelfth century to nature. It was: hierarchical, esthetic, operational (note the emphasis on mastery), and, in a certain sense, anthropocentric (as in the theme of humanity as microcosm). To this list, we should also add "spatial." For the Irenaean-Augustinian temporal theme of creation history was virtually eclipsed in this period. "Nature, the vicar of God," Chenu explains, "was insensitive to the passage of time in human history and to the sequence of Divine activities. The creation itself was detemporalized and deexistentialized, for it was thought of rather as it exists in the divine 'ideas' than as it unfolds in the six days of Genesis."[18] Nature had a certain timeless character to it, not unlike the structure of a great Gothic cathedral.

Alan of Lille as a Representative Thinker

The thought of Alan of Lille (ca. 1128–1202), called the *doctor universalis* in his own time, exemplifies many of these trends. It also points us to one further theme, which is of great importance for our explorations here, in view of its implications for further developments in the tradition, as well as with regard to its continuity with earlier constructions. Paradoxical as this may sound, although he celebrates nature, Alan also presents us with an anticosmic theology of redemption.

Like Irenaeus, Alan wrote against the claims of the tradition of Gnosticism. His work *Contra haereticos* was a refutation of the thought and practices of the Catharii movement. More positively, he celebrated the vitalities and the diversities of nature in his long allegorical poem *De planctu Naturae*, "The Lament of Nature."[19] This work, which helped set the stage for Dante's *Divine Comedy*, is about the virgin goddess Natura, a figure whose literary and philosophical history seems to stem from the Earth Goddess cults that flourished in the Greco-Roman world (and elsewhere, widely). Alan describes Natura's beauty and the fecundity of her world. The purpose of the poem is to contrast her purity and beauty with the desecrations imposed on her and her world by human sinfulness.

Alan not only takes the idea of the great chain of being for granted, it is the leitmotif of his vision. He depicts that hierarchy with great poetic power and sensual concreteness, which shows how a relatively staid conceptuality such as this could take on existential life. He describes the heavens first of all, "as the citadel of a human city, [where] resides imperially the everlasting Ruler." From God the King the command goes out that all things should be known and written in the book of his providence. Then, "in the air, as in the middle of the city, the heavenly army of angels does service, and with delegated control diligently extends its guard over man. Man, like one foreign born, dwelling in a suburb of the universe, does not refuse obedience to the angelic host."[20] Noteworthy here is the enormous ontological territory, as it were, which is allotted to the angels, this vast world of spiritual creatures. Modern readers, conditioned by a quite different set of assumptions, sometimes read the hierarchical conception of reality in the Middle Ages as if it refers chiefly to nature. It does refer to nature, as we will now see, but it offers a primary place to the angels. It is no wonder, then, that the *Celestial Hierarchy* of Dionysius the Areopagite was one of the most popular works of this century, and beyond, in the Middle Ages.

Finally, even farther from the divine citadel, Alan depicts God creating a beautiful material universe which is the domain of Natura. In so doing, God instills a marvelous sensuous harmony in the whole: "And thus He united with mutual and fraternal kisses things antagonistic from the opposition of their properties, between which the space had made its room from the contraries, and He changed the strife of hatred into the peace of friendship. All things, then, agreeing through invisible bonds of union, plurality returned to unity, diversity to identity, dissonance to harmony, discord to concord in peaceful agreement."[21]

Such is Alan's vision of the cosmic Ruler's overflowing goodness in nature, personified by the goddess Natura. There can be little doubt about his glorification of nature in its divinely given goodness. Strikingly, indeed, he even describes the goddess' virgin body erotically, and her domain, particularly the copulation among animals, with a tangible, earthy zest.

But why is this goddess there? What is her destiny? Here we see the emergence of the ambiguity given with the great chain of being conceptuality. Alan does envision creation in terms of overflowing divine goodness, thus picking up and developing some Augustinian themes. But in a sense all this goodness is going nowhere, ultimately, according to Alan's schema. At this point we witness the return of "the Good," that anticosmic, world-transcending spiritual deity in heaven. Here we see the anticosmic tradition of Origen and John the Scot is very much alive. Nature's goodness, it turns out, will finally fade to nothing. Alan expresses this succinctly in a formula in his theological *Regulae*. Irrational creatures, he says, are good only with regard to the beginning, the alpha of the world (*ab alpha*). Rational creatures, on the other hand, whose beatitude is the reason why the world is created in the first place, are good both with regard to the beginning and with regard to the ending, the omega of the world (*ex alpha et omega*).[22] Nature may be beautiful and sensuous, in other words, but she has her definite, passing place, subordinate to and instrumental for the world of rational creatures and their destiny to be partakers of grace in heaven.

Thus we encounter the tension between the logic of overflowing goodness and the logic of the world-transcending, spiritual good in a most pronounced way—given the dramatic accounts of nature's beauty and goodness. The fact remains, however, that Natura's goodness is only partial, only incomplete, compared to the goodness of rational creatures. She must step aside at the very end to allow the fulfillment of a higher, spiritual purpose for humanity and the angels. Under the impact of the idea of the good, then, the idea of the overflowing goodness of God is finally delimited, compromised. The overflowing and the ingathering, the diastole and systole, of the hierarchy of being is *asymmetrical*. As far as redemption is concerned, then, Alan's thought is formally similar to Origen's and John's—notwithstanding his rejection of the idea of a cosmic fall in favor of a rich picture of the divine goodness permeating nature.

The accent in Alan's thought, to be sure, and in the reflection of many of his theological contemporaries, was so thoroughly and so compellingly fixed on the glories of nature as created that what amounts to the final ignominy of nature, its eschatological abnegation, was largely hidden. That idea, the legacy of the metaphor of ascent and of the idea of the good, remained mostly in the background of his thought. Even so, we can see in retrospect that the goddess Natura had, in fact, a kind of dark, if hidden, *Doppelgänger*, death. Death did not equally threaten all creatures, in Alan's view. Humans were captives of the same threat to be sure; but they were also liberated by the promise of eternal life, whereas nature was not. This mostly hidden motif of duality came to a kind of aesthetic expression in Germany two centuries later, after the experience of death had become a more self-conscious theme in the culture, in the image of *Frau Welt*. The figure of this woman began to appear in the portal sculpture of many churches. On the front she is attractive and shows an alluring, aristocratic smile. The back half of her body, however, is being eaten by worms and frogs and snakes. *Frau Welt* reveals the hidden side, as it were, of the justly celebrated theological naturalism of the later Middle Ages.

THE CONCEPTUAL RESOLUTIONS OF THOMAS AQUINAS: THE SUBORDINATION OF NATURE

The affirmation of nature as a congenial, accessible, and divinely given environment, which we saw developing in the twelfth century, and that century's confidence in human mastery over nature, carried over into the thought of the Angelic Doctor Thomas Aquinas. Etienne Gilson has observed that Thomas's view of the world was permeated with a "radical optimism,"[23] and that it was. Never for a moment did Thomas doubt his ability to comprehend nature and its place in the greater scheme of things. Never for a moment did he display any lack of confidence in nature's life of its own or its goodness in itself. Thomas was at home with the diversity and the mysteries of nature in a way that is reminiscent of the contemplative mastery of the Irish saints. Thomas was also thoroughly influenced by the hierarchical ontology of Dionysius the Areopagite, which had made such a deep impression on the mind of the twelfth century.[24]

Thomas drew together the various strands of his thought, philosophical and theological, in his monumental *Summa Theologica*. The confident, logical bent of his mind is apparent throughout this work, as is the thoroughgoing influence of the philosopher from whom he learned so much, Aristotle. Accordingly, the motif of creation history, already on the wane in the twelfth century, is further deemphasized by Thomas's attempt to construct a work of rational coherence. The goal of a *Summa*, says Chenu, is to "transform sacred history into an organized science."[25] Thomas sought to hold on to the theme of creation history and yet to achieve a metaphysical intelligibility by integrating the former within the ontological dynamics of the hierarchy of being, as Origen and others had done before him. Creation history thus becomes the movement of the overflowing goodness of God (creation), on the one hand, and the movement of return on the part of the creatures to God, on the other, as it had been for Origen and, much closer to Thomas, Alan. On this universal circuit of being, as Chenu points out, the events recorded in the historical narratives of the Bible could be located, "with all the contingency . . . that their dependency on the free will of God and of man implies."[26]

The *Summa* then is organized according to this grand schema of the universe. The first part articulates the emanation of all things from God, who is here the Principle of being. The second part depicts the return of things, each according to its nature, to God, who is here the End (*telos*) of being, focusing on God's free grace, revealed by sacred history, in the God-Man, Christ. The third part studies "the Christian conditions" of the return of the creatures to God, as Chenu puts it; and here, more than elsewhere in the *Summa*, "history will dominate, because here it yields a 'revelation' in the strong sense of that word."[27]

Looking at the hierarchical schema of the *Summa*, Chenu comments: "Emanation-return are intelligibility in its fulness." By this he means that for Thomas, "all creatures, and particularly human creatures, and all events, particularly human events, are framed between two causes—the efficient cause, God the Creator and Conserver (*Ia Pars*), and the final cause, God-Beautifier and Glorified (*IIa Pars*)—as between two supreme reasons giving them meaning and value before the mind."[28] We can now follow the movement of Thomas's thought, particularly with regard to nature, as his mind proceeds from God, the Principle, to God, the End, within the categories of hierarchical thought.

God the Principle: The Accent on
the Divine Transcendence

At one point in his Compendium of Theology, also a work of his maturity, Thomas observes that the Apostles' Creed refers to God not only as omnipotent but also as "Maker." "For making," he explains, "is properly the action of an artificer who operates by his will."[29] Thomas wants to stress that God is free, and under no constraint, to create. At the same time, another nuance is implicit here, which characterizes Thomas's thought about God's creative activity generally. God acts powerfully by his will, like a builder. In the more technical terms which Thomas prefers, God is the "efficient cause" of the creation. The nuance at this point, then, is more that God *posits* the world by fiat, rather than that the world flows into being, as it were, by a process of emanation, shaped by the omnipresent, overflowing goodness of God.[30] This is not to say that the second motif is missing, by any means. The Aristotelian notion of efficient causality is balanced by the Platonic theme of emanation-participation, which we highlighted in Augustine's thought. Leo Scheffczyk reminds us that the *Summa* begins with the notion that the creation possesses "being through participation," and that therefore Thomas does not understand the world solely in terms of an external, efficient causality.[31] Thus Thomas can affirm the traditional idea, given prominence by Basil the Great in the East, that the image of the Spirit "moving over the face of the waters" in the Genesis account suggests God fostering and quickening the world, "and impressing vital power, as the hen broods over her chickens."[32] And he can even envision God as rejoicing in his works, suggesting again that the divine relation to nature is more than external: ". . . the words, God saw that it was good, signify that the things that he had made were to endure, since they express a certain satisfaction taken by God in his works, as an artist in his art."[33] Still, the overall accent in Thomas's thought, as far as God's relationship to the creation is concerned, tends to be fixed on the idea of efficient causality. That there is a certain distance, accordingly, between God and the creation—strictly speaking, an infinite distance, as far as Thomas is concerned—is a keystone of Thomas's thought.[34]

The motif of a distance between the Creator and the creation is further reenforced by Thomas's understanding of God's governance of the creation. As far as the creation's *being* is concerned, on the one hand, Thomas's concept of God's presence in all things is strong. God, for Thomas, is the Living God, "He Who Is." And this signifies, as Gilson points out, the immanence of the divine efficacy in all his creatures, functioning at the same time as the cause of their being and their duration. He quotes Thomas: "Being is innermost in each thing, and most fundamentally present within all things. . . . Hence it must be that God is in all things, and innermostly."[35] Thomas expresses this point still more forcefully in his *Compendium*: "We are not to suppose that the existence of things is caused by God in the same way as the existence of a house is caused by its builder. When the builder departs, the house still remains standing. . . . But God is, directly, by Himself, the cause of the very existence, and communicates existence to all things just as the sun communicates light to the air and to whatever else is illuminated by the sun. The continuous shining of the sun is required for the preservation of light in the air; similarly God must confer existence on all things if they are to persevere in existence. . . . Therefore God must be in all things."[36]

On the other hand, as far as the creature's *being governed* is concerned, God is variously removed from creatures, according to their place in the hierarchy of being. Here God "governs some things by means of others."[37] Thomas considers this to be a sign of God's dignity, that he perfects things by giving them a government, "as a master, who not only imparts knowledge to his pupils, but gives also the faculty of teaching to others."[38] But, again, we see the theme of the divine immanence in the creation being qualified and the theme of the divine transcendence being underlined.

The implicit image here is akin to Alan of Lille's picture of the great universal kingdom with the Ruler residing at the exalted heights of the hierarchy, and issuing orders, which then are carried out, like ripples on a still pond when a stone is dropped, by one descending rank of intellectual creatures after another. So Thomas often quotes Augustine's statement in his treatise on the Trinity: "As the inferior angels who have less universal forms are ruled by the superior; so are all corporeal things ruled by angels."[39] Or, characteristically in his own words:

Among intellectual substances, therefore, some are divinely governed by others, that is, the lower by the higher. Similarly lower bodies are controlled in God's plan, by higher bodies. Hence every movement of lower bodies is caused by the movement of heavenly bodies, just as the intelligible exemplars of things descend to lower spirits through higher spirits.[40]

Now it is surely an indispensable teaching of the classical Christian tradition that God wholly transcends the creation. The world is not God, in any sense. Thomas gives clear and compelling expression to that doctrine. But it would also seem that the way he expresses the idea, particularly with regard to the theology of nature, forces him to pay a high price. Highlighting God's efficient causality and the mediated character of God's rule the way he does makes it difficult for him to convey the powerful immediacy and the gentle care of the Creator in and for the creation, as Irenaeus and Augustine were able to do. The motif of divine externality seems to qualify everything else for Thomas.

At this point, we see, within his theology of creation, a theme that we will see in a still-more-pronounced fashion in his theology of salvation: the ambiguity of thought shaped by both the metaphor of fecundity and the metaphor of ascent, and the concomitant ambiguity of their conceptual expressions in Thomas's hierarchical thinking. Thomas holds the motions of the self-sufficient good (the legacy of Aristotle) and overflowing goodness (the legacy of Plato) in a certain tension, but it is the metaphor of ascent which is finally the more influential, so much so that the meaning of the overflowing goodness of God begins to lose its existential concreteness and its analogical tangibility. Overflowing goodness now tends to appear as a construct of abstract thought rather than as a mysterious work of God calling forth awe and wonder. The divine immanence and the divine governance of all things appear more as a rational judgment in Thomas's thought than a personal encounter with the *tremendum* of the divine presence in creation, as they were for Augustine. It would be difficult to say of the Creator as Thomas depicts him—although the cognitive ingredients for this utterance are not missing—what Augustine might readily have said himself, that the whole world is charged with the glory of God.[41]

Creation as Good: The Accent on Creaturely Autonomy

When we turn to Thomas's view of creation as such, that is, creation viewed horizontally, as it were, instead of vertically in relationship to God, we meet a corresponding kind of ambiguity.

To begin with, for Thomas each creature has a life and function of its own, as part of a larger whole. Each is set in motion—created—by God to realize some specific potential. "The universe, as represented by St. Thomas," Gilson comments, "is not a mass of inert bodies passively moved by a force which passes through them, but a collection of active beings each enjoying the efficacy delegated to it by God along with actual being."[42] In keeping with, and indeed advancing, the scientific spirit of the twelfth century, Thomas definitely wants to affirm the importance and integrity of secondary causes, as well as the first cause of the created order. In his view, the Creator is powerful enough to give others genuine efficacy. If God were the immediate cause of things, Thomas explains, "the order of cause and effect would be taken away from created things: and this would imply lack of power in the Creator."[43] Further, Thomas will have no part of Origen's notion of a cosmic fall, an idea which he self-consciously rejects.[44] Nature did not fall when humankind fell. *This* world around us—even with its signs of violence—is in fact the good world God created. "For the nature of animals," he says, "was not changed by man's sin, as if those whose nature it now is to devour the flesh of others, would have lived on herbs, as the lion and the falcon."[45] This is not to say that human sin does not color the human relationship with nature; it does.[46] But it is to say that the world of nature which we experience around us is in fact, according to Thomas, the good world God created, not some other alien world, not, as for Origen, a kind of divine afterthought occasioned by sin.

Likewise, Thomas has a consistently positive regard for the human body. The body, for him, is surely no prison. On the contrary, "the natural condition of the human soul is to be united to the body." The soul, accordingly, has a natural longing for union with the body. Their separation is contrary to nature.[47] In the same vein, the whole range of natural human knowledge of God—for example, that God is the first cause of all things—is obtained through the senses. Thus, although the body is definitely intended by God, according to Thomas, to serve the soul, and although in this world it "does obstruct and slow down the soul, so that the soul can neither devote itself to uninterrupted contemplation nor reach the heights of contemplation,"[48] the body is, nevertheless, a good and essential servant of the soul, and will be all the more so in the life to come.

Yet for all this impressive emphasis on the goodness and self-efficacy of the creatures, an ambiguity still is evident. Thomas seems to stress that self-efficacy so much that the divine efficacy seems to fade from any kind of sustained, compelling significance. Seen from another angle of vision, this is the same point we were considering earlier, in our evaluation of Thomas's accent on the Creator as efficient cause as compared to the more Augustinian accent on God as overflowing goodness, in which the creatures participate for their being and movement. The self-efficacy of the creatures, by accent, tends to become autonomy in Thomas's thought. Nature, in particular, tends to become, by accent, a self-enclosed, independent whole ruled by an inviolable inner law. Nowhere is this accent more clearly expressed than in Thomas's understanding of miracles.

Augustine, we saw, put forward an omnimiraculous view of nature. For him nature was intrinsically an open system, a field of wonder, from the least of the creatures to the greatest. Thomas, in contrast, holds that in order for God to intervene miraculously in nature God must *set aside*, by fiat, the order of nature: "An occurrence is miraculous when it surpasses the power of every created thing."[49] The nuance seems to be that a *real* act of God, as distinct from a general, universal communication of being to all things, has to break through the closed order of nature. Thus there is a kind of de facto deistic accent in Thomas's thought about nature, alongside his consistent emphasis on God's communication of being to nature at all times. This ambiguity seems, in turn, to be attributable to the role the Aristotelian idea of the good plays in his thought about creation, compared to the Platonic-Augustinian idea of goodness.

The Diversity of the Creation and Its Anthropocentric Structure

A similar ambiguity appears when we survey Thomas's elaborate ideas about the diversity of creatures in the world. Why is the universe the way it is? Why is there such a vast variety of creatures, some of them offensive or dangerous? Thomas responds with a theocentric answer: an infinite God wishes to communicate his goodness to a finite world. Only a vast world of graduated perfection could adequately receive and represent the infinite goodness of God:

> For he produced things into being in order that His goodness might be communicated to them; and because his goodness could not be adequately represented by one creature alone, he produced many and diverse creatures, that what was wanting to one representation of the Divine goodness might be supplied by another. For goodness, which in God is simple and uniform, in creatures is manifold and divided; and hence the whole universe together participates in the Divine Goodness more perfectly, and represents it better than any single creature whatever.[50]

We have already encountered this set of ideas in Augustine, but Thomas projects it with a kind of rigor and clarity that it did not have in Augustine's thought.

That larger system, for Thomas, also helps to explain why some creatures objectionable to humans are present in the world, a point which Augustine made also, and which Thomas self-consciously appropriates for him.[51] Thomas further affirms Augustine's suggestion that human sinfulness has compounded the problems humans have with the hostile side of nature. Thomas imagines, indeed, that the human creature before the fall "would have used the things of this world conformably to the order designed," hence "poisonous animals would not have harmed him."[52] This discussion of the variety in nature is highly suggestive.

Yet this theocentric view of nature goes hand in hand with a thoroughgoing anthropocentrism in Thomas's understanding of creation. To approach this idea, it will be helpful to recall that in Thomas's mind the hierarchy of being is not a cone shaped with the human creature at the apex, not precisely. If any image can suggest Thomas's meaning, it may be the hierarchy as an inverted cone. As for Alan of Lille and many other medieval thinkers, the weight of the hierarchy for Thomas is, so to speak, not with the material creatures, but with the angelic. Thomas was not called the Angelic Doctor for naught. His universe is

populated mainly with angels: ". . . angels, even as they are immaterial substances, exist in exceeding great number, far beyond all material multitude."
Even more: ". . . immaterial substances as it were incomparably exceed material
substances as to multitude."[53] This, clearly, is because God is spirit and therefore to mirror himself fully in a finite world most of the creatures would have to
be spiritual, according to such a logic. So Thomas's vision of creation is tilted
heavily to the side of the spiritual realm.

Now for Thomas the material creatures, like all others, were created that
they "might be assimilated to the divine goodness."[54] But all creatures lower
than the "spiritual" human creature in the hierarchy, in fact, assimilate the
divine goodness *by serving the human creature!* Thomas reasons that although all
creatures are ordained to the divine goodness as their end, "some are closer to
the end than others, and so participate in the divine goodness more abundantly." Hence lesser creatures, having a smaller share in the divine goodness,
"are in some way subordinated to higher beings as to their ends." More specifically, "lower beings realize their last end chiefly by their subordination to
higher beings." Then Thomas points to the concrete order of the universe itself:
"As we observe . . . , imperfect beings serve the needs of more noble beings;
plants draw their nutriment from the earth, animals feed on plants, and these in
turn serve man's use. We conclude, then, that lifeless beings exist for living beings, plants for animals, and the latter for man." Further, he argues, since intellectual nature is superior to material nature, "the whole of material nature is
subordinate to intellectual nature." This means, in turn, "that the whole of material nature exists for man, inasmuch as he is a rational animal."[55] One might
refer to this line of argument as Thomas's *intramundane anthropocentrism.*[56] All
material and vital creatures fulfill their raison d'être chiefly as they serve the rational animal in their midst.[57] They serve the good of the whole by being subordinate to human needs. This is why they are also preserved by God: "The life
of animals and plants is preserved not for themselves but for man."[58]

These human needs, for Thomas, are surely not independent values. They are
subject to a range of ethical norms. Thomas's anthropocentrism here is not yet
that of a Descartes, for whom knowledge is essentially power over nature. Nor
is it by any means the anthropocentrism of later industrial society, according to
which nature is a storehouse of resources available for human exploitation. But
Thomas's view is not totally dissimilar from those approaches to nature either.
When he sees nature, he sees something created essentially to satisfy basic human needs and to aid the human quest for God. The sense for communion with
nature, both in its vertical and its horizontal dimensions—the accent on the
presence of God in nature and on human cooperation with nature (*concursus*)—which we saw in Augustine here begins to fade from the picture. Domin-

ion over nature is, in Thomas's thought, in the process of becoming domination of nature. Nature is seen more as an object for human use, which satisfies biological needs and serves spiritual knowledge, than as a subject in its own right, as it was for Augustine. This is the accent:

> We believe all corporeal things to have been made for man's sake, wherefore all things are stated to be subject to him. Now they serve man in two ways, first as sustenance of his bodily life, secondly, as helping him to know God, inasmuch as man sees the invisible things of God by the things that are made. (Rom. 1:20)[59]

This kind of anthropocentrism surely stands in an uneasy relationship with Thomas's theocentric understanding of the diversity and gradation of creatures in the universe, where all things are created, primarily, to mirror God's goodness. Thus each one has a kind of integrity of its own, a niche of divinely bestowed value, one might say. This ambiguity, like others we have noticed in Thomas's thought, seems again to arise from his attempt to synthesize goodness and the good, the overflowing universal creativity of God, on the one hand, and the spiritual otherness of God and all rational creatures, on the other.

God the End (telos): The Virtual Negation of Nature

The same tension between the motifs of overflowing goodness and the nature-transcending spiritual good is evident, only all the more so, when we turn our attention now to the return of the creatures to God, to the end of all things.

Thomas's view of the return of the creatures to God could be looked at as an extended—and at points somewhat convoluted—commentary on the principle we have already encountered in Alan of Lille, that nature is created good *ab alpha*, while spiritual creatures, humans and angels, are created good *ex alpha et omega*. Thus from the very start, among the visible creatures, Thomas sees humanity alone as created in a "state of grace." This gift (*donum indebitum*) is what is lost in the fall and restored in redemption.[60] In this sense, with the exception of the human creature, the whole of nature is *not* created in a state of grace, although it is surely created good, as we have seen. Neither is nature intended or predestined for salvation in any sense, at the very beginning. Predestination for Thomas is "a plan existing in the Divine mind for the ordering of some persons to eternal salvation."[61]

Accordingly, when Thomas surveys the whole created world, he sees a *twofold perfection*. "The first perfection," he says, "is the completeness of the universe at its first founding, and this is what is ascribed to the seventh day [of the creation account, when God 'rested']."[62] This is the theme of the divine goodness, which we have already encountered in various forms in Thomas's thought. The second perfection of the universe has to do with human redemption, the vision of God, at the very end of all things. This is why the world, most fundamentally, is created by God. "The final perfection," Thomas says, "which is the end of the whole universe, is the perfect beatitude of the saints at the consummation of the world."[63] Thus the grand movement of divine causality for Thomas, as for thinkers such as Alan of Lille, is essentially asymmetrical. The overflowing goodness of God extends to all things. The return of all things to God is intended only for rational creatures.

But Thomas is not satisfied with the implications of this formal, asymmetrical dialectic of creation and human redemption. At this point his mind seems to have been much more thoroughly shaped by biblical theology than Origen's was. Thomas's affirmation of nature's goodness, consonant with biblical attitudes, would not allow him to rest content with a totally spiritualized view of redemption. For Thomas, the concrete biblical themes of the resurrection of the body and the new heavens and the new earth had to be dealt with on their own terms. And this he attempts to do in the third part of his *Summa Theologica*, which, as we have seen, focuses on the revealed "Christian aspects" of the return of all things to the Creator. But his discussion here is not always compelling; indeed, it often appears contrived, as far as his theology of nature is concerned.

So we find Thomas, as a matter of course, speaking often about the renewal of the whole world. But why should the world of nature be renewed, since it was not created in a state of grace with regard to the final perfection of the universe? Thomas gives several answers for this question, all of which revolve around the needs of the human creatures. So this renewal of the world, such as it is, is for Thomas a radically anthropocentric consummation, self-consciously and explicitly.

One answer is that "the dwelling should befit the dweller." This logic, given the premise, is clear: "But the world was made to be man's dwelling. Therefore it should befit man. Now man will be renewed. Therefore the world will be likewise."[64]

One can ask here: if the end of human life is the vision of God, seeing God face to face, why should there be a renewed cosmos in eternity for the human creature at all?[65] If we recall Thomas's teaching about the soul and the body, in contrast, given their essential togetherness, there is a compelling Thomistic logic for the resurrection of the body: human nature is essentially corporeal and cannot attain its *telos* otherwise.[66] But why does the human environment have to be renewed? Since its end is to fulfill human needs on earth, during which epoch humans receive the redeeming grace they need to attain the beatific vision, when the time of that vision arrives, what use can that environment possibly be anymore? Why should it not simply be discarded by God?

Such a line of questioning is evidently on Thomas's mind. So he finds yet another reason, again anthropocentric in character, and again of doubtful force—especially in view of what he says later, as we will see, about the final fate of the animals, plants, and minerals: "the corporeal creature will be rewarded for its services to man."[67] Here he has in mind, curiously, only the four material elements and the heavenly bodies, not the animals, plants, and minerals, as such.[68]

Notwithstanding these arguments by Thomas, whatever one might think of their effectiveness, *the fundamental asymmetrical logic of the two orders of perfection triumphs in the end.* With regard to this actual dwelling of humankind, this visible, tangible world of animals and plants, minerals and all mixed bodies, *there will be no renewal* at the "consummation of the world." Thomas tells us that they will "altogether cease after the renewal of the world."[69] Why? At this point Thomas's logic is fully consistent with his view of the biophysical world as essentially the servant of humanity:

> If the end ceases, those things which are directed to the end should cease. Now plants and animals were made for the upkeep of human life. . . . Therefore, when man's animal life ceases, animals and plants should cease. But after this renewal, animal life will cease in man. Therefore neither plants nor animals ought to remain.

Again, from a slightly different perspective:

> Dumb animals, plants, and minerals, and all mixed bodies, are corruptible both in their whole and in their parts, both on the part of the matter which loses its form, and on the part of their form which does not remain actually; and thus they will not remain in this renewal. . . .

All of these creatures are "not capable of renewal."[70]

Assessment: The Ambiguity of Nature

Sic transit gloria mundi. The celebrated Thomistic principle that grace does not destroy nature, but perfects it, turns out to be narrowly anthropocentric, when all has been said. For, in effect, grace *does* destroy the animals, the plants, the minerals, and all mixed bodies. It only perfects spiritual creatures.

This is the uncertain legacy of the subordination of the metaphor of fecundity to the metaphor of ascent at the roots of Thomas's hierarchical thinking. This is the uncertain legacy of a theology which is virtually untouched by the metaphor of migration to a good land.

We are offered a theology that both affirms nature and denies nature: a theology that stresses, under the rubric of creation, the overflowing goodness of God, yet which highlights, under the rubric of redemption, the nature-denying finality of fulfillment in God. With regard to his theology of salvation as it pertains to nature, Thomas stands more in the tradition of Origen than is often realized, notwithstanding his evident dependence on Augustine and the theological naturalism of the twelfth century in other respects.

The tradition of Origen influences his understanding of the divine goodness in the creation as well, given Thomas's accent on God's transcendence over nature, nature's self-efficacy, and his anthropocentric view of nature's purpose in the greater scheme of things. On the other hand, Thomas also gives voice to the more Augustinian themes concerning the divinely ordered diversity in nature, the divine immanence in nature, and the fact that nature has not fallen. In this sense, Thomas does display a kind of optimism about this world, as Gilson observes, which sets his thought far apart from Origen's.

We are thus at a sobering moment in these historical explorations, given the enormousness of Thomas's later influence in Christian thought, explicit in Catholic theology, implicit more often than not in the theology of the Reformation tradition. Thomas's conceptual resolutions define what the theology of nature is to be, in its overall shape, for many theologians for many centuries to come. And the last word of those resolutions, as far as the theology of nature is concerned, is—ambiguity.

Grace does not destroy nature
But perfects it.

6

THE ASCENDANCY OF THE AMBIGUITY
AND AN EMBODIMENT OF THE PROMISE

Bonaventure, Dante, and Francis of Assisi

Many of the themes familiar to us in the thought of Thomas are also to be found in the works of two more visionary celebrants of nature, each champions of Francis of Assisi in a way that Thomas was not: the renowned Franciscan theologian St. Bonaventure (1221–74) and the great poet of the Middle Ages Dante Alighieri (1265–1321). A review of their patterns of thinking will show how consistently the internalized ambiguity we have been discussing is in evidence throughout the later Middle Ages, in the ranks of those who stand within the tradition of Plato, no less than those, such as Thomas, who stand more with Aristotle, as far as their formal theological conceptuality is concerned. Indeed, we will witness in the thinking of Bonaventure and Dante the ascendancy of the ambiguity now before us, so much is their rich vision of the created order to be contrasted with their anticosmic images of human redemption.

Then we will attempt to interpret the meaning of the life of Francis of Assisi (1182–1226). Francis is immensely attractive to many, yet he is still enigmatic in some ways, when seen in the context of his own theological milieu. Precisely to assess his historical particularity, and not to abstract his meaning from his own world (as tends to happen in many interpretations of Francis), we will view his significance contextually, looking back on the twelfth century, on the one hand, and looking beyond Francis to the constructions of Thomas, Bonaventure, and Dante, on the other hand. We will try to see him, as it were, in the company of his predecessors and successors, as well as in the midst of the social and religious trends of his own period. This approach will permit us to explore the often implicit theology in "the Francis event" with some confidence that we are reading from the constellation of theological meanings surrounding Francis, and not reading in our own modern—perhaps romantic—assumptions. When he does come into view, in that context, we will witness a truly remarkable phenomenon. In Francis's life as it is portrayed in the most reliable sources available to us, we will discover an embodiment of the ecological promise of classical Christian thought about nature, notwithstanding the ascendancy of the ambiguity in his own theological milieu.

THE COSMIC VISIONS OF BONAVENTURE AND DANTE:
NATURE AS A LADDER TO HEAVEN

Bonaventure's thought about the created world is formally reminiscent of Alan of Lille's. It is thoroughly shaped by the vision of the hierarchy of being and the motif of overflowing goodness.[1] But, materially, Bonaventure appears to be much more the systematic thinker, as well as the poetic visionary.[2] He builds on the hierarchical pattern of thinking, bequeathed to him by Dionysius, in a way that combines, on the one hand, a rich and coherent theological ontology and, on the other, the thoroughgoing existential impact of St. Francis's life and personality. For Bonaventure, as for Augustine, Alan, and then Francis— and here, materially, different from Thomas's theology—the whole world is charged with the glory of God. In the spirit of Augustine, Bonaventure self-consciously seeks to transcend the spirit-matter dichotomy of some forms of Neoplatonic thinking: where the wholly other spiritual One is markedly separated from the biophysical world by a series of descending emanations, so that the One influences the lower levels of the hierarchy, especially the material levels, only through the mediation of other spiritual realities. For Bonaventure, emphatically, each being is equally close to God, although he does maintain that the mode of that relationship differs according to the capacity of the creature.[3] Here we see the theme of ontological participation returning to occupy the prominence it had in Augustine's thought, compared to the emphasis on efficient causality in Thomas's thinking. Bonaventure consistently emphasizes the divine immanence in the created order. Even at the lowest levels of the hierarchy of being, in the regions of sheer matter, Bonaventure sees the influences of the Divine. Matter for him is not a mere passive potentiality. Rather, as Leonard Bowman observes, it is "pregnant with a multiplicity of positive possibilities and bears within itself a kind of dim mirror image of the Eternal Art."[4] At this point we are worlds away from the anticosmic hierarchical thinking of Origen and John the Scot.

God the Principle: The Fecundity of the Triune God

The theological fulcrum of this vision of God in nature for Bonaventure is his thought about the Trinity.[5] In striking fashion Bonaventure begins by internalizing the theology of divine goodness, as it were, within the Divine Life. Overflowing goodness, then, happens in the communication between the Father and the Son in eternity, and this is an infinitely rich, unimaginable intradivine fecundity. The diffusion of the divine goodness, he holds, which "occurred in time in the creation of the world is no more than a pivot or point in comparison with the immense sweep of the eternal goodness."[6] This innerdivine fecundity is the principle of God's transcendence, since it is so immense, so infinite.[7]

Now when God expresses himself externally, for Bonaventure, he does so out of the ultimate mystery of the Trinitarian fecundity. Within the Trinity, the Father generates the Son or the Word, coeternal with himself, and in so doing expresses his own likeness. In so doing he expresses "all the things that he could make." The world then is actualized from possibilities given in the eternal Word, and so as a whole the world is like a mirror reflecting God. "While remaining radically contingent," Ewert Cousins explains, for Bonaventure "creation *ad extra* is an overflow of the Father's fecundity and always remains deeply grounded in the Word. . . . In a most emphatic way for Bonaventure, God is in the world and the world is in God."[8]

To illustrate this coinherence Bonaventure frequently employs the image of water, as Zachary Hayes observes. "The God of fecund love is compared with a vast and living fountain," Hayes writes. "Flowing from that fountain as something willed and loved by God is the immense river of creation. The world of nature is a vast expression of a loving will. . . . Like the water of a river, the world flows in such fecundity and richness that it cannot be contained in only one form or category."[9] This is Bonaventure's compelling vision of the created order, understood as reflective of the divine power, wisdom, and goodness:

> The *greatness* of things also—looking at their vast extension, latitude, and profundity, at the immense power extending itself in the diffusion of light, and the efficiency of their inner uninterrupted and diffuse operation, as manifest in the action of fire—clearly portrays the *immensity* of the power wisdom and goodness of the Triune Good. Who, uncircumscribed, exists in all things by his power, presence, and essence. Likewise, the *multitude* of things in their generic, specific and individual diversity of substance, form, or figure, and the efficiency which is beyond human estimation, manifestly suggests and shows the *immensity* of the three abovementioned attributes in God. The *beauty* of things, too, if we but consider the diversity of light, forms, and colors in elementary, inorganic, and organic bodies, as in heavenly bodies and minerals, in stones and metals, and in plants and animals, clearly proclaims these three attributes of God. Insofar as matter is full of forms because of the seminal principles, and form is full of power because of its active potentialities, while power is capable of many effects because of its efficiency, the *plenitude* of things clearly proclaims the same three attributes. In a like manner, manifold *activity*, whether natural, cultural, or moral, by its multiple variety, shows forth the immensity of that power, art, and goodness.[10]

"This passage," Bowman comments, "beautifully expresses Bonaventure's delight in the variety of creatures, and his consciousness of that variety as a shadow of the infinity and immensity of God." The impact of Augustine's theology of goodness is apparent at this point. But we may attribute the most formative influence to Francis's vivid sense of the presence of God in nature.

Bonaventure's treatment of God's immanence in nature—without weakening his accent on the infinitude of God's transcendence over nature—stands in marked contrast to Thomas's thought at this point. While God is fully transcendent for Bonaventure, we see little of Thomas's characteristic emphasis on the distance between the Creator and creature—no suggestion of any deistic accent. For Bonaventure—who as a matter of fact points to light as the ultimate form of the creation which discloses God's presence (a theme to be picked up by Dante)—the whole world is charged, richly and thoroughly charged, with the glory of God.

Bonaventure further envisions a kind of Trinitarian unity as permeating the whole created order. The triune Creator constitutes, shapes, and perfects *all* things according to his own image—the Word—not just the human creature. This is Bonaventure's movement of thought: (1) as the Son is begotten by the Father, (2) as the Son perfectly mirrors the Father, and (3) as the Son is joined with the Father through the bond of the Holy Spirit; so the order of created being (1) emanates from God, (2) reflects God throughout, and (3) is finally reunited with God. This way of thinking has been called "cosmic exemplarism." In this sense, strikingly, Bonaventure sees all creatures, as they participate in the Trinitarian dynamics of emanation, exemplarity, and consummation, as charged with the glory of God. All creatures, for him, form a kind of ladder leading the human spirit up to God above, yet that ladder communicates God's presence at every level, as it points the human mind ever more to the reality of God, with each ascending step.

The Anthropocentric Meaning of the Creation

At this point we meet a theme in Bonaventure, which is by now familiar to us from the constructions of Alan and Thomas. As Bonaventure envisions the great hierarchy of being which is the creation, notwithstanding his rich sense for the power, wisdom, and goodness of God in the world of nature, he appears to be most concerned with the dynamics of the hierarchy *above* the natural level, that is, the life of humanity and the angels. Indeed, the very category of hierarchy, which Bonaventure uses to describe the innerdynamics of the Trinitarian life of God, seems to be employed in his thought, in a strict sense, to apply to spiritual creatures alone, not to nature as well, as Hayes notes.[11] Below the divine hierarchy, then, "is the angelic hierarchy consisting of three groups of three choirs of angels, each group and each choir reflecting a property of God. Beneath this is found the ecclesiastical hierarchy consisting of three groups of three."[12] It appears that for Bonaventure "the irrational creatures" participate in the hierarchy of the creation "only mediately," as Hayes says, "through their relation to the rational."[13]

In particular, Bonaventure sees the whole of nature as finding its fulfillment in the human creature, where hierarchy, in the strict sense, begins. This is ex-

pressed in his allegorical treatment of the six days of creation, as Hayes observes, "according to which man appears on the sixth day thereby bringing the
work of the first creation to an end."[14] This general accent on the spiritual in
Bonaventure's thought about the creation, and in particular his focus on the human creature as the apex of the visible creation, shows that Bonaventure's
thought about the overflowing goodness of God, rich as it is, nevertheless is
shaped already by the metaphor of ascent—by anticipation as it were —as well
as by the metaphor of fecundity. In delineating the first great movement of
God, the overflowing, Bonaventure already knows and also shows what the final
tendency of the whole process will be, what will become of that vast overflowing of goodness, when it begins to return to its source, to God above. That
return, as we shall now see, will be chiefly a return intended for spiritual creatures, not for the whole creation. Bonaventure's theology, like Alan's and
Thomas's, is thus asymmetrical. The final ingathering of the Many is not com-
mensurate concretely with the original overflowing of the One. This, again, is
the heritage of Origen making itself felt, mediated, in all likelihood, through
the writings of Dionysius the Areopagite.

God the End (telos): The Virtual Negation of Nature

As this whole magnificent creation, charged with the glory of God throughout, returns to God; as the descending goodness of the creation is now recapitu-
lated in the ascending perfections of redemption; the whole biophysical order is,
as such, left behind. As for Alan and Thomas, nature is good *ab alpha* for Bonaventure, whereas the spiritual creatures, including humanity, are good *ex alpha
et omega*.

But Bonaventure, like Thomas, cannot rest content with the inner logic of
the grand theme of overflowing and ingathering thus shaped asymmetrically by
the metaphor of ascent. Like Thomas, Bonaventure is aware that the Bible
speaks of a cosmic renewal at the end of all things, as well as a spiritual consummation. But the more immediate influence for Bonaventure at this point,
surely, stems from Francis, his mentor, who called all creatures brothers and
sisters. Does one really want one's brothers and sisters to be finally dissolved
into nothingness? That is the logic of the dynamics of the great chain of being
when it is shaped primarily by the metaphor of ascent, rather than by the metaphor of fecundity.

Bonaventure's treatment of the theme of nature's final fulfillment differs
from Thomas's attempt to resolve the same question. But it is doubtful that
Bonaventure is any more successful in dealing with the challenge than Thomas
was. At this point he introduces what can only be judged to be, in retrospect—
notwithstanding its firm place in the theology of both Roman Catholicism and
Eastern Orthodoxy at least from that time to the present—a remarkable, but fi-

nally unconvincing theological tour de force. The point revolves around the idea that the human creature is the *microcosm*, a theme which we have already encountered in our review of twelfth-century thinking.

As this world in miniature, Bonaventure holds, the human creature not only reflects but also *embodies* all the levels of the hierarchy of being below, the material and the vital. So—this is the logic—insofar as humanity will be consummated at the end, and insofar as the human creature contains all the levels of the biophysical world, to that extent the whole creation will be consummated at the very end in eternity.[15] Also part of the microcosm theme in Bonaventure's thought, it seems, is the idea that nature is taken into the human soul, somehow, as the human mind ranges over it and employs it as a ladder by which to ascend to God. Thus the meaning of the whole of nature is, as it were, swallowed up by human meanings or, more precisely, the very being of the whole of nature is swallowed up by human beings, somehow. This is how Bowman has summarized Bonaventure's teaching at this point:

> The consummation of material creatures or their return to God is accomplished primarily through man's recognizing the vestiges of God in them and ascending through them, as upon a ladder, to the contemplation of God. It is accomplished secondarily because man embodies and brings with him all levels of creation, so that the material world participates in his ascent to God.[16]

But what if the trees called a parliament? What if the birds to whom Francis preached gathered together to consider their future? What would they make of this so-called consummation? Would they consider it a consummation for themselves or rather an annihilation? What if Noah told all the creatures at the door of the ark that, since he had contemplated them and since he embodied all their qualities, it would not be necessary for them to come along after all?

This is to suggest that a microcosmic consummation of nature is actually no consummation of nature at all. A microcosmic consummation of nature is in fact what it appears to be, a consummation of humankind. Bonaventure's thought, notwithstanding his intentions to the contrary, is thus formally similar to Thomas's. For Bonaventure, in fact, there is no room for the world of animals, plants, and minerals in eternity. They are, in fact, left behind at lower rungs of the ladder of being, as humans ascend to perfect spiritual communion with God above.

The Ascent of the Soul Above the Earth

Bonaventure's spirituality seems to point in the same direction. Cousins comments that "in Franciscan fashion" creatures, for Bonaventure, are a reflection of God, like a stained-glass window.[17] He then quotes Bonaventure: "Just as you see that a ray of light entering through a window is colored in different ways according to the different colors of the various parts, so the divine ray shines forth in each and every creature in different ways and in different properties." Cousins is surely justified in calling this reflection theme Franciscan. But the contrast between Bonaventure and Francis at this point is the more striking, as a juxtaposition of Bonaventure's *The Soul's Journey Into God* with the *Canticle of the Sun* will disclose.

In Bonaventure's great work of mystical spirituality the movement up the ladder of creation is so stressed that virtually no direct attention is given to nature at all. The divine glory and immanence in nature are surely attested, but Bonaventure never once mentions the name of one particular creature in nature. Still less does he suggest that an insect or a fish or even the sun is his brother, as Francis does of the latter. It is the goal, God above, that most fascinates and allures Bonaventure, not so much his fellow creatures along the way. As he writes toward the end of his *Soul's Journey*: "For transcending yourself and all things, by the immeasurable and absolute ecstasy of a pure mind, leaving behind all things, and freed from all things, you will ascend to the superessential ray of the divine darkness."[18] We will reserve judgment about Francis's vision at this point, but it should be clear that Bonaventure's understanding of the final goal of life, both ontologically and spiritually, is shaped most fundamentally by the metaphor of ascent.[19]

The Contrast Between the Fecundity and the Ascent

This is why it is appropriate to think in terms of the ascendancy of the ambiguity when we encounter the thought of Bonaventure. In Thomas's thought that ambiguity is clearly there. He holds to an asymmetrical view of the overflowing goodness of God and the return of all things to God, understood as the good. But in Thomas's case the metaphor of ascent visibly shapes his thinking about the overflowing of the divine goodness, too, already in the context of his doctrine of creation; indeed, one might argue that it also shapes his understanding of God in significant ways.[20] Thomas accents the divine otherness and the quasi-independent status of nature, as we have seen.

But Bonaventure incorporates the theme of fecundity into his thought at its most fundamental point, in his doctrine of God. God is by definition a God of fecundity. Further, for Bonaventure, that real and pervasive quality of the divine overflowing throughout the whole creation is accented with a compelling theological power. It is all the more striking then that when he comes to his theology of redemption, that theme of fecundity is eclipsed as the influence of the metaphor of ascent becomes dominant. We can only speculate what Bonaventure's thought might have looked like if he had followed through with the fecundity theme, as he might well have if he had viewed all things not only as created and cohering in the eternal Word of God but as consummated and glorified in the same Word at the very end. In particular, what if his thought had been more tangibly shaped by the metaphor of migration to a good land and less by the metaphor of ascent? But this kind of question is indeed speculative. Bonaventure, in fact, leaves us where Thomas did—with the ambiguity.

The Poetry of Creation

We see a similar pattern of thought in the elegant poetry of Dante. In the *Divine Comedy* we can contemplate the whole landscape of the medieval mind. Again, the shape of the vision is hierarchical. Dionysius had a profound impact on Dante.[21] This influence extended also to Dante's characteristic mode of thinking. Dionysius had distinguished between what for him were two equally valid approaches to God, the one philosophical, the other theological, the one attending to the visible and proceeding by demonstration, the other presupposing an experiential initiation, attending to the ineffable, and proceeding by the use of symbols.[22] Dante self-consciously chose the second way. His spiritual voyage of discovery sought to express the ultimate truth of things by interpreting the universe as the poetry of God.

Dante's universe is indeed a poem of God. If one could say of any single theologian or poet that in his or her vision the universe is charged with the glory of God, it would be Dante. For him, material light is the substantial form of the whole visible universe, as spiritual light is the very reality of the invisible God. Joseph Mazzeo has written of the meaning of that material light that "it establishes excellence and dignity in every corporeal thing in proper degree, giving it power to act and preserves it in being."[23] For Dante, "things are so constituted that a certain bodily aspect reveals directly, if partially, their innermost essence, translates their form. This aspect of things is what we call their beauty."[24] In Dante's mind, all things observe a mutual order; this is what makes them like God. And each thing moves toward its own proper place: "they move to diverse parts o'er the great sea of being, and each one with instinct given it to bear it on."[25] Such is the familiar medieval theme of overflowing goodness and world harmony in Dante's vision. It is clearly reminiscent of much that we have already seen in thinkers like Alan and Bonaventure.

Ascending Above the Earth to the Heights of Paradise

But it is the ascent that most captivates Dante's piety. For Dante, every level in the created order has its own kind of love or desire for its own proper place. But the proper place for human love is not in this world. "As fire moves upward by its form," he tells us in the *Purgatorio*, "being born to mount where it most abides in its matter, so the mind thus seized enters into desire, which is a spiritual movement, and never rests until the thing loved makes it rejoice."[26]

So in his *Comedy,* Dante descends to the Inferno and then exits to begin his cosmic ascent. He climbs a mountain at the summit of which is the earthly paradise. The very skies, he says, are a lure to him.[27] The heavens, like a voice, call to him.[28] Here, in the Garden, where Adam and Eve were first created, Dante is then greeted by a different kind of Eve: "A lady, alone, going on her way, singing and plucking the flowers, one by one, with which was covered all her path."[29] Guided by this lovely creature from heaven—reminiscent of Alan's goddess Natura—the pristine Beatrice, Dante then begins to leave the material world behind. She leads him upward through the various heavenly spheres—as commonly understood in the astrology and the theology of the fourteenth century. "If I am right," she tells him, "thou shouldst no more wonder at thy ascent than at a stream falling from a mountain height to the foot; it would be a wonder if, freed from hindrance, thou hadst remained below on earth. . . ."[30] Dante's proper end is nothing less than the beatific vision of God, face to face, at the heights of the hierarchy of being.

But to obtain this vision he must leave all materiality behind. This is the significance of Beatrice's departure: "she was . . . in the body the most beautiful of all created things in either the field of nature or that of art. . . . But bodily beauty is imperfect. When it has reached its maximum it must pass over into a disembodied beauty. . . ."[31]

Dante then experiences still more refinements of spiritual purity after Beatrice leaves him. He first sees, immaterially, the heavenly host bathed in God's immaterial light. That is one level of spiritual vision. But he finally must ascend still higher in order to obtain the most perfect vision of God himself in his triune glory. This vision is imageless, immediate, and inexpressible.[32]

Assessment: The Ambiguity of Nature

The goal of Dante's cosmic pilgrimage is thus perfect, transparent spirituality, total release from the biophysical order. This is the alluring vision he leaves with us. Its consonance with some traditions of mystical and monastic piety, which we have not explored in this study, should also be apparent.[33] Yet this vision again illustrates the profound ambiguity of such thinking when it is shaped primarily by the metaphor of ascent. For the most part, Dante sees the cosmos charged with divine glory, as did Bonaventure. But like the latter, too, for Dante the last word is not ambiguous. The last word is denial. His home is emphatically not on this earth,[34] surrounded by the birds and snakes and trees and streams. His home is far above in the ethereal regions of absolute, pure, and imageless spiritual transcendence. In this respect, Dante's vision has much in common with Bonaventure's. Whether he also was articulating the vision of Francis, as both he and Bonaventure thought of themselves as doing, in different ways, is another question.

THE LIFE AND SIGNIFICANCE OF FRANCIS OF ASSISI:
THE EMBRACE OF NATURE

St. Francis is a challenge to the interpreter in many ways. He is the hero of a thousand points of view. His image is easily portrayed so as to reflect the face of the investigator's ideals. Hence we are turning to the meaning of this simple but highly complex man of faith only after we have reviewed his theological context thoroughly. We will attempt to assess his concrete theological meaning with a view to twelfth-century naturalism behind him and the theological constructions of Thomas, Bonaventure, and Dante yet to come, as well as against the background of the religious and social context of his own world.

Clearly, Francis was no schoolman, nor a writing poet. He left us no *Summa*, no *Divine Comedy*. Therefore, in order to ascertain his theology of nature we cannot simply read what he wrote. But we can venture to read his life, which is rich with theological meaning and has a kind of poetry all its own.

Therefore, we must be prepared to use a more synthetic, less analytical interpretive method than we have hitherto employed. For Francis's deeds are at least as important as his words. His theology is evident at that primary level, as was Jesus', whom he sought to imitate throughout his life. Jesus' eating with publicans and sinners, for example, was a living parabolic act, theologically as pregnant with meaning as was the verbal communication of his message in the story of the shepherd and the lost sheep. So we must attend to both the words and the deeds of Francis, if we are to understand him aright.

Further, we will not want to be overly attentive to which words and deeds seem to belong to Francis himself, and which have apparently been added by his followers and interpreters. Our synthetic method of interpretation will allow us to bypass, with due caution, a whole range of critical questions such as those. For our purposes here, a "search of the historical Francis" need not be our chief concern. Which of the historical materials at our disposal stem from Francis himself? Which stem from his disciples and interpreters? While we will surely want to be aware of such questions, we can readily focus our attention on a broader field of theological meaning, which can be called the "Francis event." We can raise this general but pointed question of theological significance: what view of nature comes to expression in this process of human interaction, in the words and deeds of Francis himself, on the one hand, and in the minds and hearts of those who were so overwhelmed by his influence, on the other? We can leave most of the detailed historical questions—that is, which meanings belong to Francis and which to the responding minds of his followers and interpreters—to other investigators.

Francis as a Representative Figure

Francis is best known, perhaps understandably, for his captivating *Canticle of the Sun*. But viewed in context, that remarkable song of thanksgiving stands in a certain visible kind of continuity with the—not nearly so well known—theological naturalism of the twelfth century. When Francis praises God on high for all his creative works, most of his praises apparently refer to the way those works serve human creatures: the sun for the light by which we see, the wind for the air we breathe, the water for its usefulness, the fire for illuminating the night, the earth for giving us food and fodder. On the other hand, if the Italian is translated differently, as it legitimately may be, something else comes into view. In this case we hear Francis calling to the whole creation to join in praising the Creator, reminiscent of the ancient psalmists: "Be praised, my Lord, by sister moon and the stars . . . ," instead of "*for* sister moon and the stars. . . . " We will return to this point presently.

Francis is also much celebrated for his perfect attunement with other creatures and for their responsiveness to him. But this also is familiar to us from the preceding tradition. Francis's perceived contemplative mastery over the animals—so much so that he is seen as frequently commanding them to do his bidding—is very much reminiscent of the reported lives of the wandering Irish saints, which we considered previously.[35] One can think of Francis's famous "stilling of the swallows," which may be one of those instances of evident elaboration by his followers,[36] but which, in any case, shows his sublime attunement to the animals, and his judicious mastery over them, akin to the traditional image of Adam and Eve in the Garden. His reported encounter with the ravaging wolf at Gubio, commanding the wolf to lie down, which the animal then did "gentle as a lamb," is another such instance.[37] This account has many parallels in earlier saints' lives.

Francis's preaching and teaching is also replete with symbolic allusions to the spiritual life or the events of salvation, a motif which has its roots in the moralizing exemplarism of the early medieval bestiaries, and which would later be developed systematically and with great sophistication by Bonaventure. The lark, say Francis, "is like a good Religious, flying she praises God most sweetly . . . , condemning earthly things, always intent on praising God."[38] He is said to have cared for worms, likewise, because the Savior said "I am a worm and no man,"[39] and to have seen the sign of the cross in the interlacing of twigs in a hedge.[40] But, notwithstanding the luminescent power of Francis's own spirit, such motifs were not unprecedented.

Even Francis's dedication to poverty, the life lived in the forests, and his commitment to live on the basis of the generosity of the people, had numerous precedents,[41] although the repudiation of communal as well as individual property by monastic and semimonastic groups was not common. Likewise, Francis's self-consciously chosen role as a troubadour of Christ obviously has its roots, however far removed, in the ethos of courtly love which flourished in his time and in the preceding century.

Precedented or not, however, Francis's life would have been remarkable enough in the foregoing terms. But we have yet to see Francis in terms of his own (and his circle's) particular creativity.

Francis's Theological Creativity: Love for All the Creatures of God

Dante, we have seen, was captivated by the prospect of ascent. He told a story of being drawn up the scale of being, from the very moment that he emerged from the Inferno, toward his true home in heaven, guided by a woman of radiant heavenly beauty. Alan of Lille, in contrast, showed us the alluring goddess Natura. The theological imagination of the twelfth century was in no hurry to climb the scale of being to its apex. It came to a certain kind of rest, indeed, with the experience of the overflowing, descending goodness of God, perceived in the visible, accessible world of nature. Although we have no reason to doubt that the vision of ascent to God shaped Francis's spirituality in significant ways, it seems clear that in accent he was much closer to Alan in the twelfth century, in this respect, than to Dante after him. Nothing illustrates this more forcefully than his persistent habit of calling all the creatures of God brother and sister, and his accompanying expression of care and affection for them.

"He overflowed with the spirit of charity," his biographer Celano states in his first edition, "pitying not only men who were suffering need, but even the dumb brutes, reptiles, birds, and other creatures without sensation."[42] As this record indicates, there was much more in Francis's relationship to the creatures of nature than an aesthetic delight and a theocentric devotion, although those elements were certainly there. Francis *loved* those lowly creatures as brothers and sisters. At this point he stands apart from the theological naturalism of the twelfth century, as well as at a distance from the cosmic exemplarism and the fascination with the ascent familiar to us in the works of Bonaventure and Dante. Francis's love for the creatures was something different from either the cooperative or the contemplative mastery over nature that came to expression in the twelfth century.

Moreover, Francis did not merely use the creatures of nature as an instrument for his own and his fellows' ascent to God, as Bonaventure tended to do. He rested his affection in them. They were for him, in a certain sense, centers of value in their own right. So the worm, for example, did remind him of the humiliated Savior, but he did not use the worm merely as an occasion to enhance his own or others' relationship with Christ, or to rise higher in the scale of being to a more perfect communion with God. He loved the worm, Celano tells us, "he glowed with exceeding love . . . , wherefore he used to pick them up in the way and put them in a safe place, that they might not be crushed by the feet of passers-by." Nor, as this instance shows, did he focus his attention chiefly on the popularly "more spiritual" or ethereal creatures such as the birds, although he is most remembered for that. He cared for fish[43] and insects, even though that kind of "going the extra mile" with love for all the creatures, we may say, did not always suit his tastes. "He ordered honey and the best wine," says Celano, "to be provided for the bees that they might not perish from want in the cold of winter. He called by the name of brother all animals, though in all their kinds the gentle were his favorites."[44]

Indeed, Francis became a kind of advocate for the creatures, as one might imagine a prophet becoming an advocate of the poor and the oppressed within the human community. "Nor is it strange," one of our sources tells us, "if the fire and the other creatures were obedient to him and venerated him, for, as we who were with him have very often seen, he was so much drawn to them, and rejoiced in them so much, and his spirit was moved with so much pity and compassion for them that he would not see them badly treated and he used to speak with them with inward gladness, as if they had reason, whence by these occasions, he was often times wrapt up in God."[45]

This loving, self-giving relationship with the creatures reached perhaps its most vivid expression in the reports of Francis's duet with the nightingale. He and brother Leo were enjoying a meal together when Francis proposed that they "sing the praise of God antiphonally with this bird."[46] Leo declined, but Francis and the nightingale, we are told, continued singing antiphonally from vespers until lauds, until at last Francis was forced to stop due to exhaustion. Then the bird fluttered to his hand, where he fed it, praised it enthusiastically, and gave it his blessing. At that moment, the songful creature flew away.

Thus Francis was perceived as knowing how to apply some of the most subtle canons of human friendship to the creatures of nature, to this extent: that he could readily give up his own sense of mastery, his own power to control, in order to join in a cooperative relationship, and finally defer to the other.

The Theology of Descent and the Kenotic Christ

When Francis approached nature, we may say, he saw first neither a goddess Natura, nor yet a Beatrice, but rather—Lady Poverty. His piety surely included an element of ascent. This was memorably enacted in his climbing to the top of Mt. LaVerna. But we should remember here that the metaphor of fecundity also contains within it the nuance of climbing to the mountaintop. In this case, however, the purpose of the climbing is not to leave the material conditions of this world behind, but better to stand in solidarity with that world. Indeed, the movement of the Divine which typically emerges in thought shaped by the metaphor of fecundity is the movement of *descent*. It is apparent, then, that we can see in the life of Francis an inversion of the characteristic piety of his time, even as that piety was later to come to expression in Bonaventure and Dante. The image of Lady Poverty, for him, signals that inversion. Hearkening back to the paradoxical richness of biblical images—to become rich, one must become poor; to gain one's life, one must lose it—Francis seems to envision the way of spiritual ascent as in fact being the way of spiritual descent. "A man must be naked and free of every burden," we hear him saying in the *Sacrum Commercium* regarding Lady Poverty, "if he would attain the mountain top where she has taken refuge. Take also with you companions who will help you in your painful ascent."[47]

But why does the idea of descent appear in Francis's life and thought instead of the more familiar singular accent on ascending to the spiritual heights above and leaving the earth behind? To answer this question, we may first recall the familiar twelfth-century theological emphasis on the overflowing, descending goodness of God, and imagine that Francis saw that fecund divine benevolence all around him, with peculiar clarity and intensity. Indeed, as he loved all the creatures, so he readily understood the overflowing goodness of God as *God's love* and caring for all the creatures. This is from his memorable sermon to the birds:

> My little sisters, the birds, many are the bonds that unite us to God. And your duty is to praise Him everywhere and always. . . . Praise Him likewise for the food He provides you without your working for it, for the songs He has taught you, for your numbers that His blessing has multiplied, for your species which He preserved in the ark of olden time, and for the realm of the air He has reserved for you.

> God sustains you without having to sow or reap. He gives you fountains and streams to drink from, mountains and hills in which to take refuge, and tall trees in which to build your nests. Although you do not know how to sew or spin, He gives you and your little ones the clothing you need.

> How the Creator must love you to grant you such favors! So, my sister birds, do not be ungrateful, but continually praise Him who showers blessings upon you.[48]

The theology of divine goodness is thus vivid, even overwhelming, in Francis's thinking. But it does not stand alone, by any means. And this is Francis's pecu-

liar genius or, better, his inspiration. He joined the image of the divine goodness with a concrete christocentric devotion of radical proportions.

"Many a time," Celano tells us, "as he was walking on his way, meditating
and singing of Jesus, did he forget where he was going, and invite all the elements to praise Jesus."[49] This relationship with Jesus—with whose wounds he
was to be stigmatized—lay at the heart of what modern interpreters sometimes
unfelicitously think of as his "nature mysticism." Francis espoused Lady Poverty
—the theme of descent—because she had been "the inseparable companion of
the Most High Son of God" and because for twelve centuries, it appeared to
Francis, she had wandered about forsaken.[50] Francis's "nature mysticism" is, in
fact, more adequately thought of, if the term is to be used at all, as a "Christ
mysticism."

"Have this mind among yourselves," the apostle Paul had written, "which
you have in Christ Jesus, who, though he was in the form of God, did not count
equality with God a thing to be grasped, but emptied himself, taking the form
of a servant, being born in human likeness. And being found in human form,
he humbled himself and became obedient unto death, even death on a cross"
(Phil. 2:5–8). Francis petitions Lady Poverty with virtually the same christological confession:

> We beseech you to join us and become our way leading to the King of Glory, as
> you were the way for Him when He came to help those sitting in the shadow of
> death.
>
> For, leaving His royal abode, the Son of the Most High sought you whom all
> men fear. Enamoured by your beauty, it was you alone whom He descended to
> wed on earth. You had prepared for Him a fitting throne within a poor Virgin;
> from which He came forth to manifest Himself to the world. It was you again who
> provided Him an abode in that miserable stable when at His birth there was no
> place for Him in the inn. There you became His whole lifelong, His inseparable
> companion. For the foxes have holes and the birds of the air their nests, but He
> had no place to lay his head.[51]

Francis's relationship with nature had a *cruciform* character. He became the
Christ-like servant of nature. He impoverished himself in order that he might
give himself to others, both to human and to natural creatures. So in his life and
thought (and in the meanings that resonated in the hearts and minds of some of
his followers) he, in effect, united two grand theological themes: on the one
hand, the vision of the descending goodness of God, which makes all things
good and worthy of respect in their own right, since they are indeed of God and
for God; on the other hand, the vision of the descending love of God in Christ,
the self-giving, self-humiliating Savior, who, in turn, mandated sacrificial love
for the world.

This is the profound significance of the famous Christmas tableau that Francis created. Its meaning has often been obscured by later sentimentalities. But this was in truth an enacted parable of Francis's faith in the kenotic or self-emptying Christ, in the midst of the overflowing goodness of God. Two weeks before Christmas he asked his friend, the Lord of Grecco, for his aid in making that place "a new Bethlehem."[52] A crib was set in place, lined with hay, and an ox and ass were brought in. Mass was celebrated above the manger, beside which the animals were standing. "The night was lit up as the day," we are told by Celano, "and was delightsome to men and beasts . . . the woodland rang with voices, the rocks made answer to the jubilant throng."[53]

Theologically speaking, the implication of Francis's action seems clear. Identification with the kenotic Christ restores one, in an otherwise sinful world, to perfect communion with the overflowing goodness of God in the whole creation. Identification with the kenotic Christ, then, is not the occasion for dying to this world in order to ascend above to a world-transcending union with God. Identification with the kenotic Christ is the occasion for living in this world, imitating that Christ, yes, but at the same time imitating the Father of the same Christ, who is constantly descending to care for and to bless all of his creatures.

For this reason Francis can stand in solidarity with all the creatures of God and can call on them to share in his joy in the event of the divine descent in the stable of Bethlehem. "Sing joyfully to God our helper . . . ," we hear Francis saying in his *Office of the Lord's Passion,* which he apparently used regularly in addition to the offices of the canonical hours:

> Sing joyfully to God our helper. . . . For the Lord is terrible and great, the Great King over all the earth. Because the most high Father in heaven, our King before all ages, has sent His beloved Son from on high; and He has been born of the Blessed Virgin, Holy Mary. . . .

> For the most holy and beloved Child is given us and born for us on the way and laid for us in a manger; because He found no place in the inn. Let the heavens be glad and the earth rejoice: let the sea be moved, and the fulness thereof; the fields and all things that are in them shall be joyful. . . ."[54]

These words are reminiscent of the *Canticle of the Sun,* when it is more properly translated to accent the theocentric, rather than the anthropocentric meanings: "Be praised, my Lord, *by* sister moon and the stars." Identified with the kenotic Christ, Francis sees the descending goodness of the Creator everywhere, blessing all things, and therefore he calls on all things, human and natural, to praise the Creator.

To see all this, according to this Franciscan way of thinking, one must indeed be identified with the kenotic Christ. In this sense, Francis was not a romantic.

He did not go directly to nature, at least at first. At first he went directly to Christ. This meant that the only way to see nature as it truly is, as universally blessed and cared for by the Creator, was the way of *humility* again, the way of Lady Poverty. So, in his *Office on the Lord's Passion,* after having called all things to praise their Creator, he turns to the nations of the world and prays: "Offer your bodies in sacrifice and carry His Holy Cross: and follow unto the end His most holy commandments."[55]

Here a colloquialism is instructive: the kenotic Christ brought Francis's piety "down to earth." That is to say: the self-giving, descending Christ, Son of the Creator who is overflowing goodness, brought Francis's piety down to earth. And on the earth it stays. From thence it never ascends.

Living the Life of "Last Things"

But we must still ask a key question in this respect. For Francis, who is this kenotic Christ who binds him in humility to imitate the universal goodness of God? This question points us to an aspect of Francis's life and thought which is missing from most popular presentations of the saint, nor does it play a visible role in many scholarly interpretations: Francis's eschatological consciousness.

The expectation of the end of the world was very much alive in Francis's time, in popular circles, if not among the theologians. It was a constant source of "human tension and social upheaval," as Ray Petry has observed.[56] Francis shared in this popular eschatological consciousness. Ernst Benz has highlighted Francis's exposition of the Lord's Prayer, in this connection, in particular his interpretation of the petition for daily bread.[57] Francis identified this bread, for which he was praying, with the Christ who is to come.[58] With that identification, Benz points out, Francis gave expression to two themes, which were characteristic of his life and thought. First there is Francis's burning anticipation of the coming consummation, the coming of the kingdom, which for Francis is so real and so near that he undertakes the impossible, to live in terms of the laws of the coming kingdom—humility, love, self-giving, poverty, chastity, obedience—already in the midst of the realities of this world. The second element Benz sees implicit in Francis's identification of "daily bread" with the coming Christ is the affirmation of the meaningfulness of the life of the church in this world, above all its sacraments.[59] The latter means that Francis, notwithstanding his intense and overwhelming eschatological consciousness, did not break with the church in order to enter into the coming age, which he so vividly envisioned as the context for his own life.

This means further that Francis stands with and against another medieval figure who was well known for his particular kind of eschatological consciousness, the Cistercian abbot, Joachim of Fiore (1145–1202). Scholars debate the extent of Joachim's direct influence on Francis, but Joachimite ideas were surely widely known in Francis's time, and beyond. The saintly John of Parma, for example, Minister General of the Franciscan Order before Bonaventure, was thoroughly influenced by Joachim.[60] A comparison of Joachim and Francis, in any case, is revealing.

Joachim projected a vision of three successive ages, during which different aspects of the Trinity would be manifest: the age of the Father, the Old Testament; the age of the Son, the church; and the age of the Spirit.[61] The last, as Joachim depicts it, is akin to some of the eschatological ideas we have already seen in Irenaeus. Joachim envisions this age of the Spirit as a time of voluntary poverty and peace on earth, when a new race of children of God would inherit the earth, love one another and all the creatures of nature, and give praise to God in all things. Joachim apparently thought of himself and his followers as harbingers of the new age. So, once, in a paradigmatic action, when the clouds cleared away from over the church in which he was officiating, he saluted the sun, sang the "Veni Creator"—the hymn of invocation to the Creator Spirit—and led the congregation forth to contemplate the shining landscape.[62]

Now Francis was an obedient son of the church all his days. As Benz indicates, Francis's petition for his daily bread presupposes his acceptance and affirmation of the sacraments of the church. He never thought of leaving the church and its ordinances behind, as Joachim did, in order to enter into some new age where there would be no church. But it is surely not imagining too much at this point to think of him as sharing in the kind of penchant for realized eschatology current in Joachimite circles, in other respects: living a life of childlike simplicity, loving all the creatures of the earth, being transfixed with joy in the presence of the God who is, in some sense, already "all in all," living at peace with the world of nature, in short, living the life of the new heavens and new earth already in this world.

This brings us to an answer to our question about the kenotic Christ who so captivated Francis's soul. Was not this humble Christ, in Francis's eyes, already the Christ who was to come? In particular, was not Francis's creation of the Christmas tableau an act of eschatological piety? Was this not in some sense intended to be a parabolic enactment of the "peaceable kingdom" of the end time, a realized eschatology, a partial but tangible manifestation of life in the future world of God, promised by God throughout the ages?

The Isaianic vision of peace entailed the lamb lying down with the lion, and a little child leading them (Isa. 11:16), but it also included a vision of the *mountain* where the Temple stands being established as the highest of all mountains, whereto the nations of the world would flow, and beat their swords into plowshares (Isa. 2:1–4; 11:9). Later, in the same book, we are shown a vision of the Lord "on this mountain" making for all peoples "a feast of fat things, a feast of wine on the lees . . . And we will destroy on this mountain the covering that is cast over all peoples . . ." (Isa. 25:6–8).

What we see emerging here is the influence of yet another metaphor in Francis's life and thought, mediated to him by the eschatological consciousness of his time, and not really shared by the likes of Alan, Bonaventure, and Dante: the metaphor of migration to a good land. Christ has brought Francis's piety down to earth, in this eschatological sense. He has introduced Francis, as it were, to the fecundity of the divine characteristic of the end times, and called Francis to embody the life of childlike innocence and peace with nature, among other things. Francis's ascent to the mountain, which for him is really a descent, following the example of Christ and then living in imitation of the descending goodness of God throughout the creation, was in fact for him his descent to the promised land.

It is possible to read the story of the famous "welcoming of the birds" with such biblical nuances in mind. One day with a company of close friends, Francis set out for LaVerna, the mountain donated by the Lord of Chiusi, where some huts and a small chapel served as a devotional center for the brothers.[63] This was where his final ecstasy and stigmatization were to take place. Here, in his ascent, we are told, Francis chose to rest and to look back at all the country about him. Then the famous avian friends of the saint arrived—knowing, indeed, we may imagine, from the mind's eye of the narrator of this story, that this holy man was their friend—and they showed great joy.

> When they were come right to the foot of the very rock of LaVerna, it pleased St. Francis to rest awhile under the oak tree that stood by the way, and there standeth to this day [is this at some level a figure for "the tree of the cross"?]; and retiring beneath it St. Francis began to consider the lay of the place and of the country round about. And lo, while he was thus pondering, there came a great multitude of birds from diverse parts that, with singing and fluttering of their wings, showed forth great joy and gladness, and surrounded St. Francis, in such wise that some settled on his head, some on his shoulders, and some on his arms, some on his bosom, and some around his feet. His companions . . . beholding this marveled greatly, and St. Francis rejoiced in spirit, and spake thus: "I do believe dearest brothers, that it is pleasing to our Lord Jesus Christ that we abide on this solitary mountain, since our sisters and brothers, the birds, show such joy at our coming."[64]

Is it accidental that Celano should think of Francis in terms of the eschatological vision of Paul in Romans 8, the theme of the whole creation groaning in travail, waiting for the revelation of the children of God? "He discerned the hidden things of creation," Celano says, "with the eye of the heart, as one who had already escaped into the glorious liberty of the children of God."[65]

If these suggestions for an approach to Francis's life and theology in terms of realized eschatology have merit, then we are in a position to understand his celebrated preaching to the birds and the flowers as events of theological significance, not merely matters of personal genius or idiosyncrasy. This preaching seems to be very much more than sentimental rhetoric, exaggerated hagiography, or some unfortunate pathetic fallacy. It is rather an expression of Francis's position of living in this world, in terms of the next, when all things are to be renewed.

Renewal of the whole creation—that is surely good news for all those creatures! It was in this spirit, a spirit of hope for a fully renewed creation, that the ancient psalmist called to all creatures to praise the Lord, for his coming salvation would be a blessing for them too. So on the basis of such a hope, which for Francis would include eschatological brotherliness and sisterliness, Francis could then speak in the present to the creatures as brothers and sisters. Again the testimony of Celano is illuminating, once more with reference to the eschatological theme of the groaning of the whole creation:

> When he found many flowers growing together, it might happen that he would speak to them and encourage them, as though they could understand, to praise the Lord. It was the same with the fields of corn and the vineyards, the stones in the earth and in the woods, all the beauteous meadows, the tinkling brooks, the sprouting gardens, earth, fire, air and wind—all these he exhorted in his pure childlike spirit to love God and to serve Him joyfully.
>
> He was wont to call all created things his brothers and sisters, and in a wonderful manner inaccessible to others he would enter into the secret things as one to whom "the glorious liberty of the children of God" had been given.[66]

In light of this eschatological horizon of his life and thought, we can understand, finally, why he was able to relate to death and suffering in the world so forthrightly and with such an inner peace. When he had but a short time to live, he is said to have stretched out his hands and cried, "then be welcome sister death."[67] He knew the world into which he was about to enter. He had been living in that world, by anticipation. Therefore he was not afraid. Therefore he welcomed it.

The actual scene of Francis's dying, as we see it in the sources we have, is remarkable in many ways, not the least of which is pertinent to our concerns here. We do not see Francis ecstatically transfixed in ethereal glory, in immaterial luminescence, as Bonaventure and Dante were to imagine such a final state of union with god. It is reported that as Francis lay dying, he again and again returned to sing the hymn for which he is still most famous, the *Canticle of the Sun*.[68] Here, at the very end, as throughout his life, Francis lives and dies in solidarity with all the creatures of God. He lives and dies surrounded by the fecundity of God, partaking of the ecstasies of the promised land.

Assessment: The Triumph of the Ecological Motif

Francis's life and his death, we may therefore conclude, were shaped by the ecological motif of Western theology. In this respect we may view Francis and Augustine side by side. Both looked forward to a good land, to the final consummation of the cosmos as a whole, as well as to the consummation of human history. Both looked forward to a time when God would be all in all and when the whole universe would be transfigured with divine glory. Both, in turn, viewed existence in this world as a pilgrimage, as a life-and-death migration to that ultimate world of divine glory. At the same time, both saints maximized the potential of the metaphor of fecundity, with regard to this world as well as the next. The theme of the created world as a rich and variegated expression of God's overflowing goodness permeated their thinking and their piety. Both also shaped their thought and spirituality in response to the self-giving love of God manifest in the Christ figure, the humiliated, humble Son of God. Both Augustine and Francis were, in this sense, champions of the grace of God, which they perceived, in their own ways, as constantly overflowing, constantly descending to this earth, throughout the whole created order as well as in the specific context of the history of human salvation, mediated through the sacramental ministries of the church.

The differences between the two, as far as their approaches to nature are concerned, are mainly differences between a man of thought and a man of action. With the African doctor we witness a flowering of Christianity's ecological promise expressed in terms of an articulate, panoramic theological vision. With the Poverello from Assisi we witness a flowering of Christianity's ecological promise in terms of a vivid, personal engagement with the world of nature. Augustine reflected about nature. Francis embraced nature. Francis, indeed, shows in this respect the impassioned existential possibilities latent in Augustine's sometimes dispassionate theological discourse. Francis, we may say, is an embodiment of Christianity's ecological promise.

To say this much, however, is not yet to begin to project a systematic theology or to design an ethical program. This has not been the purpose of any of these explorations. The intent here, and throughout, has consistently been historical, not systematic. This perhaps needs to be underlined at this point, in view of the immense popularity of Francis in our day, and with particular reference to the discussion of Francis and Benedict initiated by René Dubos. Dubos has recommended Benedict as his patron saint of ecology, as it were, rather than Francis, because Dubos attributes a certain passivity before nature to Francis, whereas he sees in Benedict, as we already have had occasion to note, a spirit of "creative intervention in the earth." Dubos argues, moreover, that that ecologically sensitive, but activist spirit is what the human race needs today, more than what he considers to be the contemplative Franciscan spirit.[69]

Dubos surely deserves a hearing at this point. It may be that the Benedictine spirit, as he interprets it, needs to be seen as a valuable theological resource in its own right, alongside the Franciscan spirit. One obviously cannot discern any "theology of technology," for example, surely not explicitly, in the Francis event. And such a theology is undoubtedly called for in our own era. At the same time, a reading of Francis more sympathetic than Dubos's would probably show that Francis's life incorporates many "Benedictine" nuances, as a matter of fact, in particular the Benedictine emphasis on cooperative mastery. Also, a closer comparison of Francis and Benedict might well uncover elements in Francis's life which are missing from the theology implicit in the Benedictine spirit, Francis's eschewing of private property, for example, or his love for the poor and his commitment to serve them rather than, let us say, simply committing himself to his own community and to the contemplative life.

In any case, this point needs to be stressed here: to suggest that Francis embodies the ecological promise of the classical Christian tradition is not to suggest that he represents everything that must be affirmed today by a responsible "ecological theology." It is to suggest, however, that Francis's vision of the descending, universal goodness of God, his obedience to the kenotic Christ, his hope for the consummation of all things, and his childlike love of all the creatures of God commend themselves to us today, probably more than the contributions of any other single individual who stands within the context of the classical theological tradition, as compelling data for our own theological reflection.

If we see Francis in this light, moreover, as an embodiment of the ecological promise of classical Christianity, it is also possible to think of his life and thought instructively in terms of some of the questions raised at the beginning of these historical explorations, in our review of Kaufman's analysis of Western theology generally. As we have acknowledged that Kaufman's analysis makes sense when we are considering Origen's thought, we may also allow, when sufficient qualifications have been made, that it has some applicability to Alan, Thomas, Bonaventure, and Dante also, all of whom finally think in terms of the spiritual motif. But as Kaufman's analysis does not readily apply to Irenaeus or to Augustine, both of whom thought in terms of the ecological motif, neither does it apply, surely, to the theological meaning given in the Francis event.

Here are the rudiments for a theology that has indeed a special vocabulary for nature, the vocabulary of friendship; that envisions a close ontological bond between God and humans, on the one hand, and nature, on the other; that presupposes an understanding of God which readily highlights those qualities of the divine life which show God as immanent in, and as befriending all creatures; and that, accordingly, encourages humans to do the same, by an *imitatio Christi* and an *imitatio Dei*, by following the example of the Son of God who emptied himself in order to minister to all the creatures of God, especially the least of them, even as his Father was already ministering to them.

7

THE LIABILITIES OF THE AMBIGUITY

Reformation Theology and the Modern Secularization of Nature

To have an argument, one must be on speaking terms with one's opponent. This truism of historical studies can be readily applied to the theology of the magisterial Protestant Reformers, Martin Luther (1483–1546) and John Calvin (1509–64), as we witness them taking issue with the theology that they inherited from the Middle Ages. Although they frequently present answers that differ from the ones their predecessors articulated, the way they pose their questions, above all their central preoccupation with the theme of human salvation, has much in common with the assumptions of earlier theologians.

The inaugural question of the Reformation tradition was Luther's: "How can I find a gracious God?" Paradigmatically, that question, as it was given in the medieval tradition, could be paraphrased: "how can I ascend and finally be with God?" In the Middle Ages, as we have seen, the goal of human existence was often construed in terms of the Christian's pilgrimage within this lowly earth to the beatific vision or union with God in the heavenly Jerusalem above. Major trends in medieval thought about redemption, whether they were articulated by a Thomas, a Bonaventure, or a Dante, were all shaped, in a thoroughgoing way, by the metaphor of ascent.

The Reformers did not essentially change the form of the medieval question itself. Rather, they gave it a forceful, paradoxical answer: "You cannot ascend and finally be with God—God has descended to be with you, finally." Human striving was in vain, they argued, even human striving enabled by an indwelling of divine grace. God in his gracious favor had supplied all that humans needed for eternal salvation in Christ, the Word made flesh, right at the lowly level of human existence itself. The Reformers thus took over the form of the question from the Middle Ages at the very moment they were offering a revolutionary answer. One can say, as it were, that they inverted the metaphor of ascent: it was no longer a question of humanity ascending to God, whether by meritorious works or by indwelling gifts of grace or by any other way; now it was a question of God descending to humanity. But the legacy of the metaphor of ascent is still to be seen in their preoccupation with God and humanity, in general, and with the theme of human salvation in particular. At the same time, the ambiguity we have been tracing also emerges in the Reformer's thought. While their theology focuses on God and humanity, it also gives vivid testimony, at times, to the power and the glory of God in nature, to human solidarity with nature, and also to the eschatological fulfillment of nature. To this extent, their thought is shaped by the ecological motif.

The Reformer's preoccupation with human salvation helped to set the stage for—one is well-advised here *not* to say that it *caused*—further developments in Western thought which resulted in what we can call the secularization of nature. Focused so intensely on the anthropocentric dynamics of grace, in other words, Protestant theology in the four centuries after the Reformation, tended to open itself anew to the influence of the metaphor of ascent: Protestant theology tended to give up its claims—God's claims—on nature and the life of humanity in nature altogether. Rising above nature in order to enter into communion with God became a hallmark of Protestant thought.

This happened precisely at a time when Western culture at large was breaking away from the theological and ethical influence of classical Christian symbols and norms, and giving free reign to a spirit of aggrandizement—as well as progress—in human affairs, and policies of exploitation—as well as development—directed toward nature. In the nineteenth and early twentieth centuries, Protestant theology by and large washed its hands of nature, as it were, and thereby gave the spirit of modern industrialism its de facto permission—sometimes its de jure encouragement—to work its will on nature. For this reason, we will conclude, the ecological ambiguity of classical Christian theology had become a severe theological liability by the middle of the twentieth century.

LUTHER AND CALVIN:
THE ANTHROPOCENTRIC DYNAMICS OF GRACE
AND THE WONDERS OF NATURE

To understand Luther and Calvin rightly in the context of our concerns in this study, it is important to distinguish between the focal and circumferential elements of their thought. Clearly these elements are inseparable; they must be understood reciprocally. Yet the distinction is useful nevertheless. We will see that it is the focal elements of Reformation theology that mainly survive in modern Protestant theology, while the circumferential elements tend to slip from sight, if they do not disappear altogether.

The Focal Elements of Their Thought: Human Salvation

The focal elements of the Reformers' thought can be described as theanthropocentric. This is a term given currency in the twentieth century by Karl Barth.

He used it to refer to a theology that focuses on God and humanity as its chief subjects.

To say that the Reformers' thought is theanthropocentric is not, as such, to suggest that it was shaped by the spiritual motif whose history we have been following. The Reformers surely tended to think first and foremost about God and humanity; and that kind of thought pattern is indicative of a kind of theology that is shaped by the spiritual motif. On the other hand, the theme of rising above nature in order to enter into communion or to seek union with God is not characteristic of their thought; and that theme is an essential nuance of the spiritual motif, as we have seen its influence in numerous cases. We will return to the question about the spiritual motif in their theology presently.

Luther and Calvin present us with a vision of God and humanity in dynamic interpersonal communion, established by the gracious Word of God. This theanthropocentric focus of their thought reflects Western theology's increasing preoccupation with human salvation—soteriology—in the post-Augustinian centuries. It was already visible in a major chapter of Augustine's life which we did not consider earlier, his confrontation with Pelagius. The meaning of grace in human experience was of utmost important to Augustine. It is for this concern that he is most remembered—as the *doctor gratiae*. The intense interest in human salvation reached another peak of visibility in Anselm's deliberations in the eleventh century, in his work *Cur Deus Homo?* Much attention and many controversies in the later Middle Ages also focused on the meaning of God's redemption of humankind—atonement, predestination, the sacraments, and justification, for example. The Reformers did not take issue with this preoccupation as such. If anything, they heightened it.

For Luther, accordingly, the most important doctrine of all was the doctrine of justification. He says that it is the "master and prince, the lord, the ruler, and judge over all kinds of doctrines."[1] This central doctrine, clearly, treats God and humanity. It is concerned with persons seeking God and God coming to persons in judgment and grace. Hence it is no surprise to find Luther saying at one point, "the knowledge of God and of man is the divine and properly theological wisdom."[2]

For Calvin, we can safely say, the most important doctrine of all is the doctrine of the knowledge of God.[3] And here, as in the case of the doctrine of justification, God and humanity are the chief objects of attention. As Calvin writes, introducing his *Institutes*, "Our wisdom, in so far as it ought to be deemed true and solid wisdom, consists almost entirely of two parts: the knowledge of God and of ourselves."[4]

The theanthropocentric shape of the Reformers' most fundamental theological concerns should therefore be apparent. Further, in practice as well, they were constantly attending, in one way or another, to the right understanding of human salvation, Luther perhaps more than Calvin at this point. This comes to expression in Luther's writings in the phenomenon of his constant concern with "faith alone," *sola fide*. It is more muted in Calvin's writings; he had more systematic interests, as the comprehensive scope of his *Institutes* shows. Still, if we think of the doctrine of election as the culminating apex of his theology (it is probably best not to think of it as Calvin's "organizing principle"),⁵ then we can see that soteriological concern shaping much of Calvin's thinking too. This overriding concern with soteriology, in turn, had the effect of giving an anthropocentric accent to much of what the Reformers had to say in other contexts.

Some Anthropocentric Readings of the Creation

The theanthropocentric mode of thought of the Reformers is apparent when we consider their approach to the theology of creation. At times, indeed, their theology in this respect is so focused on God and humanity that it can appear to be radically anthropocentric. Luther remarks in his exposition of Genesis 1, for example, that Holy Scripture ". . . plainly teaches that God created all these things in order to prepare a house and an inn, as it were, for the future man."⁶ He observes that "night and day alternate for the purpose of refreshing our bodies by rest. The sun shines that work may be done. . . ."⁷ Luther's exposition of the First Article of the Apostles' Creed also has an anthropocentric tonality. It surely stands in sharp contrast to the universal scope of theological meaning entertained by some of his predecessors, such as Augustine, when they reflected about the meaning of creation. "I believe God has created me together with all that exists," Luther writes, "that he has given me and still sustains my body and soul, all my limbs and senses, my reason and all the faculties of my mind, together with food and clothing, house and home, family and property. . . . All this he does out of his pure fatherly and divine goodness and mercy, without any merit or worthiness on my part." Many of Luther's references to the beauty of creation are anthropocentric in intent, insofar as they indicate how the believer knows God rather than how they point to some theocentric value or integrity of the creatures of nature themselves.⁸

Luther also gives an indirect but forceful anthropocentric cast to his theology of creation insofar as he identifies the sphere of the created order with the rule of the hidden God, the *Deus absconditus*. Luther was very much aware of the threatening aspects of nature—the fall of a leaf, for example, which instills fear in the heart of a traveler passing through the woods. His own decision to become a monk in his early years took place when he was overcome with trepidation in the midst of a storm which had overtaken him on a lonely journey in the countryside. He had a sense, common in his time, of the alienness of the forests and of the presence of demons behind every tree. In a similar vein, he thought of the whole cosmos as a world that was running down and deteriorating.[9]

He thought that the world in his day was drawing near to the time of the apocalypse, moreover, the final, consuming cosmic inferno of universal divine judgment. More often than not, therefore, Luther tended to view the world of nature as a realm standing under the "left hand of God," the wrathful, alien hand of God. Luther took the Genesis motif of the divine curse on nature quite literally at times. "The earth," he explains, "is indeed innocent and would gladly produce the best products, but is prevented by the curse which was placed upon man because of sin."[10] Again:

> Our body bears the traces of God's wrath, which our sin has deserved. God's wrath also appears on the earth in all creatures. . . . And what of thorns, thistles, water, fire, caterpillars, flies, flees, and bedbugs? Collectively and individually, are not all of them messengers who preach to us concerning sin and God's wrath?[11]

In this respect, for Luther, nature clearly was not a milieu for communion with God, as it was, for example, for Francis. Nor did Luther generally see the great cosmic harmonies as Augustine did. Luther often tended to see nature as a concatenation of hostile energies—above all the insects!—which motivate the despairing soul to seek out and to cling to "the right hand of God," the free mercy of God communicated through Christ and mediated by the Word and Sacraments. To this extent, nature for Luther is a backdrop or, better, a kind of existential springboard for grace. Nature has the effect of drawing the despairing soul to seek the humanity of Christ. Therefore, as nature is created for the sake of humanity, according to Luther, it seems that nature also functions anthropocentrically in the order of redemption as well.

Calvin's sentiments are similar, although in his thought Luther's emphasis on the hidden God of wrath in nature gives way to a different kind of emphasis on the sovereignty of the God of grace; and other soteriological themes such as election and regeneration take on a greater importance, alongside justification by faith. The "end for which all things were created," Calvin observes in his Genesis commentary, was "that none of the conveniences and necessities of life might be wanting to men."[12] Moreover, although Calvin strongly emphasizes that the will of the Creator and its providential power rules in and through all things, the purpose Calvin often has in mind when he reflects on these themes is to show that the God who elects the believer by grace alone, for eternal salvation, is operative providentially in nature, notwithstanding the apparent evils and experienced tribulations of life in the created order.[13] For Calvin, indeed, as Langdon Gilkey explains, "the effectual meaning of the doctrine of creation" lies in its correlate providence, since the work of God's providence in our present is "the ground of that confidence in God's rule over our lives and so that hope of salvation which are a large part of a serene and active piety."[14] No matter what befalls us, in other words, Calvin wants to assure us that everything—every drop of rain[15]—is directly willed by the God of our salvation, not by some other, alien power.

So when we encounter wide-ranging affirmations of the majesty of the Creator and the glory of the Creator's dominion over all things in Calvin's writings; when we hear him speaking of the whole creation as the theater of God's glory; or when we hear him saying, strikingly, "it can be said reverently . . . that nature is God";[16] we should recall that the intent of many of these statements is to assure *believers* that *their God* is the sovereign Lord over all things, not that the Creator is carrying out some purpose with the whole creation, with nature in particular, which is somehow independent of his will for human salvation. This anthropocentric-soteriological shape of Calvin's thought is also evident in his epistemology. He often talks about the glories of God in creation in order to show us how we know—or, due to sin, do not know—God.[17]

The anthropocentric-soteriological preoccupation is further adumbrated in Calvin's eschatology, at least as a matter of emphasis. In his thought about the final fulfillment, although he holds to the traditional idea of the renewal of all things, he self-consciously avoids talking about the new heavens and the new earth. We can know very little about this, he says. Rather, he focuses all his discussion anthropocentrically on the theme of the bodily resurrection of the human creature, and related doctrinal issues.[18]

Calvin's Anthropocentric Theology of Vocational Dominion

With Calvin we also witness a heightened emphasis on the divine call to believers to transform the world, rather than to live, in faith and love, in the world as it is, or to contemplate the divinely given beauties of the world. We have already encountered this idea in our discussion of the activist Benedictine ethos and in our assessment of Thomas's teaching on the matter. But with Calvin this theme takes on a dynamism hitherto unknown in the West in this articulated form. Human dominion over history and the created order generally now receives a powerful theological validation.

This idea of "vocational-dominion," as we may call it, is rooted in Calvin's understanding of God. Calvin sets forth his doctrine of God primarily in terms of will and power—God is here the immediately ordaining sovereign—rather than in terms of a more static hierarchy of being.[19] This understanding of God, focused as it is on human life, then releases, as it were, enormous human energies which are directed at transforming human history and the face of the earth. This is how Gilkey depicts Calvin's understanding of providence and election:

"for Calvin providence expresses the rule of God over the external life of [Christians] . . . , and election represents the sovereignty of God over their inward life of faith, obedience and regeneration. With, so to speak, this outer and inner armor, both based on the sovereign will of God as directing us to salvation, human beings so chosen can face anything with serenity, humility, courage and confidence. . . ."[20] For Calvin, accordingly, the Christian's vocation is not to fulfill a given social role, and in this sense to have his or her identity formed by the society, and to love the neighbor in that context, as generally speaking it was for Luther. Rather that vocation is a call to work for new social forms and new configurations of the human environment, with the confidence born of an intense sense of chosenness and a divinely ordained historical destiny. "Thus," for Calvin, as Gilkey writes, "is the individual strengthened inwardly, given immense creative authority and sent into an 'open' world to remold it to God's glory."[21]

With this ethical dynamism of Calvin's thought before us, we can see what appears to be the influence of the spiritual motif in his thought. Although Calvin eschews any thought of humanity rising above nature in order to enter into a right relationship with God—because God in his grace elects to save people and hence there can be no valid ascent of any kind, that is, toward God—the very way he articulates the meaning of the divine election has the effect of calling the believer at a practical level, horizontally as it were, to rise above nature (and history) to transform it for the sake of the greater glory of God. This is the ethical side of Calvin's theanthropocentric thinking. As many have observed, this ethical dynamism then helps set the stage, among many other factors, for later—secularized—developments in Western mercantile and industrial society and its ethic of domination over the earth.[22]

The Reformers' Central Concern:
The Gracious Condescension of God

Neither Luther nor Calvin tightly systematized his thought about nature. We find no dialectic of world creation and human redemption in their thought, in so many words, no statement that the only divine raison d'être for the whole creation is the redemption of the human creature.[23] In this respect their thought resembles Augustine's. Given the anthropocentric dynamics of grace in their theology they might well have projected such a dialectic, as Thomas Aquinas, for one, actually did. This suggests that they were not really interested in subordinating nature to human redemption, as Thomas was. Still less did they want to project a theology, as Origen did, that would have had the effect of degrading nature. The Reformers were chiefly interested in celebrating the gracious condescension of God to the sinful human creature. This interpretation of their intentions is borne out by the fact, to which we now turn, that they also gave powerful, albeit somewhat infrequent, testimony to the wondrous works of God in nature and, especially Luther, to human solidarity with nature, reaching even to the end times.

The Circumferential Elements in Their Thought:
The Divine and the Human Engagement with Nature

As we survey the theology of the Reformers, attending to its circumference as well as to its center, we do encounter a number of striking attestations to the glory and the power of God in nature, to nature's own intrinsic wonder and beauty, and, especially for Luther, to humanity's solidarity with nature, which suggest a theocentric-ecological rather than a merely anthropocentric-soteriological reading of nature's being and value in the greater scheme of things. There is an extra charge in their thought, as it were, which cannot be explained only in terms of their interests in human salvation. We see signs here—at the circumference, to be sure, but vital signs nevertheless—of the influence of the ecological motif.

Calvin can be quite exuberant in his praise of nature's beauty in itself. The created world, he says, is God's "most beautiful theatre" where, "in a wonderful series, he distinguishes an innumerable variety of things," endowing "each with its own nature, assigned functions, appointed places, and stations."[24] The creation, he says, is "quite like a spacious and splendid house, provided and filled with the most exquisite and at the same time the most abundant furnishings."[25] Everything tells us of God, Calvin writes lyrically—and here he presents us with a picture of not only a world charged with divinity, but also a world which carries the stamp of that divine glory in its very being:

> In every part of the world, in heaven and on earth, he has written and as it were engraven the glory of his power, goodness, wisdom and eternity. . . . For all creatures, from the firmament even to the centre of the earth, could be witnesses and messengers of his glory to all men, drawing them on to seek him and, having found him, to do him service and honour according to the dignity of a Lord so good, so potent, wise and everlasting. . . . For the little singing birds sang of God, the animals acclaimed him, the elements feared and the mountains resounded with him, the river and springs threw glances toward him, the grasses and the flowers smiled.[26]

Calvin even suggests that we should not immediately pass from nature to God, but that we should ponder the beauty of nature in itself:

> While we contemplate in all creatures, as in a mirror, those immense riches of his wisdom, justice, goodness, and power, we should not merely run them over curso-

rily, and, so to speak, with a fleeting glance, but we should ponder them at length, turn them over in our mind seriously and faithfully, and recollect them repeatedly.[27]

Moreover, he seems to stand awestruck before nature at times as if he had some sense that nature has value in itself before God, that it is more than merely of instrumental value for humanity with respect to the blessings of creation and redemption. "You cannot in one glance survey this most vast and beautiful system of the universe," he writes, "in all its wide expanse, without being completely overwhelmed by the boundless force of its brightness."[28]

With Luther, there are also indications of a perhaps even more profound theological apperception of nature, beyond and behind the anthropocentric-soteriological foreground. Luther often speaks powerfully of the immanence of God in nature, of the Creator's dynamic presence "in, with, and under" all the creatures of the natural world. We meet here none of the nuances of distance between the exalted, infinite Creator and the finite creaturely earth that we encountered in Thomas Aquinas. Rather, we see some evidences of the influence of the metaphor of fecundity—with the nuance here being not so much overflowing goodness, as in Augustine and Bonaventure, but more a charged, even fearful sense for the overflowing *power* of God in nature.

Luther can envision the whole creation as "the mask of God."[29] For Luther this means, to be sure, that God is *hidden* there. But it also means that God is *powerfully present* there. Luther thinks of the Creator as being "with all creatures, flowing and pouring into them, filling all things."[30] For Luther, therefore, creation is not merely a transcendental event at the beginning of time. The divine act of Creation is also now:

> If God were to withdraw his hand, this building [the creation] would collapse. . . .
> The sun would not long return its position and shine in the heavens, no child would be born; no kernel, no blade of grass, nothing at all would grow on earth or reproduce itself if God did not work forever and ever.[31]

In this connection Luther has a rich and sophisticated, albeit paradoxical, understanding of the dynamism of the divine immanence:

> God is substantially present everywhere, in and through all creatures, in all their parts and places, so that the world is full of God and He fills all, but without His being encompassed and surrounded by it. He is at the same time outside and above all creatures. These are all exceedingly incomprehensible matters; yet they are articles of our faith and are attended clearly and mightily in Holy Writ. . . . For how can reason tolerate it that the Divine majesty is so small that it can be substantially present in a grain, on a grain, over a grain, through a grain, within and without, and that, although it is a single Majesty, it nevertheless is entirely in each grain

separately, no matter how immeasurably numerous these grains may be? . . . And that the same Majesty is so large that neither this world nor a thousand worlds can encompass it and say: "Behold, there it is!" . . . His own divine essence can be in all creatures collectively and in each one individually more profoundly, more intimately, more present than the creature is in itself; yet it can be encompassed nowhere and by no one. It encompasses all things and dwells in all, but not one thing encompasses it and dwells in it.[32]

Luther explicitly rejects hierarchical thinking, moreover, the idea that God's creative and sustaining activity is mediated through various levels of angelic powers, a theme we already have encountered in Thomas's thought and elsewhere. He states, for example:

It is God who creates, effects and preserves all things through his almighty power and right hand, as our Creed confesses. For he dispatches no officials or angels when he creates or preserves something, but all this is the work of the Divine power itself. If He is to create it or preserve it, however, he must be present and must make and preserve His creation both in its innermost and outermost aspects.[33]

This has the effect of making Luther's witness to the overflowing creative power of God in the whole creation all the more vivid and concrete.

Luther also fastens his eyes, as Calvin did, on the wonders of nature in themselves. He affirms that with the eye of faith one can see miracles all through nature, miracles even greater than the sacraments, he says. If we truly understood the growth of a grain of wheat, he observes, we would die of wonder.[34] Luther has a kind of omnimiraculous view of nature, reminiscent of Augustine's treatment of the same subject. To this extent, the metaphor of fecundity and the theology of overflowing goodness—now shaped by the nuances of power—are still dramatically influential in Luther's thought.

Luther at times can present an almost Franciscan approach to human identity in nature. The motif of human solidarity with nature is on occasion strikingly portrayed by Luther, particularly with regard to human corporeality. So in his Genesis commentary, in a context where countless doctors of the church had sung the praises of human rationality and spirituality, under the rubric of the image of God, Luther states that the fact that Adam and Eve walked about naked was their greatest adornment before God and all creatures.[35] In the same vein, Luther envisions Adam and Eve as enjoying a "common table" with the animals before the fall.[36] In this respect, Luther's statement in his Small Catechism concerning the meaning of the First Article of the Creed should be read as something more than an anthropocentric affirmation: "I believe that God has created me, *together with all creatures*. . . ."[37]

Further, Luther holds that the redemption made available to the believer by God through Christ opens up the eyes of the believer to new and glorious perceptions of God's creative activity in nature and of the wonders of nature itself. Redeemed existence, in other words, brings with it a new and more vital relationship with nature. As Luther comments:

> We are now living in the dawn of the future life; for we are beginning to regain a knowledge of the creation, a knowledge forfeited by the fall of Adam. Now we have a correct view of the creatures, more so, I suppose, than they have in the papacy. Erasmus does not concern himself with this; it interests him little how the fetus is made in the womb. . . . But by God's mercy we can begin to recognize His wonderful works and wonders also in flowers when we ponder his might and goodness. Therefore we laud, magnify, and thank him.[38]

Again, Luther writes:

> Now if I believe in God's Son and bear in mind that He became man, all creatures will appear a hundred times more beautiful to me than before. Then I will properly appreciate the sun, the moon, the stars, trees, apples, pears, as I reflect that he is Lord over and the center of all things.[39]

Similarly, as Luther looks forward to the divine consummation of the creation at the very end of time, he is not reluctant, as Calvin generally is, to imagine a final transformation of all things, a new heaven and a new earth, as well as the gift of a resurrected body to the redeemed human creatures. We will indeed be made whole bodily, he explains, and

> Then there will also be a new heaven and earth, the light of the moon will be as the light of the sun, and the light of the sun will be sevenfold. . . . That will be a broad and beautiful heaven and a joyful earth, much more beautiful and joyful than Paradise was.[40]

This vision of the end time articulates and completes Luther's consistent emphasis on the solidarity of the human creature with the rest of nature and his occasional but forceful statements about the wonders of nature itself.

To this extent, we can also say that the metaphor of migration to a good land is influential in Luther's thinking, although not nearly so pervasively as it was in Irenaeus's thought or Augustine's. Luther had an intense eschatological consciousness, as we have seen. He believed that the world was going to end during his own lifetime. But that idea mainly functioned as an interpretive lever, so to speak, for the events of his own time (seeing the Pope as the antichrist, for example). It did not often open up positive vistas of the new heavens and the new earth, beyond the day of judgment. But such vistas are, nevertheless, part of the landscape of Luther's theology.

Assessment: The Ambiguity of the Center
and the Circumference

In retrospect, we can see the ambiguity we have been tracing in this study emerging in a particularly poignant way in the thought of the Reformers. The central elements of their thought, even quantitatively speaking, are dramatically focused on soteriological-anthropocentric themes, as we have seen. Their thought in this sense is shaped by the spiritual motif of the received tradition, we may now conclude, insofar as the tradition presented the Reformers with the question with which they were chiefly concerned, the question of human salvation. They accepted that question—how can I find a gracious God?—at the very moment they sought to offer a revolutionary answer. Formally they were still very much concerned with God and humanity and the dynamics of human salvation, but materially they accented the divine descent, not the human ascent. In this sense, if such an improbable statement might be made, they were not "re-formers." They accepted the form of medieval theology as they found it in this respect. If they were not re-formers, in this sense, however, they were "inverters." They inverted the kind of theology of grace that they understood to have been bequeathed to them by the tradition.

This, then, explains how they could also give testimony, limited but powerful, to the wonders of God in nature, to human solidarity with nature, and to the final renewal of nature in the end times. In the focal regions of their thought the influence of the metaphor of ascent had been held in check, if not neutralized altogether. This meant that the influences of the two other metaphors which we have been observing—the metaphor of fecundity and the metaphor of migration to a good land—could come into play, at least to some extent, in the circumferential regions. The ecological motif did shape their thinking in significant ways, particularly Luther's. In the case of Calvin, as we have had occasion to note, we already see the seeds of future developments which point in a different direction, given the dynamics of his theology of vocational-dominion. In this respect, Calvin seems to have laid hold of the metaphor of ascent with a new kind of resolve, and to have given it a practical orientation which was to be of immense significance in ensuing centuries.

All in all, however, the Reformers never really resolved the tension in their thought between the soteriological-anthropocentric focal point and the ecological-theocentric circumference. Perhaps they were never aware of it. Nor probably should we expect that they ought to have been aware of it. The agenda of reworking the whole theology of grace of the church catholic was itself an enormous challenge, not only in the context of reflective-discursive theology but in the world of practical Church affairs as well. That they said as much as positively as they did about the theology of nature should attract our attention.

THE REFORMATION TRADITION AND THE MODERN SECULARIZATION OF NATURE

Something happened to the Reformers' thought about nature as the Reformation tradition unfolded. The tradition was decisively impacted to begin with, by three external cultural forces, each one intimately related to the others: *first* from the side of the natural sciences; *second,* following in the wake of the natural sciences, the philosophy of Immanuel Kant; *third,* from the context of the sociopolitical world of modern industrialism. With their vision of reality influenced by these trends, many nineteenth- and twentieth-century Protestant thinkers came to view nature no longer as a theater of God's glory and power in which humanity is essentially embodied, as it was for the Reformers; even less as a grand symphonic, albeit finite, realization of divine goodness, as it was for Bonaventure and Augustine; still less as a world of friends and fellow travelers, as it was for Francis. Nature now was approached as a self-enclosed, machinelike structure without any value or life of its own before God, set apart from both God and humanity.

In view of these developments, we may legitimately speak of the secularization of nature in the Reformation tradition in the nineteenth and twentieth centuries. Formally, every theologian of importance would still assert that nature is created good by God. But, materially, these theologians would generally tell a story quite different from the theological narratives of thinkers such as Augustine or even the Reformers. Nature came to be viewed by many modern Protestant thinkers as a mere thing, a world of objects, closed in upon itself, moved only by its own laws, not open to any other dimensions of reality, and therefore a world which humans must constantly transcend if they are to be rightly related to God.

The Rise of the Industrial-Mechanical Approach to Nature

Through the influence of figures such as Galileo (1564–1642), Descartes (1596–1650), and Newton (1642–1727), the modern mind more and more took the mechanical view of nature for granted. According to this view, qualities such as color or taste are secondary. Only mass and motion are primary qualities of nature. The beauty and wonder of nature, accordingly, had to be traced exclusively to the realm of human subjectivity: beauty is in the eye of the beholder. Likewise for any notion of value or purpose. As a machine, moreover, set in motion by God, many believed in the wake of the Newtonian synthesis, the cosmos would more or less run itself. It no longer needed God. Nor could one attribute any purpose to it. This is the way Edwin A. Burtt has described the rise of the mechanical view of nature:

> The gloriously romantic universe of Dante and Milton, that set no bounds to the imagination of man as it played over space and time, had now been swept away. Space was identified with the realm of geometry, time with the continuity of number. The world that people had thought themselves living in—a world rich with color and sound, redolent with fragrance, filled with gladness, love and beauty, speaking everywhere of purposive harmony and creative ideals—was crowded into minute concerns in the brains of scattered organic beings. The really important world outside was hard, cold, colorless, silent, and dead; a world of quantity, a world of mathematically computable motions in mechanical regularity. The world of qualities as immediately perceived by man became just a curious and quite minor effect of that infinite machine beyond. [41]

Fatefully, Immanuel Kant (1724–1804) was typical of his time when he took it for granted that natural science had reached its apex in Newton's work. [42] Kant held, as a matter of course, that objective empirical judgments could not be incompatible with the principles of Newton's physics. And, as far as his own picture of nature was concerned, Kant strongly stressed the quantitative, "necessary" aspects of nature. For him, these were decisive. [43] Like Newton, Kant believed that nature is composed of immutable, hard, and dead conglomerations of moving particles. [44] Although in a certain sense, which we cannot consider here, it is proper to say that Kant "relativized" the mechanical view of nature (nature for him is an "appearance," not the "thing in itself"), he nevertheless took over the major features of the view bequeathed him by Newton.

A corollary of Kant's acceptance and affirmation of the mechanical picture of nature was his separation of the ideas of God and nature. This separation was undoubtedly well on its way to fruition before Kant began to write. The English deists had already given it currency. But with Kant the notion was given what for many ensuing Protestant theologians would be a compelling philosophical foundation. God, Kant held, is definitely not an object of theoretical knowledge (that knowledge which gives us access to nature or what Kant calls the world of appearances). God, rather, is that reality that is subjectively necessary for our practical or moral reason to postulate. With regard to nature as it is apprehended by theoretical reason, according to Kant, the idea of God can legitimately be treated as a regulative principle which helps us to understand the unity of nature. [45] But, as Kant says, "God" is an idea which is "always transcendent," which allows "no immanent employment, that is: employment in reference to objects of our experience."[46] Thus, for Kant, nature remains a "self-subsisting whole," the "sum of appearances insofar as they stand, in virtue of an inner principle of causality, in thorough-going interconnection."[47] Correspondingly, Kant views humanity as fundamentally distinct from nature. Humanity's greatness—freedom—is the human creature's transcendence of the allegedly deterministic sphere of nature. "As regards the empirical character [of humanity]," Kant remarks, "there is no freedom."[48]

We can instructively think of Kant's philosophy as an ecological sieve. As the flow of the Reformation tradition passed through his thought—which has been profoundly influential ever since within the Reformation tradition—the theocentric-ecological circumference of Reformation thought was largely filtered out. Most major Protestant theological systems after Kant would be radically theanthropocentric. God would be viewed essentially in isolation from nature, and humanity would be viewed essentially in isolation from nature. The fundamental Reformation intuition, the focus on God and humanity, would remain intact and thrive. But it would no longer presuppose the Reformers' circumferential theology of nature. It would be highly spiritualized. This was already dramatically apparent in Kant's use of the concept of the kingdom of God. For him the picture of a divine kingdom referred chiefly to an "ethical commonwealth" or a "people of God under ethical laws."[49] This spiritualizing use of the fundamental Christian concept is to be contrasted with the sense it has in the writings of the Reformers. Both Luther and Calvin conceive of the kingdom of God as tangibly comprehending the sphere of nature.[50]

But we should not give Kant all the credit, such as it was, for establishing the hegemony of the mechanical view of nature within the mainstream of modern Protestant theology. The mechanical view of nature was strongly buttressed by the rising socioeconomic influences of the fast-developing industrial society in the West. As Lewis Mumford, a careful student of capitalism's approach to nature, has observed, "The power that was science and the power that was money were, in final analysis, the same kind of power: the power of abstraction, measurement, quantification."[51] In a word, the entrepreneur who needed natural resources for his factories found it easy to measure the value of nature in money, because it was easy for him to conceive of nature in itself as a valueless, dead, indifferent, God-less machine. The converse of course is also true. The economic requirements of capitalism surely paved the way for a widespread acceptance of the mechanical view of nature. Thus the scientific-philosophical doctrine and the ideology of the bourgeoisie tended to coalesce; so much so that we are probably best advised to refer to the "industrial-mechanical view of nature" rather than merely the mechanical view of nature.[52]

It was a heady age. Toward the middle of the eighteenth century, Alexander Pope expressed the temper of modernity in his famous epitaph for Sïr Isaac Newton:

Nature and Nature's Laws lay hid in Night:
God said, Let Newton be! and all was Light.

In 1837, the English historian Thomas MacCaulay uttered a still more exuberant paean for science:

It has lengthened life; it has mitigated pain; it has extinguished diseases; it has increased the fertility of the soil; it has given new securities to the mariner; it has furnished new arms to the warrior; it has spanned great rivers and estuaries with bridges of form not known to our fathers; it has guided the thunderbolt innocuously from the heaven to earth; it has lighted up the night with the splendor of day. . . . These are but a part of its fruits, and of its first fruits; for it is a philosophy which never rests, which has never attained, which is never perfect. Its law is progress.[53]

Progress was indeed a reality in the nineteenth century, in many ways, and its fruits, several of which MacCaulay mentions, were surely a boon to many. No wonder that Kant, and many ensuing philosophers and theologians, found it easy to take the industrial-mechanical view of nature for granted. It seemed to be proving itself before their eyes. But there were more ominous trends gaining momentum in the shadows of progress. Not the least of these was a growing rejection, either self-consciously or unconsciously, of the all-embracing system of Christian symbols and norms which society in the West had taken for granted from the time of the Middle Ages on, however much it might have honored them in the breach.[54] This was particularly true of the modern Western approach to nature.

The industrial-mechanical view of nature was, in fact, a secularized view of nature. God had been removed, for all intents and purposes, from the picture, notwithstanding attempts by popular exponents of liberalism and some of its theological apologists to place God at the apex of the whole culture of industrialism, as a kind of ultimate validation of what was coming into being. It was indeed relatively easy for some to identify progress, as it was understood in the nineteenth century, with an immanental unfolding of the kingdom of God. But the underlying spiritual forces of the culture which carried the industrial-mechanical view of nature were immanental: a faith in human autonomy and a commitment to pursue scientific and industrial development as an end in itself.[55] The symbols and norms of Christian theology no longer consistently impacted this culture spiritually, at its deepest levels. Friedrich Nietzsche (1844–

1900) was perhaps closer to the pulse of his times than he knew. It was an era of will-to-power in many respects, particularly with respect to nature. What was a theology of vocational-dominion for Calvin, shaped by classical Christian symbols and norms, became in the nineteenth century a secular ideology of domination—which at times was presented in the guise of traditional theological constructs. In this context one can see what could well happen if the energies of the Calvinistic spirit were to begin to lose their theological moorings. Remove the righteous divine will and the holiness of the community, and one is left with an autonomous individual—or an autonomous ruling class— and a valueless world of nature, together with an immense surplus of psychosocial energy which can be employed individually or collectively to dominate other individuals or groups. In this connection also, a heterodox tradition apparently had a key role to play, as William Leiss and others have argued. Leiss, following Eliade, detects the influence of the ancient alchemist's dream— using knowledge as power over the elements—as being "the driving spirit of the modern age."[56] This was "the Faustian bargain" of modernity.

Whatever its source or sources, however, it is clear that an unbridled quest for domination over nature was a hallmark of nineteenth-century culture in the West. This is nowhere more apparent than in some of the expressions of socialism generally, and in the thought of Karl Marx (1818–83) in particular. The Saint-Simonians, for example, announced, as William Leiss points out, that modern industrial society would change the whole course of history, through the exploitation of nature: "The exploitation of man by man has come to its end . . . the exploitation of the globe, of external nature, becomes henceforth the sole end of man's physical activity."[57] As Karl Löwith has stated regarding Marx: "[Marx] took it for granted that nature is a mere means and material for the purpose of developing the historical forces of human production."[58]

The Abandonment of Nature in the Reformation Tradition

In 1933, the sponsors of the Chicago World's Fair chose a memorable motto for that event: "Science Explores, Technology Executes, Man Conforms." This was the world in which Protestant theologians found themselves writing during the nineteenth century and beyond. And many of them made a fateful decision: to hold firmly to the Kantian framework as the metaphysical basis of their theology and thereby, by default, to accept the mechanical view of nature, as it flowed into the ideational patterns channeled out by the socioeconomic forces of modern industrial society generally. Their theology, accordingly, as a matter of course, became more and more a theology of God and humanity apart from nature, a highly spiritualized theanthropology. The Reformation tradition lost its ecological dimension at almost every point. Nature was thus handed over by default to the forces of secularism.

This was especially true for Albrecht Ritschl (1822–89) and his followers. Ritschl's theology takes its root, as no other influential theology prior to his time, in the problem of the value of humanity in relationship to the value of nature. Ritschl maintains that all religions ask this question: how humans, recognizing themselves as part of nature, while at the same time being capable of spiritual personality, can attain to that dominion over nature as opposed to limitation by it, which this capability gives them.[59]

Christianity provides the answer to this question, Ritschl suggests, in its message of the kingdom of God.[60] By the latter expression Ritschl means a community of moral or spiritual agents. People rise into this kingdom, above nature, when they appropriate the message of the kingdom. Christianity, says Ritschl, establishes the principle that "personal life is to be prized above the whole world of nature." But Ritschl also wants to say more than this. He also wants to argue and he does argue, that nature itself gains its *sole* value through its association with humans. Thus he says of God's providential activity that "all things" are governed "on the principle that mankind are ordained to be the final end of the world, through trust in God and as members of his spiritual Kingdom."[61] The world, in other words, exists solely for the sake of humans. This point is made undeniably clear when Ritschl equates the kingdom of God with God's self-end and then says that the world of nature is a means to that divine end:

> If it be an essential part of God's personal end that He should create a multitude of spirits, formed after their own kind, and that He should bring them to perfection in order to manifest Himself to them as love, then the world of nature, viewed as distinct from the world of man, cannot be viewed as a mere arbitrary appendix, but must rather be regarded as a means to the Divine end.[62]

In this way, Ritschl concludes, the statement that God has created the world out of love receives its proper limitations, and the creation of nature by God is given the value of a relative necessity, the necessity, namely, of serving as a means to God's previously chosen end of calling into being a multitude of spirits akin to himself.[63] Did Ritschl know at this point that he was reaffirming an approach to nature, formally speaking, which was given classic expression by Thomas Aquinas? That is not clear. But what is clear is this, that here the spiritual motif becomes dominant in Western theology once again.

Many other nineteenth-century Protestant thinkers took similar positions. The Ritschlian set of assumptions lies behind the thought of Wilhelm Herrmann (1846–1922), for example, when he developed his idea that Christianity has chiefly to do with the communion of the Christian with God. It is also evident in the theology of Adolph von Harnack (1851–1930), who specified that the content of theology is "God the Father and the human soul so ennobled that it can and does unite with him."[64] Standing apart from these developments, the existence theology of Søren Kierkegaard (1813–55) nevertheless points in the same direction. From a Kierkegaardian perspective, indeed, interest in nature and in the cosmos can be just as threatening to authentic human existence as an interest in world history after the fashion of Hegel.[65]

The existential theology of Rudolf Bultmann (1884–1976) stands in the tradition of both Ritschl and Kierkegaard. It is most immediately shaped, however, by the philosophy of Neo-Kantianism, as Roger Johnson has shown.[66] Bultmann is preoccupied with authentic human existence made possible through hearing the Word of God, the *kerygma,* which calls the believer away from identification with nature, the realm of objectification.[67] Bultmann distinguishes forcefully between an abstract or speculative "world-view" and a more personal "self-understanding." Faith, he argues, can have nothing to do with the former; its proper domain is the realm of personal self-understanding. Accordingly, Bultmann holds that God cannot be understood properly as being active throughout the cosmos at all! To do that would be to transform faith into a world view. "Only statements about God are legitimate," Bultmann explains, "as expressing the existential relation between God and man. Statements which speak of God's actions as cosmic events are illegitimate."[68]

God's actions generally in nature, Bultmann contends, are as hidden to the believer as they are to the nonbeliever.[69] God can only be talked about, in other words, as *one who acts on persons.* As Bultmann says, "Images which describe God acting are legitimate only if they mean that God is a personal being acting on persons."[70] Indeed, for Bultmann, faith properly removes God from nature, thereby opening it up to human activity. By faith, Bultmann tells us, "the world becomes a profane place and is thus restored to its true place as the sphere of man's action."[71]

Nature in itself emerges in Bultmann's writings again and again as a self-enclosed whole—this is his Kantianism—which is not part of, indeed which tends to obstruct, authentic human existence in relation to God. For Bultmann, evidently, nature is first and foremost to be described as a realm where the "cause and effect nexus" is dominant.[72]

One could say, in retrospect, that Bultmann baptized the post-Kantian secularization of nature in the Reformation tradition.

Emil Brunner (1889–1966) also stands firmly in this theanthropocentric Protestant mainstream, with this important difference: he develops and shapes it systematically. This systematic elaboration, as we noted, was not characteristic of the Reformers themselves. Brunner states that the "supreme coordinating concept" of his dogmatics is "the self-communication of God."[73] By the latter expression, in typical post-Kantian fashion, Brunner specifically means God's "self-communication to man." The systematic implication of this for Brunner, already drawn in passing by Kant and systematically by Ritschl, is that the world of nature is theologically what it (allegedly) was for the biblical writers, "never anything more than the 'scenery' in which the history of mankind takes place."[74]

In keeping with such an approach to nature, modern Protestant theology has generally given little or no substantive thought to the eschatological future of nature. This is not surprising since the dominant assumption has been that nature, at most, is the scenery for the divine-human drama; and therefore it must have little or no abiding value. The apocalyptic vision of the New Testament with its pictures of a new heaven and a new earth in which righteousness dwells, and the lavish images of early theologians such as Irenaeus, depicting a good land of glorious fecundity as the final destiny of all things—all this was conveniently forgotten by many Protestant thinkers in the nineteenth century and beyond, or it was self-consciously "demythologized," as in Bultmann's thought, in terms of human self-understanding.[75]

For Bultmann and for Brunner, therefore, as for Kant and for Ritschl, and many other Protestant theologians in the modern period, ultimate fulfillment —whether "future" or "realized"—is essentially and exclusively a theanthropocentric concept. Humanity rising above a self-enclosed and often threatening world of nature in order to enter into communion with God—that is the last word about nature spoken by post-Kantian Protestant thought. The spiritual motif has triumphed here, almost to the extent, at times, that the theme of creations' goodness, the last bulwark against Gnosticism, seems to be in jeopardy.[76]

Some Countervailing Trends

There were, to be sure, other streams of thought abroad in the modern period than the ones we have highlighted in this chapter. Rightly interpreted, the emergence of romantic thinking in the modern era can be viewed not only as a protest directed against the dominant industrial culture in the West but as a protest against modern Protestant theology as well, which was so thoroughly identified with that culture's approach to nature. In England, Wordsworth (1770–1850) and Coleridge (1772–1834) developed what M. H. Abrams has referred to as a "Natural Supernaturalism,"[77] drawing extensively on what might be called the fecundity tradition of classical Christian thought, as well as on other, more heterodox traditions in the West. In the United States, the nineteenth century witnessed the birth of the Transcendentalist movement which, especially in the thought of Henry David Thoreau (1817–62), turned to the vitalities of nature, now understood as *Natura Naturans*, both as a way of finding relief from what it perceived to be the sterilities of rampant industrial society and as a way of finding a new and more powerful experience of God. On the continent, Friedrich Wilhelm Joseph von Schelling (1775–1874) projected a new metaphysics of nature, a "Philosophy of Life," which also stood radically apart from the mechanistic views which Kant took for granted.

Of theologians of renown in the late nineteenth and early twentieth centuries, it was perhaps Paul Tillich (1886–1965) who drew most self-consciously and most systematically on the intuitions of the romantic movement.[78] From the time of his dissertation on Schelling to the end of his life, when he was exploring the insights of Buddhism, his interest in the theology of nature did not waver. He had little tolerance for the post-Kantian Protestant surrender of nature to the natural sciences and to industrial society generally.[79]

His understanding of God as the ground of being transcended the post-Kantian preoccupation of theology with a God who was understood as a moral personality, a God who had little or nothing to do with the cosmos.[80] Tillich reached back to Luther and to Augustine, among others, to find resources for a theology of nature which emphasized at once the *mysterium tremendum* of God in nature and the fecundity of nature as it participated in the divine life. Tillich developed a kind of sacramental theology of nature, as his profound essay "Nature and Sacrament" indicates.[81] According to this theology, the presence of the Divine is to be found not only in what traditionally has been called the sacraments but, through the ecstasy of faith, in, with, and under the whole constellation of natural reality.

But notwithstanding his popular appeal, and the interest which his work provoked in scholarly circles in many fields, Tillich remained an isolated figure in theological circles as far as his theology of nature was concerned. Although he was influential among students of theology in many ways—perhaps most especially for his theology of culture—his self-confessed romanticizing approach to nature simply did not elicit any visible following in the dominant schools of theology in his own time. An either implicit or explicit Kantianism, with its mechanistic understanding of nature presupposed, generally held sway within Protestant theological circles.

Assessment: The Fateful Triumph of the Spiritual Motif in a Secular Culture

These developments signaled the end of any widespread influence of the ecological motif—if not the total eclipse of that motif—in the Protestant tradition. Modern Protestant thought, with some notable exceptions, such as Tillich, has been mainly shaped by the spiritual motif. The influence of the ecological motif, however powerful it had been on occasion in the Reformers' theology, was already circumferential there. Nineteenth- and twentieth-century Protestant thought, through midcentury, then proceeded to push it out of the picture almost totally, as it gave full sway to the spiritual motif.

At this point Gordon Kaufman's analysis of the Christian tradition's approach to nature seems to have what is perhaps its most immediate relevance. Kaufman argues, as we noted, that Christian theology generally has no special vocabulary for nature, as it does for grace; that it presupposes, structurally, a fundamental ontological dissimilarity between God and humans, on the one hand, and nature, on the other hand; that it is predicated on a definition of God which itself presupposes a depreciation of nature; and that, finally, nature is mainly understood as a field for moral activity, not for contemplation.

We have seen that this analysis rings true in certain contexts: with regard to Origen's thought, surely; for Thomas and Bonaventure to some extent; but definitely not for Irenaeus, Augustine, or Francis. Whether it also holds true for the Reformers can be a matter of discussion, depending on how marginal one judges the circumferential ecological elements of their thought to be. But we can now say, without a doubt, that Kaufman's analysis applies most precisely to the post-Kantian tradition in Protestantism—so much so that one can wonder whether this is not the voice which is really speaking in the formidable argument of Kaufman's important essay.

It is possible, then, to lay Kaufman's analysis to rest, with gratitude. He has given us, we may now conclude, an instructive schematic description of theologies shaped by the spiritual motif in Western Christian thought. But his analysis, it should now be clear, does not begin to do justice to those theologies which have been shaped by the ecological motif.[82] This is the pathos of his argument. In reading the whole Christian tradition through the lenses of post-Kantian Protestantism, he has not been able to see, much less to focus on, one of the two major trajectories of classical Christian thought about nature. Conversely, he has not been ready, given his single-minded focus on the patterns of thought shaped by the spiritual motif, to see the liabilities of that motif, particularly in the modern period. Those liabilities have been substantial.

During the very period when Western culture at large was giving up traditional Christian symbols and norms with abandon; when the human "ego" and the industrial enterprise were emerging as the undisputed, albeit sometimes conflicting, deities of the modern age; when God was being either self-consciously dethroned, or simply abandoned by default, as the modern spirit sought to build its own subjective inner paradise or an objective industrial utopia, guided by symbols and norms of its own invention[83]—at this very time, the dominant theology of the Reformation tradition gave up all claims on the world of nature.

That may have been a necessary retreat. To stand up for the cause of God and humanity in a world where human subjectivity, on the one hand, and nature, construed either romantically or materialistically, on the other hand, had become the deities of the day was surely an enormous challenge. But that stance was not without its costs.

For, could a theology of God and humanity really lay claim to "the human" without laying claim to the cosmic? And even more so, could it really lay hold of "the Divine" if it had no way of drawing any tangible lines from God to the immensities of the universe in which the modern consciousness found itself immersed? Could the human be truly human and the Divine truly divine, if theology had little or nothing to say about nature, except that it was somehow a function of the relationship between God and humanity?

The force of such questions was not lost on the minds of two of the greatest and still among the most renowned theologians of the first half of the twentieth century, Karl Barth and Pierre Teilhard de Chardin. They reached out to embrace the universe, as it were. Drawing on New Testament themes, especially from Ephesians and Colossians, which depict the universal lordship of Jesus Christ, they attempted, each in his own way, to lay theological claim on the whole creation once again, in the grand theological manner of Thomas and Bonaventure. We now turn to Barth and Teilhard to conclude our explorations of the ambiguous ecological promise of classical Christian thought.

8

THE TRIUMPH OF PERSONALISM

Karl Barth and Pierre Teilhard de Chardin

The end of our historical investigation of classical Christian thought about nature is now in sight, and our concluding discussion of biblical thought about nature is coming into view. In this chapter we will consider the theologies of two preeminent thinkers of the twentieth century, Karl Barth (1886–1968) and Pierre Teilhard de Chardin (1881–1955). Notwithstanding their differences, or perhaps precisely because of their differences, they illustrate well what has happened to classical Christian thought concerning nature in the twentieth century.[1]

They are strikingly dissimilar thinkers in many ways. The one is a confessional theologian and a Protestant. The other is a philosophical theologian, more particularly a process thinker, and a Roman Catholic. The one began his theological work with a ringing rejection of the highest aspirations of Western culture. The other began by appropriating many of those aspirations as his own, above all belief in progress. Yet they were united in this perception of the theological challenge facing them: since the twentieth century is a time of secularization and cultural disintegration, only a theology which can make universal claims, and which, further, can anchor those claims in the revelation of God in Jesus Christ, can expect to speak to all those who dwell in despair and uncertainty, whether inside or outside the church.

Without judging their theologies in other respects, however, we will have to conclude that their monumental efforts to claim all of reality, in the name of Jesus Christ, fall short of the mark as far as their theologies of nature are concerned. As we examine their approaches to the theology of nature, we will see how the ambiguity we have been tracing in classical Christian thought has tended to give way to a consistent and comprehensive dominance by the spiritual motif. In their thought, the predominating influence of the nature-denying metaphor of ascent, on the one hand, and the radical subordination of the two nature-affirming metaphors, fecundity and migration to a good land, on the other, signals a crisis in classical Christian thought about nature, as it finds itself situated in the midst of a thoroughly secularized culture. For both Barth and Teilhard, the spiritual motif of the tradition has triumphed, in the form of a rigorous and thoroughgoing attention to personal being, at the expense of

145

natural being. Notwithstanding significant countervailing trends, especially in Teilhard's thought, in both these theologies the ecological motif of the tradition has been pushed to the background, if not out of sight altogether. Their thought is haunted by a profound inner tension in this respect. Their purpose is to claim all things for the lordship of Jesus Christ. In fact, notwithstanding their efforts to lay hold of nature firmly, their thought, in effect, extends that claim chiefly to persons.

KARL BARTH: THE HUMANITY OF GOD

Karl Barth's theology burst upon the Western theological world like a tidal wave from some distant, unknown geological upheaval. His "Theology of Crisis" in his early years represented a radical challenge, a divine no, as he thought of it in those days, to the culture and the theology of nineteenth-century Europe. He objected passionately to what he thought of as nineteenth-century theology's accommodation to Western culture and its concomitant obfuscation of the radical claims of the Word of God. In the spirit of the biblical prophets, he championed a "Wholly Other" God, and the Word of judgment—*krisis*—that that unknown, transcendent God directed to the culture of the West and to the church which, Barth felt, had so thoroughly sought to adjust its message of judgment and grace to the canons of that culture.

The roots of this Theology of Crisis were manifold. Not the least of these was Barth's own grappling with the Letter to the Romans, which led him to many of his revolutionary insights, as it had Luther four centuries earlier. Also, Barth was thoroughly influenced by Platonic thinking in those years, a fact especially evident in the first edition of his epochal *Commentary on Romans* of 1919. The Platonic notion of the two realms, the world of eternal ideas set over against and above the world of sense and mere opinion, apparently helped Barth to articulate his strong convictions about the absoluteness of the divine transcendence and to give expression to what he called in his early writings, following Søren Kierkegaard (who had drawn on Platonic thought in a similar way), the "infinite qualitative distinction" between God and the world.

Decades later, Barth looked back on his Theology of Crisis and allowed that that theology had some serious shortcomings. He did not withdraw his critique of the culture and the theology of the preceding century, but he did note how he had revised his own response to that theology. In a memorable 1957 essay, "The Humanity of God," he narrated how he had come to qualify his earlier accent on the transcendence of God and the limitations of the finite: not by rejecting that accent as such but by construing it anew in terms of the humanity of God. "What began forcibly to present itself upon us about forty years ago," he wrote in 1957, "was not so much the humanity of God as His *deity*—a God absolutely unique in His relation to man and the world, overpoweringly lofty and distant, strange, yes, wholly other."² Barth granted that his early critics were not altogether wrong in suggesting that he had made God great at the cost of humanity.³

By 1957 Barth's own mature theology had begun to unfold, massively, in his multivolumed *Church Dogmatics*. In Barth's own judgment, what we may call his theology of dogma represented a thoroughgoing attempt to redress what he considered to be the one-sided accents of his theology of crisis. Hence the theme, "the humanity of God," as he explained:

> Who God is and what He is in his deity He proves and reveals not in a vacuum as a divine being-for-Himself, but precisely and authentically in the fact that He exists, speaks, and acts as the partner of *man*, though of course the absolutely superior partner.⁴

That is to say, for Barth, "it is precisely God's *deity* which, rightly understood, includes *his humanity*."⁵

As we now turn to consider Barth's mature theology, as it came to expression in his *Church Dogmatics*, we will see that he is indeed, as he stated, fundamentally interested in articulating the significance of the divine yes, and so expressing the *positive* relation of God to the world, as contrasted to his accent on the divine no in his early writings. Seen in light of this emphasis on the divine yes, his mature theology therefore definitely signals, as Berkouwer has suggested in his interpretation of Barth's theology, "the triumph of Grace."⁶

But we must be careful to heed Barth's own words at this point. As he depicts the developments in his thought, from his *Comentary on Romans* to his *Church Dogmatics*, those developments have to do exclusively with the divine-human relationship, as the title of his seminal essay, "The Humanity of God," attests. Does this mean, then, that Barth's view of the relationship between God and nature—and thereby the corresponding relationship between humanity and nature—is continuous with the strong *negative* accent on the divine transcendence and creaturely limitations that characterized the Theology of Crisis? Is his dogmatic theology of nature still predominantly a theology of the divine no? Do we encounter the triumph of grace in this context also, or is that triumph exclusively to be found in the context of Barth's anthropology? If, further, that negative accent does remain, in what relationship does the resultant theology of nature stand to the secularization of nature that occurred in modern Protestant thought? We will return to these questions as we proceed.

The Fundamentals of Barth's Mature Thought:
His The-Anthropology

The *Church Dogmatics* is not an easy work to interpret. The sheer length of the dozen volumes gave Barth occasion to say much about many things in widely differing contexts. Also, much of his argument is presented as a direct exposition of Scripture, especially his doctrine of creation, which is a long commentary on Genesis 1 and 2. Barth attempts to remain faithful to the Scriptures —with the result that along the way he sometimes makes assertions which, although they may appear to be exegetically valid, stand in tension with his own unfolding theological logic. The best approach to Barth's dogmatic thought, therefore, is to adhere as closely as possible to his own explicit argument and to view his exegetical explorations as contributing to that argument, wherever possible.

When we turn to the theology of nature in his dogmatics, however, we immediately encounter what appears to be a serious obstacle. Barth does not deal with the theology of nature substantively at any one place. He believes, indeed, that dogmatic theology cannot rightly contain a substantive doctrine of nature as such. But Barth does in fact have a systematic approach to the theology of nature, which is decisive for his—often implicit—thought about nature. And, as we will see presently, he also has a number of things to say about nature in itself and regarding nature's relationship to God and to humanity; these observations are consistent with his overall systematic approach to the topic. Both formally and materially, in other words, Barth has a theology of nature, even though he does not seek to develop it self-consciously and explicitly.

We can appropriately begin our exploration of Barth's theology of nature by attending to the underlying logic of his thought. If one were to diagram the theology of the *Church Dogmatics,* a suitable image would be the arch. This image could aptly illustrate the important positions that two doctrines occupy in his thought, the doctrine of election and the doctrine of the Word. The keystone of the arch would have to be Barth's christological doctrine of election. Without the latter the structure of Barth's thought would fall to pieces.[7] Nevertheless, Barth's doctrine of election cannot be treated as a logical principle from which he deduces everything else. His theology remains within the bounds of hearing and confessing faith, hence the word "Church" in the title of his dogmatics. The means of doing theology are for Barth in keeping with the whole Reformation tradition, that theology should first and foremost be thought of as an exposition of the Word of God, proclaimed in and by the church. Hence, if we are to think of election as the keystone of his thought, the Word should be viewed as the springer stones, the foundational noetic elements, sustaining the whole structure.

The Word of God Addressed to Humanity

Barth thinks of the Word of God as the personal address of God to humanity, which as God's Word accomplishes what it says and thereby establishes his lordship.[8] This Word, Barth suggests, has various forms: the Scriptures, the proclamation of the church based on the Scriptures, and the core-revelation itself, attested by both the Scriptures and the church's proclamation, the event of Jesus Christ. Here Barth's famed christocentrism comes into view—what he at one point himself referred to as his "christological concentration."[9] The Word is God's address to humanity *in Jesus Christ.* Also we here catch sight of Barth's radical theanthropocentrism: the Word is not first and foremost the principle of creation (the *logos asarkos*) which gives all things their created being; the Word is first and foremost *God's* address to *humanity* in Jesus Christ. Christian doctrine, as Barth says, in so many words, "has to be exclusively and conclusively the doctrine of Jesus Christ as the living Word of God spoken to us men."[10] In reading Barth's doctrine of the Word, one must think first not of God addressing the whole creation, as in the first chapter of Genesis, but of God addressing the human predicament, as in the first chapter of the Fourth Gospel, through the Word made flesh. These are the epistemological foundations for Barth's theological ontology (his assumption is that the order of knowing *is* the order of being), which, as we will now see, comes to its apex in his christological doctrine of election.

We may note in passing, however, that given the way Barth understands the Word of God the theology of nature seems to be pushed to the periphery, if not out of the picture altogether, at this foundational level of his thought. This is the fundamental noetic expression of his unifying theme, "the humanity of God."

The Eternal Election of Jesus Christ and the People of Christ

We now shift our attention from the springer stones to the keystone. For Barth the "here and now" of the church's proclaimed Word is wholly dependent on the "there and then" of the Word made flesh.[11] There is no Word of God above or beyond Jesus Christ. The "God-man," in turn, for Barth, is the embodiment of God's eternal election. The "God-man" is the very reality of that eternal election.

When, with Barth, we first fix our eyes on election, we see that the scene has undergone a radical shift, from the epistemological foundations to the ontological principle, to the keystone of all created reality; from God's address to humanity in the world, to an eternal drama that begins to unfold before the world begins and which is the basis of everything else that transpires in world history. Barth signals this by including the doctrine of election within his doctrine of God. Election is a "supralapsarian" doctrine for him not only in the sense that he treats it before he discusses themes such as "the fall" but also in the sense that it defines the very being of God. In eternity, Barth says, God chose another for communion with himself. This "internal work" of God is the eternal beginning of all the ways and works of God. It tells us most fundamentally who God is and what his purposes are.[12]

That eternal, internal work by God, according to Barth, is specifically the election of Jesus Christ. God would not be God without the Son sitting at his right hand, from eternity, as far as Barth is concerned. Barth means "Son" here specifically in the sense of *Incarnate* Son, as he did in his doctrine of the Word. In eternity, in the person of his only Son, God unites himself with Jesus of Nazareth.[13] Jesus Christ, therefore, is both the subject and the object of God's eternal decision. As the eternal Son, Jesus Christ is the electing God. As the Son in the flesh, Jesus Christ is the elected human.[14] If Barth thus directs us to a scene in eternity as the keystone of his thought, he leaves no doubt about who the dramatis personae are—*God* in Jesus Christ and *humanity* in Jesus Christ; or, seen in their unity—God and humanity in *Jesus Christ.* In this sense God and humanity in Jesus Christ are the "ground of being," the *Realgrund,* of everything else. Election, in this theanthropocentric, christocentric sense, for Barth is the first and last of God's works, the alpha and omega of the whole history of creation, reconciliation, and redemption. Election, he says, is "the principle and essence of all happening everywhere."[15]

Yet if we continue to survey the same scene with Barth, we see more than *the* God and *the* human being united in Jesus Christ. We also see the ontological prefiguration of a *community of humans* united together in the person of the "God-man."[16] The gracious election of God in eternity for Barth refers not only to the one who is elected but also to a people of elect ones.[17] Barth makes this point strongly when he says:

> A Christ without his community would be a phantom figure, and a community without Christ would be more than ever a phantom figure. The one divine act of election is the election of this head *and* body.[18]

So the humanity of God means for Barth not only the existential address of God to humanity, not only the eternal election of the "God-man" Jesus Christ, but also the eternal election of the church, which is chosen with the "God-man." This divine act of election Barth also refers to explicitly and frequently as the eternal covenant of grace. The triumph of grace is thereby established at the central point, at the keystone, of his thought.

One should remember that all this happens in Barth's thought *before* the created world comes into view. Barth holds that "man-as-such"—an important technical term—has not yet been created. "Man-as-such" is an expression employed by Barth to allow him to assert the preexistence of the eternal human,

Jesus, and the concomitant preexistence of the eternal community of humans, the church. "Man-as-such" and "creation-as-such" only come into being when the world is created.

The radically theanthropocentric character of Barth's doctrine of election, as well as his doctrine of the Word, should thus be apparent. Barth is silent about nonhuman creatures, as far as God's eternity is concerned. Barth knows about the Platonic theme, found in Augustine, Thomas, and elsewhere in the tradition, that the "ideas" of all creatures preexisted eternally in the mind of God. But Barth subjects that construct to a characteristic christological-anthropological concentration. He remarks that "the inner necessity which led the Church and its theologians to speak of the fulness of the Divine ideas in the mind of God stemmed from the sphere of anthropology."[19] Nature, in Barth's schema, is noticeable by its absence, in eternity.

In terms of the root metaphors we have been tracing in this study, we can say at this point that as far as the fundamental principles of Barth's thought are concerned, the metaphor of ascent is clearly dominant, exclusively dominant, it would seem. As he hears the Word of God addressed to humanity, Barth lifts up his eyes to God's eternity and sees God and humanity above, the Son at the right hand of the Father, and the people of God united in the Son. There is no hint at this point of any imaginative influence exercised by the metaphor of fecundity or the metaphor of migration to a good land. Barth rejects the construct that all the "ideas" or archetypes of all creatures preexisted in the mind of God. Likewise, he depicts the scene of eternity, which for him is the alpha and omega of all things, the ontological principle of everything, as essentially a *landless* event. "God and man" above—that is Barth's first and last word, as far as the keystone of his dogmatic thought is concerned. Barth formally begins this thought where Thomas and Bonaventure and Dante materially ended theirs, with the saints alone with God in eternity, far above the earth—so far above, indeed, that the earth does not even come into view.

Creation: The Space for the Realization of Election

It is only when the inner work of God—the covenant of grace—is finished, according to Barth's schema, that the created world "as such" and its history with God come into view. We now observe the second act, as it were, of Barth's eternal theological drama. God in his love, Barth says, is not satisfied with his "eternal covenant as such." God also wants to "give it form outside the Divine realm."[20] God's aim, therefore, according to Barth, is now the "actualization," the "realization," the "happening," or the "fulfillment" of his eternal covenant with humanity.[21]

This takes place, Barth tells us, through the history of salvation, that is, the history of the covenant, specifically through God's works of reconciliation and redemption, which have their beginning, middle, and end in Jesus Christ.[22] But this history of salvation, Barth's reasoning continues, cannot in fact happen if there is no place for it to occur. It needs a "theater" outside of God.[23] This, then, is why God brings the created world into being.

Barth asserts that "creation is the construction of the space for the history of the convenant of grace."[24] Creation, Barth holds, is the "external ground" for the establishment of the covenant. To that degree, creation is essential to the greater scheme of things. But its being is purely instrumental, "pure service."[25] As a showplace for the saving works of God, it cannot be the subject of a work directed to it.[26] Everything is created—including "man-as-such"— solely for the sake of the realization of God's covenant with humanity in Jesus Christ. This is so also for God's preservation of the world, following its creation: "Because of the *servatio,* therefore the *creatio* and therefore also the *conservatio.*"[27] Because of election, the world is created; because of election the world is also sustained. "There is a history between God and the world," Barth explains, "but this history has no independent meaning. It takes place for the sake of the primal history which is played out between God and this one man [Jesus Christ] and His people. It is the sphere in which the primal history is played out."[28]

We now see formally speaking that nature for the first time has come into view in Barth's schema, as a kind of stage to allow the eternally founded drama between God and humanity to run its course. So, whereas humanity has a dual status—it is elected in eternity and it is also created "as such," in order to fulfill its eternal determination—the whole world of nature, outside of humanity, has a single status only. It has no eternal determination. Its reality is purely instrumental. It is merely the temporal setting for the really real, for the exfoliation and the consummation of the eternal convenant of grace with humanity.

The Anthropocentric Meaning of "Creation as Such"

Given Barth's radically theanthropocentric doctrine of election, and the concomitant radically theanthropocentric doctrine of reconciliation and redemption, it comes as no surprise to find Barth also presenting us with a radically anthropocentric view of "creation-as-such." What other meaning could creation have in his schema but an anthropocentric meaning?

Humanity, Barth suggests, is the whole point (*der Inbegriff*) of the created world.[29] In the realization of human creatures, the whole creation, he says, receives its peak and meaning.[30] Humanity is the light in the middle, he comments, the positive meaning of all existence.[31] Everything created prior to humanity is only relatively necessary, compared to the human creature.[32] The whole creation, therefore, can be fittingly called a house built for humanity.[33]

As Barth concludes in one striking statement about the cosmos: "It is created on the foundation of God's counsel of grace. So it has its goal in man, so this reality stands or falls with this, that there is also human reality in it."[34]

With this anthropocentric accent of his doctrine of creation-as-such before us, we can only conclude that the metaphor of ascent, so dominant in the fundamentals of his thought, is also the ruling metaphor in Barth's thought in the context of his doctrine of creation. Everything, for him, happens for the sake of the covenant between God and humanity. Nature, in particular, has no divinely bestowed meaning of its own. Nature for Barth, as for Origen, is a kind of divine afterthought that allows God's primary purpose—redemption of the eternally chosen ones—to be fulfilled.

This is not to suggest, however, that the natural cosmos is an evil or alien place, as far as Barth is concerned. Here Barth's thought stands in sharp contrast to Origen's. For Barth, nature is totally shaped by grace. The very being of nature, Barth tells us, shows this to us: the covenantal history of God with humanity needs a "corresponding space."[35] Barth introduces here a creation-symbolism which is reminiscent of Bonaventure's. The cosmos mirrors "the primary Divine activity," the covenantal history of God with humanity.[36] "The history of creation . . . ," we read, "from its origins and its whole structure, is planned to reflect these [saving] deeds of God, to give them an echo."[37]

Barth also takes up the traditional theme, the goodness of creation, with little evidence of Origen's suspicion of matter. Creation, Barth wants to stress, stands under the divine yes, it is a blessing.[38] Yet one should hear Barth carefully at this point. He does not want the expression "very good" of Gen. 1:31 to be "understood abstractly" as a description of the cosmos! Surely, Barth says, the Creator does justify the cosmos as such. But God does this "because it is created according to his will and plan and therefore with the determination for the construction and the consummation of the covenant between him and man."[39]

As we look at Barth's creation symbolism and his view of creation's goodness, we see that they do hold in check any thoroughgoing implications that would suggest that nature is evil or somehow alien to God or humanity. But at the same time it is apparent that those themes do little more than set limits against purely negative views such as the Gnostics', or against the kind of only slightly guarded degradation of nature we encountered in Origen's thought. Barth's creation symbolism and his theology of creation's goodness surely do not accent the positive. The metaphor of fecundity, which so richly shaped Augustine's imagination and occasioned his panoramic vision of the overflowing goodness of God throughout the whole cosmos, is mainly noticeable in Barth's thought by its absence. That Augustinian reading of the "very good" in Gen. 1:31 Barth rejects, for his own reasons, as "abstract." The cosmos *is* a mirror of God's gracious election of humanity for Barth. The cosmos *is* a home that is rightly built to contain that covenantal history. But intrinsically before God, in Barth's view, the cosmos still amounts to nothing apart from humanity. It has no evident permanent meaning in the greater scheme of things, as the human community obviously does.[40]

Divine Transcendence and Human Mastery Over the Earth

With regard to the human relation to nature, furthermore, and nature-in-itself, there are numerous suggestions that Barth—who refuses to deal with such matters directly—actually presupposes the modern, post-Kantian secularized view of nature more often than not. In this context the legacy of the theology of crisis, with its notion of the wholly other God and its assumption that the finite cannot receive the infinite (*finitum non capax infiniti*), looms large indeed. All we know about created beings outside of humanity, Barth tells us, is that God "stands over against them in his majestic dissimilarity."[41] This accent on the divine transcendence of nature, reminiscent not only of Kant but also of the Platonic thought patterns Barth drew on in his *Commentary on Romans,* is further reinforced by Barth's identification of "heaven" as the proper dwelling place of God in the world created by God. For Barth, God's immanence in the created world of heaven and earth, in other words, is in the realm of the spiritual, with the angels, not on the earth.[42] Gone is Luther's emphasis, for example, on God as the creative power of nature, pouring over, in, and through nature. Moreover, heaven, Barth explains, serves as a *limit* over against the earth.[43] And God is nearer to heaven than to earth, Barth says; it is the *terminus a quo* of all God's activity.[44] This sounds very much like the "infinite qualititative distinction" between God and the world which Barth championed in his theology of crisis.

Barth calls "earth," in contrast, the lower, visible part of the cosmos. The human creature is created under heaven, on earth, Barth says.[45] By speaking this way Barth wants to accent the human's creatureliness. Yet at the same time he is attempting to display the human creature as the lord and master of the creation. Barth regularly thinks of nature correspondingly as an "It," that is, as an object to be manipulated.[46] He variously attempts to set limits to that manipulative relationship, above all the canons of prudence. But that the created relationship between humanity and nature is essentially one of mastery he leaves us no doubt.

What becomes of the Augustinian, Franciscan, or Lutheran wonder before nature in such a theological framework? Cultural historians of the past, who have traced such themes as "the development of the modern feeling for nature," that is, the trends which eventually flourished in the romanticism of the likes of Wordsworth or Goethe, have marveled that Martin Luther made his famous journey to Rome as a young monk and apparently never once said anything about his experience of the Alps afterward. One can readily think of reasons why Luther might not have had occasion or reason to do this, but not so with Barth. For one who spent so much of his life in Switzerland, and who certainly knew how to celebrate the aesthetic wonders of this life, above all the music of Mozart, it is striking that we read nothing, or next to nothing, in his vast corpus about the beauties of nature. Presumably he thought that the Alps were too "abstract." Nature-in-itself, for Barth, appears mainly as an object to be manipulated, over against which God stands in his majestic dissimilarity.

Assessment: The Dominance of the Spiritual Motif

What we see happening in Barth's approach to nature in his dogmatic thought, as we saw in Bultmann's thought also, is the unconscious baptism of the modern secularization of nature in the West. He refuses to develop an explicit, substantive theology of nature—although he clearly wishes to claim all things for the lordship of Jesus Christ—and the result is that the divine grace —as he envisions it and which so thoroughly shapes his thinking—has little to do with nature other than exercising a kind of absolute domination over it, pursuant to human redemption. Barth offers no forceful corrective to the post-Kantian secularization of nature in Protestant thought. He more or less accepts the status quo in this respect, although in other contexts he takes consistent and urgent issues with the theology he inherited.

Barth presents us by default with a view of nature that is radically interpreted in terms of personal being. It therefore allows little room, if any, for a sense of human solidarity with and cooperation with, not to speak of wonderment before, nature as a realm of fellow creatures worthy of respect in their own right. Could Barth ever have said, with Francis, "sister earth"? That is doubtful— when, for Barth, only humans elected in Christ have any ultimate meaning in the greater scheme of things. Notwithstanding exegetical elements in his dogmatics that sometimes point in other directions, the inner logic of Barth's thought at this point is abundantly clear. His theology is fundamentally a theology of personal being, of God and humanity, and that is virtually all. Everything else in the visible creation, as far as he is concerned, is subservient to, and instrumental for, that theme.

This is the legacy of the exclusive dominance of the spiritual motif in Barth's thought. He begins with a vision of God and humanity alone, above in eternity, and when all has been said and done he essentially ends with that vision.

PIERRE TEILHARD DE CHARDIN:
A PERSONALISTIC UNIVERSE

Karl Barth directed a radical protest against the received theology of his time and against what he perceived to be its unholy alliance with modern culture.

Barth's theology, in this sense, was first of all a theology of antithesis. Barth then proceeded to develop his theology in his *Church Dogmatics* as an exposition of the revealed Word of God, independent (he claimed) of any substantive dependency on cultural assumptions or metaphysical constructions. His thought as a whole, therefore, can be considered to be both a theology of antithesis and a theology of thesis. This is why it is appropriate to think of him as a "confessional theologian."

As we look now at the thought of the French paleontologist, philosopher, and theologian Pierre Teilhard de Chardin, we encounter a radically different kind of thinker. Teilhard is a theologian of synthesis. Teilhard self-consciously thinks within the parameters of modern culture, although not uncritically. He attempts to show the unity of what can be known generally, in principle, by anyone—this is his "phenomenology"—and what can be known only particularly, through divine revelation, mediated by the Catholic tradition. In this sense, like Thomas Aquinas, Teilhard can be called a "philosophical theologian." Or, better, to use one of his own expressions, his thought can aptly be called a theology of "creative union." In view of the poetic and intuitive character of his thinking, indeed, it seems appropriate to approach his thought as some of his interpreters have, as a "theological vision of reality," rather than as a theology in any traditional dogmatic or philosophical sense of that word.

Rather than stand in judgment over modern culture, Teilhard chose to enter into its anguish, in order to lead it beyond itself to something higher. He saw a world around him dominated by the motif of entropy, a universe with no hope, nothing to look forward to but a vast, cosmic "heat death," and little to be thankful for in the present, given the brutal experiences of two world wars. Throughout his life he was passionately committed to overcome the pessimism and the despair which, in his judgment, were endemic in the modern consciousness. He wanted to offer our "age of anxiety" a forceful and universal optimism which would be scientifically, metaphysically, and theologically respectable.

An Integrating Theme: Evolution

To develop his vision, Teilhard seized upon a theme that hitherto had either been totally rejected or respectfully neglected by many, although not all, Christian thinkers in the late nineteenth and early twentieth centuries: evolution. He adopted this theme, given wide currency by Darwin, and made it his own, critically and constructively, much as Thomas Aquinas had adopted and adapted the principles of Aristotle in the thirteenth century. Yet it would be a mistake to think of Teilhard's enterprise solely in the context of modern theological responses to Darwin, although certainly Darwin's discoveries were constantly on

Teilhard's mind. Teilhard's employment of evolution as a fundamental theme is rooted in earlier intellectual epochs, as the names of those who either directly or indirectly influenced his synthesis will show, thinkers such as Plato, Aristotle, and Plotinus; Origen, Augustine, and Thomas; Leibnitz, Schelling, and Hegel. Teilhard wrote from within the mainstream of "perennial" metaphysics in the West; in particular, from within the tradition of ongoing reflection about the great chain of being, a conceptuality we have encountered often in this study. Teilhard's thought about evolution has its roots in this venerable intellectual milieu.

Among the various developments in thinking about the great chain of being that occurred in the medieval and modern periods, two need to be noted here if we are to understand Teilhard's most fundamental assumptions about the character of reality and its evolutionary forms. The first idea has to do with *what* evolves, the second with *how* the evolutionary process unfolds.

Arthur Lovejoy pointed out that the conceptuality of the great chain of being has been construed both morphologically and psychologically at various points in its history. On the one hand, every creature has been viewed as having a distinct *form* of being, within a hierarchy of forms. On the other hand, the emanation of the One to the many and the return of the many to the One has also been depicted in terms of gradations of *consciousness*. The seventeenth-century German philosopher Gottfried Wilhelm Leibnitz (1646–1716) is a good example of a thinker who adopted the psychological emphasis, according to Lovejoy. Leibnitz espoused a metaphysical panpsychism; for him, the whole of reality was essentially a gradation of varying levels of consciousness. Teilhard combines the morphological and the psychological motifs. He speaks, as we shall see, of a "without" and a "within" of things, and posits a universal principle of being, the law of "complexity-consciousness." He depicts the hierarchy of being accordingly, as evolving levels of morphological complexity and spiritual consciousness.

The second development in the tradition of reflection about the great chain of being which we need to note here is what Lovejoy refers to as "the temporalizing of the Chain of Being," which, he shows, occurred dramatically in the eighteenth century. Schematically, it is helpful in this connection to think of the hierarchy of being as being rotated forty-five degrees to the right and to see the process of universal emanation, in its most noteworthy phase, moving now not down from the One to the many, but fundamentally from the many up toward the One. This, as Lovejoy sees it, was the shift of thought that occurred when philosophers gave up the more or less timeless vertical metaphysics of ancient philosophy and adopted the temporal, more horizontal metaphysics of modernity. In the wake of this shift of perspective, the concept of emanation would eventually give way, in this tradition of reflection, to the concept of evolution.[47] Interestingly, this temporalized chain of being appears forcefully in some of the writings of Leibnitz, coupled with the familiar Enlightenment idea of indefinite progress. The timeless chain of being thus becomes a universal program of endless becoming. We will see that Teilhard follows Leibnitz implicitly in this respect, as well as in the context of a metaphysics of consciousness.

But Teilhard's integrating theme—evolution—is informed still more deeply, beneath the level of the metaphysical tradition and the theme of evolution, by his own self-conscious choice of metaphors, a thought that will be readily apparent to anyone who has followed the course of our historical explorations thus far. As a visionary thinker, indeed, Teilhard is perhaps more consciously aware of the formative function of metaphors than any other single thinker we have encountered in this study.

With this level of his thinking in view, however, we encounter a profound tension. This tension tends to belie the viability of Teilhard's intention to claim the whole of reality for the "cosmic Christ." On the one hand, his conscious purpose is to project a universal vision, which not only encompasses the vast world of nature, but which demonstrates that nature has an indispensable place in the evolution of the whole. On the other hand, his mode of thought points in a different direction. As we will see, Teilhard thinks primarily in terms of the metaphor of ascent, which as we have often noticed is markedly anticosmic in its implications. We do see the influence of the metaphor of fecundity in his thought: at the beginnings of his vision, as it were, with his picture of the many, and with his thought of Christ as exerting influence throughout the whole creation, not just within the realm of human affairs. But the metaphor of fecundity finally gives way to the dominance of the metaphor of ascent, as Teilhard proceeds to show us what is clearly his primary theological interest —the ascending cosmic process of evolution, from the many to the One. Further, we see little or no influence from the metaphor of migration to a good land in his thought. Solidarity with the land, for Teilhard, is a stage that must be left behind, as the human species ascends to higher and higher levels of consciousness and spiritual union.

At the categorical level we see a way of thinking that begins with the vision of overflowing goodness. The "cosmic Christ," in Teilhard's schema, functions in a way that is akin to the metaphysical dynamics of overflowing goodness in the traditional great chain of being conceptuality. But Teilhard's mind definitively comes to rest with the triumph of the acosmic, spiritual-rational good. The two "gods" of the great chain of being conceptuality, as Lovejoy has identified them, are evidently present in Teilhard's thought—but it is the suprasensible good, rather than overflowing goodness, that is finally dominant. "Nothing in the world is really of value," Teilhard once stated in a letter, "except what happens in the end."[48] This statement underlines the permanency and the completeness of the influence exercised in his thought by the metaphor of ascent and by its metaphysical expression in the idea of the good.

As we will concretely see, Teilhard's thought about creation and redemption is asymmetrical, as was the case for Thomas and Bonaventure. The many are created, but only the few are redeemed. As a matter of fact, much in Teilhard's thought calls to mind the fecundity theme in Bonaventure, yet it has the same outcome for Teilhard as for Bonaventure: the metaphor of fecundity is finally eclipsed by the metaphor of ascent, and the metaphor of migration to a good land is scarcely ever to be seen.

We will begin our exploration of the course of Teilhard's argument by examining what can be called his phenomenology of evolution. This is Teilhard the scientist and metaphysician at work.[49]

The Unity of His Evolutionary Thought:
The Ascending Axis of Hominization

The unity of Teilhard's phenomenological vision, in his own terms, is personalism. Teilhard interprets the whole of reality in terms of personal being, divine and human. Everything hinges for Teilhard accordingly on what he refers to as the "ascending axis of hominization."[50]

To underline this point Teilhard revives a scientific concept which has been widely rejected, in its traditional form, by most biologists today: orthogenesis. Literally this word means coming into being in a straight line. By invoking this contested concept Teilhard seeks to reaffirm the centrality of humanity in the story of evolution. With Darwin and the neo-Darwinians, Teilhard does accept the anti-orthogenetic notion of natural selection. The process of evolution is not simply a straight line to humankind, by any means, according to Teilhard. The process of evolution, he holds, "proceeds step by step by dint of billionfold trial and error."[51] It is an infinite process of groping or "cosmic drift." That explains why the whole process has taken such an extended time.

At the same time, for Teilhard, evolution has always had one goal. It has followed a line toward the coming into being of human life on planet earth. This line surely has been more like a highly erratic spiral upward than a straight line, according to Teilhard. Nevertheless, he maintains, there has been, there is, and there will continue to be one inner drive—one main axis of evolution—of the whole universal evolutionary process, however random its morphology.

In this connection Teilhard introduces the concept of a universal law—complexity-consciousness—to which we have already referred. For him this law is as fundamental to nature as is the law of gravity, the second law of thermodynamics, or the law of the conservation of energy. The law of complexity-consciousness means simply that the process of evolution represents an ever-increasing development toward higher organization and more intense and unified forms of consciousness. There are, then, Teilhard points out, two axial lines in the universe. One is the impressive quantitative one which runs from the subatomic world to the galactic worlds, the axis of physical infinity. This material aspect of the world, Teilhard grants, is ultimately tending toward death, according to the second law of thermodynamics. Then there is the evolutionary axis of complexity-consciousness. According to this law, in the midst of the dying physical cosmos, life and consciousness are gradually emerging and intensifying. This is the axis—complexity and consciousness—that Teilhard sees as the key to understanding the meaning of the whole universe and the history of evolution in particular. This is the orthogenetic line of evolution.

The law of complexity-consciousness, Teilhard maintains, applies everywhere, even where it cannot be observed. All entities in the universe have both a "without," a certain state of organization, and a "within," a certain state of consciousness. Where the one increases, the other will increase too. A larger and more organized brain, for example, will soon be the occasion for a more intense form of consciousness. Moreover, the higher the level of organization of a natural entity, the more consciousness it will possess.[52]

Teilhard feels compelled to postulate a primitive state of consciousness in all material things on the basis of the scientific principle, much emphasized by Darwin and intrinsic to the conceptuality of the great chain of being, *natura non facit saltum.* Nature does not proceed by leaps. If consciousness is a reality now, of which we are subjectively certain, it must have been real in some sense at primitive levels of physical reality.

The concept of orthogenesis and the law of complexity-consciousness show how deep the current of personalism is in Teilhard's phenomenology of evolution, and why the term "radical" is appropriate at this point. The whole infinitely variegated evolutionary process of the universe has one axis, one goal: the life and future of the human creature, as humanity is destined to come into being and to be unified spiritually. The ultimate law of the universe—complexity-consciousness—focuses teleologically on human reality; humanity is its final product.

But Teilhard's personalism is more than just a passive phenomenological observation of a universal process that has its final goal in the glorification of the human creature. Teilhard's radically personalistic vision of reality also has an activist thrust, not unlike the thought of Karl Marx. According to Teilhard the human species is now in a position to bring the whole universe to its originally intended fulfillment *by its own action.* In this sense the future of the whole universe hinges on the proper exercise of human freedom. Humankind, Teilhard suggests, is "evolution conscious of itself." Evolution, therefore, will only ascend to its next level through the proper use of the human consciousness. In theological terms, the kingdom of God will not come unless humans consciously work to make it come. This is a striking doctrine, indeed. It attaches a kind of significance to moral action that dwarfs even the dynamism of Calvin's doctrine of vocational-dominion. Never for once would Calvin have allowed the thought that human action can in any sense have a part to play in bringing in the kingdom.

The Particulars of His Evolutionary Thought:
Stages of Becoming

When we examine the particulars of Teilhard's phenomenological vision, in turn, we see a picture of universal *genesis* or becoming.

The whole universal evolutionary process begins with cosmogenesis, the coming into being and the increasing organization of physical matter. Over a period of billions of years, from a state of almost totally disintegrated physical matter, the history of our universe began. By apparent accident, moreover, a habitable place finally came into being—the earth. Again, through a billion-fold process of trial and error, life emerged on Planet Earth. This was biogenesis. Through a similar lengthy process, life covered the earth; henceforth this could be called the biosphere. In this sphere, complexification then proceeded on a vast scale. Retrospectively we can see that life's greatest density passed through those creatures possessing a central nervous system. Teilhard calls this facet of evolution cephalization. With cephalization, Teilhard points out, one can see the first signs of emergent consciousness.

Then comes a step in the history of evolution comparable only to the birth of life. This is the birth of mind or self-consciousness in the human creature, the most cephalized of the living creatures. This, Teilhard calls noogenesis or homogenesis. Quantitatively speaking, the appearance of humanity was almost totally without significance. Here Teilhard agrees with Darwin and Darwin's twentieth-century followers. In almost all respects the human creature was dwarfed by other creatures; it appeared as but one weak product of a billionfold cosmic drift. As Teilhard says with his characteristic sense of drama, "Man came silently into the world." Nevertheless here was a phenomenon expressing the flow of the universe itself:

> However solitary his advent, man emerged from a general groping of the world. He was born a direct lineal descendent from a total effort of life, so that the species has an axial value and a preeminent dignity.[53]

Human life emerged, like everything else, as a result of natural selection, but it was a natural selection which was drawn forward by the very life force of the universe itself. With human life, moreover, the interiority of matter, the "within" has finally become the dominant factor. Here, finally, spirit rules over matter, or it can. Humans are self-conscious beings. They know themselves as selves and are free to lead a rational life.

But evolution does not stop here, Teilhard stresses. It continues to press forward and upward, in two partially overlapping phases. The first phase is expansion or planetization. The human creature multiplies and fills the earth. Concomitantly, the quality of human life—that is, culture—develops or intensifies. This is the second phase, the phase of compression or convergence. As Teilhard writes:

> Traditions became organized and a collective memory was developed. Slender and granular as the first membrane might be, the noosphere there and then began to close in upon itself and to encircle the earth.[54]

Beginning about the middle of the nineteenth century, this dual process of human evolution by expansion and compression began to reach its limits, according to Teilhard. This process was helped along by the social compression of humankind on continents and by the worldwide social interaction made possible by modern technology.

In the human sphere, Teilhard believes, evolution is now approaching its limits; evolution is ready for another major step forward. Teilhard sees signs of this impending new development in the growing social organization of the world.[55] He does see the evils of certain totalitarian states in the twentieth century, for example; but at the same time he sees them as pointing to new possibilities for a world society. More important than social organization, however, Teilhard sees the noosphere arriving at a critical point of development through the scientific discovery of evolution. Now finally in our period, evolution has become conscious of itself. This awareness Teilhard calls the involution of evolution.[56] We are now coming to realize that the whole universal process is passing through us and to that extent depends on us. As Teilhard writes, with reference to the similar Marxist point of view:

> Like sons who have grown up, like workers, who have become "conscious," we are discovering that something is developing in the world by means of us, perhaps at our expense. And what is more serious still, that we have become aware that, in the great game that is being played we are the players as well as being the cards and the stakes. Nothing can go on if we leave the table. Neither can any power force us to remain.[57]

This conception of a humanity that has reached the limits of its terrestrial expansion and is fast approaching the limits of its spiritual cultural compression leads Teilhard to pose the question of the omega point; that is, the question whether it is not reasonable to assume that the whole evolutionary process has a

final cone, which is the end-goal of the universal efficacy of the law of complexity-consciousness. This takes Teilhard's thought to the boundary of theology explicitly, since he has discerned that the whole process is tending toward
the production of purer and purer forms of personalized spirit.

As human life is progressively integrated and spiritualized, Teilhard asks, is
it not conceivable that evolution will pass through one final cosmic involution
into the reality of sheer personalized-spirit? When that time comes, evil—
which for Teilhard is disintegration and disunion of reality—will have been
abolished. Perfect union of spiritualized, personal reality, an ultrasynthesized
humankind, will have come into being.

The Apex of Evolution: Christ Omega and
the Body of Christ

One can now see how smoothly Teilhard's phenomenological account of evolution passes over into his explicit theology of evolution. Teilhard affirms that
the exalted Jesus Christ is the central point of the whole universe, of all visible
and invisible powers. In this context, Teilhard states that the whole universal
process of cosmogenesis, biogenesis, and noogenesis is ultimately a process of
Christogenesis, the growth of the living, fulfilled Christ. The exalted, resurrected Christ, and the body of believers united to him, is the omega point of the
universe. Teilhard frequently alludes to Colossians and Ephesians as the biblical
basis for this cosmic Christology. In particular, he often refers to Col. 1:15f.,
where the Pauline author depicts Christ as the firstborn of creation.

For Teilhard, the glorified, fulfilled Christ is the ultimate goal and therefore
the ultimate reality of the universe. Teilhard expresses this by drawing on the
New Testament word "pleroma" ("fullness") and refers to Christ's role in the
universe as pleromatization or totalization, that is, drawing all things to himself. All things, Teilhard maintains, have their being and their becoming
through the universal Christ.

In metaphysical terms Teilhard sees the exalted Christ functioning as the first
mover of the universe; not as its efficient cause, as the "God way back there"
who set all things in motion. No, God is not way back at the beginning, in isolation as the efficient cause, the watchmaker. Rather God is the ever-present final cause. The "Prime-Mover," he says characteristically, "is ahead."[58] Christ,
in other words, is a kind of spiritual magnet which draws the universe to itself,
and which organizes and orders the universe, a process that will allow it one day
to attain fulfillment in Him.[59] More specifically the ultimate spiritual energy
which radiates from Christ and which draws all things to him and orders all
things for him is—divine love. Ultimate reality is charity. Charity is the spiritual force that draws all things toward final union with God in Christ. This is
the spiritual force that was working from the beginning of time on the "within"

of primordial matter, drawing it forward and upward along the axis of complexity-consciousness.

Teilhard further sees historical Christianity as being in some sense already at the omega point. He holds that historical Christianity is the most universal religion and the religion most able to inspire humankind to deeds of love and peace. More particularly, he believes that the Church of Rome occupies the portion closest to the main axis of evolution, according to the evolutionary principle of cephalization. The Roman Church, and especially the Roman pontiff as Teilhard seems to suggest, is, as it were, the central nervous system of the body of Christ. But it is not the organization of the body of Christ as much as its redemptive reality that fascinates Teilhard, particularly the reality of the universal Christ experienced in the Eucharist. Celebration of the Eucharist, according to Teilhard, is participation in the reality of the final, fulfilled Christ, the finally formed body of Christ or the divine milieu. In the Eucharist, ultimate charity is immediately real and accessible in our own period of evolutionary history.

Teilhard thus has a certain pervasive mystical bent. He deeply values the mysteries of the church as the reality of the end time in this world. Still, he is much more concerned with moral action. He holds that the logical-existential result of the evolutionary process is that Christians are called to join with all people of good will in building a world society of peace and justice. Indeed, insofar as any individual or group works on building that society, they are building up the body of Christ. As Teilhard suggested in a note in 1918, Christ needs the results of human labor so that he can reach his plenitude, his own fullness.

When Christ does reach his own fullness, his highly intensified, infinitely spiritualized body will be the only surviving reality. Biophysical reality generally will die a death of heatlessness and will disintegrate toward nothingness. But human reality will be transfigured into the white spiritual heat of ultimate charity, in the fullness of Christ. The members of the mystical body will then be united once and for all to the head. That will be the final cephalization of the universe, which Teilhard refers to as an act of spiritual ecstasy in God. Then the vast universal process of evolution—cosmogenesis, biogenesis, homogenesis and Christogenesis—will come to an end. The cosmic ascent of humanity will have reached its final goal, union with the universal Christ, and through him, union with God, who will then be all in all.

Assessment: The Dominance of the Spiritual Motif

Teilhard has been celebrated as a profound and creative theologian of nature.[60] In some ways he is, as we will have occasion to observe more fully in conclusion. But this judgment should not be allowed to stand unqualified. The underlying tensions in his thought between his evident intention to embrace and to affirm the whole of nature, on the one hand, and the dominance of the nature-denying metaphor of ascent, on the other hand, must be recognized. And when we do, we must conclude that it is the latter, rather than the former, that most fundamentally shapes Teilhard's thought.

To be sure, we see in Teilhard nothing of the anticosmic spirit that was in evidence in Origen or the early Augustine. Teilhard is by no means hostile to matter and to life. On the contrary, he consistently seeks to celebrate the biophysical order and rejoice in its complexities and immensities. But—and this is his fateful accent—he unquestionably celebrates the biophysical in order to celebrate the spiritual or the personal all the more; and in that process of thought the celebration of the biophysical tends to take a second place, and then to fall by the wayside. "Matter and spirit are not opposed as two separate things, as two natures," he tells us, "but as two directions of evolution within the world."[61] In this world of evolution, according to the law of complexity-consciousness, the process of unification as Teilhard depicts it unfolds hierarchically, with each stage being the precondition of the next and each stage being largely left behind except insofar as some of it is taken up and transformed at the next level of ascent. "At the heart of our universe," Teilhard explains, "each soul exists for God, in our Lord. But all reality, even material reality, around each one of us, exists for our souls. Hence, all sensible reality around each one of us, exists, through our souls, for God in our Lord."[62] Again, he tells us: "In our universe where all spirit moves toward God, Our Lord, everything that is sensible exists for spirit."[63]

The biophysical is good, as far as Teilhard is concerned, only because it produces the spiritual. Once the spiritual has been produced, moreover, the biophysical essentially loses its raison d'être, as far as Teilhard's logic is concerned. At that point, he depicts the biophysical order as drifting back into the nothingness of the multiple, whence it came, while the spiritual is unified one more time, in Christ. The final word of Teilhard's schema, as it was for both Thomas and Bonaventure—ironic as this may sound in the context of a discussion of one who is so widely praised as the contemporary theologian of nature par excellence—is the *abolition of nature,* except for those small portions of the biophysical order that have been taken up, and spiritualized, in human souls. This point can be documented extensively from Teilhard's writings, if it is not already overwhelmingly apparent.[64]

Teilhard's schema, in this respect, is akin to Barth's, who holds that creation is the external ground of the covenant between God and humanity, and conversely, that the covenant is the internal ground of the creation. Yet Teilhard seems to go much further than Barth in his tonality, if not in his logic. At times Teilhard even verges on a kind of spiritual narcissism, as far as nature is concerned.[65] He loves nature fundamentally, not in itself as Francis did. He seeks to embrace the creatures of nature not in a Franciscan mode, as brothers and sisters with whom he stands in solidarity, but because these are the objects that have been destined to produce the world of personality. Nature is beautiful for Teilhard not in itself, but because it is a kind of mirror that shows those who have eyes to see how great their own spiritual destiny is going to be. Thus Teilhard can celebrate the material order with affective abandon, as in his "Hymn to Matter." Yet matter for him is always an occasion for something better, for human progress and mastery:

> Blessed be you, harsh matter, barren soil, stubborn rock, you who yield only to violence, you who force us to work if we would eat. Blessed be you, perilous matter, violent sea, untamable passion: you who unless we fetter you will devour us.[66]

He blesses matter in its "totality" and in its "true nature."[67] But what does this mean? Clearly, it means that matter is the stage for something far greater—for the birth of spirit: "You I acclaim as the inexhaustible potentiality for existence and transformation wherein the predestined substance germinates and grows."[68] This tendency in Teilhard's thought—to celebrate the biophysical, yet to celebrate it only as a passing stage on the way to what is truly important—can be further illustrated, lest there be any doubt about its pervasiveness in his thinking, by looking carefully at his striking essay on chastity.

Teilhard rejects what he considers to be the traditional approach to chastity, with its assumptions "that sexual relations are tainted by some degradation or defilement."[69] The latter view, in his judgment, is rooted in a general ambivalence toward the material order in classical Christian thought and practice. While Christianity has never condemned matter, he says; while, indeed, it has defended it against the likes of the Manichees; while, further, it has always drawn nourishment from sacramental practices and has lived with the hope of the resurrection of the body; this traditional affirmation of the human body and the material order generally was combined, in Teilhard's view, with an "odd mistrust of the earth's resources," as if the world, created good, nevertheless contained within it a "hidden perversion."[70]

In contrast, Teilhard wants to affirm the goodness of the biophysical world, in particular the goodness of the human body. Humans are deeply rooted in their evolutionary history, in his view, and those roots need to be affirmed. Still, he wishes to take his readers one step further. Along with all things, he points out, humans have "a drive toward completion." It is "from this primordial impulse that the luxuriant complexity of intellectual and emotional life develops and becomes more intense and diverse." So the all-encompassing spiritual aspects of human life "have their roots deep in the corporeal. It is from man's storehouse of passion that the warmth and light of his soul arise, transfigured."[71] The body is not to be rejected—in other words, it is to be used, transformed, and sublimated—for a spiritual end.

Teilhard then depicts "woman" as "the symbol and personification of all the fulfillment we look for in the universe." The "feminine" is that which calls forth what lies at the heart of matter—spirit. Older views, Teilhard says, depicted the woman either as merely an instrument of generation or as having no spiritual significance whatsoever. He affirms the importance of woman's identification with maternity, to be sure, but he observes that this is "almost nothing in comparison with her spiritual fertility."[72] As such she has an essential role in the spiritual growth of the species. The challenge, as Teilhard sees it, is to "harness" that spiritual energy and to release thereby "the spiritual power of matter."[73] Teilhard develops such thoughts with lavish expressions of passion in his prose poem "The Eternal Feminine."[74] What we see emerging in this essay on chastity, then, is an instrumental view of the biophysical that is concretely symbolized for Teilhard by the feminine. Nature *is* good, in other words. But it is good because it elicits the spiritual. It is not good in itself.

At this point we also encounter Teilhard's enthusiastic activist-ascetic ethos of conquest. Theory and practice are intimately related in his schema, as we have seen. The kingdom of God will finally come for Teilhard only through the contributions of human mastery over the world. In the context of this essay now before us, this means not the rank conquest of woman, as in rape, but engagement with women in such a way that they become the stepping stones to the mastery and the sublimation of masculine passion. This, accordingly, is the picture we see emerging in this essay. The human (male) faces the biophysical, plunges into the nexus of its passionate allurement, and in the process moves toward a higher spiritual maturity wherein the natural is no longer to be touched. Human passion then rises above, and detaches itself from, the natural. Teilhard summarizes:

> Material creation no longer stretches between man and God like a fog or a barrier. It develops like an elevating, enriching ambiance; and it is important not to try to escape from this or release oneself from it, but to accept its reality and make our way through it. Rightly speaking, there are no sacred or profane things, no pure or impure: there is only a *good direction and a bad direction*—the direction of ascent, of amplifying unity, of greatest spiritual effort; and the direction of descent, of constricting egoism, of materializing enjoyment."[75]

This is his ethic of spiritual conquest, the subjugation of nature for the sake of spirit:

> Hitherto asceticism has been a pressure toward rejection—the chief requirement of holiness used to be self-deprivation. In the future, because of our new moral outlook on matter, spiritual detachment will be something much more like a con-

quest; it will mean plunging into the flood of created energies, in order both to be uplifted and to uplift them—and *this includes* the first and most firey [the sexual] of those energies.[76]

For Teilhard, elements of the material order, and human erotic attraction in particular, are to be cherished for what they can elicit, for what they can draw forth in terms of spirit, not for what they are as such.

This is why, finally, he argues that the relation between the sexes is best if it is not consummated. In his view, sexual union must be avoided—at least at the highest levels of the spiritual life, in which direction the whole universe is moving—in order that the energies which the feminine has elicited might be focused on God, not on the feminine itself. "Is it really possible," Teilhard asks, "without loss, to give oneself twice?" One must not embrace nature, in other words. One must not "short circuit," as he says, the "dazzling gift of the body."[77] One must save that energy—for God alone. As male and female are drawn together, Teilhard suggests, let them direct their reaching out for each other not to one another but forward and upward instead, so that they might converge with one another at a higher spiritual level in God.

"During a first phase of humanity," Teilhard concludes, "man and woman are confined to the physical act of giving and the concern with reproduction; and around that act they gradually develop a growing nimbus of spiritual exchanges." Then "the center of attraction suddenly withdraws ahead, to infinity, we might say; and, in order to continue to possess one another more fully as spirit, the lovers are obliged to turn away from the body, and so seek one another in God."[78] This is Teilhard's last word about the whole biophysical world, too, as we have seen: having conquered nature, humans are to detach themselves and ascend to a higher spiritual plane.

It is a necessary stage, then, that nature will one day fall away as hyperspiritualized human beings are united together and taken up into the spiritual incandescence of the Divine. The biblical-eschatological vision of the new heavens and the new earth, according to which the lamb will lie down with the lion and the desert will blossom, here falls by the wayside, in favor of a picture of the final consummation that is almost totally spiritualized as it was for Thomas and Bonaventure. In his essay on chastity Teilhard puts it this way:

> The most penetrating interpretation we can give the world . . . is to regard the world as a movement of *universal convergence,* within which the plurality of matter is consummated in spirit.[79]

It is indeed appropriate to say that Teilhard's thought stands, finally, for the abolition of the biophysical world, except as some of it has been taken up into human souls.

Thomas had argued, almost in passing, that the biosphere, the world of living things, except for the human creature, would not be part of the eschatologically transfigured new heavens and new earth. Bonaventure had articulated the same point, also as a matter of course. Teilhard, much more exuberantly and expansively, makes that theme one of the principles of his thinking. For Teilhard, except as some matter has been transformed into spirit in human souls, the whole biophysical order, not just the animals and plants as for Thomas, will be abrogated, decimated to nothingness, at the very end. "The day will come," Teilhard concludes his essay on chastity, "when, after harnessing the ether, the winds, the tides, gravitation, we shall harness for God the energy of love. And, on that day, for the second time in the history of the world, man will have discovered fire."[80] The ascent of humanity to perfect union with God through Christ will have come to its glorious spiritual incandescence in the white heat of the divine glory. This is the course of the universe, as Teilhard depicts it in another essay: "Crimson gleams of Matter, gliding imperceptibly into the gold of Spirit, ultimately to become transformed into the incandescence of a Universe that is Person."[81]

The Irony of Teilhard's Thought

Such is the triumph of personalism in Teilhard's thought. Such is the legacy of the dominating employment of the metaphor of ascent. The metaphors of fecundity and of migration to a good land have been eclipsed. We are left, when all has been said, with a vision of the end that is landless, purely spiritual, and with a vision of human life with nature in this world that is predicated totally on the ideas of mastery and conquest.[82] The spiritual motif of Western theology has here become dominant, while the ecological motif has become recessive. Teilhard's thought, to be sure, is shaped by the ecological motif insofar as Christ and those who are united in Christ require the temporal and spatial vastness of the natural world in order to attain their own completeness. But in the end that ecological motif ceases to function. All that remains, in Teilhard's view, is consciousness, spirit, person. Teilhard presents us with a dialectic of creation and redemption—like the constructions of Origen, Thomas, Bonaventure, Dante, and Barth—that is asymmetrical. The many are created. But only the few are redeemed.

There is a sad irony in all this. In the case of Barth, who claims not to want to deal with nature as such, and who develops his theology as an heir of the conceptually constricted tradition of Kant and Ritschl, the reader's expectations might not be high to begin with, notwithstanding Barth's evident intent to claim the whole of reality for the lordship of Jesus Christ. But Teilhard begins without that self-imposed restriction and without those categorical constrictions. He self-consciously sets out to develop a viable theology of nature, and he seems to have the conceptual resources in hand, above all the construct of evolution—with its important, albeit largely implicit, metaphysical meanings and its explicit scientific relevance—to allow him to honor his intention. But he finally fails, dramatically, to realize the promise with which he begins.

Teilhard surely takes us far beyond the construct of nature the machine. In this sense he qualifies his nineteenth-century inheritance in impressive fashion. Nature is alive for him. It is an ocean of energy and universal motion. Nature is also shaped, even to the rudiments of matter, at the subatomic level, and beyond also, in its spatial and temporal immensities, by universal vectors of divine purpose. In this sense Teilhard gives the vast temporal and spatial reaches of the cosmos, as we know them today, their due. He *sees* them. He does not look the other way, as many modern Christian theologians have done. Indeed he sees them as charged with their own *mysterium tremendum*. He stands before the sixty million galaxies of our universe in awe, and he looks back on the billion-fold drift of cosmic evolution and its history on our little planet with a profound sense of reverence. He has a speaking acquaintance, as it were, with the textures and the tectonics and the grand vitalities of nature, which may be unequaled in the whole history of Christian theology. He knows the creatures of nature. He seeks to name them. He wants to claim them all, concretely, for the lordship of Christ and the providence of God.

All this we can count as a sure and certain gain, especially when it is compared to Teilhard's nineteenth-century inheritance. But all this, no sooner than it is won, so to speak, is radically qualified by his resolute and unbending adherence to a way of thinking that is shaped by the metaphor of ascent. This then constricts his theology of nature fundamentally so that its great promise is never realized.

Teilhard finally presents us with a phenomenological and theological anthropocentrism so comprehensive that it shapes everything else in his thought. This in turn leads him to project what appears to be a virtually unbridled ethic of conquest directed toward nature. When Teilhard contemplates the *mysterium tremendum* of nature, as it were, he waits eagerly to see in the midst of it all the emergence of a human face. And as he finally sees that face it is as if he feels impulses to struggle with, to master, and to dominate nature, in order that that human countenance might come more fully to light and radiate throughout all things. In this respect, it turns out, his thought is not all that far removed from his nineteenth-century inheritance. Nature is, for him, finally a field for conquest, especially with the instruments of modern technology, which he consistently celebrates. Nature, for him, lies there, as it were, for the human taking —it is either take or be taken, eat or be eaten, as far as Teilhard is concerned—

ready to be used, even exploited, in order to build that kingdom of spirit which is the final goal of the whole evolutionary process.

BARTH AND TEILHARD:
THE UNSPOKEN ECOLOGICAL PROMISE

This means that after traversing a vast circuit of thought Teilhard ends up standing next to Barth—who never really attempted such a heroic intellectual pilgrimage with his own theology of nature. Both Teilhard and Barth reach out to claim the whole of reality, nature as well as humanity, for God and his Christ. But nature slips from their hands, from Teilhard's finally, from Barth's quickly. In the end, for both thinkers, nature is not redeemed. It is merely used. It is totally at the disposal of God's history with the human community, its future, its needs. Persons are redeemed. Nature has no divinely bestowed meaning or value apart from the meaning and value of redeemed human existence. In this twentieth-century expression of classical Christian thought about nature, it turns out that the whole of reality is the story of "the humanity of God" (Barth). The whole of reality is the drama of a "personalistic universe" (Teilhard). Barth and Teilhard thus represent the triumph of personalism in the classical tradition and, with that, the triumph of the spiritual motif. And this happens in a cultural situation—for which they themselves have a profound empathy—in which the forces of secularization, impacting on attitudes and policies regarding nature as well as in other areas, are taking the whole culture to the brink of one kind of disaster after another. This is the sad irony of their thought. They know that they must reclaim nature for the lordship of Jesus Christ and the providence of God, but they finally fail to do that.

On the other hand, there is another way of looking at the irony of their thought. That is to see not so much what they actually did produce, but what they might have produced, precisely because of their universal claims for God and his Christ. Some hypothetical questions may be able to point to the fact that that irony can be considered to be a sign of promise too, as far as their theologies of nature are concerned.

What if Barth and Teilhard had been more open to the influence of the ecological motif in their theological reflection? What if they had thought consistently in terms of the metaphor of migration to a good land and the metaphor of fecundity, instead of the metaphor of ascent?

Would it be impossible, in a Barthian mode, to think of God electing nature, as well as humanity, in Christ? Would it be impossible to picture a community of many creatures, not just persons, gathered in the ark of eternity, as it were, as the ultimate beginning and the ontological foundation of all the ways and works of God? Would it be anything but an enhancement of God's grace, from a Barthian perspective, not to begrudge the generosity of God, rather to confess that the creatures of nature also have an eternal determination, that God intends to have a history also with the galaxies and the dinosaurs and the birds of the air, that they also, in due proportion, along with all our fellow human beings, are our "covenant partners"?

Would it not be possible in a Teilhardian mode, to envision the line of complexity-consciousness not as *the* axis of universal cosmic history, but as *one* line, *prima inter pares* surely, but still one of many lines of creaturely emergence, each with its own eschatological value? Could we not see the tree of life coming to fruition with many branches, not just with one? Might it not be possible, in this connection, to draw on the theme, well-attested in the thought of Augustine, Thomas, and Bonaventure, that many eternal ideas in the mind of God are actualized in the whole creation—but now see them as being actualized throughout the whole history of creation, not just at its initial moment, and see them also as attaining their fullest actualization only at the very end? Would it not be possible to envision the end of the universe, accordingly, not as an omega point, but as an omega world, a commonwealth of creaturely being, where the light of the divine fire unites and permeates all things, *ta panta,* not just spiritual creatures, where a genuinely cosmic peace is finally established, where God is truly all in all? A one-dimensional unification of spirit in God would not be the *telos* of the universe; but a multidimensional consummation of all creaturely existence in God would be the *telos* of this universal history.

Further, given such an ecological renewal of their theological conceptualities, would it not also be possible, in both the Barthian and the Teilhardian modes, to draw substantively on the Trinitarian fecundity-theology of Bonaventure, as the ultimate validation of the divine fecundity in the creation and the final vindication of the divine fecundity in the consummated omega world, the eschatological promised land, when God is to be all in all? This would as a matter of course open up their theologies, their doctrines of God in particular, to a new kind of emphasis on the divine *life*, reminiscent of the biblical theme, "the living God," along with other more familiar, basal affirmations about the Divine, that God is love or that God is spirit.

Would not the ethical result of such theological constructions, moreover, whether Barthian or Teilhardian, be *an ethos of concomitance* with nature, rather than an ethos of dominance over nature? Would it not be consistent with Barth's and Teilhard's deepest commitments to extend the liberating triumph of grace and the unifying ultimacy of charity, in proper proportion, to include all the creatures of nature, not just the human creatures: so that those who would take either Barth's or Teilhard's theology seriously would then seek to cooperate with nature and to care for nature—even to wonder at nature first of all—rather than attempting to master or to conquer nature, or rather than being prompted to pass nature by, as it were, on the other side? Could not a theology of cosmic justice—*suum cuique,* to each creature its own—be projected according to which all creatures would be given their due and considered in some measure as brothers and sisters and as common children of the one Creator and Redeemer of all things?

But such questions take us to a threshold of systematic theology and constructive ethics, and that is beyond the scope of this study. They do disclose or at least intimate, however, that the ecological ambiguity of the classical Christian tradition need not be a permanent state of affairs, even when the spiritual motif has triumphed as completely as it has in this twentieth-century theological personalism: that the ecological promise of the tradition, so apparent in the minds of Irenaeus, Augustine, and Francis, and also expressed, in more limited ways, in the works of thinkers such as Thomas and Bonaventure, Luther and Calvin, need not be a chapter of the classical theological tradition which must remain forever closed.[83]

9

RETROSPECT AND PROSPECT

From Classical Christian Thought to the Bible

To understand the travail of nature in Western Christian thought—this has been our goal from the outset. To comprehend the ambiguous ecological promise of Christian theology—this has been the challenge continually before us. We have explored the classical Christian tradition in order to determine, through judiciously chosen historical investigations, what the shape of the theology of nature actually has been, to lay bare those foundations, in order to prepare the way for new theological constructions or to make it possible for theological constructions already underway to be better supported. We have been attempting to look down "into the deepest roots of Western religious sensibility and vocabulary" (Kaufman) in order to grasp the contours of traditional Christian thought about nature, as a foundational step toward a more fully developed and more fully viable Christian theology of nature in our time.

It is time to assess those findings, to highlight the overall metaphorical shape of classical Christian thought about nature and thereby to accent, in conclusion, both the ambiguity and the promise of traditional Christian theology as a basis for a contemporary theology of nature.

But this ending must also be a beginning. For we have yet to attempt to discover the deepest foundations of all, the biblical theology of nature. This whole study, in a sense, depends on that additional step. For the Bible is *the* authority, insofar as any historical document is authoritative, for every kind of Christian theology. If we do not know what the Bible says about nature, therefore, the whole enterprise of historical exploration of the classical theological tradition could easily be questioned.

This is especially true in this particular instance. For twentieth-century theology has witnessed what can only be thought of as a striking, if not always unanimous, agreement about the biblical understanding of nature. Many, if not all, biblical scholars were themselves a part of this near-consensus for several decades, although some have recently begun to reconsider the whole matter as they have been rethinking the "biblical theology movement" which flourished at mid-century and beyond.[1] That near-consensus can be identified this way, in

175

capsule form, already alluded to in chapter 1: *the Bible has to do primarily with history, not with nature.* This approach to biblical thought about nature is still enormously influential in sophisticated theological treatises, in distinguished biblical studies, and in popular articles in church magazines.

If the Bible does indeed have to do primarily with history, not with nature, what difference does it make that the classical theological tradition might have something else to say? That might be traced to any number of postbiblical influences, for example, to the so-called hellenization of Christianity. Hence, at the end of this study, we must take one more crucial step, in order to extend, if not totally to complete, the course of the argument we have been pursuing. We must ask what the implications of our findings are for envisioning a new reading of the biblical theology of nature. That step will occupy our attention in the last chapter of this study.

To set the stage for that concluding discussion in this chapter, we will review what can be called "the anthropocentric view" of the biblical theology of nature, in conjunction with our assessment of the overall shape of classical Christian thought about nature. We will see that this widely held anthropocentric view has its own assumptions, which are remarkably similar to another set of assumptions—the spiritual motif—familiar to us from our study of the classical tradition.

THE AMBIGUOUS ECOLOGICAL PROMISE
OF CLASSICAL CHRISTIAN THOUGHT:
THE HISTORY OF THE SPIRITUAL AND
ECOLOGICAL MOTIFS

We have seen that much depends on the root metaphor that mostly shapes any given theological system. We saw that Irenaeus thinks chiefly in terms of the metaphor of migration to a good land. There are signs that his thought is also influenced by the metaphor of fecundity, particularly in the context of his eschatological visions, although not exclusively there. This results in a consistent affirmation of the natural order in terms of goodness in Irenaeus's thought. Nature for him is tangibly good and ultimately significant. Irenaeus celebrates the flesh of this world, both now and in the age to come. The symmetry of Irenaeus's understanding of creation and redemption, moveover, could not be more pronounced. His vision of God's grand design begins with the moment of creation of all things—Irenaeus will not have us probing into any pretemporal divine events—and it concludes, vividly, with the renewal of all things. This symmetrical, ecological view of first things and last things, protology and eschatology, is the legacy of the dominance of the metaphor of migration to a good land in Irenaeus's thought.

For Origen, in contrast, the nature-denying metaphor of ascent is so dominant that the material order, as he depicts it, has lost much if not all of its tangible texture of goodness. For this reason, we concluded, Origen degrades the world of nature. In the same vein, also in contrast to Irenaeus, Origen presents us with an asymmetrical dialectic of creation and redemption. This is one of the legacies of the dominance of the metaphor of ascent in his thinking. Origen does attempt to affirm the goodness of the created order—we would expect nothing less, since that doctrine was for all intents and purposes a dogma of the Christian tradition, right from the start. For him, all things *are* created good; although even this doctrine, in his thought, has at most a kind of marginal efficacy. But for Origen all things are *not* saved at the very end. Only spiritual creatures remain. The material order, therefore, has no permanent goodness in the greater scheme of things, as does the spiritual order. It is, for Origen, as if the material order were a stage—a punishing, frequently hostile arena at that—which collapses into nothingness once the primary drama of salvation of the spiritual creatures has run its course.

Sum. of Augustine's thought, over the course of his life, covers a spectrum that is at early
Aug. once more radical in its degradation of nature than Origen's negative schema Aug,
and yet richer in its affirmation of nature than Irenaeus's positive schema. His Late
thought represents a kind of microcosm of the possibilities latent in classical Aug,
Christian thought about nature. He begins with a Manichean vision of the world, which is thoroughly dominated by the metaphor of ascent. Then, for many complex and interrelated reasons, ranging from his existential quest to his biblical studies, his theology shifts more and more to the point where the metaphor of migration to the good land dominates his thinking; this undergirds his mature interest in historical categories. As this shift occurs—we have left open the question which comes first—another shift, of equal importance, is also underway: the emergence of the influence of the metaphor of fecundity, in conjunction with the influence of the metaphor of migration to a good land.

What was for Irenaeus mainly an eschatological vision of overflowing goodness is developed by Augustine into a universal principle for interpreting the whole divine economy in its fullness. For Augustine, the whole creation is brought into being by God as a realm of blessing and divine glory; it is sustained as such; and it is consummated as such. His mature view of creation and redemption, accordingly, is symmetrical,[2] as Irenaeus's was, yet it is more richly symmetrical than Irenaeus's. Augustine celebrates the world of the flesh, in this sense, more fully than Irenaeus, since he finds a way, under the aegis of the metaphor of fecundity, to show how all things, the creatures of nature as well as human creatures, have their own integrity, their own value, their own necessary place in the greater history of the created order. Such thoughts are evident but remain mainly underdeveloped in Irenaeus's theology. In this sense, Augustine's thought represents the flowering of the ecological promise of classical Christian theology.

Sum. of St. Francis

What Augustine wrote with words, Francis wrote with his own life history. If Augustine's thought represents the flowering of the ecological promise of classical Christian thought, Francis's life story represents the flowering of the ecological promise of the classical Christian ethos. The mind and life of Francis are shaped, as Augustine's vision was, by the metaphor of migration to a good land and the metaphor of fecundity. Francis climbs the mountain of God's creation in order to stand in universal solidarity with all God's creatures, both in this world and in the world to come, for which he so passionately yearns. Then he descends, as he perceived God's love always to be overflowing, in order to embrace all the creatures of God, not only the specially elected and specially blessed human creatures. His view of creation and redemption, moreover, appears as a matter of course to be symmetrical, as was Augustine's and Irenaeus's: Francis follows the overflowing goodness of God, as the humble servant of God, into every corner of the creation. And he evidently awaits an eschatological world which he believes will also be blessed with the fullness and the glory of all God's transfigured creatures, material and spiritual.

Of the medieval thinkers we studied, Francis is an isolated figure. His sensibility for nature clearly places him far apart from the sense of alienation from nature that pervaded the early Middle Ages. He also stands apart from the theoretical expressions of that alienation, as for example in the schema of John the Scot in the ninth century, who more or less reproduces the system of Origen. But Francis also stands apart from what we can think of as the theological mainstream of the later Middle Ages, represented in our explorations by the Aristotelian synthesis of Thomas Aquinas, on the one hand, and by the Platonizing visions of Bonaventure and Dante, on the other.

Sum. of Aquinas Bonaventure Dante

In the thought of Thomas, Bonaventure, and Dante, the metaphor of ascent once again assumes a dominant position, a certain relative dominance. This is the significance of the thoroughgoing influence that the hierarchical categories of Dionysius the Areopagite exercised variously in the schemata of Thomas, Bonaventure, and Dante. Each of these writers shapes his thought according to a hierarchical vision, predicated on a teleology of ascent. Thus while we do meet the theme of overflowing goodness in the constructions of Thomas, Bonaventure, and Dante, familiar to us from Augustine's thought, that theme is subordinated to a dialectic shaped by the metaphor of ascent, rather than by the metaphor of migration to a good land which predominated in Augustine's thought. The influence of the latter metaphor tends to fade from the center of these medieval theological constructions, if it does not disappear altogether. As

a result, Thomas, Bonaventure, and Dante present us with an asymmetrical dia- ✳
lectic of creation and redemption, as Origen did, and as Augustine did not.
God is the Creator of all things, but not the redeemer of all things. Overflowing
goodness is a reality, but it is finally delimited and reduced by the ascent of the
spiritual creatures to the good.

When all has been said, Thomas, Bonaventure, and Dante leave us with an
eschatological vision of God, the angels, and the body of redeemed humans
transfixed above in eternal glory. We see here no tangible signs of the gloriously
full and abundant vision of the new heavens and the new earth, a vision that
variously but powerfully inspired the minds of Irenaeus, Augustine, and Francis. For all the beautiful images of God that Bonaventure can detect in the created order, for example, he finally shows us an eschatological world akin to
Thomas's—and Origen's—where the biophysical world has been largely abne-
gated. His view of creation and redemption is thus markedly asymmetrical,
ironically perhaps, given his self-conscious interest in the theme of fecundity.
Much the same can be said of Thomas and Dante. In the constructions of these
three thinkers the ecological ambiguity of classical Christian thought about nature comes to the fore in a pronounced way. They affirm the goodness of the
whole created order, on the one hand (Bonaventure more convincingly than the
other two), yet they finally reject that theme in the context of their doctrine of
redemption, on the other hand.

With Luther and Calvin we witness a certain theological realignment. They
self-consciously reject the idea of ascent to God as it was bequeathed to them by
the later Middle Ages. For them, the center of theological reflection must focus
on the descent of God to his creation. They find it accordingly congenial to
think of nature as "the mask of God" or as "the theater of God's glory." They
highlight the immanence of the descending God of grace throughout nature.
These affirmations have a tonality, moreover, that resonates with the expressions of faith characteristic of Irenaeus, Augustine, and Francis. The influence
of the metaphor of fecundity is therefore apparent in the Reformers' thought,
especially in Luther's theology. The latter envisions a Creator who is creatively
and powerfully "pouring" himself in, with, and under all things. Luther also
has a strong sense of the solidarity between humans and other creatures, both in
this life and in the life to come. In addition, both Luther and Calvin articulate a
profound sense of wonder before the mysteries and miracles of nature and the
conviction tht one day all things will be made new; although, again, of the two
Luther presents the more convincing statement of the matter.

All the same, the Reformers are preoccupied with soteriological issues—
issues pertaining to human salvation. This anthropocentric-soteriological
concern, we suggested, is the center of their thought, whereas the other em-

phases, pertaining to God's creative providence in nature and human solidarity with nature, lie more at the circumference of their thinking, however vivid those elements can sometimes be. The Reformers, moreover, never really self-consciously draw together those circumferential and central elements in any explicit, systematic way. Creation and redemption are significant givens in their thought; and they are symmetrically delineated. But human redemption tends to assume the position of central importance, mainly because of the attention they devote to it, in their particular polemical situation.

By the time of Kant, and in succeeding generations of theologians influenced by him, the anthropocentric-soteriological center of the Reformer's thought would become, more or less, the singular point of theological reflection. The theology of creation in the meantime, strongly attested in the circumferential regions of the Reformers' thought, would be deemphasized—even stripped away—by post-Kantian theologians in favor of what from the perspective of the preceding tradition must be viewed as a more narrow theanthropology. In the thought of Kant and Ritschl, in particular, we see the influence of the metaphor of ascent reasserting itself in tangible ways. Ritschl said, for example, that "man rising above nature" to commune with God is the central point of his theology. Correspondingly, the metaphor of migration to a good land would, as a matter of course, fade from significance in the thought of Kant and Ritschl. The land or nature really has no substantive place in their thought.

This set the stage for the emergence of Karl Barth's thought. He is dependent on the Kantian tradition and behind that, of course, on Reformation thought. But the roots of his theology, in this respect, go much deeper. He has sometimes been described as the Protestant Thomas Aquinas. In light of the findings of this study, ironically perhaps, we can now say that the likeness is substantive as well as formal. Barth's approach to the theology of nature is in many ways akin to Thomas's (which may help to explain why his theology has been of such great interest to some Roman Catholics). In Barth we meet the muted emphasis on the overflowing goodness of God, as we did in Thomas; to this degree the metaphor of fecundity is still effectual in his thinking. Yet Barth develops a dialectic of creation and redemption, again akin to Thomas's, which portrays the chief end of all things as human salvation. In this sense, from the beginning of his thought (the Word and election) to the end (redemption), the metaphor of ascent dominates Barth's reflection. This is Barth's "theanthropology." This is the meaning of his central theme, "the humanity of God." This also, more particularly, is the legacy of the Reformation tradition's preoccupation with human redemption, as it was shaped by Kantian thinking. In addition, once again akin to Thomas, Barth so accents the transcendence of God and humanity over nature that as a result the theme of the overflowing goodness of God manifest in nature is further circumscribed to the point where it is left with only a certain formal or abstract meaning in his thought. Notwithstanding his lengthy exegesis of Genesis 1, and his attention, in this context, to all the creatures of God, Barth is clearly preoccupied with—not to say fixated on—the story of the human creature, from the beginning to the end of the divine economy. His theology of nature is thus predominantly shaped, as Thomas's was, by the metaphor of ascent. The influence of the metaphor of migration to a good land is minimal; at times, as in his doctrine of election, it is altogether absent. Barth presents us accordingly, as Thomas did, with an asymmetrical doctrine of creation and redemption.

If Barth's approach to the theology of nature is reminiscent of Thomas's, albeit in a post-Reformation, post-Kantian form, Teilhard de Chardin's approach to the theology of nature is reminiscent of Bonaventure's, albeit in a post-Leibnitzian, post-Darwinian form. One can instructively recall here Bonaventure's rich picture of the overflowing goodness of God and the universal return of the whole scale of being, proclaiming the Creator at every level, to unity with God above. This vision can be taken to be the traditional theological roots of Teilhard's thought. Many of the features we saw in Bonaventure's synthesis are evident in Teilhard's vision, above all its hierarchical character, predicated on the metaphor of ascent.

Teilhard presents us with a vision of spirit, when all has been said, rising and unifying itself above and beyond the material order. The whole divine economy, indeed, is for Teilhard one universal ascent of spirit, over vast epochs of time. The material order for him *is* shaped by overflowing goodness, as it was for Bonaventure. Yet, again akin to Bonaventure, Teilhard subordinates the metaphor of fecundity to the metaphor of ascent. Hence the vast biophysical order for Teilhard is in fact a colossal kind of stage—or a constellation of stages, teleologically ordered—whose purpose it is to produce a final unified world of pure spirit. Like Barth, and before him Thomas, Bonaventure, and Origen, Teilhard presents us with an asymmetrical view of creation and redemption. In his schema, only "the within" of the many is saved. The material "without" is more or less abrogated.[3] Accordingly, Teilhard likes to think self-consciously in terms of a "personalizing universe." Further, since for Teilhard the material order is essentially that which is left behind in the evolutionary ascent of the spiritual, it is not surprising to see him interpreting the human relationship to nature, as Barth does, chiefly in terms of domination, mastery, and human transformation. This is the practical legacy of the dominance of the metaphor of ascent in his thought.

As we survey the whole course of classical Christian thought about nature, as it is known to us in these several instances, we can speak of a struggle in the Christian mind between the metaphor of ascent, on the one hand, and the metaphor of migration to a good land, on the other. The metaphor of fecundity, in the context of such an imaginative flux, is positioned in the middle.

If the metaphor of ascent is dominant, then the metaphor of fecundity—insofar as it is influential—will be systematically subordinated to the metaphor of ascent. Categorically, the overflowing goodness of God will be viewed as the first stage in a universal divine economy whose final goal is the ascent of the spiritual creatures alone to union with God.

If, on the other hand, the metaphor of migration to a good land is dominant, then the metaphor of fecundity may be fittingly conjoined with it and thereafter have the effect of expanding and developing the theme of the land as a place of blessing.

The persistence of either one of these trends in the imagination produces the two motifs to which we have often referred, the spiritual motif and the ecological motif. The struggle within the Christian mind is in this respect essentially the struggle between the spiritual and the ecological motifs.

For the sake of further clarification, it may be helpful to note here at this culminating point in our discussion that the influence of each of the root metaphors—when it has been dominant outside the classical tradition—whose history we have been following can give shape, and in fact has given shape at various points, to a heterodox extreme. These extremes hover at the edge of classical Christian thought but by definition are not found as such within the pale of the normative tradition.

We have seen how the metaphor of *ascent* can lead to a thoroughgoing religio-metaphysical *dualism*, as in Gnosticism. Here the material world is envisioned as a vast prison, not in any sense a place of blessing, to which the only appropriate response will be the desire to escape: to rise to the highest levels of true being, far above the evils of nature.

Another option, which is visible in Stoicism and in some forms of Romanticism, is for the metaphor of *fecundity* to be employed more or less exclusively. This can lead to the extreme of *monism* or pantheism. Here God and humanity are, as it were, swallowed up in nature now understood as *natura naturans*.

Finally, it is possible for the metaphor of migration to a good land to be employed in such a way that the end result is *secularism*. This happened, as we saw, as Western culture was developed more and more apart from the symbolic and normative influences of Christianity. In its classical setting, as it shapes Western theology at various points, the metaphor of migration to a good land always results in a theology where the land or the earth is understood to be divinely given and given concomitantly within certain comprehensive divine prerogatives. This is the legitimate traditional basis for the contemporary theological reflection about "responsible stewardship." Within the imaginative energies of the metaphor of migration to a good land, in other words, the themes of divine grace and divine command are always implied. On the other hand, in anti-

Christian or post-Christian contexts where the lordship of God and his goodness is no longer affirmed or taken seriously, the land or the earth can be viewed as a mere object, whose only purpose is to be available for exploitation and satisfaction of human need, greed, or pleasure. Anyone familiar with the history of technological innovation in the modern West will be aware of the sad result of this story, when human mastery over nature—now outside a defining theological framework—was championed merely for the sake of exploitation and self-aggrandizement, either by individuals or by groups.

In this connection it is interesting to observe that the metaphor of fecundity seems to have functioned, throughout the history of Christian thought about nature, as a corrective imaginative energy that has helped to hold the influence of both the metaphor of ascent and the metaphor of migration to a good land firmly within the orthodox mainstream. On the one hand, the metaphor of fecundity, conjoined with and subordinated to the metaphor of ascent, has kept the latter from shifting too far (even in Origen's thought) toward dualism. On the other hand, the metaphor of fecundity, conjoined with and interpretive of the metaphor of migration to a good land, has kept the influence of the latter from leaning too much toward the side of secularism. If, in other words, someone seriously and passionately believes that "the earth is the Lord's and the fullness thereof," then it will be difficult for that believer to interpret the earth either as a prison or as a mere object intended solely for human exploitation.

But such considerations already begin to take us to the edge of constructive theological reflection. Our purpose here rather has been to further clarify the historical trends we have been examining by identifying certain limits of those trends.

In conclusion, the classical theological tradition in the West must be judged to be less than ecologically promising at many points, insofar as it has been shaped by the metaphor of ascent, that is, when it has been construed in terms of the spiritual motif. But we must also acknowledge the ecological promise of the tradition—which more than a few contemporary interpreters of the tradition have failed to see. This comes to the fore under the aegis of the metaphor of migration to a good land and the metaphor of fecundity. That promise is especially striking when those two metaphors are regularly conjoined with one another in the form of the ecological motif of the tradition.

TOWARD A NEW READING OF THE BIBLICAL THEOLOGY OF NATURE: BEYOND THE CLAIMS OF THE SPIRITUAL MOTIF

The anthropocentric understanding of nature in biblical thought was well-summarized by G. W. H. Lampe, in a paper read at the Faith and Order Commission of the World Council of Churches in 1964.[4] This paper is representative of a wide range of scholarly opinion about nature in the Scriptures, including the positions of G. Ernest Wright[5] and Gerhard von Rad[6] in Old Testament studies, and Rudolf Bultmann and many of his well-known pupils in New Testament studies.[7]

Lampe deals first with the Old Testament understanding of creation. He tells us that the views of the Hebrew writers are in a sense wholly anthropocentric. "Man stands at the centre of the whole picture," he explains, "and the rest of the animate and inanimate world is seen as a kind of backcloth for the drama of human history." Even more:

> What we ourselves call "nature" derives its significance from the activity within it of mankind and, in particular, of the chosen people of God. In this sense, what we call "the natural order" revolves around man as the central point and focus which gives meaning to the whole.[8]

Hebrew attention to God the Creator, he asserts, is logically and theologically dependent on the experience of redemption, that is, the experience of divine election, manifested primarily in the deliverance from Egypt and the covenant of Sinai.[9] God's revelation to Israel came primarily to Israel in terms of election, covenant, and the manifestation of judgment and salvation in the events of the national history, not through the natural order. Hence the world of nature and indeed the creation as a whole was viewed as a stage for God's dealing with humanity or, more particularly, with Israel:

> Therefore, when we say that the Old Testament view of creation is man-centered, we mean, not that man as such occupies a position of supreme importance in the universe, but that man in his relation to God, or rather God in his dealings with man, is at the centre. The story of creation forms a setting of the stage for the history of God's activity towards mankind, and in the first place towards those whom he calls to be a peculiar people to himself and a royal priesthood.[10]

Given the centrality of human history in its thought and life, moreover, Israel regularly viewed "nature cults" as an enemy. Worship of nature or the "deified forces of nature" was viewed as a turning away from the fundamental belief that it is by God's uttered Word that all things come into being and upon his will and purpose that they depend. Also worship of nature, or the deified forces of nature, denies the human creature's proper role in nature—to have dominion over the earth.[11]

Lampe further observes that those in the Hebrew tradition who stood within God's covenant and acknowledged him as the Lord of history could then view the natural order as pointing to its maker and can affirm it as good. Indeed he traces a kind of progressive knowledge of God:

> In light of their conviction that God revealed himself in the mighty acts at the beginning and in the whole subsequent course of their history, Israel came to believe

that God who thus disclosed himself in the history of this one nation must be the sovereign Lord of all the peoples in the world. The Lord of Israel was found to be the only God. Moreover, through knowing God to be the author of redemption and of the covenant which made Israel a people dedicated to his service, they came to the belief that the God who sustained and renewed their life and restored what has been overthrown must also be the original source of all life. [12]

He also points out that the Old Testament humanity and nature are bound together so that when humans sin that disruption carries over, as it were, into the world of nature.

When Lampe turns to consider the prophetic and apocalyptic contributions to the Old Testament understanding of nature he notes that their picture of the redeemed future of the people of God includes a renewal of the whole creation. [13] But here he takes pains to stress again the anthropocentric character of this promised renewal:

> The transformation of the lower creation, as this is imagined by the prophets, is not the completion of a natural process of development. It is not a perfecting of the lower creation for its own sake. It is the accompaniment and the extension, or perhaps the projection on to the wider screen of the whole of heaven and earth, of the redemption of God's people and the consequent transformation of the human situation. [14]

It is hard to say, he adds, how much the prophetic language about the transformation of the animals is to be regarded as "poetical fancy," akin to the calls of the psalmist to the floods to clap their hands. But this is sure, he concludes: "the *eschaton* involves all of God's world, but it does so because a transformed world is included in the realization of God's creative and redemptive purpose for his people." [15]

Lampe argues that the New Testament understanding of the created order is very much akin to the Old Testament approach. "Above all," he tells us, "the created universe is still seen in the New Testament as the setting for God's dealings with mankind." [16] Yet the New Testament picture of creation is anthropocentric in a new sense. Its center and focus is Christ, and "the new man in Christ, that is the renewed people of God who are the body of Christ." The New Testament, moreover, discloses a progressive movement of thought, similar to that of the Old Testament, in Lampe's view: first the experience of the lordship of Christ, then the experience of his lordship over the nations, finally the attribution to him of lordship over the whole creation, from beginning to end: "As the goal of creation he must also be the origin of creation, since the end is the fulfillment of God's purpose in the beginning. He is alpha and omega." [17] The very New Testament term for creation (*ktisis*), Lampe maintains, often refers to the human creature alone. Indeed, he allows that perhaps Barth was correct in his *Shorter Commentary on Romans* when he maintained that this focus on humanity is "the primary meaning [of *ktisis*] in the new Testament and that only secondarily is it extended to refer to the animals and inanimate nature which were created for man's sake."[18]

Lampe refers to Paul's vision of the groaning of the whole creation in this connection, but he insists that "whatever he [Paul] has to say about the creation as a whole is incidental to his praises of God's work in [human] redemption."[19] It may be, Lampe suggests, that the whole creation is included in the New Testament expectation of the end times because the hope of the re-creation of the human body leads naturally to the idea of the re-creation of the natural order of which it forms a part.[20] Paul's allusion to the groaning of the whole creation, in any case, Lampe regards as "a kind of cosmic extension or projection of the conscious expectation of mankind."[21] This is also true, he holds, regarding one of the most widely discussed New Testament texts in this connection, Col. 1:15ff., where the writer depicts Christ as the firstborn of the creation and as reconciling all things, visible and invisible. "What is chiefly in mind" in this passage, Lampe tells us, "is God's action in rescuing us from the authority of darkness and transferring us into the kingdom of Christ in whom we have the deliverance which is the forgiveness of sins. This renewal of sinful man in Christ is primary; from this point the writer looks back, as it were, to the original creation."[22] In other words, the writer of the letter to the Colossians asserts that Christ, who is the originator of the new creation through his resurrection, is the originator also of the original creation of which this is the fulfillment.[23]

Lampe summarizes his argument this way:

> In the Old Testament nature forms the setting for the drama of man's creation and redemption, and it is itself involved in man's fortunes as the drama unfolds, just as the scenery of a play has to be changed. So also in Paul's thought [and in the letter to the Colossians] the whole creation is the stage and scene of man's adoption into sonship and it is involved in man's transformation since man is both a physical being himself and also the head of creation.[24]

Although Lampe does not deal with questions of historical development at length in his short article, the anthropocentric interpretation of the biblical theology of nature which he essentially reproduces here actually does presuppose a dialectical theory of historical development, which has a familiar Hegelian structure: thesis, antithesis, and synthesis. This is worth noting here not because Hegelian thought is self-evidently true or false, nor because somehow it is possible to write history without presuppositions: but precisely because it does demonstrate that the anthropocentric view has its own set of presuppositions which like all others employed in historical study must be tested in terms of their helpfulness in interpreting the historical data.

G. Ernest Wright, for one, is aware that he is employing such dialectical categories. He even refers to Hegel's interpretation of nature in the ancient Near East with approval.[25] The thesis, in Wright's schema, is ancient Near Eastern polytheism, with its virtual identification of God's activity with the processes of nature. The antithesis is the emergence of Israel's historical faith: "While living in the world of natural religion, they [the Israelites] focused their attention not on nature and the gods of nature, but on the God who had revealed himself in an extraordinary series of historical events."[26] The synthesis is the projection of the power of the Lord of history, who was discerned as all-powerful there, back into the world of nature: "This meant that nature could not be left to the prerogatives of the pagan Baal. The epithets and functions of this Canaanite god of the storm were taken over for Yahweh."[27] Nature according to Wright was viewed by Israel as a stage for history: "Nature was not an independent object nor the kingdom of powers to be worshipped; it was instead a handmaiden, a servant of history."[28]

A similar, if not so self-conscious, set of presuppositions about historical development can be found in the works of Rudolf Bultmann. Here the thesis once more is a culture dominated by religions of nature (Hellenistic); the antithesis is a religion of historical existence (Christian, and to a certain extent, Gnostic); and the synthesis is a religion of history which sees that nature is a stage God rules for the sake of his history with humanity (Christian).[29] This is how Bultmann describes the theology of nature in the Old Testament; but what he says in this context also represents the way he approaches nature in the New Testament:

> Man is a creature. But this does not mean that he is just a part of nature or its processes. He is not a part of the objective world, but stands over against it. This aspect of human nature is never a problem in the Old Testament as it is with the Cynics, the Stoics, and the Epicureans.

> For the Old Testament the world is the field of man's experience, the stage on which his work and destiny are played out. Man is not interpreted in light of the world, but the world in light of man.

> If the world as nature is the sphere of God's sovereignty and the stage for man's labors and the working out of his destiny, that means that in the last resort it is regarded as history, rather than nature. The real sphere where God rules is in history.[30]

Again, the point of this discussion of historical development here is not that this particular set of presuppositions is necessarily something pernicious or, for that matter, that it is necessarily helpful in interpreting the historical data. The point here is rather that this dialectic *is* presupposed by the anthropocentric view of the biblical theology of nature. A different set of presuppositions presumably would call forth a different interpretation of the data. The question, then, is one of the adequacy of presuppositions, not whether the interpreter can live without them.

At the same time, it is instructive to view that set of presuppositions in its own historical context, and to consider what we might learn from some form-critical analysis. When we do, it becomes apparent that the presuppositions of the anthropocentric view of the biblical theology of nature are remarkably similar, formally speaking, to what we have called in this study the spiritual motif of Western theology. From Origen to Ritschl, from the early Augustine to Kant, from Thomas and Bonaventure to Barth and Teilhard de Chardin, the theme of humanity rising above nature in order to enter into communion with God has been much in evidence in Western theology. This in essence is the sustained influence of the metaphor of ascent. Indeed, in some of the historical examples of theologies shaped by this spiritual motif which we have examined, we have witnessed the projection of precisely the kind of dialectic that the anthropocentric view attributes to biblical theology.

Thomas, for example, presents us with this universal kind of reflective schema: creation or the divine moment of overflowing goodness (thesis); redemption or the divine moment of calling humanity out of this world to the beatific vision above (antithesis); and sanctification or the use by humans of the things of this world (by reason) and of supernatural things, especially the sacraments (by faith), in order to ascend to God above (synthesis). For Thomas, in modern terms, nature is the context in which the history of salvation emerges and nature is then made the servant of that salvation history. This is not to suggest that a G. W. H. Lampe or a G. Ernest Wright or a Rudolf Bultmann have been directly influenced by Thomas, or that their own theologies are somehow in substantive agreement with his. It is rather to observe that the presuppositions of the anthropocentric view of the biblical theology of nature are indeed formally similar to the spiritual motif of theological reflection about nature in the West.

A number of questions arise, then. What if we were to experiment with our biblical interpretation? What if we were self-consciously to set aside the spiritual motif of Western theology as the formative reflective matrix for our interpretive principles and to put in its place the ecological motif? What if we were to think in terms of the metaphor of migration to a good land and the metaphor of fecundity whenever possible, rather than in terms of the metaphor of ascent, as we approached the biblical materials? What picture of the biblical theology of nature might such a set of presuppositions call forth from the data?

10

A NEW OPTION
IN BIBLICAL INTERPRETATION

An Ecological Reading of Biblical Theology

Is it true that "man stands at the center of the whole picture" for the Old Testament, and that "the rest of the animate and inanimate world is seen as a kind of backcloth for the drama of human history?" Is nature, according to the Old Testament, merely the stage for God's dealings within human history? Does the new Testament presuppose, likewise, that "the whole creation is the stage and scene of man's adoption into sonship" and nothing more? Proponents of the widely held anthropocentric understanding of biblical thought about nature generally answer each of these questions in the affirmative.

Another reading of biblical theology is possible. The data of biblical theology, in both the Old and New Testaments, allow us—if they do not indubitably require us—to develop an ecological reading of biblical faith, focusing on the themes now familiar to us, especially in the works of Irenaeus and Augustine, as integrating constructs: the land of promise and the fecundity of God. The narratives of biblical experience can be read primarily in terms of the metaphor of migration to a good land and the metaphor of fecundity (the ecological motif), wherever that seems feasible, rather than primarily in terms of the metaphor of ascent (spiritual motif).

We are considering this alternative approach to the biblical theology of nature, it should be noted, *not because the protagonists of the anthropocentric approach employ historical categories* in their biblical interpretation, *but because they generally employ those historical categories too narrowly,* in terms of human history over against nature. In order to discern the ecological promise of biblical theology we can and should hold firm to historical categories in our interpretation. These categories can be taken to be self-authenticating, in line with the assumptions of the overwhelming majority of scholarly interpreters of the Bible in the last one hundred years. But it is possible to construe those historical categories more generously and more universally than the proponents of the anthropocentric approach have generally done: not in terms of God and humanity over against nature, but in terms of God and humanity with nature. This could be called an ecological hermeneutic of history. It is predicated on the assumption of a divine and human concomitance with nature, rather than a divine and human disjunction from nature.

OLD TESTAMENT THEMES: THE ECOLOGICAL MOTIF

This ecological approach to the biblical theology of nature surely can only be schematized here.[1] But enough can be said to show the possibilities inherent in the interpretive perspective it presupposes. We can fittingly begin by considering the theology of the land in the Old Testament and the related Hebraic theme, the divine blessing or the divine fecundity.

The Centrality of the Land and the Blessing of Yahweh

In the first six books of the Bible, Gerhard von Rad has observed, "there is probably no more important idea than that expressed in terms of the land promised and later granted by Yahweh, an idea found in all the sources, and indeed in every part of each of them."[2] The centrality of this theme in the life of ancient Israel has not always been recognized, particularly by Christian scholars, who have tended to approach these materials with different concerns, more particularly by those scholars who have sought to accent the mighty acts of God in human history, as over against the activity of God in nature. "Preoccupation with existentialist *decisions* and transforming *events*," Walter Brueggemann writes, with an only thinly veiled reference to Rudoph Bultmann and to G. Ernest Wright, "has distracted us from seeing that this God is committed to this land and that his promise for his people is always his land."[3]

Brueggemann himself has attempted to redress this imbalance with a study of this theme which has far-reaching implications for our understanding of biblical theology in general and of the biblical theology of nature in particular. "It will no longer do to talk about Yahweh and his people," he states categorically, "but we must speak about Yahweh and his people *and his land.*"[4] Land, he tells us, is a central—if not *the* central—theme of biblical faith.[5] That theme, according to Brueggemann, is most fully expressed in the writings of the Deuteronomic tradition, which we will review here, following Brueggemann's presentation. The land for Deuteronomy, above all, is regarded as a *gift*. It does not belong to Israel. It is not Israel's property. Yahweh alone provides the land of promise: "The land is mine and you are but aliens who have become my tenants" (Lev. 25:23). "Israel cannot and does not and need not secure its existence for itself," Brueggemann explains. "It is done for it by the same One who gave manna, quail, and water. Only now the gifts are enduring and not so precarious."[6] Indeed, this is a most gifted land:

> It fulfills every anticipation of the wilderness: water-brooks, fountains, springs; food-wheat, barley, wines, fig trees, pomegranates, olives, honey; plenty—

without scarcity . . . , without lack . . . ; minerals—iron, copper. The water does not need to come at the last moment, incredibly from a rock. Its sources are visible and reliable.

Brueggemann observes that this motif stands as a protest against "an existentialism that interprets the Bible only for dramatic events, finding meaning in intrusive, disruptive discontinuities."[7] On the contrary, he points out, the Deuteronomist can readily believe that Yahweh "grants his people enduring, wholesome continuities, enjoying the span of planting and harvest, participating in the full cycle of life with the earth—and all under Yahweh's attentive, protective eyes. Truly said that this is a fertility God."[8] This point bears emphasis.

First, it is striking because this theme is lifted up by a Hebraic tradition, whose theological roots lie in the northern kingdom, where the struggle with Baal—the "god of nature"—was much more intense than it was in the south. The Deuteronomic tradition and the tradition of the Eloist, which also has roots in the north, apparently did not preface their epic accounts of Israel's history with any creation narrative, as the Yahwist had done or as the Priestly writers were later to do. Still, Deuteronomy celebrates the divine giftedness of the land in such lavish terms.

This theme of the fertility of Yahweh's land is also striking, second, because it suggests a biblical concern which, once it has been seen in the sources, is clearly essential but which has not always been commented on or even observed by students of Israel's faith. This is the notion of divine blessing.

Claus Westermann has studied this theme with suggestive results. Westermann argues that two themes run side by side in the Bible, neither one of which may be properly subsumed under, or derived from, the other: deliverance and blessing.[9] He explains:

> When the Bible speaks of God's contact with mankind, his blessing is there alongside his deliverance. History comes into being only when both are there together. The element of contingency, essential to historical events, enters the biblical history through the presence together of God's activity in saving and blessing and through their effect on each other.[10]

In Westermann's view, therefore, "no concept of history that excludes or ignores God's activity in the world of nature can adequately reflect what occurs in the Old Testament between God and his people."[11] The theme of blessing, he observes, is lifted up most fully by Deuteronomy. Here, he points out, deliverance and blessing are self-consciously linked together, with the latter seen as something conditional, predicated on Israel's faithfulness to its covenant obligations.[12]

Each of these elements, the land-fertility theme and the blessing theme, also

has a more generalized signification in Israel's faith, which is surely worth underlining here. This is Israel's broader sense for the land and the earth as a
whole: a confession of its goodness, as in the cadence of Genesis 1, "and God
saw that it was good"; and a celebration of its rich diversity, as in some of the
Psalms, "the earth is the Lord's and the fullness thereof" (Ps. 24:1). Likewise, as
Israel could not think of itself apart from the land, neither could it finally think
of human creatures in general apart from the earth: Adam is of the earth (*adamah*). Behind this lies the notion that the very self, the *nephesh*, permeates the
land.[13]

Election Faith and Creation Faith

If the land and the earth are evidently so central in Israel's faith, what are we
to make of the claims of those who adhere to the anthropocentric approach to
Israel's theology of nature, such as von Rad, Wright, and Lampe, who maintain that concern with nature is a "secondary addition" to Israel's—alleged
—primary faith in human redemption? This judgment is, as it were, the
hermeneutical keystone of the anthropocentric approach. Therefore it merits
our most careful scrutiny.

That there was a flowering of "creation theology" in monarchical and postmonarchical Israel seems clear. But the question is, what was the significance of
that flowering? It is possible to argue—and this takes into account the findings
of Brueggemann and Westermann in a way which the anthropocentric approach
cannot—that the flowering of creation theology in Israel's monarchical and
postmonarchical periods does not signal an influx of "alien elements" from the
"nature religions" of Canaan, as the protagonists of the anthropocentric approach either argue or tend to assume, but that it represents *an exfoliation of
themes already given in Israel's premonarchical confessions* in a culture permeated by
Canaanite imagery and mythology. Israel's originating "election faith," in other
words, need not be viewed, as the proponents of the anthropocentric approach
do, solely as a faith in God's relationship with the people of Israel. That election
faith, as we will now see, can be interpreted, first and foremost, as an encounter
with the "Lord of heaven and earth" who graciously delivers the people and calls
them to obedience.

Walther Zimmerli has highlighted Exod. 20:2 as a key text that can help us
understand Israel's originating experience of God: "I am Yahweh, your God,
who led you out of the land of Egypt, out of the house of slavery." Zimmerli
stresses that Israel "did not derive her knowledge of God from a general belief in
creation." On the contrary, he comments, Israel "is conscious that this knowledge is founded on a quite concrete encounter in the course of her history. It is
not the general which stands at the beginning; rather it is the concrete encoun-

ter. Israel knows her God from the experience of being saved."[14] Gerhard von Rad makes much the same kind of statement: "The Yahwistic faith of the Old Testament is based on the notion of election and therefore primarily concerned with redemption."[15] Such statements can be affirmed as generalizations.[16] But they require explication, lest their level of generalization obscure some of the particulars of Israel's originating election faith. For election was *not an idea* as such in the mind of Israel; it was, as Zimmerli suggests, an encounter, *an experience of Yahweh* delivering his people. Israel's election faith was radically *theocentric* in this experiential, nonspeculative sense.[17] Ludwig Koehler comes close to the heart of the matter, therefore, when he observes that "the one fundamental statement in the theology of the Old Testament is this: God is ruling Lord. . . . Everything else derives from it. . . ."[18] Hence we must ask *who* elected Israel in the events of the Exodus and Sinai, if we are to grasp fully the particularities of Israel's originating election faith.

Who is the Lord who graciously chose Israel from among the nations, who delivered the people from bondage in Egypt and revealed his will to them at Sinai? Clearly he is not a deity who has no power. On the contrary, he is a Lord of great might who can work his way in the waters of the Reed Sea and feed his people in the wilderness. He is probably not at first thought of reflectively as "the Creator," as he is when the psalmist says, "Our help is in the name of the Lord who made heaven and earth" (Ps. 124:8). For Israel apparently had no independent "doctrine of creation" in its earliest history, as von Rad emphasizes.[19]

But neither, it seems, did Israel have an "independent doctrine of redemption" in its earliest period. What captivated the minds of the people in the nation's earliest epoch was the experience of deliverance from bondage by Yahweh the Lord. Still, that very experience of lordship contained within it a vital faith in Yahweh's unsurpassable power in, with, and under the world of nature and a conviction that Yahweh knows how to exercise his power in order to achieve his gracious purposes. If Yahweh was not yet "the Creator," then he surely was "the Lord of heaven and earth."

George Landes has observed in this connection that the Hebrews spoke of their God as *Elohim* from earliest times. This is a plural of majesty, totally derived from the divine name *El*, "whose common Semitic root meaning seems to refer to power, preeminently creation power."[20] Further, he points out, "even when they came to venerate Yahweh, whom without hesitation or scruple they identified with El and Elohim, the function of divine creatorship was not lost. Indeed the very name Yahweh, which is probably to be derived from the initial verb form of a cultic epithet referring to *El* as the one who brings into existence all that exists, must have been understood in connection with creator work."

Landes even goes so far as to suggest that a self-conscious creation faith was given in Israel's experience along with that election faith:

> When Israel told her story of the Exodus, the wilderness wandering, and the giving of the land, Yahweh's delivering actions were not depicted involving only historical actors and political events, but also with the use of the forces and elements of nature—in the plagues against the Egyptian oppressors, in the parting of the waters of the Reed Sea, in the sending of the manna, quails, and water, in separating the waters of the Jordan, in making the sun and moon stand still for Joshua. Only the Creator-God, the One who made the sea, the animals, the heavenly bodies and all of nature, could employ these elements in his redemptive work.[21]

That may be. But, as we await further historical research on the subject,[22] it seems sufficient, given the data at hand, to speak of Yahweh in this context as Lord of heaven and earth, rather than "the Creator," since the latter implies a kind of reflective explication of the "compact symbolism" (Eric Voeglin) of Israel's experience which may not have been widely developed in its earliest epoch. In any case, it is safe to say and necessary to say that the Lord who delivered Israel was the Lord of heaven and earth, not just the Lord of human history.[23]

It is important to keep this point in mind when we consider the much-discussed conflict between Yahweh and Baal. Often, as in the writings of Wright, that conflict is portrayed as the struggle of the God of history, Yahweh, against the god of nature, Baal. But, in fact, it seems much more appropriate to say that this is a struggle between the Lord of nature and history, on the one hand, and a deity of natural cycles, on the other hand.

Moreover, in Israel's earliest experience of Yahweh, he is a deity who is *like* Baal in significant ways. Yahweh seems to have a relationship with nature which is totally theocentric, as it were, which is established by Yahweh solely in order to exercise his power, not just to deliver his people in their distress. The Lord who works his will majestically in the Reed Sea, in other words, and who manifests himself with great glory at Sinai, is the very God who, in addition, more generally works majestically in nature and manifests his glory throughout the earth.

This is the picture given us in Psalm 29 for example. This celebration of Yahweh's power in the thunderstorm and the mountains is sometimes discounted because it is said to be a "Canaanite Psalm" borrowed by Israel. Rather, as careful analysis by Arthur Weiser has shown, the psalm—especially in view of its link (in v. 8) with the Sinai tradition—must be seen as a composition arising within the tradition of Israel, however much it may employ Canaanite forms.[24] When Israel praised God from the very beginning, it praised him among many other reasons for the majestic power that he exercises throughout the world of nature.

In contrast to later Christian theology, Israel's originating election faith does not seem to be readily divisible into two forms, "faith in the Redeemer" and "faith in the Creator."[25] It is first of all faith in Yahweh as gracious Lord of power. Yahweh first and foremost is Israel's "king" in this dynamic and encompassing sense. He is known as the majestic Ruler, whose governance extends everywhere in the world of Israel's experience, to the overwhelming phenomena of nature, as well as to the intimacies of personal life and the structures of social existence. He is known as the one who by his mercy and power and understanding brings order out of chaos, freedom out of oppression, forgiveness out of guilt, and who will always bring his powerful judgment to bear on those who transgress his holy will.[26]

This theocentric-ecological approach to Israel's originating election faith appears to be at least as viable as the narrower interpretation taken for granted by the proponents of the anthropocentric approach to the Old Testament theology of nature. The theocentric-ecological perspective is large enough, as it were, not only to comprehend their—legitimate—concern with the centrality of human salvation in the originating faith experience of Israel, but other elements as well, particularly those pertaining to Yahweh's activity in nature. This approach also has the advantage of helping to explain why Israel's originating election faith could so easily come to focus in significant ways on the land theme and the blessing theme highlighted so suggestively by Brueggemann and Westermann respectively. Right from the beginning it appears that Israel understood God to be the Lord of heaven and earth. So it was fitting, then, to see the same God so intimately bound up with the land in particular and the earth in general. Likewise, it was fitting to see the identity of the redeemed nation, and indeed the identity of all peoples everywhere, as rooted in the land and the earth at large. Israel's originating election faith, we can then say, was the fertile soil which made possible the later flowering of its creation theology, alongside of and interpenetrating its redemption theology, in monarchical and postmonarchical times.

The proponents of the anthropocentric view of the Old Testament theology of nature do not have the hermeneutic flexibility at their disposal to interpret convincingly that flowering of creation theology in its native setting. This is apparently because their approach is essentially shaped by the metaphor of ascent (the spiritual motif), which as we have frequently seen is opposed to the metaphor of fecundity. The proponents of this view are forced by their own presuppositions, to downplay the land and the fecundity themes in Old Testament theology, to consider them secondary or even alien elements, when the historical data themselves seem to suggest something else.

It is better that we should self-consciously employ the root metaphors of migration to a good land and fecundity (the ecological motif) as a framework of interpretation: for we have seen how these two root metaphors can indeed coalesce harmoniously. Both are nature-affirming metaphors, in contrast to the metaphor of ascent (the spiritual motif), which is essentially a nature-denying metaphor. The use of these metaphors in a self-conscious way offers the prospect of allowing us to do much more justice to the complex data of Old Testament faith than does a single-minded reliance on the metaphor of ascent.

We have a way therefore to understand the flowering of creation theology in monarchical times and beyond, which more nearly seems to reflect the data themselves than the anthropocentric approach allows us to do. As the prominent positioning of the creation narrative of Genesis 1 shows, and as the uninhibited celebration of the whole creation in many of the Psalms also indicates, ancient Israel itself apparently did not understand the flowering of creation theology in its own history as something essentially alien to the people's originating election faith.[27] It is now time to consider that flowering in a summary fashion.

The Flowering of Creation Faith

By the time of the Priestly writer, the power of Yahweh in and over all things began to be thought of much more self-consciously than in Psalm 29, in terms of his creative Word, although that motif was attested widely in earlier expressions of Israel's faith, as in Psalm 29 itself (for example, v. 5: "the voice of the Lord breaks the cedars . . ."). In the Priestly account of creation, the writer draws on the image of "the Word" to display both the effortlessness of Yahweh's creative activity and its orderliness. The latter is a theme that comes to full expression here, although the notion of Yahweh as a God of understanding had never really been absent, as for example in Jer. 12:12: "It is he who made the earth by his power, who established the world by his wisdom, and by his understanding stretched out the heavens." The Priestly writer shows us Yahweh positing the world almost as a master builder, not only without effort but thoughtfully, carefully, and with aesthetic delight in the works of his own hands.[28]

With the Priestly writer in Genesis 1, the fecundity theme reaches one of its most striking Old Testament expressions, a kind of self-conscious architectonic fascination with the earth and its fullness, from the lights in the firmament of the heavens to the swarms of living creatures in the waters, from the plants and trees bearing fruit to the beasts of the earth and the cattle and everything that creeps upon the ground. One might hear resonances of this fascination with the fullness of the earth, albeit in a more compact form, in the earlier inaugural vision of Isaiah: "Holy, holy, holy is the Lord of hosts; the whole earth is full of his glory" (Isa. 6:3).

Many of the Psalms, especially the so-called Royal Psalms, likewise depict the universal reign of Yahweh as they envision the ascent of the divine king to the heavenly throne so that he might rule over all things and fill all things with his glory (for example, Psalms 47 and 97). "The ascension of God and his universal rule coincide," Edward Schillebeeckx explains. "In this capacity he is called *'elyon*, the Most High, either above all other gods (who later become *'elohim* and angels, Ps. 97:9) or above the political and military authorities on earth (Ps. 47:9). As *'elyon*, God is ruler of the world who must be praised for his majesty."[29] Ps. 97:1–5 is a characteristic statement of these songs of praise:

> The Lord reigns; let the earth rejoice; let the many coastlands be glad! Clouds and thick darkness are around him; righteousness and justice are the foundation of his throne. . . . His lightenings lighten the world; the earth sees and trembles. The mountains melt like wax before the Lord, before the Lord of all the earth.

Similar meanings come to expression in a later prayer in a different context, put on the lips of King David by the Chronicler:

> Thine, O Lord, is the greatness and the power, and the glory, and the victory and the majesty; for all that is in the heavens and in the earth is thine: thine is the kingdom, O Lord, and thou art exalted as head above all (1 Chron. 29:11).

This is the fecundity theme in another vivid expression. The image of the divine ascent in this case is to be seen as a constituent element (see chap. 2, above) of the fecundity theme. Yahweh ascends as the Most High in order to rule over and to fill all things with his glory.

Other expressions of the fecundity theme depict the relationship between Yahweh and nature less in terms of luminescent architectonics and more in terms of a quality of personal care and attention for every creature, however small, however strange.[30] Thus we hear that Yahweh knows the birds of the air (Ps. 50:1), that he calls the stars by name (Isa. 40:26), that both animals and humans are in his care (Ps. 36:5), and that he feeds them all (Ps. 145:14). Yahweh commands Noah to take the animals with him, two by two, in order to keep them alive (Gen. 6:19) and, after the deluge, he makes his covenant with "all the birds and animals" (Gen. 9:10) as well as with Noah and his descendants.

But the richest expression of the fecundity theme is undoubtedly Psalm 104. This psalm combines both the architectonic vision of the Priestly writer—it can be read as a poetic commentary on the traditions brought together by the Priestly writer in Genesis 1—and the more-personalized images evident in the Psalms and elsewhere, which we have just noted. As in some of the earliest confessions of Yahweh's creativity, the psalmist here highlights the divine power in all of nature. But at the same time we meet the themes of the wisdom of the master builder and his constant care for the whole creation. This is a sampling of its twenty-five verses:

PS.
104

> Bless the Lord, O my soul! . . . Thou art clothed with honor and majesty, who coverest thyself with light as with a garment, who has stretched out the heavens like a tent, who has laid the beams of thy chambers on the waters, who makest the clouds thy chariot, who ridest on the wings of the wind. . . . Thou didst set the earth on its foundations, so that it should never be shaken. Thou didst cover it with the deep as with a garment; the waters stood above the mountains. At thy rebuke they fled. . . . The mountains rose, the valleys sank down to the place which thou didst appoint for them. . . . Thou makest springs gush forth in the valleys; they flow between the hills, they give drink to every beast of the field . . . by them the birds of the air have their habitation; they sing among the branches. From thy lofty abode thou waterest the mountains; the earth is satisfied with the fruit of thy work. Thou dost cause the grass to grow for the cattle, and plants for man to cultivate, that he may bring forth food from the earth, and wine to gladden the heart of man.

Then the psalmist surveys this whole cosmos of variegated vitality and creaturely glory and sings: "O Lord, how manifold are thy works! In wisdom thou made them all; the earth is full of thy creatures" (v. 24).[31] Sometimes the significance of this beautiful poem about Yahweh's power and wisdom in nature has been downplayed by commentators, in light of its Egyptian parallels. But it really belongs to the unfolding center of Israel's faith in Yahweh in its monarchical and postmonarchical era, as the parallel with Genesis 1 indicates.[32]

The image of Yahweh's well-ordered power in nature also brings with it an idea which we already encountered in another form in our consideration of Psalm 29. Here, again, we see that Yahweh has a relationship with nature that is radically theocentric, but in a slightly different sense: not so much in terms of his power, but more in terms of his wisdom. Yahweh is seen as structuring the cosmos not just so that he may bless human creatures but also so that he might delight in his own works: "May the glory of the Lord endure forever, may the Lord rejoice in his works" (Ps. 104:31). The same motif is also evident in the tightly written narrative of Genesis 1. As S. R. Driver has observed, a note of divine satisfaction runs through the whole Priestly narrative of creation, indicated by the repeated expression "And God saw that it was good." The formula used marks each work, says Driver, "as one corresponding to the Divine intention, perfect, as far as its nature required and permitted, complete, and the object of the Creator's approving regard and satisfaction."[33]

The obverse side of this theme is one of the least understood themes in the

Old Testament: nature's praise of Yahweh. The fullest expression of it is Psalm 148, which calls the whole creation—sun and moon, sea monsters and all depths, mountains and all hills, as well as kings of the earth and all peoples— to praise Yahweh. One can imagine that some kind of "primitive" animism or panpsychism may be implicit here, but that should not be allowed to obscure the coherent theological assumption: that the glories of nature are enjoyable and pleasing to Yahweh, just as the right kind of sacrifice is sometimes said to be pleasing to him. Yahweh is a God, indeed, who rejoices in all his works. We can therefore hear behind these exuberant texts calling nature to praise the Lord the sober but powerful cadence of Genesis 1, "and God saw that it was good."

Such is the scope of the themes of the fertile land and the good earth and its fullness as those themes took shape in Israel's monarchical and postmonarchical centuries, in continuity with the intuitions and confessions of premonarchical times. But this is not the end of the story by any means.

The Future of the Land and the Whole Creation

As the land was seen by Deuteronomy as a place of great blessing and fertility, and as the poets of Israel celebrated the manifold fecundity of Yahweh throughout the whole earth, so in times of deepest despair the prophets, and especially the apocalyptic writers, proclaimed the hope of a renewed land and indeed a universally renewed earth, often with lavish images of overflowing fecundity. If judgment was being pronounced on Israel, all the greater, according to the prophetic tradition, would be the renewal of the land when Israel's fortunes were finally restored. This theme was celebrated with rich imagery by 2 Isaiah in the exilic period. Later, in a time when the people believed that such prophetic expectations were no longer to be thought of as realizable, the growing literature of the apocalyptic writers—such as 3 Isaiah—lifted up a still-larger hope for the whole earth, totally beyond this world: a day of new heavens and new earth, when Yahweh would make not just the land of Israel, but all things new.[34]

In the vision of those apocalyptic writers who stand in continuity with the prophetic tradition, the influence of the metaphor of migration to a good land and the influence of the metaphor of fecundity fully coalesce, in terms of the eschatological vision of cosmic renewal. The land theme itself was already a fecundity theme, in a sense, insofar as the land was viewed as the place of overflowing divine blessings (Deuteronomy) and insofar as the whole earth was seen as a gloriously beautiful cosmos of exuberant vitalities (for example, Psalm 104). But the vision of seers like 3 Isaiah gives the coalescing of the two themes—land and fecundity—its most universal and unified expression.

NEW TESTAMENT THEMES: THE ECOLOGICAL MOTIF

It is possible to read much of New Testament theology as standing in continuity with the prophetic-apocalyptic tradition, and before that with the land-blessing theology of Deuteronomy and the fecundity theology of the Priestly writer and the Psalms. Here we can follow the lead of Ernst Käsemann, who memorably said that apocalyptic is the mother of all Christian theology.[35] In this sense, we can approach the New Testament as we approached the old: we can see its theology as thoroughly shaped by the ecological motif, albeit eschatologically construed, for the most part.

The Apocalyptic Proclamation of Jesus: The Renewal of the Whole Creation

Teachings of JC.

Jesus and his proclamation are to be viewed accordingly in terms of the world of apocalyptic thought for our purposes here. His apocalypticism, then, not his celebrated—and often romanticized—concern for the lilies of the field and the birds of the air, is the critical point to be underlined as we pursue the theology of nature given in his life and his teaching.

Jesus' proclamation of the kingdom of God was focused on the present as the time of the kingdom's dawning. To this extent, it surely had an anthropocentric focus since it called people to decision, as Bultmann often emphasizes. But Jesus also took for granted, as the parables of growth show, that there would be a final transformation of heaven and earth, in keeping with the prophetic-apocalyptic expectations he had inherited.[36]

Further, although scholars have long ago given up the attempt to write biographical accounts of Jesus' life or to give detailed description of his consciousness of his own vocation (due to the complexities of the data available in the New Testament), thoughtful consideration of the materials we do have, as Schillebeeckx has shown, allows us to draw some probable conclusions: Jesus in all likelihood saw himself generally and was seen by his first followers as Israel's final, eschatological prophet, whose vocation was in some sense to inaugurate the last days of the whole creation in judgment and grace.[37] Jesus' self-understanding, then, and the view of him held by his first disciples, as this image of him can be cautiously reconstructed, also has this bipolar structure akin to his proclamation of the Kingdom of God—on the one hand, present claims for discipleship in response to God's latterday acts of mercy and, on the other hand, future expectations of a universal transformation of heaven and earth.

The latter point, concerning the earth, bears underlining here since in some forms of apocalyptic thought a pronounced form of dualism was in evidence, a dualism which negated the earth as God's domain (this dualism presumably helped to pave the way for gnostic influence, after apocalytpic thought began to lose favor). "The recession towards eternity of the movement which begins in the Incarnation," W. Manson has commented on the early Christian perspective, "does not cut out the earth, or by-pass it in process, but takes the world and history up into itself." Again: "The scene of the Eschaton, the Age of Glory, is, it would seem, the world in which man's life is lived and in which Christ died and rose. New Heavens and a New Earth signify not the final destruction or displacement of the cosmos, but its renovation." Manson points out, further, that the basic passage about the Son of man in Daniel 7, on which text the New Testament hope is mainly formed, says nothing about the celestial figure there likened to a Son of man as coming back to earth; but early Christianity took this for granted.[38]

We can appropriately read the "compact symbolism" (Voeglin) of Jesus' proclamation of the kingdom of God, then, along with his evident self-understanding in particular and the Son of man imagery more generally (which was in all likelihood employed by groups of his earliest followers in response to him, if he did not employ it of himself) as being multidimensional: first in its temporal scope and second in its substantive comprehensiveness. First, temporally, the meanings given in this symbolism encompassed both the future and the present, as we have seen. Second, substantively, those meanings comprehended the fullness of the creation, not just the dimension of human affairs. Those substantive meanings were more explicit insofar as they projected a coming world-transformation; they were more implicit insofar as they presupposed the universalistic traditions of the Old Testament which we considered earlier, from the Exodus and Sinai confessions to the affirmations of Genesis 1 and Psalm 104, from the prophetic utterance of 2 Isaiah to the apocalyptic claims of writers such as 3 Isaiah.

This means that the historical Jesus, insofar as we have access to him through the faith-colored lenses of the New Testament writings, can be thought of as an ecological figure as well as an eschatological figure. As liberation theologians in recent years have sought to show that his life has meanings given in it which transcend the immediate existential dimension of personal salvation and which comprehend the world of sociopolitical reality,[39] so we may carry this unveiling of his meaning fittingly yet another step: to identify its cosmic claims and its cosmic implications. The God with whom Jesus evidently shared such intimate communion, with whom he identified himself profoundly when he called him *Abba*, was after all, in Jesus' eyes and in the eyes of Jesus' first followers, not only the God of individual souls, not only the God of historical peoples such as the Hebrews, he was also the Maker of Heaven and Earth, the gracious and powerful Creator and Consummator of the whole creation. We have this picture of the God whom Jesus calls *Abba*: he knows when a sparrow falls (Matt. 10:29) and he knows when he will bring the whole to its ending and its final fulfillment (cf. Matt. 24:36). The heavenly Father of this eschatological prophet, Jesus, is at once the Father of all things of the earth.

The Apocalyptic Theology of Paul:
The Renewal of the Whole Creation

St. Paul

We may read the theology of Paul in much the same way, as standing in continuity with the Old Testament themes we have already considered, especially as those came to expression in the final stages of the prophetic-apocalyptic tradition. This kind of approach to Paul has been developed with compelling insight by J. Christiaan Beker.[40] He highlights Romans 8, in particular, as a key to understanding the whole of Paul's theology. Here Paul speaks about the groaning of the whole creation and thereby anticipates the day of the new heavens and the new earth, familiar in apocalyptic expectation. This interpretation of Romans 8 is to be contrasted with the assumptions of the anthropocentric view of the biblical theology of nature: that the travail of creation envisioned in Romans 8 either refers chiefly to human history (Bultmann, Barth) or it is some flight of poetic fancy, related obscurely to the fact that humans have a body which is to be redeemed (Lampe).

The integrating center of Paul's apocalyptic thinking is, as Beker emphasizes, the apostle's understanding of the death and resurrection of Jesus Christ. Apocalyptic thought is here fundamentally defined by its christological focal point. Paul is not interested in speculative apocalyptic timetables. He is overwhelmingly concerned to show the particular meaning of the lordship of Jesus Christ for every concrete historical situation. It is in this context, according to Beker, that the theme of justification by faith, which looms so large in the theology of the Reformation and in the biblical interpretation of modern Protestant exegetes, has its legitimate and essential place. Still, as Beker shows, Paul *does* construe that concrete lordship of Jesus Christ apocalyptically. Paul's vision of the lordship of Christ, in this respect, comes to its most vivid expression in 1 Corinthians 15, which depicts the Lordship of Christ as serving the greater world-historical purposes of God:

> For as in Adam all die, so also in Christ shall all be made alive. But each in his own order: Christ the first fruits, then at his coming those who belong to Christ. Then comes the end, when he delivers the kingdom to God the Father after destroying every rule and every authority and power. For he must reign until he has put all his enemies under his feet. . . . When all things are subjected to him, then the Son himself will also be subjected to him who put all things under him, that God may be all in all. (1 Cor. 15:22–28)

Paul is indeed passionately concerned with the individual's faith in Christ and with the life of the church, the body of Christ, but all the more so because he is concerned to understand faith and the church as having their part in the universal history of God: "For from him and through him and to him are all things. To him be glory forever. Amen" (Rom. 11:36).[41] Paul's thought soars within, and is shaped by, his universal vision of all things, *ta panta*, under the lordship of Christ, moving toward the day of final renewal which is near at hand, when God will be all in all.

This is a way to read the theology of Paul, as we can read the proclamation of Jesus, in terms of the ecological motif: as bringing together the influence of the metaphor of migration to a good land and the metaphor of fecundity, in terms of apocalyptic expectation.

Colossians and Ephesians: The Cosmic Lordship of Christ

It is also possible to read the so-called Deutero-Pauline theology of Colossians and Ephesians in a similar way. With these epistles, to be sure, we are no longer in the context of apocalyptic thinking. Rather we are in the milieu of what has sometimes been called "monarchical" thought. The intense expectation of the future dawning of the last day in its fullness, which so captivated the minds of Jesus and Paul, has given way here to a profound, even serene, confession of the *present* rule of God and his Christ, throughout all things. Still, the impact of the theme of human rootedness in the cosmos (the land theme) and the theme of the universal divine immanence (the fecundity theme), continuous with both the Old Testament and the thought world of Jesus and Paul, is very much apparent.

As we look at Colossians and Ephesians in the second half of the first century, we enter a cultural world quite different from the prophetic-apocalyptic thought-world taken for granted a generation earlier by Jesus and Paul in their own ways. The apocalyptic manner of thinking, as Schillebeeckx frequently observes, generally was characterized by two dimensions, both of them essentially temporal: first, a heavenly world prepared in eternity, waiting to descend from its eternal locus to the earth; second, the anticipated future coming of that heavenly world.[42] So the seer of the Book of Revelation envisions (1) the Jerusalem above (2) descending to earth in the midst of a renovated creation (Rev. 21:1–4). In Asia Minor, in contrast, particularly in cities such as Colossae and Ephesus, the religious world view, although in some respects similar, was at base qualitatively different. Here the perspective—given in a vast diversity of religious expression—was mainly *spatial*, not temporal as in the prophetic-apocalyptic tradition of Judaism. Reality was generally seen as a towering hierarchy of overlapping dimensions extending from the earth upward, through many levels of "powers" or "angels," finally reaching up to the realm of the eternal heavens. In this context, as Schillebeeckx explains, first-century people of cities such as Colossae and Ephesus "were aware of a cosmic fault, a kind of catastrophe in the universe, a gulf between the higher (heavenly) and the lower (earthly) world."[43] Theirs was an existential world of radical cosmic fragmentation and pronounced cultural instability. Their quest for salvation accordingly took the form of a longing for the restoration of the unity of the cosmos by the reestablishment of spiritual linkages to the heavenly realms above. The desire to commune with the world of the powers or the angels was therefore intense on the part of many people. It comes as no surprise to learn in this connection that belief in a descending-ascending redeemer figure was a commonplace of this syncretistic culture, not, as has been sometimes assumed, a feature only of Gnosticism.[44] The idea of a redeemer figure who descends to the earthly realm and then ascends to the eternal world above was one way often chosen to see the radical fault between the two dimensions overcome.

This is the syncretistic world in which Colossians and Ephesians apparently were written—also, as we will see presently, were the Gospel of John and the Letter to the Hebrews. These Deutero-Pauline letters take many of its features for granted. But at the same time they take issue with some of its most fundamental assumptions, especially by means of their uncompromising identification of the crucified and exalted Jesus as the descending-ascending redeemer and by their subordination of all powers and angels to him in such a way as to show that he is the Lord of the fullness of finite reality. Colossians and Ephesians see the radical cosmic fault of the universe being overcome, not by the redeemer figure's removal of elect humans from the lower regions as in some Gnostic systems, but by the redeemer figure's healing of the fault by means of his filling all things with his salvific power. This cosmic restoration of unity, importantly, is inaugurated in their view by the crucifixion of the redeemer and by his calling together a new people blessed by his peace and united in him; but the scope of his redeeming work is nevertheless cosmic. It encompasses all things, *ta panta*, as we will see now as we consider each letter in turn. As we do, the more spatial conceptuality of these letters, as contrasted with the temporal prophetic-apocalyptic conceptuality of Jesus and Paul, will also be apparent.

The Letter to the Colossians has been the subject of an intense debate in recent years, above all concerning the meaning of the christological hymn in chapter one:[45]

> He is the image of the invisible God, the first-born of all creation; for in him all things were created, in heaven and on earth, visible and invisible, whether thrones or dominions or principalities or authorities—all things were created through him and for him. He is before all things, and in him all things hold together.

He is the head of the body, *the church*; he is the beginning, the first-born from the dead, that in everything he might be preeminent. For in him all the fulness of God was pleased to dwell, and through him to reconcile to himself all things, whether on earth or in heaven, making peace *by the blood of the cross*. (Col. 1:15–20)

The italicized phrases were apparently added to a hymn known to the Colossian church by the Pauline author of Colossians in order to correct what from his point of view was a one-sided emphasis on the universal lordship of the exalted Christ. The result of that emphasis, he apparently believed, was a failure on the part of some Christians to grasp the importance of the missionary function of the church and the reality of the cross as the sign of Christian existence before the final consummation. Still, we can appropriately interpret this hymn—in continuity with Paul's thought—in the sense of both/and: both cosmos and church, both exalted Lord and crucified Savior, both strophe one (on creation) and strophe two (on redemption). In contrast, the disjunctive view—either/or—championed by many who have been influenced by Bultmann, seems to be more an expression of Bultmann's presuppositions about the theology of nature than a straightforward reading of the text in its own historical context.[46]

In the Letter to the Colossians the exalted Christ is fully and explicitly identified with the Creator of all things. Paul had already accepted that identification at any early date, in his Letter to the Corinthians:

> There is one God, the Father, from whom are all things and for whom we exist, and one Lord, Jesus Christ, through whom are all things and through whom we exist. (1 Cor. 8:6)

In Philippians he refers to the power of Christ "which enables him to subject all things to himself" (3:21). In Colossians that identification is extrapolated in a way that shows that even the invisible powers of the creation were created in Christ. Then Christ himself is identified as the vital principle of the creation now, as its source of unity: "in him all things hold together" (Col. 1:17). This seems to be the writer's way of articulating Paul's theme of the reign of Christ (cf. 1 Cor. 15:25), although the apocalyptic reference to the future consummation, characteristic of Paul (cf. 1 Cor. 15:24–28), has faded into the background, if it is not totally absent.

Christ, therefore, according to Colossians, has an immanent cosmic role akin to Wisdom in Hebraic and later Jewish thought. His rule is with the Father, from beginning to end of the whole creation. He is, in this sense, the Father's creative Word (cf. John 1:1). One can envision his power and his wisdom as permeating all things, as Wisdom did in the thought of Hellenistic Judaism. We here begin to see vivid signs of the influence of the metaphor of fecundity.

The power of Christ fills all things. It overflows to all things, as it were, and thereby holds them together (Col. 1:17). "As 'image of the invisible God,'" F. W. Beare comments, "the Son is God manifest, the bearer of the might and majesty of God, the revealer and mediator of the creating and sustaining power of the Godhead in relation to the world."[47]

All things, in turn, are supple, as it were, in response to Christ's lordship. They surely are not mechanical, self-contained, eternally determined by fate— or Christ would not be their creative principle. His continuing embrace of the creation from beginning to end is depicted—compactly—by verse 16: "in him all things were created." This refers not to his agency as such at this point but to what F. W. Beare calls his "spiritual locality." Although there is no doubt whatsoever about his transcendence of all things (the term "the All" is probably avoided, in favor of "all things" because of the former's pantheistic associations, according to Beare), Christ can be thought of—precisely because he is transcendent Lord of all—in the vision of this hymn as the transcendent divine whole, which is greater than the sum of the created parts of the universe. In the thought of the hymn "all things 'stand created,'" Beare explains, "through him and for him. As they had their origin ('were created') in him, so they owe their settled state, as a created universe, to his mediation, and move toward him as toward their goal."[48]

The Letter to the Ephesians picks up and develops the same kind of themes. It depicts God having a plan or purpose—this is the "divine economy" (*oikonomia*)—for the whole universe, revealed and fulfilled in Christ: "to unite all things in him, things in heaven and things on earth" (1:10). It depicts Christ, accordingly, as descending through all levels of the universe, so that he might ascend far above the universe and then "fill all things" (4:10). Henry Chadwick has described Ephesians' image of Christ this way: "He is the linchpin of the great chain of being, transcendent over it and at the same time immanent within the whole. . . . By this language Paul [or the Pauline author of Ephesians] imports a specifically Christian content into the contemporary cosmology for which there was no more pressing question than the source of harmony in a world of diversity and freedom. That immanent power of God which providentially guides the universe is identified with Christ."[49]

The theology of Ephesians reads as if it were profoundly conversant with the syncretistic culture of the ancient Mediterranean world. It was indeed immersed in that culture, as Schillebeeckx observes: "Cosmic reconciliation consists in the fact that the division of these two halves of the world [the heavenly and the earthly] by an impregnable wall is shattered by a heavenly hero and that these worlds are reconciled: in one man, the great macrocosm. A cosmic drama on high brings redemption and salvation for men. Similar ideas were to be found throughout the ancient world."[50] Still, the contrast between the syncretistic images of the culture at large and the particularistic focus of Ephesians is just as great, for "instead of a mystical drama we have a historical crucifixion. . . ."[51]

Further, the roots of this Ephesian theology seem to be substantially nourished by underlying Old Testament traditions, even as they grow in a hellenistic environment. We can readily detect the influence of Hebrew images, especially from the Royal Psalms. In these psalms, as we have seen, we are often presented with images of Yahweh, the Most High, ascending beyond the heavens in order to establish his universal rule over all the things and to fill all things. Although that ancient Hebrew name for God, the Most High, apparently was out of favor in the times immediately before Christ,[52] it must have been an obvious connection for the writer of Ephesians to make, as Schillebeeckx observes, in order to illuminate the confession that God has visited Israel in the person of Jesus: "to use the model of Yahweh's *anabasis* and *katabasis* and to connnect the resurrection of Jesus with these Royal Psalms: the enthronement of Christ as ruler of the world, as victor over all heavenly powers."[53] This, we may observe, is the legacy of the metaphor of the land and the metaphor of fecundity; the image that "the earth is the Lord's and the fullness thereof" is given new expression in a syncretistic first-century culture.

Although Teilhard de Chardin has made much of these texts from Colossians and Ephesians, it appears that he has misinterpreted their meaning fundamentally. We see in these letters not a vision of all things moving toward Christ or being drawn to him, so that they might be united to him spiritually, in a kind of a hierarchical evolution. The picture here is quite different. Christ *is*, as Teilhard suggests, the one who is the active agent of the divine creativity—here the Pauline theme of the rule of Christ with the Father emerges once again. Christ *is* also the receptive matrix of the divine providence, as Teilhard maintains, the goal as well as the beginning of all things. But it is precisely *all things* (*ta panta*) through and in which Christ exercises his lordship and to which he extends his power to draw them to himself: all things, visible and invisible, *not* by any means just spiritual things, as Teilhard again and again suggests as he looks to the consummation of the world. For these letters, that consummation in Christ, is both visible and invisible, both material and spiritual. In this respect they preserve one of the important themes of Paul's own apocalyptic thinking. This indeed is the metaphor of fecundity that is influential in these letters, not the metaphor of ascent.

Interpreting the Universal Lordship of Christ

What we then should make of all this theologically is emphatically another question. The Pauline apocalyptic framework and the Deutero-Pauline monar-

chical framework stand in a certain tension with each other. A theological statement of the teleological agency of Christ in the whole creation would surely
have to take that tension between the future and the present into account. We
might well wish to distinguish between the *logos-asarkos* and the *logos-ensarkos*,
between the creative Word of the Father and the Word made flesh, as many
doctors of the church have done (Athanasius and Calvin, for example) in order
to make coherent theological sense out of the notion that Christ, along with the
Father, is the active principle of the whole creation from beginning to end.[54]
But such questions lie beyond the scope of this study.

Our purpose here has been to show that the lordship of Christ was readily understood in early Christianity, in nonapocalyptic as well as in apocalyptic terms,
as extending to the whole creation—powerfully, immediately, and extensively—along with Christ's lordship in the church and in human history generally. Lampe's interpretation of these majestic christological themes in terms of
anthropology alone falls far short of the mark. What they are about is revealed
in their vision of the outcome, and that is a cosmic consummation and a cosmic
dominion. Obviously, such themes *are* invoked also—perhaps primarily at
times—in order to deal with crucial anthropological and ecclesiological issues.
But their epistolary occasions and emphases should not be allowed to subtract
from their universal meaning.

It was also important for us to identify how the metaphor of migration to a
good land and the metaphor of fecundity functioned in early Christian thought,
at various points. We saw that the influences of those metaphors came together
already in the Old Testament. But here that confluence occurs in universalizing
christological context, variously adumbrated first by Jesus and Paul in apocalyptic terms, and then by Colossians and Ephesians in the monarchical mode of
thought.

The Mission of the Church and the Universal Lordship of Christ

Beyond the proclamation of Jesus, the theology of Paul, and the theology of
Colossians and Ephesians, it must be noted that much of the New Testament is
preoccupied not with these universalizing cosmic concerns, but more with the
immediate life of the church, with what happens in "the center of time." That is
the original title of a major study of Luke's writings by Hans Conzelman.[55]

The Gospel of Luke and the Book of Acts, along with writings such as 2 Peter, still hold in principle to the apocalyptic vision of "new heavens and a new
earth in which righteousness dwells" (2 Peter 3:13). But they more or less assume that that end has been postponed; they are interested chiefly in other

themes.[56] "Luke aptly uses the solution of apocalyptic postponement," Beker explains, "to concentrate on the missionary demands of the church. It is displaced, as it were, by the geographical end of the mission to the ends of the earth (Acts 1:1–8), that is, to Rome as the center of the Roman Empire (Acts 28)." Likewise in Mark and Matthew the emphasis seems to rest most fully on the present lordship of the exalted Christ in the life of the church.[57] The creation and consummation of the world, and the rule of the Father with the exalted Christ between those times, are the limits and the context within which the Synoptic Gospels focus their concerns about the life and mission of the church as it lives, sacramentally and sacrificially, under the lordship of Christ and as it is empowered by the Spirit.[58] So the Gospel of Matthew ends memorably with the risen Lord's words to his disciples: "All authority in heaven and on earth has been given to me. Go therefore and make disciples of all nations, baptizing them in the name of the Father and of the Son and of the Holy Spirit, teaching them to observe all that I have commanded you; and lo, I am with you always, even to the close of the age" (Matt. 28:18ff).

This emphasis on the center of time and the mission of the church surely bears underlining in a context where we have explored the Pauline and Deutero-Pauline teachings about the cosmic lordship of Christ as much as we have. Any attempt to build a theology of nature on a biblical basis must take into account this widespread New Testament interest—very much present in Paul, Colossians, and Ephesians too—in the life of the church and its mission. There can be no shortcuts to a theology of nature, which can legitimately claim New Testament warrant, which at the same time explicitly or implicitly encourage the church today to avoid the life of self-sacrifice (Mark), to avoid the discipline of piety and learning about the righteous demands of Jesus (Matthew), or to avoid the life of mercy offered to the poor and the public witness of the gospel, empowered by the Spirit (Luke-Acts). No biblically legitimate creation theology or cosmic Christology will prompt its adherents to forsake the life and mission of the people of God under the cross.

At the same time, we also need to hear the witness of Paul in this respect. Paul was no less passionately concerned with the mission of the church and the theology of the cross than any other early Christian writer. But it may just be the case that his apocalyptic theology, predicated on his vision of the eschatological triumph of God, might be best suited, of all the other New Testament theological "trajectories" or traditions which we know, to offer us the framework to preserve the integrity of the church's life and mission, in all its aspects, in a world dominated by a spirit of alienation from nature and the threat of universal death. As Beker observes:

The collapse of apocalypticism into Christology or anthropology causes a disorientation of Paul's proclamation of the resurrection, which has grave consequences for Paul's thought. Individualism and spiritualization—if not ecclesiastical self-aggrandizement—are the inevitable results of such an interpretation. Moreover, the neglect of Paul's apocalyptic thought leads to a neglect of his "ecological" and cosmic themes and so to a misconstrual of both his anthropology and his ecclesiology, for the somatic worldly component of his anthropology cannot be spiritualized away. . . . Paul's church is not an aggregate of justified sinners or a sacramental institute or a means for private self-sanctification but the avante-garde of the new creation in a hostile world, creating beachheads in this world of God's dawning new world and yearning for the day of God's visible Lordship over his creation.[59]

Further:

Because the church is not an elite body separated from a doomed world, but a community placed in the midst of the cosmic community of creation, its task is not merely to win souls but to bear the burdens of creation to which it not only belongs, but to which it must also bear witness.[60]

The outpouring of the Spirit, in other words, and the mission of the church in the midst of the nations, is at once an eschatological witness on behalf of the whole creation, as it groans in travail. The mission of the church among the nations can only be pursued in light of Paul's theology if is predicated on the divine promise for the whole earth and the hope of that day of universal fulfillment of all things.

It would seem possible to interpret the widely attested New Testament concern with "the middle of time" in the context of a more fully developed and self-consciously construed apocalyptic kind of thinking as in Paul without doing violence to the theological focus on life in the middle of time, yet at the same time allowing that focus to be charged circumferentially as it probably was in practice in early Christianity with the universal meanings of an apocalyptic vision of all things familiar to us in Paul's theology.

AMBIGUITY IN THE NEW TESTAMENT WITNESS: THE INFLUENCE OF THE SPIRITUAL MOTIF

Even this ecological reading of the New Testament theology of nature, however, has its limits. This portrayal of the mind of early Christianity, wherein we see the influence of the metaphor of migration to a good land and the metaphor of fecundity—the ecological motif—coming to expression in one grand vision of the ultimate realization of the divine purpose for all things, in the coming new heavens and the new earth, or in the integration and unification of the whole creation under the cosmic rule of Christ, does not represent the dominant thinking of all those New Testament writings which portray Christ in a cosmic context.

Once again we encounter the ambiguity of Christian thought about nature. Once again we encounter thought patterns that have been shaped, it seems, by the metaphor of ascent, that is, by the spiritual motif. We see this happening in two forms, the one is oriented on first things, protology, the other is oriented on last things, eschatology.

First Things: Christ and His Church According to John   *Protology*

The Gospel of John presents us in many ways with a protological vision of salvation, which is shaped by the metaphor of ascent. It may be true that "the Johannine trajectory" brings together a variety of theological expressions, including the antignostic emphasis on the flesh, which is characteristic of 1 John, and the earth-affirming apocalyptic vision of the Seer who composed the Book of Revelation.[61] Even so, the force of the Fourth Gospel itself, notwithstanding redactions that may point in a different direction, comes down heavily on the side of a kind of thinking which seems to be thoroughly influenced by what we have called in this study the spiritual motif.

In the Gospel of John the apocalyptic framework of Paul and many other first generation Christians has virtually disappeared altogether. For John, the future becomes chiefly an unfolding of what has already happened in the Christ-event.[62] The identity of the Jesus of history with the risen Christ as Beker points out, is asserted in such a way by John that Christ is portrayed as "divinity in the flesh" on earth.[63] Likewise, "the resurrection of Christ is interpreted as the exaltation of Christ, that is, as his present lordship in heaven and his present activity in the Spirit, but in such a way that it is no longer connected with the imminent resurrection of the dead and the cosmic renewal of creation."[64]

Schillebeeckx has argued, with some force, that the theological background of these protological perceptions of Christ lies not in Gnosticism (which he believes was probably a later phenomenon that drew on many of the same traditions the Johannine school took for granted)[65] or hellenistic syncretism as such (which we considered in our discussion of Colossians and Ephesians), but in certain heterodox Jewish circles in Palestine, "marginal communities with a Jewish spirituality within the Jewish syncretism of the first century A.D."[66] After 2 Isaiah, he explains, "the theme of an eschatological prophet like Moses developed in early Judaism into a 'Moses mysticism,' a phenomenon which is also called 'Sinaitism' in exegetical literature."[67] This literature views the death of Moses as an exaltation, an *anabasis*, as an ascension to heaven, just as the death of Jesus is for John. Further, the same thought-world presents us with the image of Moses, thus glorified, mediating access to the vision of God, through the grace of a new birth. This Moses mysticism was apparently strong among the first-century Samaritan communities in Palestine, moreover, so much so that scholars speak not only of Sinaitism, but also of Samaritanism.[68] This connection with the Samaritans is striking, because many exegetes also see strong ties between the Johannine community and the Samaritan mission, to which the name of Stephen is usually related.[69]

With this heterodox theological background in view, the centrality of the Johannine model of descent (*katabasis*) and ascent (*anabasis*) for depicting the protological Christ comes into sharper focus.[70] This is particularly the case with regard to its dominant spatial aspects, already familiar to us from our consideration of the not dissimilar, albeit Hellenistic, cultural background of Colossians and Ephesians. For John, Jesus "comes from above" (John 3:31). This is perhaps John's single most important theological construct. On the basis of this protological vision John then "ascribes to the earthly Jesus characteristics which elsewhere in the New Testament are assigned to the risen Christ or are put on the lips of the earthly Jesus by the exalted Christ."[71] In this context we meet a striking image of "the Son of Man," not found in the other Gospels, "a descending and ascending Son of Man."[72] This and other evidence which points in the same direction prompts Schillebeeckx to observe that the Fourth Gospel reinterprets all primitive Christian traditions regarding Jesus in terms of the *katabasis-anabasis* model,[73] which the Johannine community found in its heterodox Jewish traditions in Palestine.

To this degree we can observe a formal similarity between the Deutero-Pauline materials we have already considered and the theology of the Fourth Gospel. But Colossians and Ephesians are concerned with the unity of all things, with Christ descending, as Ephesians has it, so that he might ascend and fill all things. The Gospel of John shows us a different kind of descent, not so much to the end that Christ might fill all things—although all things were created in him, according to John—but more so that he might ascend and carry those whom he has called away from "this world," which is consistently thought of in John in negative, even hostile, terms.

John often seems to suggest that salvation means the removal of believers from this world to some higher heavenly sphere, to the beginning when the Word alone was with God. This is suggested by John's Christology. So Käsemann writes that the "Incarnation in John does not mean complete, total entry into the earth, into human existence, but rather the encounter between the heavenly and the earthly."[74] Indeed, it is not just an encounter, it is an encounter which is part of a divine movement, from heaven to earth and then back again. Again, as Käsemann says: "Jesus is pictured as the one who is on the way and this picture is repeated on a higher level, since his way on earth is simultaneously his way back from earth via the Cross to heaven. The dimension of the past is retained only insofar as it points forward to his presence; all of the future is nothing but the glorified extension and repetition of his presence. . . . The sole theme of history is the *praesentia Christi*. Whatever else may happen on earth is only scenery and props for this theme."[75]

Many interpreters have noticed in this connection that the famous celebration of love as *agape* in the Fourth Gospel seems to focus chiefly on the life of the Christian community, that is, those people who have the new "heavenly" identity in Christ, as contrasted to those who identity is rooted in "the world."[76] "Love in John," Käsemann comments, "is inseparably bound to the event of the Word, to speaking the Word on the one hand and to receiving and preserving it on the other. This is just as true for the Father's relationship to the Son as it is for the relation of both to the community."[77] Notwithstanding the oft-quoted words of John 3:16, about God loving the world (which Käsemann takes to be a traditional formula used for the purpose of glorifying Christ),[78] the disciples in John's view go out into a world which "at its core is an alien realm . . . just as according to John, Jesus himself has been an alien sojourner in this world below."[79] The world for John is "the object of mission only insofar as it is necessary to gather the elect."[80] Käsemann concludes, "the notion of the liberated community takes the place of the new world."[81]

However we may finally wish to read the Fourth Gospel in detail, it seems clear that John represents a tradition that was predicated on a vision of Christ and the community of Christ first and foremost and that John has very little positive regard for human history in general or for the biophysical world as such. "A characteristic trait of our Gospel," Käsemann comments, "is the tension between universalism and predestination. Jesus is designated 'savior of the world,' who has come not to judge, but to save the world, yet it is only believers, the elect, his own, who are in fact saved."[82] Further: "The possibilities inherent in apocalypticism no longer have validity, even if traditional formulae and a few phrases here and there are distant reminders of it. . . . [John] recognizes the new creation only in the form of reborn disciples. They, however, no longer represent the earthly but the heavenly world and therefore are not the representatives of a restored creation."[83]

It is almost as if the dimensions of human history and the universal world of nature did not enter into John's mind, except in terms of the negative connotations associated with his image of "the world." No wonder that Rudolf Bultmann—who himself has a theology that is predicated on the theme of disjunction from nature, which for him is the realm of "objectification"—has seized upon the Gospel of John as the most profound expression of the early Christian message.[84]

Hebrews

Last Things: Christ and His Church
According to Hebrews —eschatology

The Letter to the Hebrews, although different from the Fourth Gospel in many ways, seems to move in the same orbit of thought as far as the theology of the divine economy is concerned. Here, however, the accent is not on protology, but eschatology. We are presented with a vision of a final fulfillment which is totally spiritual (with the possible exception of the resurrected bodies of the saints). Hebrews refers, to be sure, to the Word as the principle of all creation (11:3), as does John. But that theme should be seen in terms of its theological *telos*: the eschatological salvation of those who believe. The primary focus of Hebrews is on the church, the people of God, as the end and goal of the whole creation.

Some commentators have argued that in Hebrews the eschatological expectation of Christ's return—the horizontal-temporal line—disappears and the Hellenistic pattern of a world of different stories—the vertical-spatial line—takes its place. While it seems clear that spatial categories do assume a special importance for Hebrews, as for the Gospel of John, the former is distinct from the latter in this respect as in others: the writer of Hebrews accents both the temporal and the spatial dimensions. "In Hebrews," Schillebeeckx explains, "the Greek view of the world is incorporated into the Jewish conception of time, which runs between proton and eschaton. Time and space are essential to the author's view of the world, just as they are in the Jewish apocalyptic of the two ages. Thus the author of Hebrews looks both upwards and forwards into the future."[85]

Still, Hebrews was written in a context of first-century religious syncretism, already familiar to us from our consideration of Colossians and Ephesians, on the one hand, and the Johannine tradition on the other. And this world view has shaped the theology of the letter markedly. The author may well have been a diaspora Jew from Alexandria before his conversion to Christianity, as Schillebeeckx suggests, one who was "familiar with a number of Greek ideas which were current in Egypt at the time, but particularly drawn to Jewish spirituality, above all the so-called 'Sinaitic spirituality' of the less 'orthodox' or mystical trends within early Judaism in the second half of the first century A.D."[86] The vision of Hebrews, like that of the Johannine tradition, is accordingly shaped by the model of the descending and ascending redeemer figure, although it is construed more eschatologically than in the Fourth Gospel.

For Hebrews, faith is the "conviction of things not seen" (11:1–4). This faith envisions a high priest, Christ, in a heavenly sanctuary above, which has been built by God (8:1–2). The high priest, the letter informs us, came to earth in order to abolish the old sacrificial rites here on earth and to open the door to the sanctuary of God in heaven. This is where he went, then, as he "passed through the heavens" (4:14).

The famous narrative about the Old Testament saints in Hebrews 11 has the purpose accordingly of displaying the aforementioned heavenly tabernacle as the place of salvation. The Old Testament saints all were "strangers and pilgrims on the earth" (11:13). They all looked forward, as Abraham did, "to the city which has foundations, whose builder and maker is God" (11:10; cf. 11:16; 13:14). The author uses the language of pilgrimage to a good land, but he leaves no doubt that he attaches a purely spiritual meaning to that image: those saints, he tells us, looked for "a better country, that is, a heavenly one" (11:16). Nor are we left in doubt about which metaphor is shaping his vision of salvation. It is the metaphor of ascent and as always it shapes a vision that ends with a purely spiritual world:

> But you have come to Mount Zion and to the city of the living God, the heavenly Jerusalem, and to innumerable angels in festal gathering, and to the assembly of the first-born who are enrolled in heaven, and to a judge who is God of all, and to the spirits of the just men made perfect. (12:22–23)

The Pauline vision of the Christian standing in solidarity with the whole creation at the very end is thereby eclipsed. Likewise for the image of the Book of Revelation which shows us the New Jerusalem coming down from heaven to be established on a glorified earth. In contrast, we are left with a vision of "men and angels" communing with God and Christ above, in the ethereal regions at the top of Mount Zion.

The church on earth, in the meantime, occupies a kind of middle position in the "vestibule" of heaven, that is, the sphere of the angels (cf. Heb. 8:5–6). "Thus Jesus," Schillebeeckx comments, "who is exalted to God, is not just the minister in the heavenly sanctuary, where God dwells with his attendants and where from now on Jesus always intercedes for us." He is also the church's minister in the heavenly vestibule, where the church dwells. This contrasts sharply with Rev. 21:2—and indeed with the fundamental assumptions of both Jesus and Paul, as we have interpreted them here. What Hebrews calls "the city of the living God" (Heb. 12:22) or the "heavenly Jerusalem" (Heb. 12:22) does *not* descend to earth. Rather the church ascends: "Christians are already taken above into the heavenly Jerusalem, the vestibule."[87]

The universal economy of God, according to the Fourth Gospel and Hebrews, is clearly shaped by the metaphor of ascent. The metaphor of migration to a good land and the metaphor of fecundity have receded into the shadows. The spiritual motif has triumphed over the ecological motif.

A QUESTION FOR INTERPRETERS:
THE TRAVAIL OF NATURE AT THE
END OF ALL THINGS

Which way of thinking should be the norm in our interpretation of the Scriptures, and which should be interpreted in light of that norm? Should we interpret the whole movement of Hebraic experience and much of early Christian experience—especially the faith of Paul, Colossians, and Ephesians—in terms of the Gospel of John and the Letter to the Hebrews, or vice versa?

This question concretely highlights both the ambiguity and the promise of Christian thought about nature. This question shows concisely why it is appropriate to think of the travail of nature in Christian theology. Our review of Christian thought about nature, now carried through in this preliminary way to the Scriptures themselves, confronts us with this fundamental interpretive question on whose answer the whole Christian theology of nature hinges. John or Paul? Spiritual motif or ecological motif? Which one offers us the normative interpretive framework for our reading of the Scriptures?[88]

But the question can be sharpened still further. It comes to its most dramatic expression in the context of eschatology, heightened and highlighted so much in early Christianity. Here we see the travail of nature most vividly—at the end of all things.

This is the question before us, as it arises in the context of eschatology. What is the grand design of God? What is the goal of the divine economy? Is the divine economy asymmetrical or symmetrical?

The classical theological tradition is of a divided mind in this connection, as we have seen. At times the spiritual motif is dominant, at other times the ecological motif. To read the classical theological tradition, then, as a guide to the Bible is to move from one ambiguous promise to another.

The Spiritual Motif as an Interpretive Framework

Origen depicted the goal of all things as the return of the fallen rational spirits to perfect union with God. Thomas, after having affirmed the goodness of creation in a way that Origen never did, nevertheless asserted asymmetrically that the end (*telos*) of the whole creation is chiefly the beatitude of the saints (and the angels) alone in heaven with God. Bonaventure and Dante offer us similar images of the *telos* of all things. In our time, Karl Barth, with his radically protological vision of God's election of Jesus Christ and the people of Christ in eternity—formally reminiscent of the Fourth Gospel—and Teilhard de Chardin, with his radically eschatological vision of the union of humanity with Christ in a world of pure, divinized spirit—formally reminiscent of the Letter to the Hebrews—stand in the same tradition. This is the tradition of the spiritual motif.

Standing within that tradition the biblical interpreter would as a matter of course gravitate to the Gospel of John and the Letter to the Hebrews as the purest theological expression of what the rest of the Bible is attempting to say.

The Ecological Motif as an Interpretive Framework

There is, we have seen, another way of reading the Scriptures, through the eyes of thinkers and seers such as Irenaeus, the mature Augustine, Francis, and, to a significant degree, Luther and Calvin. Standing in this theological tradition with one's thought shaped primarily not by the metaphor of ascent but primarily by the metaphor of migration to a good land and the metaphor of fecundity, one will as a matter of course look to the dynamics of Hebraic faith, to the proclamation of Jesus, and to the theology of Paul and the Pauline authors of Colossians and Ephesians as the normative biblical tradition. For this way of thinking, when all has been said, the divine economy is, at once, the divine ecology. Creation and redemption, redemption and creation, are symmetrical, held in unity by the overarching and undergirding power and wisdom of God's gracious lordship. "For from him and through him and to him are all things," says the apostle. "To him be glory for ever. Amen" (Rom. 11:36). According to this vision of reality, all things are created good by God and cared for by God in proper proportion. All things are sustained by God and governed by God, even while—within the human environment—they are being ravaged by sin. All things finally shall be consummated in glory by God, when every creature shall enjoy the glorious liberty of the children of God.

The Future of Nature

This is the question, then, more than any other, that this study bequeaths to all who wish to learn about, and to learn from, the New Testament theology of nature in particular and the biblical-classical theology of nature in general.

Is the final aim of God, in his governance of all things, to bring into being at the very end a glorified kingdom of spirits alone who, thus united with God, may contemplate him in perfect bliss, while as a precondition of their ecstasy all the other creatures of nature must be left by God to fall away into eternal oblivion?

Or is the final aim of God, in his governance of all things, to communicate his life to another in a way which calls forth at the very end new heavens and a new earth in which righteousness dwells, a transfigured cosmos where peace is universally established between all creatures at last, in the midst of which is situated a glorious city of resurrected saints who dwell in justice, blessed with all the resplendent fullness of the earth, and who continually call upon all creatures to join with them in their joyful praise of the one who is all in all?

With the question posed this way, a large majority of modern biblical scholars would self-consciously, or as a matter of course, choose the first option—the way of the Fourth Gospel and the Letter to the Hebrews—in keeping with their interpretive assumptions which have been so thoroughly shaped by the spiritual motif.

Our review of classical Christian thought about nature highlights a fresh interpretive possibility: an ecological reading of biblical faith. If contemporary Christian theologians took that kind of approach to biblical theology seriously, instructed along the way by teachers such as Irenaeus, Augustine, and Francis, that could lead to a new birth of Christian thought about nature. The travail of nature in Christian theology could come to a blessed ending.

What about the feminist interpretation of nature?

NOTES

CHAPTER 1

1. See, for example, Alan W. Watts, *Nature, Man and Woman* (New York: Pantheon Books, 1958; reissued, Vintage Books, 1970); and Duane Elgin, *Voluntary Simplicity: Toward A Way of Life That is Outwardly Simple, Inwardly Rich* (New York: William Morrow, 1981), especially chap. 10.

2. See especially Vine Deloria, Jr., *God is Red* (New York: Grosset & Dunlap, 1973).

3. Ian L. McHarg, "The Place of Nature in the City of Man," *Western Man and Environmental Ethics: Attitudes Toward Nature and Technology*, ed. Ian G. Barbour (Reading, Mass.: Addison-Wesley, 1973), 175.

4. Lynn White, Jr., "The Historical Roots of Our Ecologic Crisis," *Science* 155 (1967): 1203–7.

5. Ibid., 30, 27.

6. McHarg, "Place of Nature," 175. McHarg mentions Duns Scotus, John Scotus Erigena, Francis of Assisi, Wordsworth, Goethe, Thoreau, G. M. Hopkins, and "the nineteenth and twentieth century naturalists." For a similar but much more extensive critique and rejection of the classical Western theological tradition, see Watts, *Nature, Man and Woman*, chap. 1.

7. This estimate is also shared by the exponents of the so-called Deep Ecology philosophy, a newly developing expression of metaphysical naturalism. See George Sessions, "Shallow and Deep Ecology: A Review of the Philosophical Literature," in *Ecological Consciousness: Essays from the Earthday X Colloquium*, University of Denver, 21–24 April 1980, ed. Robert C. Schultz, Jr., and Donald Hughes (Washington, D.C.: University Press of America, 1981), chap. 19.

8. Rosemary Radford Ruether, *Liberation Theology: Human Hope Confronts Christian History and American Power* (New York: Paulist Press, 1972), 115. See also idem, *New Woman/New Earth: Sexist Ideologies and Human Liberation* (New York: Seabury Press, 1975).

9. Ruether, *Liberation Theology*, 115.

10. Ibid.

11. Ibid., 122.

12. Ludwig Feuerbach, *The Essence of Christianity*, trans. George Eliot (New York: Harper & Row, 1957), 287.

13. Deloria, *God is Red*, 70.

14. See Thomas Sieger Derr, "Religion's Responsibility for the Ecological Crisis: An Argument Run Amok," *Worldview* 18:1 (January 1975): 39–45.

15. Thomas Sieger Derr, *Ecology and Human Need* (Philadelphia: Westminster Press, 1975). For a review of this work, see H. Paul Santmire, "Ecology and Ethical Ecumenics," *Anglican Theological Review* 59:1 (January 1977): 98–101.

16. Derr, *Ecology and Human Need*, 17.

17. See, for example, Mary Evelyn Jegen and Bruno U. Manno, eds., *The Earth is the Lord's: Essays on Stewardship* (New York: Paulist Press, 1978).

18. Derr, *Ecology and Human Need*, 7.

19. Ibid., 23.

20. Many twentieth-century theologians work essentially within the framework of theological anthropocentrism or, more precisely, with the presupposition that theology is most properly thought of as the-anthropology, the doctrine of God and humanity. "The-anthropology" is a term given currency by Karl Barth, whose thought we will examine in chapter 8. Here our concern is chiefly with those theologians who have addressed themselves to ecological issues with these the-anthropocentric assumptions. They are numerous, and many of them have made contributions in the context of discussions within the World Council of Churches. Of these, the following can be mentioned: G. W. H. Lampe, "The New Testament Doctrine of *Ktisis*," *Scottish Journal of Theology* 17:4 (December 1964): 449–62; also published in German, in *Kerygma und Dogma* 11:1 (January 1965): 21–32, discussed below, chap. 9 (175–88); Paul Evdokimov, "Nature," *Scottish Journal of Theology* 18:1 (March 1965): 1–22; and Hendrikus Berkof, "God in Nature and History," reprinted in C. T. McIntire, ed., *God, History, and Historians: Modern Christian Views of History* (New York: Oxford University Press, 1977). Side by side with these representative works, we can also mention the monograph of Paulos Gregorios, *The Human Presence: An Orthodox View of Nature* (Geneva: World Council of Churches, 1978), which has been given the place of a major World Council of Churches study book, as was Derr's. Gregorios's approach differs widely from Derr's in many respects, but as its title indicates his argument finally comes to rest within the same orbit. For Gregorios, both ontologically and ethically speaking, nature stands or falls with "the human presence." Gregorios does not transcend anthropocentrism; rather he celebrates it and attempts to define all ecological issues from the perspective of his particular—Eastern—the-anthropology.

21. See n. 14.

22. Gordon Kaufman, "The Concept of Nature: A Problem for Theology," *Harvard Theological Review* 65 (1972): 337–66.

23. Ibid., 350.

24. Ibid., 351.

25. Ibid., 312.

26. Ibid., 352.

27. Ibid., 353.

28. Ibid., 355.

29. See esp. John Cobb, *Is It Too Late? A Theology of Ecology* (Beverly Hills, Calif.: Bruce Books, 1972); Charles Birch, "Nature, Humanity and God in Ecological Perspective," in *Faith and Science in an Unjust World: Report of the World Council of Churches'*

Conference on Faith, Science and the Future, ed. Roger L. Shinn (Philadelphia: Fortress Press, 1980), vol. 1, pp. 62–73; idem, "Creation, Technology and Human Survival: Called to Replenish the Earth," *Ecumenical Review* 28:1 (January 1976), 66–79; idem, *Nature and God* (Philadelphia: Westminster Press, 1965). Cobb's work has been subjected to careful scrutiny by Claude Stewart, "Nature In Grace: A Study in the Theology of Nature," NABPR Dissertation Series, No. 3 (Macon, Ga.: Mercer University Press, 1983).

30. Some descriptive study has been done on Western attitudes toward nature generally, including religious attitudes, by Clarence Glacken, *Traces on the Rhodian Shore: Nature and Culture in Western Thought From Ancient Times to the End of the Eighteenth Century* (Berkeley, Calif.: University of California Press, 1976).

Keith Thomas has focused his attention on the development of attitudes toward nature in modern English culture, including the contributions of popular theological writers, in his thorough study *Man and the Natural World: A History of the Modern Sensibility* (New York: Pantheon Books, 1983). N. Max Wilders has traced the interaction between the natural sciences and cosmological metaphysics on the one hand and Christian theology on the other, from medieval to modern times, in his detailed history *The Theologian and His Universe: Theology and Cosmology from the Middle Ages to the Present,* trans. Paul Dunphy (New York: Seabury Press, 1982): what he thinks of as "the influence of man's evolving world picture on the current interpretation of Christianity" (234). While each of these works educe significant materials and draw noteworthy conclusions, they remain within the general field of the history of ideas. They are not studies in historical theology, which read the tradition from the inside, so to speak, in terms of its own metaphors and categories.

Focused historical study of Christian thought about nature is noticeably limited. Allan D. Galloway, *The Cosmic Christ* (New York: Harper & Brothers, 1951), has traced the theme of cosmic redemption from biblical times to the twentieth century. Leo Scheffczyk has studied the history of the doctrine of creation (with amazingly little attention to the theology of nature, as such, ironically), *Creation and Providence,* trans. Richard Strachan (New York: Herder & Herder, 1970). George H. Williams has followed the history of the wilderness and paradise motif, from biblical times to the present, *Wilderness and Paradise in Christian Thought: The Biblical Experience of the Desert in the History of Christianity and the Paradise Theme in the Theological Idea of the University* (New York: Harper & Row, 1962). Some of the few studies that have been done on biblical thought about nature will be cited below. All of these works, in one way or another, help us to understand Christian thought about nature, but none of them deals directly and extensively with this theme itself. Perhaps the most illuminating material on our theme comes from the research of George H. Williams in the form of a long two-part essay, "Christian Attitudes Toward Nature," *Christian Scholars Review* 2 (Fall 1971, Winter 1972): 3–35, 112–26. But this work, as we might expect, is limited in scope.

31. From among a vast literature, see the following: *Global Future: Time to Act,* Report to the President on Global Resources, Environment, and Population, by the Council on Environmental Quality (Washington, D.C.: United States Department of State,

1981); Lester R. Brown, *World Without Borders* (New York: Random House, 1972); idem, *Building a Sustainable Society* (New York: W. W. Norton, 1982); and, still valuable, Richard Falk, *This Endangered Planet: Prospects and Proposals for Human Survival* (New York: Random House, 1971).

32. For an early attempt at this kind of study, see H. Paul Santmire, *Brother Earth: Nature, God, and Ecology in a Time of Crisis* (New York: Thomas Nelson, 1970). This work has been analyzed and evaluated by Stewart, "Nature In Grace," along with the works of John Cobb (see n. 29) and Teilhard de Chardin.

For an updating of the argument in *Brother Earth*, see H. Paul Santmire, "The Future of the Cosmos and the Renewal of the Church's Life with Nature," *Word and World*, 4 (Fall 1984). Of the many studies in the theology of nature which have appeared in the last twenty years, the most suggestive and illuminating is still Joseph Sittler's volume, *Essays on Nature and Grace* (Philadelphia: Fortress Press, 1972). A representative introduction to an important allied field, environmental ethics, is the work by Albert J. Fritch, *et al.*, *Environmental Ethics: Choices for Concerned Citizens* (Garden City, New York: Anchor Press/Doubleday, 1980).

33. See the article by H. Paul Santmire, "Alienation from Nature in Contemporary Western Experience" (forthcoming) which details the rise of the Gnostic spirit in our time with specific reference to attitudes toward nature. More generally, see Carl A. Raschke, *The Interruption of Eternity: Modern Gnosticism and the Origins of the New Religious Consciousness* (Chicago: Nelson-Hall, 1980); and Hans Jonas, *The Gnostic Religion: The Message of the Alien God and the Beginnings of Christianity*, 2d ed., revised (Boston: Beacon Press, 1958), especially the Epilogue, "Gnosticism, Nihilism, and Existentialism."

34. See the detailed discussion of this point in Santmire, *Brother Earth*, chap. 2.

35. There is, as yet, no comprehensive review of the contemporary discussion of the theology of nature, which emerged in many countries in the late 1960s and which now includes more than twenty-five book-length studies and hundreds of articles. This is symptomatic of the discussion itself, which has generally been fragmented and occasional. Books continue to appear which betray no awareness that an international discussion of the theology of nature has been underway for twenty years. The single most insightful study in this context is the volume of essays by Joseph Sittler, *Essays on Nature and Grace* (Philadelphia: Fortress Press, 1972). The best available summaries of the overall discussion are to be found in Derr, *Ecology and Human Need*, chaps. 2 and 3, and in Stewart, "Nature In Grace." Reference can also be made to H. Paul Santmire, "'Toward a New Theology of Nature': A Theme Whose Time Has Passed" (forthcoming), which attempts to review the entire contemporary discussion.

For a review of the development of, and debate about, "cosmic christology" in the modern period, see J. A. Lyons, *The Cosmic Christ in Origen and Teilhard: A Comparative Study* (Oxford: Oxford University Press, 1982), chap. 1.

36. Augustine *Soliloquies* 1.2.7.

37. Arthur Lovejoy, "Nature as an Esthetic Norm," *Essays in the History of Ideas* (New York: G. P. Putnam's Sons, 1948), chap. 5. See also Arthur Lovejoy and George Boas, *Primitivism and Related Ideas in Antiquity* (Baltimore: Johns Hopkins, 1935), especially the discussion "Some Meanings of 'Nature.'"

38. See Kaufman, "Concept of Nature." See also s.v. "Nature," *New Catholic Encyclopedia* (New York: McGraw-Hill, 1967). For a review of Western philosophical ideas of nature, see R. G. Collingwood, *The Idea of Nature* (New York: Oxford University Press, 1945).

39. In this sense, we are bracketing the complex metaphysical history of the word, for example, nature as creative principle *(natura naturans)*. Cf. s.v. *"physis," Theological Dictionary of the New Testament* (hereafter cited as *TDNT*), ed. G. Kittel et al. Nature is being defined here, again, *theologically* in terms of the biblical image, "the earth." Cf. s.v. *"ge," TDNT*: "As part of the world created by God . . . [the earth] is 'creature' *(ktisis)*, not 'nature' in the sense of the philosophical concept of nature. That is to say, it exists only by the will of the Creator and the creative Word of almighty God. Its existence is bordered by an absolute beginning and an absolute end like that of the whole world of heaven and earth."

40. The word "environment" will be used in the popular sense of the "nonhuman world of nature." The word "ecological" will be employed in a nontechnical but generally familiar sense to denote a system of interrelationships in the world of nature or, by analogy, a system of interrelationships in the world of human action and/or reflection, with regard to nature and perhaps other aspects of reality, created and divine (cf. Joseph Sittler's use of the term in the title of his volume, *The Ecology of Faith* [Philadelphia: Fortress Press, 1970]). The word "cosmos" will be used also, although sparingly. Cosmos will be taken here simply as a synonym of "nature" or "the earth." The word will be avoided since it is sometimes used theologically to include both "heaven and earth," that is, the realm of the angels and the transcending human dimension of the creation, as well as nature (as here defined). Also "cosmos" sometimes, as in the Gospel of John, has the nuance of "that which is condemned," that is, "the world," that which is a threat to the life of faith; it can mean, in particular, "the hostile human world" (cf. s.v. *"kosmos," TDNT*). The "earth," in contrast, does not readily carry these negative or particularly anthropocentric nuances. Likewise, since "cosmology" is often used to refer to a branch of physics or astronomy, or to speculative philosophical discourse (à la Alfred North Whitehead), this term will be avoided altogether.

41. See Ludwig Schütz, *Thomas-Lexikon*, 2d ed. (New York: Ungar, 1957), s.v. "natura."

42. We are rejecting the theological definition of nature as "the nonhuman creation," because that arbitrarily excludes the human body and human fabrications from nature. We are also rejecting the popular definition of nature as the unspoiled or untouched part of the material-vital creation, since so much of nature is in fact touched by human hands, in one way or another, and since all of nature bears the impress, as far as faith is concerned, of the divine intentionality. Much of nature is touched by human hands, directly or indirectly. All of nature is touched by the divine hands, so to speak, all of the time. Further phenomenological distinctions can be made, to be sure. So it is sometimes helpful to speak of fabricated, cultivated, and wild nature (for example, a building, an apple orchard, a star).

43. Should anyone care to ask, this field of study might be called, with a due sense of caution, "historical terrology," which would take its place alongside of historical an-

thropology and angelology. Those three are subfields of "historical ktisiology" (the history of the doctrine of creation *{ktisis}*), which, in turn, is a branch of the well-known academic field, historical theology.

CHAPTER 2

1. A critical yet empathetic awareness of the theological tradition of the church can sometimes, perhaps more often than not, be most helpful in leading us to understand the traditions of biblical faith. This is precisely the point where the highly regarded and still valuable discussion of biblical hermeneutics by Krister Stendahl, s.v. "Biblical Theology," *Interpreter's Dictionary of the Bible* (Nashville: Abingdon Press, 1962; hereafter referred to as *IDB*), begins to show some signs of internal stress. Stendahl distinguishes between two interpretive methods, the one the province of historical research, he suggests, the other the province of preaching and constructive theology. The first method approaches the text by asking "what it meant," the second by raising the question "what it means." For our purposes here, we can let that distinction stand as it is, as one viable and widely accepted option in the contemporary theological discussion of hermeneutics; on this approach to hermeneutics, see James Barr, s.v. "Biblical Theology," *IDB*, Supplemental Volume (Nashville: Abingdon Press, 1976). But within the framework of this plausible option, refinements are necessary.

The mind of the historian, who asks "what it meant," however "objective" or "unbiased" it may be, is not a tabula rasa. The questions which historians bring to the texts in order to determine "what it meant" will obviously be influenced by their own historical context, particularly by where they stand—or do not stand—within the Christian tradition. Stendahl himself demonstrates this fact when, in an important article, he juxtaposes Augustine and Luther, on the one hand, over against Paul, on the other, in terms of the post-Pauline "introspective conscience" which he believes has shaped the tradition's exegesis of Paul to our own day, but which no longer is fully valid as an interpretive framework (idem, "The Apostle Paul and the Introspective Conscience of the West," *Harvard Theological Review* 66:3 [July 1963]: 199–216). This article by Stendahl suggests a refinement in his own hermeneutic, which he seems to presuppose, but which he does not articulate as such.

In order to pursue the question "what it meant" as "objectively" as possible (more precisely: as "intersubjectively" as possible), one has to know where one stands in one's own tradition of interpretation. One has to be conscious of the manifold questions that have been put to the Bible in one's own community of exegesis and exposition. One is well advised to ask, in other words, not only "what it meant" with regard to the Bible itself but also, in service of that question, "what it *has* meant" in the history of interpretation. The latter question can help one clear the exegetical air, so to speak, and allow one to find some critical distance from the text when one asks the question "what it meant."

Martin Luther said memorably, for example, that the Bible is the cradle of Christ. By this he meant hermeneutically that the central teaching of the Bible is the good news of God's justification of the ungodly by grace alone, apart from the works of the law, through faith alone. Lutheran exegetes ever since have approached the Scriptures eager to discern this message. Rudolph Bultmann is a noteworthy modern example of this history of interpretation. It is important to be aware of this hermeneutical trajectory when one reads biblical exegesis by scholars influenced by Bultmann, however "objective" their interpretation may appear. "What it has meant" surely shapes the Bultmann school's overall approach to the question "what it meant" and thus their approach to the constructive question "what it means."

This same issue has also occupied the attention of Karlfried Froehlich, although from a different perspective. He has been concerned about viewing the tradition of exegesis in the church as a *resource* which allows one to see the adumbration of various potential meanings of the text. Cf. Froehlich, "Church History and the Bible," *Princeton Seminary Bulletin* 1:4 (New Series 1978): 213–24, especially 218:

> Historical "understanding" of a biblical text cannot stop with the elucidation
> of its historical "*Sitz im Leben*," with its focus on the intentions of the author.
> Understanding must take into account the text's post-history as the paradigm
> of the text's own historicity, i.e., as the way in which the text itself can func-
> tion as a source of human self-interpretation in a variety of contexts, and
> thus, through its historical interpretations, is participant in the shaping of
> life.

Froehlich has also summarized some recent developments in the general discussion of biblical hermeneutics, in particular the movement toward a "post-critical" approach to biblical exegesis. See idem, "Biblical Interpretation on the Move," *Word and World* 1:2 (Spring 1981): 140–52. His remarks about the work of the New Testament scholar Peter Stuhlmacher (p. 151) are of special interest:

> In antithesis to one of the basic dogmas of biblical criticism, Stuhlmacher
> holds that the exegetical tradition does not necessarily hinder understand-
> ing but may give access to its full potential. . . . Drawing on a philosophical
> tradition that extends from Dilthey to H. G. Gadamer, he states that "every
> serious historical interpretation must fulfill the requirement of having con-
> sciously reflected on the impact of the text in history." . . . The history of in-
> terpretation thus becomes part of the "horizons" which have to be 'fused' in
> the exegetical endeavor (Gadamer).

In principle, going through the classical theological tradition, rather than around it, as a mode of access to biblical meanings seems to have significant hermeneutical potential.

2. In more technical terms, this undertaking can be called an "eidetic reduction." This is Langdon Gilkey's somewhat ponderous expression (chosen no doubt to assuage anxiety about the validity of the whole endeavor); see idem, *Reaping the Whirlwind: A Christian Interpretation of History* (New York: Seabury Press, 1976), 134–47. Gilkey suggests that there are four levels to self-conscious theological discourse, this eidetic reduction being the first. It is necessary because Christian theology must be able to draw on its own tradition substantively. To do this, theologians must know what the various symbols of the past "have meant in all the ways that are relevant, in their orig-

inal form in the biblical witness, and as they have been interpreted in the life of the Christian community" (140). But, Gilkey observes, given the wealth of the historical material in the ensuing tradition, the symbols of the past "must be 'reduced' from the plurality of their historical variations to some unity and coherence of form" (140) before the symbols can be employed creatively in a contemporary context. This reduction, Gilkey notes wryly, will no doubt horrify biblical scholars and historians of Christian theology, "but nothing can be said by any of us (even by them) *theologically*, i.e., concerning the meaning and value of these symbols *for us*, without a reduction" (143).

3. Cf. David Tracy, "Metaphor and Religion: The Test Case of Christian Texts," in *On Metaphor*, ed. Sheldon Sacks (Chicago: University of Chicago Press, 1978), 89: "That all major religions are grounded in certain root metaphors has become a commonplace in modern religious studies. In a particular religion root metaphors form a cluster or network in which certain sustained metaphors both organize subsidiary metaphors and diffuse new ones."

4. Stephen Pepper, *World Hypotheses: A Study in Evidence* (Berkeley: University of California Press, 1966).

5. Alfred North Whitehead, *Science and the Modern World* (New York: Macmillan, 1925).

6. Langdon Gilkey, *Religion and the Scientific Future: Reflections on Myth, Science and Theology* (New York: Harper & Row, 1970), 103.

7. Ibid., 104.

8. See the instructive discussion by Sallie McFague, *Speaking in Parables: A Study in Metaphor and Theology* (Philadelphia: Fortress Press, 1975). She argues that metaphor is not first of all owned by the poets, so to speak, but the common possession of ordinary language (43). The human mind, indeed, constructs its world through the use of metaphors: "Reality is created through [an] incredibly complex process of metaphorical leaps, of seeing this or that." Hence metaphor is not merely a stage on the way to conceptual language, which can be superseded. It is "always crucial to the creation of linguistic significance" (52). McFague summarizes her illuminating thesis with these words:

> Metaphor is not only a poetic device for the creation of new meaning, but metaphor is as ultimate as thought. It can be *the* source for new insight because all human discovery is by metaphor. Metaphor unites us and our world at a level below subject-object, mind-body; it is the nexus of "man in the being of the world," the intimation of our original unity with all that is. (56)

In the terms being employed here, "root metaphors" are organizing or integrating metaphors, which come with families, as it were. As such they have a certain durability that many other metaphors lack. They are *prima inter pares*.

9. The term "motif" is used here without any conscious intent either to adopt or to qualify the "motif-research" method of certain Scandinavian scholars such as Anders Nygren. See, for example, Nygren's *Agape and Eros* (Philadelphia: Westminster Press, 1935).

10. Although root metaphors and models do indeed have much in common, they should nevertheless be distinguished. Cf. the discussion by Ian G. Barbour, *Myths, Models, and Paradigms: A Comparative Study in Science and Religion* (New York: Harper & Row, 1974). He explains that religious models "serve as 'organizing images' which give emphasis, selectively restructuring as well as interpreting our perceptions. Models, like metaphors, may help us to notice particular features of the world. In all of these functions—the evocation of attitudes, the guidance of behavior, the interpretation of experience, and the organization of perceptions—a metaphor is used only momentarily, whereas a model is used in a sustained and systematic fashion" (16). For our purposes here, a root metaphor can be thought of as a prereflective or borderline-reflective model. Or, alternatively, a model may be a self-consciously employed root metaphor.

11. These words are borrowed from Arthur Lovejoy, *The Great Chain of Being: A Study of the History of An Idea* (New York: Harper & Brothers, 1936), 7, who is addressing himself to a slightly different, but related point.

12. Samuel Taylor Coleridge, "Hymn Before Sunrise, In the Vale of Chamouni," lines 5–16.

13. See Marjorie Hope Nicolson, *Mountain Gloom and Mountain Glory: The Development of the Aesthetics of the Infinite* (Ithaca, N.Y.: Cornell University Press, 1959).

14. Richard J. Clifford, *The Cosmic Mountain in Canaan and the Old Testament*, Harvard Semitic Monographs (Cambridge: Harvard University Press, 1972), 5.

15. Edwyn Bevan, *Symbolism and Belief* (London: Allen & Unwin, 1938). On the mountain and the experience of awe, see chaps. 2 and 3.

16. Ibid., 63f.

17. Mircea Eliade, *The Sacred and the Profane: The Nature of Religion* (New York: Harper & Row, 1957).

18. Ibid., 43.

19. Ibid., 38.

20. Ibid.

21. Ibid., 44.

22. Ibid., 117.

23. John Milton, *Paradise Lost*, V, 511.

24. Quoted by George S. Hendry, *Theology of Nature* (Philadelphia: Westminster Press, 1980), 90.

25. Lovejoy, *Great Chain of Being*.

26. Carl Boberg (Swedish); Stuart K. Hine (English), "How Great Thou Art."

27. Lactantius *Institutes* 7.24.

28. Edward Johnson, *Wonder-Working Providence of Sions Savior*, in Perry Miller, Thomas H. Johnson, *The Puritans* (New York: Atlanta Book Co., 1938).

29. The experience of the promising journey should probably be sharply distinguished from another familiar Western experience, *wandering*, although the two have some things in common. The classical instance of wandering is, of course, the story of Odysseus. As Homer tells the story, Odysseus, already apart from his homeland, is swept off course by circumstances beyond his control. Thenceforth his mind is shaped

by two antithetical sets of motives. On the one hand, he appears to be the weary traveler, far from home, who would like nothing better than to return to his family. On the other hand, he appears as the supreme adventurer, driven by his desire for constantly new experiences. In either mode, however, he is not embarked on a promising journey to a good land. Either he is on his way home (here "the end is like the beginning") or he is without any definite goal ahead of him, except his desire to gain more experience of life. In the latter instance, there is no ending envisioned for his wandering, either terminally (*finis*) or in terms of a final fulfillment (*telos*). The people of Israel, in contrast, did wander in the wilderness and did yearn, at times, for a return to Egypt, but their overriding goal, as it is described for us in the biblical texts, was clear: not to return, nor to gain more experience through their journey, but to arrive in the land promised to them by God.

30. Thomas Olivers, "The God of Abraham Praise."

CHAPTER 3

1. See Wolfhart Pannenberg, *Basic Questions in Theology*, Vol. 2, trans. George H. Kehm (Philadelphia: Fortress Press, 1971), chap. 5: "The Appropriation of the Philosophical Concept of God as a Dogmatic Problem of Early Christian Theology."

2. Allan D. Galloway, *The Cosmic Christ* (London: James Nisbet & Co., 1951); for example, 99:

> He [Irenaeus] takes the attitude that Scripture has given us all the knowledge that is necessary for salvation, and any questions that are not fully answered by Scriptures must be left severely alone. Thus, instead of attempting to formulate a real interpretation of Biblical eschatology, he is content to confine his argument against the Gnostics and the cosmic problems they raise, firstly, to demonstration of the difficulties and inconsistencies in the heretical solutions which they adopt; and secondly, to a simple reassertion of the Biblical position, without enquiring too closely as to whether it does not involve similar difficulties itself.

3. See Gustaf Wingren, *Man and the Incarnation: A Study in the Biblical Theology of Irenaeus*, trans. Ross MacKenzie (Philadelphia: Muhlenberg Press, 1959); John Lawson, *The Biblical Theology of St. Irenaeus* (London: Epworth Press, 1948); Philip Hefner, "Theological Methodology and St. Irenaeus," *Journal of Religion* 44 (1964): 294–309; Leo Scheffczyk, *Creation and Providence*, trans. Richard Strachan (New York: Herder & Herder, 1970), 66ff.

4. Pannenberg's positive estimate of Irenaeus's stature is even more far-reaching. Cf. *Basic Questions*, Vol. 2, p. 178:

> The work of Irenaeus offers a broadly sketched attempt to develop a historical understanding of the totality of reality from the standpoint of the freely acting God of the Bible, while appropriating the philosophical concepts of simplicity and incomprehensibility. Although the goal of a theological-philosophical synthesis was not the foremost aim of his endeavors, Irenaeus

achieved such a synthesis by means of his view, taken over from Justin, of the history of redemption as a sequence of dispensations of the incomprehensible God. In many respects it was more impressive than what Alexandrian theology was able to develop despite its much more deliberate striving for such a synthesis.

5. T. E. Pollard, *Johannine Christology and the Early Church* (Cambridge: Cambridge University Press, 1970), 88, following G. Bardy, "Pour l'histoire de l'école d'Alexandrie."

6. On Origen generally, see the standard works cited by Pollard, *Johannine Christology*, and also the bibliography provided by Scheffczyk, *Creation and Providence*, 64ff. For a concise overview of Origen's thought, see Henry Chadwick, *Early Christian Thought and the Classical Tradition* (New York: Oxford University Press, 1966).

7. On Gnosticism and related trends generally, see E. Blackman, *Marcion and His Influence* (London: SPCK, 1948); Robert Grant, *Gnosticism and Early Christianity*, revised ed. (New York: Harper & Row, 1959) and idem, s.v. "Gnosticism," *IDB*; Hans Jonas, *The Gnostic Problem: The Message of an Alien God*, revised ed. (Boston: Beacon Press, 1958); R. M. Wilson, *Gnosis and the New Testament* (Philadelphia: Fortress Press, 1968); Elaine Pagels, s.v. "Gnosticism," *IDB*, Supplemental Volume, and idem, *The Gnostic Gospels* (New York: Random House, 1979); Pheme Perkins, *The Gnostic Dialogue: The Early Church and the Crisis of Gnosticism* (New York: Paulist Press, 1980).

8. Jonas, *Gnostic Problem*.

9. Wilson, *Gnosis and New Testament*, 84. According to Jonas, *Gnostic Problem*, 32f., modern research has shown that Gnosticism was a pre-Christian phenomenon, rooted both in Judaism and in the Hellenistic milieu. This, however, is still debated.

10. Jonas, *Gnostic Problem*, 7f.

11. Cf. Wilson, *Gnosis and New Testament*, 82: "In the New Testament we are faced only with an incipient Gnosticism. The false doctrines which are refuted in Colossians and in I John are still far removed from later elaborations, although they show already the main characteristics of the movement."

12. The subtitle of Jonas's book *The Gnostic Problem* is *The Message of an Alien God*.

13. Wilson, *Gnosis and New Testament*, 70.

14. Jonas, *Gnostic Problem*, 43.

15. Ibid., 44.

16. Ibid., 42: "The cardinal feature of gnostic thought is the radical dualism that governs the relation of God and the world, and correspondingly that of man and the world."

17. Ibid., 17.

18. Ibid., 45.

19. Ibid.

20. In her widely publicized study already cited, *The Gnostic Gospels*, Elaine Pagels concentrates chiefly on gnostic teachings about Christ, God, the church, and the human self, without giving much sustained attention to the gnostic view of the material order. This approach has the effect of glossing over the profound alienation from the

world that shaped the gnostic mind. Her position has the further effect of presenting a picture of Irenaeus chiefly as a representative of church authority (incipient authoritarianism) over against gnostic individualism. Pheme Perkins, *Gnostic Dialogue*, has criticized Pagels's interpretation of Gnosticism, in this regard, as a modernization. Her view, according to Perkins, owes more to modern individualism and the modern concern with subjectivity than to a reading of the gnostic mind itself. Rather, Perkins argues, the Gnostics were not individualists, as such, but representatives of a fast-fading second-century cultural dependence on oral tradition. Irenaeus, in addition to everything else, according to Perkins, therefore stands most fundamentally against Gnosticism as one who is a proponent of the new—written—scriptural authority.

Gérard Vallée has provided what is perhaps the most balanced statement of Irenaeus's motives, in his essay "Theological and Non-Theological Motives in Irenaeus's Refutation of the Gnostics," in *Jewish and Christian Self-Definition*: Vol. 1, *The Shaping of Christianity in the Second and Third Centuries*, ed. E. P. Sanders (Philadelphia: Fortress Press, 1980), 174–85. Theologically, according to Vallée, Irenaeus's most central concern is to reject the Gnostics' most basic dualism, which divides the Divine, separating "the true God" and the Creator, as that division gives rise to "diverse expressions of a *metaphysical dualism* [his italics] opposing the world above to the world below, spirit to matter" (180). From this single overriding theological concern of Irenaeus all his other criticisms of Gnosticism emerge, Vallée argues: christological dualism (the Gnostics wrongly separate Christ from Jesus), soteriological dualism (they deny the universality of salvation), scriptural dualism (they reject the Old Testament), ecclesiastical dualism (they distinguish between simple believers and pneumatics), social dualism (they teach that some people are essentially good, others essentially evil), practical dualism (they distinguish between common and esoteric moralities). Irenaeus also had sociopolitical motives for his rejection of Gnosticism, in Vallée's view: "In the confrontation with the Gnostics it is obvious where Irenaeus's sentiments lie. He imagines himself as the spokesman of the masses, strongly anchored in the tradition and the faith of the average Christian" (181). The Gnostics, on the other hand, he saw as potential or actual revolutionaries, who unduly drew the attention of the civil authorities to a church which still lived in a precarious sociopolitical situation. Irenaeus's influence in ensuing centuries, according to Vallée, then turned out to be twofold. Irenaeus's rejection of the Gnostic anticosmicism and antisomaticism helped to establish those limits for Christian teaching about creation throughout the centuries. On the other hand, his defense of the church against the spirit of gnostic freedom also helped set the stage for an authoritarian pattern for meeting heretical challenges.

21. Wingren, *Man and the Incarnation*, 44ff.

22. Aloys Grillmeier, *Christ in the Christian Tradition: From the Apostolic Age to Chalcedon (451)*, trans. J. W. Bowden (New York: Sheed & Ward, 1965), 101.

23. Cf. Wingren, *Man and the Incarnation*, 81: "Recapitulation means the accomplishment of God's plan of salvation, and this accomplishment is within a history, in a time sequence at one particular time. It is a continuous process in which the *oikonomia, dispositio*, of God is manifested by degrees."

24. Irenaeus *Against the Heresies* 3.16.6.

25. Ibid., 5.36.1. Cf. Grillmeier, *Christ in Christian Tradition*, 101: "The significance of the *anakephalaiosis* [recapitulation] in Irenaeus must be assessed in light of the *oikonomia* [Divine plan and providence]. The *anakephalaiosis* as an act of Christ is the specific contribution which Christ makes to the realization of the one *oikonomia* of the Father in Christ and the Spirit."

26. Galloway, *Cosmic Christ*, 116. Cf. also Philip Carrington, *The Early Christian Church*, Vol. 2 (Cambridge: Cambridge University Press, 1957), 325:

> The chiliasm of Phrygian prophets and elders to whom he had listened in his younger days, takes possession of his imagination. . . . His preoccupation with this world and its destiny leads him too close to the vision of the redeemed earth; and now Asian mysticism with its dreams of an earthly paradise takes complete control. He accepts all the promises of the prophets with a childlike literalism which is in complete contrast to his profound analysis of the symbolism of soteriology.

27. Irenaeus *Against the Heresies* 5.23.2.

28. Ibid., 5.36.1.

29. Cf. ibid., 5.32.2.

30. Ibid.

31. Cf. ibid.

32. Ibid., 5.36.1.

33. Irenaeus *Demonstration of the Apostolic Preaching* 4.

34. Irenaeus *Against the Heresies* 4.38.3.

35. Ibid., 4.20.1.

36. Ibid., 5.28.3.

37. Ibid., 2.28.1.

38. Ibid., 2.2.5.

39. Ibid., 2.28.7.

40. Ibid., 5.3.2.

41. Ibid., 5.2.2.

42. Ibid., 5.29.1.

43. So, for example, Joppich Godehard, *Salus Carnis: Eine Untersuchung In der Theologie des hl. Irenaeus von Lyon* (Munster-Schwarzach: Vier Turne Verlag, 1965), passim.

44. Cf. R. A. Markus, "Pleroma and Fulfillment: The Significance of History in St. Irenaeus' Opposition to Gnosticism," *Vigiliae Christianae* 8 (1954): 193–224, especially 211f.: For Irenaeus, in opposition to the Gnostics,

> there is no room for two worlds, anymore than there is for two Gods, for a cosmos and an *aion*, of a world of history and a timeless world of spirit. For God in his infinity contains all things: if there were anything beyond his immensity, "he would not be the pleroma of all things," and would be limited by what fell outside him and be contained in a more inclusive Pleroma (AH 2.1.2.3). . . . What he opposes to the Gnostics is a single world full of God's glory and one God who contains it all and governs its history by his providence (AH 3.25).

45. Irenaeus *Against the Heresies* 5.29.1. Italics added.

46. Ibid., 4.37.7.

47. Thus Irenaeus's thought stands in the tradition of those Eastern fathers, and some in the West, such as Duns Scotus, who held that the incarnation would have happened even if Adam had not sinned.

48. Irenaeus *Against the Heresies* 2.25.2.

49. Ibid., 4.19.2.

50. Ibid., 5.22.2.

51. Ibid., 5.33.3.

52. Ibid., 5.33.4.

53. Ibid., 5.36.1.

54. This image of God was common in Hellenistic culture, as the popular writing *De Mundo* shows (attributed mistakenly at that time to Aristotle).

55. Overall, the preceding account of Irenaeus's thought is incomplete. We have not done more than notice Irenaeus's teaching about "Man and the Incarnation," studied instructively by Wingren, in his book which bears that title. Those themes are obviously of great importance to Irenaeus. That is not in question here.

56. See the references cited above, n. 6.

57. Arthur Lovejoy, *The Great Chain of Being*, 62.

58. Ibid., 82.

59. Ibid., 34f.

60. Cf. A. H. Armstrong and R. A. Markus, *Christian Faith and Greek Philosophy* (New York: Sheed & Ward, 1960), 35.

61. This is not to impose a value judgment on the tradition at this point, as some have done, such as Harnack, who decried the "Hellenization of Christianity" as a fall from its original biblical purity. Here the intent is only descriptive. As it spread around the Mediterranean basin, Christianity as a matter of course, and often as a matter of conscious intention, became Hellenized. For a balanced, positive estimate of Hellenization, by one who seeks to go beyond its categories, see Leslie Dewart, *The Future of Belief: Theism in a World Come of Age* (New York: Herder & Herder, 1966), 132–35. For a general description of the period, see E. E. Peters, *The Harvest of Hellenism: A History of the Near East from Alexander the Great to the Triumph of Christianity* (New York: Simon & Schuster, 1970).

62. E. R. Dodds, *Pagan and Christian in an Age of Anxiety: Some Aspects of Religious Experience From Marcus Aurelius to Constantine* (Cambridge: Cambridge University Press, 1965).

63. Ibid., 6f.

64. Ibid., 28.

65. This is not to suggest, however, that the early Church never proclaimed the God of creation as part of its message. Cf. Edward Schillebeeckx, *Christ: The Experience of Jesus as Lord*, trans. John Bowden (New York: Crossroads Publishing Company, 1983), p. 526: "When the New Testament proclamation of faith is addressed to Jews, there is hardly any mention of belief in creation; there was no doubt at all about this among Jews (see Acts 4:24). When speaking to non-Jews, however, Christians, like Jews

themselves had to stress the one true God, the Creator of heaven and earth. . . . The coming of a Gentile was not only a conversion to Christ, but also conversion to a monotheism centered on the Creator, the one living God. Thus creation was an element taken from the ancient view of the world, purified by Israel's salvation history and by the historical ministry of Jesus—to become the first article of faith in the Christian kerygma (it was later incorporated into the Apostles' Creed) as a matrix of faith in God's grace in Christ." Still, it was the experience of the foreground (redemption) rather than the background (creation) that tended to receive the most attention among Christian thinkers, once the status of the background had been secured. On Marcion, see Jaroslav Pelikan, *The Christian Tradition: A History of the Development of Doctrine.* Vol. 1: *The Emergence of the Catholic Tradition (100–600)* (Chicago: University of Chicago Press, 1971), 73.

66. The eschatological consciousness of the first- and second-century church undoubtedly also had its impact in this context, as did the force of Roman persecutions and the influence—often perceived as negative—of Roman urban culture. The martyrs and the first monks, each in their own ways, passionately looked toward the coming of the next world. In that sense, their *praxis* had a world-denying character to it. At first, it seems, this world-denying tendency was mainly Jewish, apocalyptic, and ascetic, reminiscent of Qumran. Later, for example under the influence of Basil the Great (ca. 330–79), it became more characteristically Hellenized. On this, see Peters, *Harvest' of Hellenism*, 635ff.

67. Origen *De Principiis* 1.5.1.

68. Origen *Commentary on Romans* IV. Quoted by Thomas E. Clarke, *The Eschatological Transformation of the Material World According to St. Augustine* (Woodstock, Md.: Woodstock College Press, 1956), 7.

69. Origen *De Principiis* 1.5.1.

70. Ibid., 5.6.2.

71. Ibid., 1.5.5.

72. Ibid., 1.7.2.

73. Origen *Against Celsus* 4:81–89.

74. Ibid., 4:74. Cited by Williams, "Christian Attitudes Toward Nature," *Christian Scholars Review* 2 (Fall 1971, Winter 1972): 23.

75. Origen *Against Celsus* 4:78.

76. See H. Koch, *Pronoia und Paideusis: Studien über Origenes and sein Verhältnis zum Platonismus*, in *Arbeiten zur Kirchengeschicte* 22 (1932): 36–38.

77. Origen *De Principiis* 1.6.2.

78. George Florovsky, "The Concept of Creation in St. Athanasius," *Studia Patristica* 7 (1962): 243.

79. Origen *De Principiis* 1.8.2.

80. Ibid., 1.6.4.

81. Rowan A. Greer, trans. and introduction, *Origen* (selections) (New York: Paulist Press, 1979), "Homily 27 on Numbers," par. 2.

82. Ibid., par. 3.

83. Cf. ibid., par. 4.

84. Ibid.

85. Ibid.

86. Some of Origen's critics accused him of believing in the idea of the transmigration of souls. His extant works rather suggest that the soul is variously embodied in successive worlds (as the divine process of "educating" the free *logikoi* to achieve salvation continues). In any case, this motif of multiple embodiments further indicates how, for him, the self's center of identity is essentially the soul, not soul and body—still less is the essential self seen as an integrated psychosomatic whole.

CHAPTER 4

1. Frederick Copleston, *A History of Philosophy*, Vol. 2: *Mediaeval Philosophy: Augustine to Bonaventure* (Garden City, N.Y.: Doubleday & Co., 1962), Part 2, p. 55.

2. Paul Tillich was wont to observe that only a few geniuses in the history of theology were able to unite both the philosophical and confessional modes of theological discourse. He considered Augustine to be one of these.

3. See Peter Brown, *Augustine of Hippo: A Biography* (Berkeley, Calif.: University of California Press, 1967), chap. 5.

4. Hans Jonas, *The Gnostic Problem: The Message of an Alien God*, revised ed. (Boston: Beacon Press, 1958), 227f.

5. Brown, *Augustine*, 99.

6. Augustine *Confessions* 7.13. Cited by Brown, *Augustine*, 100.

7. This work was polemical, as in *Against the Manichees* (388–89). It was scholarly, exegetical, and reflectively theological, both in his "literal commentary" (393–94) and his justly famous longer commentary, *De Genesi ad Litteram* (ca. 402). It was existential, and intensely personal, in his *Confessions* (401). And, finally, it was lucidly synthetic of all his preceding discoveries, and integrated with the historical insights of the great work of his maturity, *City of God* 11, 12 (417).

8. This kind of theological reflection on Genesis was already well underway, it is worth noting, before Augustine's time. Origen himself had written a commentary on Genesis. A break with Origen's thinking, however, clearly occurs in the commentary of Basil the Great, the *Hexaemeron*. This work radically diverges from the acosmic and sometimes anticosmic sensibilities of Origen, in virtue of its positive, even euphoric appreciation for the biophysical world. Many other major theologians also wrote commentaries throughout the centuries on Genesis 1. This tradition, the "hexaemeral literature," extends through Thomas Aquinas, to Luther and Calvin, and down to Karl Barth in our century. This body of material has not yet received the scholarly attention it merits, except, in part, by Frank E. Robbins, in an older study, *The Hexaemeral Literature* (Chicago: University of Chicago Press, 1912).

9. Paul Tillich, "The Struggle Between Time and Space," *Theology of Culture*, ed. Robert C. Kimball (New York: Oxford University Press, 1959), chap. 3.

10. R. A. Markus, *Saeculum: History and Society in the Theology of St. Augustine* (Cambridge: Cambridge University Press, 1970), 18.

11. Ibid., 80.

12. Augustine *Soliloquies* 1.2.7.

13. See *City of God* 12.20, where Augustine observes that Christ is the straight way by which the mind escapes the circular maze of pagan thought.

14. Brown, *Augustine*, 317.

15. Augustine *Epistle* 138.1. Cited by Brown, *Augustine*, 317f.

16. Augustine *Epistle* 137.15. Cited by Christopher Dawson, "St. Augustine and His Age," *Enquiries into Religion and Culture* (New York: Sheed & Ward, 1937), 253.

17. Arthur Lovejoy, *The Great Chain of Being: A Study of the History of an Idea* (New York: Harper & Brothers, 1936), chap. 9.

18. Cf. Langdon Gilkey, *Reaping the Whirlwind: A Christian Interpretation of History* (New York: Seabury Press, 1976), 162: ". . . there is no question that Augustine is also rightly credited with giving to time and so to historical process an intelligibility and a meaning which they had not possessed before. With Augustine, the Western, and so the modern, sense of temporal passage comes to definitive and formative expression: historical time is a linear significance, each of whose moments contains the possibility of ultimate significance, and so whose course as a whole possesses an intelligible unity relevant to the gaining of final salvation."

19. Dawson, *Enquiries*, 234, 239.

20. Cf. ibid., 238:

> If we compare the *City of God* with the works of the great Greek apologists, the *Contra Celsum* of Origen, the *Contra Gentes* of Athanasius, and the *Preparatio Evangelica* of Eusebius, we are at once struck by the contrast of his method. He does not base his treatment of the subject on philosophic and metaphysical arguments as the Greek fathers had done, but on the eschatological and social dualism, which, as we have seen, was characteristic of the earliest Christian teaching and to which the African tradition, as a whole, had proved so faithful.

21. In view of these findings, the standard reading of Augustine will have to be revised. Cf. John Herman Randall, Jr., *Hellenistic Ways of Deliverance and the Making of the Christian Synthesis* (New York: Columbia University Press, 1970), 191: "Like Socrates, Augustine turned his back on trees and stones and sought man."

22. Augustine *Confessions* 1.4.

23. How far Augustine had moved from the days when he was most influenced by the world-transcending aspects of Neoplatonism toward an affirmation of God's immediate, caring presence in the world, is indicated by a somewhat qualified compliment paid him by a scholar whose primary affinities lie with Thomas Aquinas, not Augustine. Etienne Gilson, *The Christian Philosophy of St. Thomas Aquinas*, trans. L. K. Shook (New York: Random House, 1956), 134, indicates how little Augustine's earlier idea of an all-transcending One influences his mature thought (Gilson also wants to suggest that Thomas supplies the philosophical substructure which Augustine, he believes, lacks):

> By a strange paradox, the philosopher who most completely identified God with the transcendent immutability of Essence was the Christian most aware of the Divine efficacy in nature, in the universal history of humanity, in the

personal history of the individual conscience. When he speaks of these things as a theologian, St. Augustine seems infallible. Here he is without rival in the history of Christian thought. . . . His greatness is not the philosopher's but the theologian's whose philosophy lags behind his theology without retarding its progress.

Augustine's entire religion, as it appears in the *City of God*, is based on a history dominated by the memory of two major events, Creation and Redemption, and upon a third, the Last Judgment. In order to make a philosophy of history out of this theology of history Augustine drew but slightly on his ontology of the immutable.

24. Augustine *Confessions* 12.7.

25. Augustine *City of God* 12.24.

26. For example, Augustine *De Genesi ad Litteram* 4.21.38.

27. Ibid., 5.5.16.

28. Augustine *Confessions* 12.7.

29. Cf. Augustine *City of God* 12.7.

30. Ibid., 11.22.

31. Ibid., 22.24.

32. Ibid., 12.4.

33. Ibid.

34. Ibid., 12.4; cf. 12.5.

35. Augustine *Confessions* 13.28.

36. Augustine *De Genesi ad Litteram* 5.23.46.

37. Alfred North Whitehead, *Process and Reality* (New York: Macmillan, 1919), 523, has given currency to this general view. He criticizes "the deeper idolatry, of the fashioning of God in the image of the Egyptian, Persian, and Roman imperial rulers. . . . The Church gave unto God the attributes which belong exclusively to Caesar." There is, however, at least one important area where Whitehead's judgment about the Deity of classical Christianity seems to hold true; that is the doctrine of double predestination, to which Augustine and many other theologians adhered (mainly for a whole range of pressing practical reasons). The Deity who for no reason consigns people to hell sounds very much like Caesar.

38. Augustine *De Genesi ad Litteram* 12.17.32.

39. Augustine *City of God* 7.30.

40. Augustine *De Genesi ad Litteram* 1.17.36. Basil has identified the Holy Spirit with the Platonic and Neoplatonic idea of an indwelling World Soul. Augustine wavered about accepting that identification. See Christopher J. O'Toole, *The Philosophy of Creation in the Writings of St. Augustine* (Washington, D.C.: Catholic University of America, 1944), 61: "Augustine nevertheless believes that even if the world is not animated [by a World Soul] there is in it a spiritual and vital force which is exercised by the angels in dependence on God."

41. Augustine *De Genesi ad Litteram* 4.16.2.

42. Ibid., 5.21.42.

43. See Augustine *On the Trinity* 3:4.

44. Augustine *Epistle* 187. Cited by O'Toole, *Philosophy of Creation*, 98.

45. Augustine *Commentary on John* 8:1. Cited by Margaret Ruth Miles, *Augustine on the Body* (Missoula, Mont.: Scholars Press, 1979), 38. On Augustine's theology of miracles, cf. further Louis Monden, *Signs and Wonders: A Study in the Miraculous Element in Religion*, no trans. (New York: Desclee Company, 1960), 41ff.

46. Miles, *Augustine on the Body*, 38.

47. Augustine *Commentary on John* 7.1, "the very God, the Father of our Lord Jesus Christ, makes and rules all things by his Word; these primary miracles are effected by the Word as God; the secondary and later ones are effected by the same Word, but now incarnate and made man for us. Since we wonder at the mighty works of the man Jesus, let us also wonder at what he has done as God." Quoted by Etienne Gilson, *The Spirit of Medieval Philosophy*, trans. A. H. C. Downes (London: Sheed & Ward, 1936), 375.

48. It is generally known that Augustine finds it possible to identify "traces of the Trinity" (*vestigia Trinitatis*) throughout the created order. He may or may not use this idea in an edifying way, theologically speaking. But it should not be assumed that the grounding of the idea is some odd or arbitrary theological fancy. Augustine does not think of himself as "reading in" (eisegesis) the Trinity into nature, but rather as approaching the "Book of Nature" in order to seek traces of the Trinitarian God who in fact is, for Augustine, actually and immediately there, as Creator and Governor of all things (exegesis).

49. Augustine *On the Trinity* 3.9. Cf. further *De Genesi ad Litteram* 11.17.4, 32.

50. Augustine *De Genesi ad Litteram* 5.23.44, 45.

51. Gilkey, *Reaping the Whirlwind*, pp. 174ff. et passim, has argued that for Augustine

> history and its institutions are conceived as manifestations of a static and changeless order now fallen permanently and unredeemably from its own perfection. Providence reestablishes and supports that fallen order in its fallenness. God's purpose, therefore, is not to bring the institutions of history through higher levels of order to completion, but only to give social existence sufficient health to point individuals beyond and outside themselves to a realm of grace found in the church.

At this point Gilkey is silent about Augustine's view of God's history with nature, since Gilkey has other concerns to pursue in his illuminating study of the rise of the historical consciousness. But it seems clear that the kind of analysis he develops regarding Augustine's view of God's history with humanity will not hold, at least in the same way, regarding Augustine's view of God's history with nature. To begin with, for Augustine, nature has not fallen. Hence providence will not have as its chief purpose the restraint of sin. Second, Augustine evidently assumes that the "seminal reasons" will keep coming to fruition, in their right time, over the whole of creation history. Admittedly, he does not dwell on this idea (he was faced with the collapse of Rome, not the collapse of global ecosystems), but it is certainly there.

52. It is important to understand here how much Augustine's mature theological position stands apart from his earlier, dominantly world-transcending Neoplatonic mode of thought. Dietrich Ritschl, *Memory and Hope: An Inquiry Concerning the Presence of Christ* (New York: Macmillan, 1967), 130, has conflated the two: "The beautific vision anticipates the final fulfillment of such an extent that the expectation of the fulfillment becomes unimportant and superfluous." This scarcely reflects Augustine's later emphasis on the resurrection of the body (see below) or, more generall, on the new creation. On the other hand, that Augustine was *in ensuing centuries* interpreted, as Ritschl here interprets him, seems clear, especially given the widespread influence of Neoplatonic thought that was mediated, above all, by Dionysius the Areopagite.

53. Augustine *City of God* 20.16.

54. Gilkey, *Reaping the Whirlwind*, 162, draws the contrast between the Irenaean and the Augustinian future-expectations too sharply. He says that Augustine understood the eschatological events depicted so vividly by Irenaeus and others "as events in a supernatural, ahistorical realm; not a new age in future time and space but in a higher realm of being, a participation in God's eternity beyond death, space, historical time, the physical body and the physical earth—though each who will be 'there' will at the end recover back his own transfigured body in that supernatural realm." It seems that Gilkey has not sufficiently distinguished between Augustine's earlier development and his mature thought. In the latter, there is no question but that the world consummation lies in the future—understood in the sense of futurity, not in the sense of a symbol pointing to a rising above the temporal order. One may choose to call this future "supernatural," as Gilkey does; but that term should then be understood in the sense of "posttemporal," with the nuance that the whole of creation history is therewith fulfilled, not in the otherworldly Neoplatonic sense of the soul ascending to the above, which would be the negation of the spatiotemporal realm of creation history.

55. Augustine *City of God* 22.29.

56. See Thomas E. Clarke, *The Eschatological Transformation of the Material World According to St. Augustine* (Woodstock, Md.: Woodstock College Press, 1956).

57. Augustine *Confessions* 12.2.

58. See Clarke, *Eschatological Transformation*, 4.

59. Ibid., 34.

60. Ibid., 35.

61. Augustine *City of God* 22.24.

62. Augustine *Sermons* 241.2.

63. Augustine *City of God* 12.3.

64. Miles, *Augustine on the Body*, 7.

65. Augustine *City of God* 14.3.

66. Ibid., 14.21.

67. Augustine *De Genesi ad Litteram* 6.19.30.

68. Miles, *Augustine on the Body*, 97.

69. Ibid., 114.

70. Ibid.

71. Augustine *Sermons* 30.4. Cited by Brown, *Augustine*, 366.

72. Augustine *Sermons* 155.5.

73. See Miles, *Augustine on the Body*, 121f. Cf. also Rosemary Radford Ruether, "Virginal Feminism in the Fathers of the Church," *Religion and Sexism: Images of Women in the Jewish and Christian Traditions*, ed. idem (New York: Simon & Schuster, 1974).

74. Augustine *Retractions* 1.43.3. Quoted by A. H. Armstrong, *St. Augustine and Christian Platonism* (Philadelphia: Villanova University Press, 1967), 17.

75. See especially Augustine *De Genesi ad Litteram* 12.6.15.

76. Ibid., 12.31.59.

77. This is not to say, however, that later interpreters of Augustine were able to hold these trends in check. Both types of dualism had negative, not to say destructive influence (at times) in later years.

78. Augustine *City of God* 12.23.

79. Ibid., 13.33.

80. Gregory of Nyssa *On the Making of Man* 2.

81. E.g., Augustine *City of God* 14.27.

82. Ibid., 14.5.

83. Ibid., 12.22.

84. For a general summary statement on "peace" as an ideal, see ibid., 19.12–13.

85. Leo Scheffczyk, *Creation and Providence*, trans. Richard Strachan (New York: Herder & Herder, 1970), 101, acknowledges Augustine's unwillingness to coordinate world creation and human redemption dialectically—but he sees it as a *fault*—in view of Scheffczyk's own penchant for a theology which entertains that anthropocentric kind of dialectic. Indeed Scheffczyk's own presuppositions lead him to misinterpret Augustine at this point: "Augustine's main concern is to grasp being and the structure of the world, not the economy in which God has set them." Again: "Yet the harmony St. Augustine established at the level of ontological thought was achieved at the expense of the scriptural concept of creation as part of the economy of salvation, beginning with creation; [this] yields to a metaphysical contemplation of the nature and order of the universe." No, this is to force the broad sweep of Augustine's mature thought about creation history—there *is* a universal economy for Augustine—into categories he never intended (thinking of creation as a mere stage for human salvation) and *then* to conclude that his historical vision is really not historical after all, since it is not the particular history Scheffczyk has in mind. Actually, Scheffczyk is too good of a historian to miss this point altogether; so in a note to the first remark he more or less takes back what he has just said in the body of his text:

> This judgment is legitimate even granted the fact that Augustine, in contrast to the lack of the historical dimension of Neoplatonism, had a definite sense of the history of creation, as can be seen especially in the second part of his *City of God* (11 and 12), which demonstrates the meaning and beauty of creation even in the process of growing and becoming. Fundamentally, however, this is a Christian philosophy of history rather than an attempt to see history from the viewpoint of the economy of salvation, as emerges particu-

larly clearly from the fact that the real moving force behind this history comes into operation only after Adam's fall and the schism of the two cities. The philosophy of history underlying *De civitate dei* is concerned more with the revelation of divine justice and wisdom than the leading of the world to Christ. . . . The idea of providence, too, has its place here, though it is drawn not solely from the order of nature, but also, and particularly, from history.

86. Augustine *Enchiridion* 9.29.

87. Augustine *On Predestination* 31. See also 35.

88. Augustine recognized this. Note the "astonishment" he expresses concerning Origen's views, as he rejects them forcefully: *City of God* 10.12.

89. Ibid., 11.21.

CHAPTER 5

1. M. D. Chenu, *Nature, Man, and Society in the Twelfth Century: Essays on New Theological Perspectives in the Latin West*, ed. and trans. Jerome Taylor and Lester K. Little (Chicago: University of Chicago Press, 1968), 36.

2. Charles T. Wood, *The Age of Chivalry: Manners and Morals 1000–1450* (New York: Universe Books, 1970), 72.

3. Quoted, ibid.

4. Cf. Lynn White, Jr., "Natural Science and Naturalistic Art in the Middle Ages," *American Historical Review* 52:3 (April 1947): 421–35.

5. On Dionysius's and John's view of creation, see Leo Scheffczyk, *Creation and Providence*, trans. Richard Strachan (New York: Herder & Herder, 1970), 106–12.

6. Chenu, *Nature, Man, and Society*, 25.

7. Frederick Copleston, *A History of Philosophy*, Vol. 2: *Mediaeval Philosophy: Augustine to Bonaventure* (Garden City, N.Y.: Doubleday & Co., 1962), Part 2, p. 145.

8. Lewis Mumford, *The Myth of the Machine: Technics and Human Development* (New York: Harcourt, Brace, & World, 1966), especially 263–67. René Dubos, *Reason Awake: Science for Man* (New York: Columbia University Press, 1970), 126f.

9. Lynn White, Jr., *Machine Ex Deo: Essays in the Dynamics of Western Culture* (Cambridge: MIT Press, 1968), 71.

10. G. F. Whicher, trans., *The Goliard Poets* (New York: New Directions, 1949), 203. Cited by Wood, *Age of Chivalry*, 72.

11. Cf. George H. Williams, "Christian Attitudes Toward Nature," *Christian Scholars Review* 2 (Fall 1971, Winter 1972): 32: "The monastic and sectarian retreat to the wilderness, the interpretation of it as a provisional paradise, the taming of wild beasts by the saintly hermits and monks, the conversion of the contemplation of the external wilderness into the mystical wilderness and hence garden of delights, is a persistent thrust in Christian history. . . ."

12. See Helen Waddell, *Beasts and Saints* (London: Constable and Company, 1934).

13. Chenu, *Nature, Man, and Society*, 23.

14. Ibid., 20.

15. Ibid., 8.

16. Ibid., 29.

17. Ibid., 33.

18. Ibid., 163.

19. Alan of Lille, "The Lament of Nature."

20. Ibid., 3.120–40.

21. Ibid.

22. Alan of Lille *Theologicae Regulae* 6.626D: "Et sic omnium creatum aut est bonum ab alpha, i.e., naturaliter participes est bonitatis et hoc habet a sua auctore, aut ex alpha et omega, ut rationalis creatura, quae ad beautitudinem qua finis est omnium rerum, tendit." And "The Lament of Nature," 6.627A: "Ex fine igitur sola rationalis creatura bona est . . ."

23. Etienne Gilson, *The Christian Philosophy of St. Thomas Aquinas*, trans. L. K. Shook (New York: Random House, 1956), 189.

24. Cf. ibid., 361: "The sense of hierarchy shows the profound influence of Pseudo-Dionysius on St. Thomas."

25. M. D. Chenu, *Toward Understanding St. Thomas*, trans. A. M. Landry and D. Hughes (Chicago: Henry Regnery, 1964), 301f.

26. Ibid., 304.

27. Ibid., 305.

28. Ibid., 311.

29. Thomas Aquinas *Compendium of Theology* 96.

30. Cf. Scheffczyk, *Creation and Providence*, 147.

31. Thomas Aquinas *Summa Theologica* 1.44.1. Cited by Scheffczyk, *Creation and Providence*, 150.

32. Aquinas *Summa Theologica* 1.74.3.

33. Ibid.

34. Cf. Gilson, *Thomas*, 361: "Between the freely created universe and God the Creator there is an impassable abyss and no other continuity than the continuity of order. Properly speaking the world is an ordered discontinuity."

35. Ibid., 135ff.

36. Aquinas *Compendium of Theology* 130.

37. Aquinas *Summa Theologica* 1.103.6.

38. Ibid.

39. Ibid., 1.110.1.

40. Aquinas *Compendium of Theology* 127.

41. Cf. Scheffczyk's conclusions, *Creation and Providence*, 151, that Thomas tends "to represent creation as something self-contained, an isolated event in the past, to treat it as a mere object for rational analysis. . . ."

42. Gilson, *Thomas*, 183.

43. Aquinas *Summa Theologica* 1.105.5. Similarly, Thomas says that without such self-efficacy the things of nature, as we observe them, would be futile: "the active powers which are seen to exist in all things, would be bestowed on things to no purpose, if these wrought nothing through them. Indeed, all things created would seem, in a way,

to be purposeless, if they lacked an operation proper to them, since the purpose of everything is its operation" (ibid).

44. Aquinas *Summa Theologica* 1.47.2.

45. Ibid., 1.96.1.

46. Ibid.: "Properly speaking, a corporeal thing cannot be subject to the stain of sin, nevertheless, on account of sin corporeal things contract a certain unfittingness for being appointed to spiritual purposes."

47. Aquinas *Compendium of Theology* 152.

48. Ibid., 167.

49. Aquinas *Summa Theologica* 1.110.4. Quoted by Louis Monden, *Signs and Wonders: A Study in the Miraculous Element in Religion*, no trans. (New York: Desclee Company, 1960), 47. See his discussion of Thomas's view of miracles; he calls it a "debased conception" (pp. 46f.).

50. Aquinas *Summa Theologica* 1.47.1.

51. Ibid., 1.72.1.

52. Ibid.

53. Aquinas *Compendium of Theology* 101.

54. Aquinas *Summa Theologica* 1.50.3.

55. Aquinas *Compendium of Theology* 148.

56. Cf. John N. Wright, *The Order of the Universe in the Theology of Thomas Aquinas* (Rome: Apud Aedes Universitatis Gregogianne, 1957), 157, commenting on the *Summa Contra Gentiles* 6.2.7: ". . . the ultimate end of the whole process of generation is man. The same is true of the process of conservation. Furthermore, all things work for the utility of man."

57. Cf. Wright, *Order of Universe*, 149: "Concretely the order of the universe as tending to God means entirely the disposition of divine providence in working out the salvation of man. It would not be accurate to say 'entirely,' because the angelic activity maintaining their own beatitude belongs to this order."

58. Aquinas *Summa Theologica* 1.96.1.

59. Ibid., 3.91.1.

60. Cf. ibid., 1.73.1.

61. Ibid., 1.23.2.

62. Ibid., 1.73.1.

63. Ibid.

64. Ibid., 3.91.1. To this Thomas adds another psychological reason, pertaining to human fulfillment: "Man loves the whole world naturally and consequently desires its good. Therefore that man's desire be satisfied the universe needs also be made better" (ibid.).

65. Apart from the rather undefined idea, which Thomas does not really pursue, that human love for the world requires its renewal. See n. 63.

66. See Aquinas *Compendium of Theology* 151, 152, 153.

67. Aquinas *Summa Theologica* 3.91.4.

68. In this context, Aquinas also invokes the principle of whole and part, *Summa*

Theologica 3.91.4: "it is fitting that the whole and part should have the same disposition." But this seems to beg the question before him: why the renewal of the dwelling? He seems to assert that the whole world should be renewed because it is fitting that the whole world should be renewed. Not only does this answer look questionable on these logical grounds, moreover, but "the whole" in question is only the four material elements, the rudiments of nature, not the concrete world of nature which was the human creature's actual dwelling. But why is it fitting that *that* whole should be renewed?

69. Ibid., 3.91.5.

70. Ibid.

CHAPTER 6

1. The theme of history, not usually at home in this conceptuality, does emerge in Bonaventure's thought in a way which it does not seem to be in evidence in Alan's. Bonaventure was influenced by the apocalyptic periodization of history set forth by Joachim of Fiora. But that historicizing motif does not seem to have influenced his theology of nature, as it did Augustine's. Nature seems to be viewed by Bonaventure through the more spatial categories of hierarchical thought, here akin to Alan. History seems to be a category chiefly, if not exclusively, used by Bonaventure to interpret human experience. On Bonaventure's thought about history, see Bernard McGinn, "The Significance of Bonaventure's Theology of History," *Journal of Religion* 58, supplement (1978): S64–S81.

2. An overview of Bonaventure's thought, with numerous references to other works in the field, can be found in John P. Dourley, *Paul Tillich and Bonaventure: An Evaluation of Tillich's Claim to Stand in the Augustinian-Franciscan Tradition* (Leiden: E. J. Brill, 1975), chap. 4.

3. Leonard J. Bowman, "The Cosmic Exemplarism of Bonaventura, "*Journal of Religion* 55:2 (April 1975): 181–98, see especially 187.

4. Ibid.

5. Here following the analysis of Ewert Cousins, "St. Bonaventure, St. Thomas, and the Movement of Thought in the Thirteenth Century," in *Bonaventure and Aquinas: Enduring Philosophers*, ed. Robert W. Shahan and Francis J. Kovach (Norman, Okla.: University of Oklahoma Press, 1976), 5–23.

6. Cited by Cousins, "St. Bonaventure," 18. Bonaventure is probably indebted to Alan of Lille at this point; see Dourley, *Paul Tillich*, 119.

7. Cousins, "St. Bonaventure," 18, observes instructively, that by placing the absolute fecundity of God within the Trinity, Bonaventure "has saved both God and the world. He has rescued the divine fecundity by freeing it from the limits of creation, and he has preserved the world by protecting it from God's overwhelming power. If the only way the divine fecundity could be actualized were in creation. . . , this could produce a static world in which all possibles must be actualized or so enmesh God in the world for his own self-actualization that his transcendence would be swallowed up in creation."

8. Ibid., 19.

9. Zachary Hayes, *The Hidden Center: Spirituality and Speculative Christology in St. Bonaventure* (New York: Paulist Press, 1981), 13.

10. Quoted by Bowman, "Cosmic Exemplarism," 191.

11. Hayes, *Hidden Center*, 160.

12. Ibid., 16.

13. Ibid., 160.

14. Ibid., 161.

15. Gregory of Nyssa advanced this idea (see Paulos Gregorios, *The Human Presence: An Orthodox View of Nature* [Geneva: World Council of Churches, 1978], chapter 5), as did Theodore of Mopsuestia (see Jaroslav Pelikan, *The Christian Tradition: A History of the Development of Doctrine*. Vol. 1: *The Emergence of the Catholic Tradition 100–600* [Chicago: University of Chicago Press, 1971], pp. 234f.).

16. Bowman, "Cosmic Exemplarism," 195. Cf. Hayes, *Hidden Center*, 17:

> As the emanation of creation from God may be expressed also in the imagery of descent, it becomes clear that the return of creation to God may be expressed in the imagery of ascent. As the emanation from God involves increasingly distant levels of God-likeness, the return to God implies ever fuller levels of God-likeness. As light moves away from its source, it becomes weak and diffuse; but as it approaches nearer to its source, it is gathered together and is united. The image of the circle appears again, for the emanation-descent and the return-ascent, which represent a dispersion and a unification, appear as a circle which closes back on its beginning. The meaning of [this] reduction is best understood if we keep in mind that in Bonaventure's view, all of the physical universe is related to humankind as to its proximate end. It is, therefore, in and through the human race that the universe will come to its completion.

17. Ewert Cousins, "Introduction," *Bonaventure: The Soul's Journey Into God, the Tree of Life, the Life of St. Francis*, trans. idem (New York: Paulist Press, 1978), 26.

18. Ibid., 115.

19. Cf. Hayes, *Hidden Center*, 218:

> Bonaventure's theological vision remains in intimate contact with the experience of Francis of Assisi, reflecting similar perceptions of God, Christ, and the world. Yet, upon closer comparison, it appears that the Seraphic Doctor has integrated Francis' experience of nature and of Christ into a synthesis that includes the Augustinian way of interiority and the Dionysian approach to God. . . . The Christ-centered spirituality characteristic of Francis and the perception of the presence of God in the whole creation so characteristic of the Poverello are integrated with the inner way and the mystical tradition to form the stages of the soul's spiritual journey. Without any loss to its fundamental inspiration, the way of Francis is enriched by being integrated into a fuller context, and out of the meeting of these traditions there emerges the spirituality which moves in and through the creatures of the visible world, in· and through the world of the soul, through speculation on the mystery of God, to arrive at the threshold where stands the Exemplar in the form of the

crucified Christ who invites the soul to leave behind the efforts and the images of intellectual speculation and pass over the threshold into the mystery of divine love embodied in the form of the Crucified as He made Himself known to Francis in the experience of Alverna.

20. Cf. Cousins, "St. Bonaventure," especially 22:

> Thomas . . . represents another Christian response to the Islamic problematic. Like Bonaventure and like the orthodox Muslims, he does not place Aristotle above revelation. But unlike Bonaventure, Thomas is less of the Sufi and closer to the orthodox Islamic position emphasizing the polarity between God and the world. In so doing, he makes a stronger affirmation of the Semitic sense of God's transcendence than Bonaventure does. I am, of course, not denying that there are significant dimensions of divine immanence clearly expressed in Thomas' thought. My point here is that, seen against the background of the Islamic problematic, the emphasis on transcendence in Thomas is drawn more sharply into focus.

21. See Joseph Anthony Mazzeo, *Structure and Thought in the Paradiso* (Ithaca, N.Y.: Cornell University Press, 1958), 42.

22. Ibid., 42f.

23. Ibid., 15.

24. Ibid., 18.

25. Dante *Paradiso* 1.103–12.

26. Dante *Purgatorio* 18.28. Cited by Mazzeo, *Structure and Thought*, 53.

27. Dante *Purgatorio* 19.62.

28. Ibid., 14.148–50.

29. Ibid., 28.40–42.

30. Dante *Paradiso* 1.136. Cited by Mazzeo, *Structure and Thought*, 169.

31. Mazzeo, *Structure and Thought*, 21.

32. Ibid., 4.

33. Dante stands in the tradition of Bonaventure at this point, among other names which might be mentioned. Also, in the background is the whole world of monastic culture; see Jean Leclercq, *The Love of Learning and the Desire for God: A Study of Monastic Culture*, trans. Catharine Misrahi (New York: Fordham University Press, 1960). He writes: "The mountain of the return is the symbol of the monastic mystery. . . . The monastery is then a Jerusalem in anticipation, a place of waiting and desire, of preparation for that holy city towards which we look with joy" (68f.). "The Jerusalem above is the end the monk strives for. He will rise toward it through everything which calls to mind—and gives reality to—an ascension, and this introduces a whole series of themes" (70). He points out, in this connection, that St. Bernard left more sermons on the ascension of Christ than on the passion. He further quotes a twelfth-century monk who took the name of John of Fecamp, a highly influential writer in his time: "May your soul leave this world, traverse the heavens themselves and pass beyond the stars until you reach God" (78).

34. Erich Auerbach has argued in *Dante, Poet of the Secular World*, trans. Ralph

Mannheim (Chicago: University of Chicago Press, 1961), that notwithstanding all this emphasis on the sublimely transcendent realities of God, Dante is in fact a harbinger of the new kind of consciousness, characteristic of the modern period, with a strong this-worldly accent. Witness Dante's extensive commentary on the events of his own time in the *Inferno*. That may indeed be a proper reading of the great thirteenth-century poet. But Dante is surely, in any case, a spokesperson for his own period as well.

35. See Edward A. Armstrong, *St. Francis: Nature Mystic, The Derivation and Significance of the Nature Stories in the Franciscan Legend* (Berkeley, Calif.: University of California Press, 1973), 35–41.

36. See ibid., 71f.

37. Ibid., 209.

38. *Speculum Perfectionis* 113. Cited by Armstrong, *St. Francis*, 90.

39. Celano *Vita Prima* 80. Cited by Armstrong, *St. Francis*, 144.

40. Celano *Vita Prima* 45. Cited by Armstrong, *St. Francis*, 11.

41. See Armstrong, *St. Francis*, 23ff.

42. Celano *Vita Prima* 59. Cited by Armstrong, *St. Francis*, 171.

43. Celano *Vita Prima* 61. Cited by Armstrong, *St. Francis*, 160.

44. Celano *Vita Secunda* 165. Cited by Armstrong, *St. Francis*, 148.

45. *Speculum Perfectionis* 115. Cited by Armstrong, *St. Francis*, 10.

46. *Fioretti*. Cited by Armstrong, *St. Francis*, 68.

47. *Sacrum Commercium*. Cited by Omer Englebert, *St. Francis of Assisi: A Biography*, trans. and ed. Edward Hutton (London: B. Oates, 1950), 119.

48. Celano *Vita Prima* 58f.: Cited by Englebert, *St. Francis of Assisi*, 188f.

49. Celano *Vita Prima* 116. Cited by Armstrong, St. Francis, 221.

50. Celano *Vita Prima* 55. Cited by Englebert, *St. Francis of Assisi*, 118.

51. *Sacrum Commercium*. Cited by Englebert, *St. Francis of Assisi*, 119.

52. Celano *Vita Prima* 84. Cited by Armstrong, *St. Francis*, 133.

53. Celano *Vita Prima* 84. Cited by Armstrong, *St. Francis*, 133.

54. Francis *Office of the Lord's Passion*. Cited by Englebert, *St. Francis of Assisi*, 487, n. 5.

55. Francis *Office of the Lord's Passion*. Cited by Englebert, *St. Francis of Assisi*, 487, n. 5.

56. Ray C. Petry, "Medieval Eschatology and St. Francis of Assisi," *Church History* 9:1 (March 1940): 54–69. See literature he cites, 55–58.

57. Ernst Benz, *Ecclesia Spiritualis: Kirchen Idee und Geschichts Theologie der Franziskanischen Reformation* (Stuttgart: W. Kohlhammer, 1934).

58. Ibid., 163.

59. Ibid.

60. Armstrong, *St. Francis*, 31.

61. For an overview of Joachim's thought, see Ernst Benz, *Evolution and Christian Hope: Man's Concept of the Future from the Early Fathers to Teilhard de Chardin*, trans. Heinz G. Frank (Garden City, N.Y.: Doubleday & Co., 1966), chap. 3.

62. Armstrong, *St. Francis*, 30.

63. Ibid., 42.

64. Ibid.

65. Celano *Vita Prima* 80. Cited by Armstrong, *St. Francis*, 60.

66. Celano *Vita Prima* 80, 81. Cited by Armstrong, *St. Francis*, 9.

67. Celano *Vita Secunda* 217. Cited by Armstrong, *St. Francis*, 239.

68. Englebert, *St. Francis of Assisi*.

69. See chapter 5, n. 8 above.

CHAPTER 7

1. *Luthers Werke Kritische Gesamtausgabe {Schriften}* (Weimar), 39.1.205 (hereafter cited as *WA*).

2. *WA* 40.2.327.

3. See Edward A. Dowey, *The Knowledge of God in Calvin's Theology* (New York: Columbia University Press, 1952).

4. John Calvin *Institutes of the Christian Religion* 1.1.1 (hereafter cited as *Institutes*).

5. See n. 23 below.

6. Martin Luther, *Lectures on Genesis (Chapters 1–5)*, Vol. 1 of *Luther's Works*, ed. Jaroslav Pelikan (St. Louis: Concordia Publishing House, 1955), 47.

7. *WA* 42.31.32.

8. Cf. *WA* 48.201.5: "All creation is the most beautiful book or Bible, in it God has described and portrayed himself." Cited by Heinrich Bornkamm, *Luther's World of Thought*, trans. Martin H. Bertram (Saint Louis: Concordia Publishing House, 1958), 179.

9. *WA* 48.628.13ff.: "Heaven and earth are gradually growing old, and the strength of the rest of the creation is not as it was at the beginning of the creation." Cited by Werner Elert, *The Structure of Lutheranism*, Vol. 1, trans. Walter A. Hansen (St. Louis: Concordia Publishing House, 1962), 42. Luther believed that the flood caused most of the deterioration. See Marjorie Hope Nicolson, *Mountain Gloom and Mountain Glory: The Development of the Aesthetics of the Infinite* (Ithaca, N.Y.: Cornell University Press, 1959), 100ff.

10. Luther, *Lectures on Genesis*, 205.

11. *WA* 42.155f.

12. John Calvin, *Commentaries on the First Book of Moses Called Genesis*, Vol. 1, trans. John King (Edinburgh: Edinburgh Printing Company, 1847), 96. See *Institutes* 1.14.22.

13. See Langdon Gilkey, *Reaping the Whirlwind: A Christian Interpretation of History* (New York: Seabury Press, 1976), 175–87.

14. Ibid., 178.

15. *Institutes* 1.16.5.

16. *Institutes* 1.5.5.

17. Cf. Calvin, *Commentaries on the First Book*, 64: "After the world had been created, man was placed in it as a theatre, that he, beholding above him and beneath him wonderful works of God might reverently adore their author." On the knowledge of God "after the fall," see *Institutes* 1.6.1.

18. Cf. *Institutes* 3.25.10: "For though we very truly hear that the Kingdom will be

filled with splendour, joy, happiness, and glory, yet when these things are spoken of, they remain utterly remote from our perception, and, as it were, wrapped in obscurities, until that day comes when he will reveal to us his glory, that we may behold it face to face." On the other hand, he does affirm the traditional doctrine: "God will restore the present fallen world to perfect condition at the same time as the human race." (*Commentary on Romans* 8:21, cited by Charles Partee, *Calvin and Classical Philosophy* [Leiden: E. J. Brill, 1977], 49.)

19. Gilkey, *Reaping the Whirlwind*, 176.

20. Ibid., 177.

21. Ibid., 185.

22. This is a much-discussed and much-contested point, especially in the wake of the famous studies by Weber and Tawney. Here, however, there is no intent to suggest that the spirit of Calvinism *caused* the rise of capitalism.

23. It might be argued that Calvin has an implicit dialectic of world creation and human salvation insofar as election precedes creation, in his thinking. That being the case, so it could be said, creation becomes a kind of stage necessary for the realization of election in time. Thomas had posited such an idea, with his doctrine that human beatitude in heaven is the chief end of creation. It also became popular in much of modern theology, as we will see presently. But Calvin does not employ the idea of election that way. Although it is pretemporal for him, he consistently treats the doctrine in the context of his discussion of the church and faith. Cf. Dowey, *Knowledge of God*, 186, 187: "It was characteristic of Reformed theology orthodoxy to place the decrees of God in the theological system before the doctrine of creation. Although Calvin's view of God's predestination is supralapsarian, it always appears in his systematic work as part of soteriology." "Regardless of the fact that the decrees precede creation, *sub specie aeternitatis*, the only saving relation to God is through Christ in faith." Along with this, Calvin repeats the traditional answer, which we saw expressed by Augustine, to the question why God created the world: "If the cause is sought by which he was led once to create these things, and is now moved to preserve them, we shall find that it is his goodness alone" (*Institutes* 1.5.6.).

24. *Institutes* 1.14.20.

25. Ibid.

26. John Calvin, *Opera Selecta* 9.793, 795. Cited by Francois Wendel, *Calvin: The Origin and Development of His Thought*, trans. Philip Mamet (New York: Harper & Row, 1963), 34.

27. *Institutes* 1.14.21.

28. Ibid., 1.5.1.

29. E.g., *WA* 40.1.94.

30. *WA* 10.143; on Heb. 1:3.

31. Martin Luther, *Sermons on the Gospel of John (Chapters 1–4)*, Vol. 22 of *Luther's Works*, ed. Jaroslav Pelikan (St. Louis: Concordia Publishing House, 1957), 26.

32. *WA* 23.134.34–23.136.36. Cited by Bornkamm, *Luther's World*, 189.

33. Martin Luther, *That These Words of Christ, 'This is My Body,' etc. Still Stand Firm*

Against the Fanatics, Vol. 37 of *Luther's Works*, ed. Helmut T. Lehmann (Philadelphia: Fortress Press, 1961), 57f.

34. Ibid., 338.

35. See H. Paul Santmire, *Brother Earth: Nature, God, and Ecology in a Time of Crisis* (New York: Thomas Nelson, 1970), 141.

36. Martin Luther, *Lectures on Genesis (chapters 1–5)*, Vol. 1 of *Luther's Works*, ed. Jaroslav Pelikan (St. Louis: Concordia Publishing House, 1955), 42.

37. Martin Luther, Small Catechism, in *The Book of Concord*, trans. and ed. Theodore G. Tappert (Philadelphia: Fortress Press, 1959).

38. *WA–TR* 1:1160. Cited by Bornkamm, *Luther's World*, 184.

39. Luther, *Sermons on the Gospel of John*, 496.

40. Martin Luther, *Selected Psalms*, Vol. 12 of *Luther's Works*, ed. Jaroslav Pelikan (St. Louis: Concordia Publishing House, 1955), 119, 121.

41. Edwin A. Burtt, *The Metaphysical Foundations of Modern Physical Science*, revised ed. (London: Kegan, Paul, Trubner, 1932), 236f.

42. See S. Korner, *Kant* (Harmondsworth, England: Penguin Books, 1955), 55.

43. Ibid.

44. Cf. Immanuel Kant, *Critique of Pure Reason*, A 216, B 263.

45. Ibid., A 698, B 726.

46. Ibid., A 799, B 827.

47. Ibid., B 446n.

48. Ibid., A 550, B 578.

49. Immanuel Kant, *Religion Within the Limits of Reason Alone*, trans. T. M. Green and H. H. Hudson (New York: Harper & Row, 1960), book 3.

50. See Santmire, *Brother Earth*, 102.

51. Lewis Mumford, *Technics and Civilization* (New York: Harcourt Brace, 1934), 25. See also idem, *The Myth of the Machine*.

52. Closer analysis shows, indeed, that *class* interests, the desire of some to dominate others by dominating nature, played an important role in motivating these developments. See William Leiss, *The Domination of Nature* (New York: George Braziller, 1972), passim.

53. Cited by George Steiner, *In Bluebeard's Castle: Some Notes Toward the Redefinition of Culture* (New Haven, Conn.: Yale University Press, 1971), 7.

54. Leiss, *Domination of Nature*, has traced the growth of this secularization process. He instances Francis Bacon as an illustrative, transitional figure: "When the concept of mastery of nature is thoroughly secularized, the ethical limitations implicit in the pact between God and man, whereby the human race was granted a partial dominion over the earth, lose their efficacy. The religious casing in which Bacon had embedded his plea for a fresh conquest of nature failed, but the idea itself emerged intact and in secular dress fired the imagination of later periods" (54f.).

55. For one concrete picture of some of these developments, see Carlton J. H. Hayes, *A Generation of Materialism: 1871–1900* (New York: Harper & Brothers, 1941).

56. Leiss, *Domination of Nature*, 40f.

57. Ibid., 82.

58. Karl Löwith, "Nature, History, and Existentialism," *Social Research* 9 (March 1952): 83.

59. Albrecht Ritschl, *Instruction in the Christian Religion in Three Essays*, trans. Philip Hefner (Philadelphia: Fortress Press, 1972), par. 8. For a helpful introduction to Ritschl's thought generally, see Hefner's essay in this volume, pp. 1–50.

60. Ibid.

61. Albrecht Ritschl, *The Christian Doctrine of Justification and Reconciliation: The Positive Development of the Doctrine*, trans. H. R. MacKintosh and A. B. Macaulay (Edinburgh: T. & T. Clark, 1900), 222.

62. Ibid., 279.

63. Ibid.

64. Adolph von Harnack, *What Is Christianity?* trans. T. B. Saunders (New York: Harper & Brothers, 1957), 63.

65. Cf. Löwith, "Nature, History, and Existentialism."

66. Roger A. Johnson, *The Origins of Demythologizing* (Leiden: E. J. Brill, 1973).

67. Roger A. Johnson, *Critical Issues in Modern Religion*, ed. Johnson (Englewood Cliffs, N.J.: Prentice-Hall, 1973), chap. 2.

68. Rudolf Bultmann, *Jesus Christ and Mythology* (New York: Charles Scribner's Sons, 1958), 69.

69. Ibid., 64.

70. Ibid., 70.

71. Ibid., 85.

72. Ibid., 15, 61.

73. Emil Brunner, *The Christian Doctrine of the Church, Faith, and Consummation*, trans. D. Cairns (London: Lutterworth Press, 1949), 224.

74. Emil Brunner, *Revelation and Reason*, trans. O. Wyon (Philadelphia: Westminster Press, 1946), 33n.

75. For Bultmann, as Roger Johnson has written (*Critical Issues*, 61), "the end which the kergyma announces is not the end of the world, but the end of a worldly self-understanding; the new age which the kergyma promises is not a new heaven and a new earth, but a new self-understanding which includes a new perspective on the whole of reality."

76. In retrospect, indeed, it seems that the Kantian approach to nature does have some striking *formal*, not material, similarities with gnostic thought, as Allan Galloway has argued, *The Cosmic Christ* (New York: Harper & Brothers, 1951): "The resultant position [of Kant] is one which, despite the wide divergence in the concepts employed, has essentially the same theological implications as the Gnostic dualism which the early church had to counter by reasserting the cosmic significance of the work of Christ. This, of course, is the kind of parallel which we can draw only in the most guarded terms and with extreme caution. . . . The typical Gnostic speculations . . . Kant would disallow as involving the transcendental employment of the categories of the understanding, or else would dismiss as 'fantastical theosophical dreams'" (145). "The only real similarity is in

the practical religious outcome—that is, in the way it affects our religious attitude to our immediate situation in this physical world, the world in which we act. It is in this respect (but only in this respect) that we may justifiably compare the noumenal world of Kant with the Pleroma of the Gnostics." "The Kantian noumenal world is conceived as being of an intelligible nature as contrasted with the immediate environment, which is sensible. The Gnostic Pleroma is conceived as being spiritual and invisible, as contrasted with this world, which is material and visible. The visible phenomenal world in Kant is, by its essential nature as mere appearance, excluded from any participation in the moral and religious values realized in the noumenal world. In Gnostic dualism the visible material world is excluded, by its essential nature as matter, from any participation in the values realized in the Pleroma." "For Kant, this simply meant that the phenomenal world as such has no moral significance whatever, while for the Gnostics it meant that the physical environment was positively evil. But in the long run, the practical effect is the same. . . ." (146) "This means that, for Kant, as for the Gnostics, the final aim of the religious life was to escape from the immediate environment into a realm of spiritual values. To this process our immediate phenomenal experience remains ultimately irrelevant" (146f.) See, further, Galloway's discussion on pp. 147–53, especially the two quotations on 152f., the one from a Valentinian Gnostic, the other from Kant's *Critique of Practical Reason*, where Kant speaks memorably about "the starry heavens above and the moral law within."

77. M. H. Abrams, *Natural Supernaturalism* (New York: W. W. Norton, 1971).

78. On Tillich, see Norman Young, *Creator, Creation, and Faith* (Philadelphia: Westminster Press, 1976), chap. 6; and Clifford Green, chapter 12 of *Critical Issues in Modern Religion*, ed. Roger A. Johnson.

79. See Paul Tillich, "Nature and Sacrament," *Protestant Era*, trans. James Luther Adams (Chicago: University of Chicago Press, 1957), 77f.: "In later Ritschlianism faith became the means of elevating the ethical personality above nature to moral independence, leaving nature to technical control." "Although the faith of which, for instance, a man like William Hermann speaks, is in itself warm, powerful, and passionate, its function in the context of the technological interpretation of reality is the creation of the personality of the victorious bourgeoisie."

80. See Paul Tillich, *Systematic Theology*, Vol. 1 (Chicago: University of Chicago Press, 1951), section 3: "Being and God."

81. See n. 79.

82. In his own systematic reflection, it is interesting to note, Kaufman's approach to nature is identifiably Kantian, yet it stands at the edge of Kantianism in some respects also. In his *Systematic Theology: A Historicist Perspective* (New York: Charles Scribner's Sons, 1968), he affirms that the end (*telos*) of the creation is the creation of a community of persons, as Kant and Ritschl had said (see 322f.), but he is self-consciously *agnostic* about God having *other* purposes with nature: "Whatever additional meaning the physical universe and plant and animal life have, a central dimension of their significance is the environment they provide for the development of a community of free spirits created in God's own image" (215f.). Indeed: "God may well be working out a

variety of purposes in and through the creation, most of which are completely unknown to us; belief that God has revealed his intentions for human history does not entail the conclusion that we know everything he is doing in the world" (302). Kaufman goes still further, even, it seems, beyond his self-chosen agnosticism, in a note affirming that the way God works with humanity reveals to us how God works with the creation as a whole (290n). Then, on that—fragile—basis Kaufman suggests what he calls an ethic of "benevolence" for "all being" (295f.). It seems that Kaufman is struggling here to give expression to the ecological motif, but that his Kantian categories do not readily allow him to do this. Cf. further his essay, "On the Meaning of 'Act of God,'" in *God the Problem* (Cambridge: Harvard University Press, 1972), chap. 6, where he relates the idea of the universal divine agency to the whole creation, to both nature and human history, not just to human history alone.

83. For a more detailed description of these trends, see H. Paul Santmire, "Epilogue: The Birthing of Post-Modern Religion," *Critical Issues in Modern Religion*, ed. Roger A. Johnson, 435–44.

CHAPTER 8

1. The thought of Paul Tillich will not be considered in this chapter. This might seem like a glaring omission, in view of what we have already had occasion to observe about his theology. He clearly has a rich appreciation for nature, and that appreciation is theologically well-grounded. The ecological motif has shaped his thinking thoroughly. As such, Tillich's thought has affinities with Luther's and Augustine's, as we noted. But Tillich writes self-consciously "on the boundary" of classical Christian thought. This is indicated most dramatically, perhaps, by his "hyper-personalism," his refusal to think of God in personal terms. He asserts that the personal is rooted in God, not that God is personal. This doctrine indicates that Tillich's own assessment of his thought is appropriate; he does belong at the boundary of the classical tradition. Further, that boundary position, particularly his hyper-personalism, takes him out of the tension in the middle of the tradition, which in many ways makes the theology of nature so problematic for classical Christian thought: to confess a personal God who is Lord of—impersonal—nature. Some critics of the Christian tradition would perhaps maintain that the only way for Christians to have both God and nature is to follow Tillich's path. That may be. But that is moving outside of the classical theological tradition, as we know it in the West. And hence Tillich, and others like him, cannot rightfully be the object of sustained attention in this study. On the other hand, precisely because he does occupy a position on the boundary, and because his theology is so suggestive at so many points, Tillich can be a dialogue partner and a theological resource for anyone who is interested in the kind of issues we are dealing with in this study. For Tillich's own discussion of personalism and related issues, see especially *Biblical Religion and the Search for Ultimate Reality* (Chicago: University of Chicago Press, 1955).

2. Karl Barth, *The Humanity of God*, trans. John N. Thomas (Richmond: John Knox Press, 1960), 37.

3. Ibid., 43.

4. Ibid., 45.

5. Ibid., 46.

6. G. C. Berkouwer, *The Triumph of Grace in the Theology of Karl Barth*, trans. Harry R. Boer (Grand Rapids: Wm. B. Eerdmans, 1956).

7. This kind of observation is a commonplace in the literature on Barth. Cf. the quotations cited by Robert Jenson, *Alpha and Omega: A Study in the Theology of Karl Barth* (New York: Thomas Nelson, 1963), 18, n. 5.

8. See H. Paul Santmire, "Creation and Nature: A Study of the Doctrine of Nature with Special Attention to Karl Barth's Doctrine of Creation" (Th.D. diss., Harvard University, 1966), 30–35.

9. Karl Barth, "How My Mind Has Changed," *Christian Century* 56:37–38 (September 13, 20, 1939).

10. Ibid., 1132.

11. Karl Barth, *Church Dogmatics* (Edinburgh: T & T Clark, 1936–61), 1.1, p. 135.

12. Cf. ibid., 2.2, par. 33.

13. Ibid., 2.2, p. 8.

14. Ibid., 2.2, p. 59.

15. Ibid., 2.2, p. 183n.

16. Ibid., 2.2, pp. 116f.

17. Ibid., 2.2, par. 34.

18. Ibid., 3.2, p. 342.

19. Ibid., 3.2, p. 155n.

20. Ibid., 3.1, p. 97.

21. See the references cited by Santmire, *Creation and Nature*, 58, n. 2.

22. Cf. Barth, *Church Dogmatics*, 3.1, par. 41.

23. Ibid., 3.3, p. 48.

24. Ibid., 3.1, p. 44.

25. Ibid., 3.3, p. 46.

26. Ibid., 3.3, p. 48.

27. Ibid., 3.3, p. 80.

28. Ibid., 2.2, pp. 7f.

29. Ibid., 3.1, p. 18.

30. Ibid., 3.1, p. 213.

31. Ibid., 3.1, pp. 171, 376.

32. Ibid., 3.1, pp. 156f.

33. See the references cited by Santmire, *Creation and Nature*, 72, n. 3.

34. Barth, *Church Dogmatics*, 3.2, p. 14.

35. Ibid., 3.1, p. 44.

36. Ibid., 3.1, pp. 44, 54n.

37. Ibid., 3.3, p. 47.

38. Ibid., 3.3, p. 30.

39. Ibid., 3.1, pp. 369f.

40. Barth did not finish his dogmatics, so we will never know how he envisioned the future of nature, what he would have done with the New Testament expectation of a new heaven and a new earth in which righteousness dwells. But the logic of his thought

everywhere suggests that the cosmos indeed has no permanent value, that it could easily be discarded at the very end, because its service had been completed.

41. Barth, *Church Dogmatics*, 3.2, p. 137.

42. Ibid., 3.3, pp. 436f., n. 432.

43. Ibid., 3.3, pp. 426f.

44. Ibid., 3.3, pp. 432f.

45. Ibid., 3.2, par. 43.

46. See Santmire, *Creation and Nature*, 151f.

47. This is how Arthur Lovejoy, *The Great Chain of Being* (New York: Harper & Brothers, 1936), 244, describes the temporalizing of the great chain of being: "The *plenum formarum* [fullness of metaphysical forms] came to be conceived by some, not as the inventory but as the program of nature, which is being carried out gradually and exceedingly slowly in the cosmic history. While all the possibles demand realization, they are not accorded it all at once. Some have attained it in the past and have apparently since lost it; many are embodied in the kind of creatures which now exist; doubtless infinitely many more are destined to receive the gift of actual existence in the ages that are to come. It is only of the universe in its entire temporal span that the principle of plenitude holds good. The Demiurgus is not in a hurry, and his goodness is sufficiently exhibited if, soon or late, every Idea finds its manifestation in the sensible order."

48. Pierre Teilhard de Chardin, *Letters From a Traveller*, trans. B. Wall, R. Hague, V. Hammersley, and N. Linday (New York: Harper & Row, 1962), 296.

49. Whether Teilhard's "phenomenology" is simply good natural science, as he apparently thinks, or metaphysics done under the guise of science, as some of his interpreters think, can be left an open question here.

50. Teilhard, letter, 7 October 1948. Cited by Christopher Mooney, *Teilhard de Chardin and the Mystery of Christ* (Garden City, N.Y.: Doubleday & Co., 1968), 169.

51. Teilhard de Chardin, *The Phenomenon of Man*, trans. Bernard Wall (New York: Harper & Row, 1959), 302.

52. This seems to imply that even apparently "dead" entities such as rocks and neutrons have some consciousness. Teilhard is not a panpsychist in an unqualified sense, however. The "within" of electrons, for example, is for him extremely undifferentiated and disintegrated, approaching nothingness. Further, there can be no question, in his mind, of communion somehow with a stone or a tree.

53. Teilhard, *Phenomenon of Man*, 188.

54. Ibid., 209.

55. Pierre Teilhard de Chardin, *The Future of Man*, trans. N. Denny (New York: Harper & Row, 1964), 39.

56. Teilhard, *Phenomenon of Man*, 220.

57. Ibid., 229.

58. Ibid., 271.

59. Pierre Teilhard de Chardin, *Science and Christ*, trans. René Hague (New York: Harper & Row, 1969), 79: "God did not will individually . . . the sun, the earth,

plants, or Man. He willed his Christ; and in order to have his Christ, he had to create the spiritual world, and man in particular, upon which Christ might germinate; and to have man, he had to launch the vast process of organic life . . . ; and the birth of that organic life called for the entire cosmic turbulence." "At the beginning of the perceptible world what existed was the Multiple; and that Multiple was already rising up, like one indissociable whole, towards spirit under the magnetic influence of the universal Christ who was being engendered in it."

60. See Claude Stewart, "Nature In Grace: A Study in the Theology of Nature" NABPR Dissertation Series, No. 3 (Macon, Ga.: Mercer University Press, 1983), chap. 4.

61. Teilhard, *Science and Christ*, 51.

62. Pierre Teilhard de Chardin, *The Divine Milieu: An Essay on the Interior Life*, no trans. (New York: Harper & Row, 1965), 56.

63. Ibid. Cited by Mooney, *Teilhard de Chardin*, 161.

64. J. A. Lyons, *The Cosmic Christ in Origen and Teilhard de Chardin: A Comparative Study* (Oxford: Oxford University Press, 1982), 206, is more charitable to Teilhard than the facts of the case merit: "What is not so clear in this account of the Pleroma with its talk of material carried beyond itself is the ultimate destiny of the material matrix itself. Teilhard does not always distinguish clearly between that and the intelligent particles that arise out of it. In its transformation does the material matrix come to an end, or is the material environment itself to be thought of as continuing. This issue is left unresolved." On the contrary, the whole logic of Teilhard's thought, as well as numerous specific statements (in addition to those cited above, see the following), demonstrate that Teilhard *took it for granted* that the "material matrix" is abolished at the very end: "One day the whole divinisable substance of matter will have passed into the souls of men; all the chosen dynamism will have been recuperated: and then our world will be ready for the Parousia" (Teilhard, *Divine Milieu*, 86).

"In a convergent universe, every element finds its fulfillment, not directly in its own perfection, but in its incorporation into the unity of a superior pole of consciousness in which it can enter into communion with all others. Its worth culminates in a transmutation into the other, in a self-giving excentration" (idem, *Future of Man*, 76).

Will this not be the outcome of humankind at the end, Teilhard asks: "leaving earth and stars to lapse slowly back into the dwindling mass of primordial energy, it will detach itself from this planet and join the one true, irreversible essence of things, the Omega Point? . . . An escape from the planet not in space or outwardly, but spiritually and inwardly" (*Future of Man*, 122f.).

"The end of the world: The Wholesale internal introversion upon itself of the noosphere, which has simultaneously reached the uttermost limits of its complexity and its centrality. . . . The end of the world: the overthrow of equilibrium, detaching the mind, fulfilled at last, from its material matrix, so that it will henceforth rest with all its weight in God-Omega" (Teilhard, *Phenomenon of Man*, 287f.).

"To the extent that it is personalized, the grain of consciousness becomes free of its material phyletic support. Detached from its matrix of complexity, which draws it to the Multiple, the reflective center, unified in itself, can finally join the ultimate pole of all convergence." Cited by Catherine Regina O'Connor, "Woman and the Cosmos: The Feminine in the Thought of Pierre Teilhard de Chardin" (Ph.D. diss., Fordham University, 1970), n. 56.

"The material vastness of the universe will disappear. When the end of time is at hand, a terrifying spiritual pressure will be exerted on the confines of the real, built up by the desperate efforts of souls tense with longing to escape the earth" (Teilhard, *Science and Christ*, 84).

"The Incarnation will not be complete until that chosen portion of the substance contained in every object, spiritualized in a first time in our souls, and again along with our souls in Jesus, has finally joined itself to the Center of its fulfillment" (idem, *Divine Milieu*, 30).

"The Curve of consciousness, pursuing its course of growing complexity, will break through the material framework of time and space to escape. Somewhere toward an ultra center of unification and wholeness" (idem, *Future of Man*, 180f.).

At the end there will be nothing but consciousness: "Within a now tranquil ocean, each drop of which nevertheless will be conscious of itself, the astounding adventure of the world will have ended" (idem, *Science and Christ*, 85).

Also, see the many quotations which point in the same direction cited by Mooney, *Teilhard de Chardin*, e.g., 119, 125, 159, 161, and 196–98.

65. Cf. Thomas King, *Teilhard's Mysticism of Knowing* (New York: Seabury Press, 1981), 30: "Sometimes Teilhard is a lyrical poet speaking in praise of matter; sometimes Teilhard is an idealist philosopher speaking of the triumph of mind. The difference is found in the great paradox: matter is non-being that *is*; it only reflects. . . . Stability and consistence are reflected throughout the earth, but they are found 'behind us' where Christ bestows them on the rising Flux of Spirit. Behind us spirit is being rendered eternal, hard, firm and durable; the cement is settling; the molten alloy of spirit is in the process of solidification."

66. Pierre Teilhard de Chardin, "The Spiritual Power of Matter," *Hymn of the Universe*, trans. Simon Bartholomew (London: Collins, 1965), 68.

67. Ibid., 69.

68. Ibid.

69. Pierre Teilhard de Chardin, "The Evolution of Chastity," in *Toward the Future*, trans. René Hague (New York: Harcourt Brace Jovanovich, 1973).

70. Ibid., 65f.

71. Ibid., 68.

72. Ibid., 70.

73. Ibid., 72.

74. Cf. the summary of Teilhard's poem in Henri de Lubac, *The Eternal Feminine*, trans. René Hague (New York: Harper & Row, 1970), chap. 2.

75. Teilhard, "The Evolution of Chastity," 72.

76. Ibid., 72ff.

77. Ibid., 84.

78. Ibid., 85.

79. Ibid., 82.

80. Ibid., 86f.

81. Pierre Teilhard de Chardin, *The Heart of the Matter*, trans. René Hague (New York: Harcourt Brace Jovanovich, 1978), 16.

82. Cf. the judgment of Emile Rideau, *The Thought of Teilhard de Chardin*, trans. René Hague (Harper & Row, 1967), 186f.: "Teilhard . . . has little to say about the participation of the cosmos in the collective transfiguration of the consciousness. The material substructures of the universe, it would seem, have fulfilled their part by *releasing* [his italics] spirit, which, in a sort of coincidence, becomes one with Omega-Christ." "Mutual charity has so important a place in Teilhard's eschatology that it would justify the concept of the universe re-born through the mediation of conscious minds that have opted, in time, for the ideal of communion and justice. Every advance in human relations (whether close or distant), every improvement in social structure, is not simply an image and preparation of, but an anticipation of the eternal kingdom of charity. Only sin can prevent this approximation from being carried to its limit. Thus the 'divinization of the cosmos' should be taken as applying to matter only insofar as matter has an integral share in the progress of the spiritual communion of minds, in particular through technical transformations."

83. A historical account of any tradition obviously has to end somewhere, even though the tradition itself continues. And any point of termination will be in some sense arbitrary, just as the selection of representative figures along the way must in some sense be arbitrary. Barth and Teilhard, surely, do not bring the biblical-classical tradition in the West to a close! The reader not familiar with contemporary Christian theology in the West is encouraged to consult the writings of Protestants such as Jürgen Moltmann, Wolfhart Pannenberg, Langdon Gilkey, James Cone, Dorothee Soelle, Gordon Kaufman, and John Cobb, and Catholics such as Karl Rahner, Edward Schillebeeckx, Gustavo Gutiérrez, Hans Küng, Rosemary Radford Ruether, and David Tracy, in order to gain some sense about Western theological developments in the second half of our century. In this connection the aforementioned study by Claude Stewart, "Nature in Grace," will provide a helpful perspective about the theological models which have been employed in recent years in reflection about nature by theologians and will therefore facilitate the reader's assessment of the contemporary theological discussion generally with regard to our topic. Beyond all this, moreover, a more indigenous "Third World" kind of theological reflection is emerging in our time. This kind of theology appears to be drawing on new—to Western eyes—appreceptions of nature, rooted, for example, in African or Asian cultural traditions. Any student of the theology of nature will want to turn to such works as soon as they become available. Nevertheless, as far as Western theological reflection about nature is concerned, Barth and Teilhard do bring the biblical-classical tradition to a certain resting place, if not to an end. For they raise the questions and bequeath the ambiguous legacy with which any contemporary Christian thinker, who wishes to take the biblical-classical tradition of reflection about nature seriously, must begin.

CHAPTER 9

1. See Brevard S. Childs, *Biblical Theology in Crisis* (Philadelphia: Westminster Press, 1970), and the literature he cites, especially the works by James Barr. See also Barr's more recent summary, "Biblical Theology," in the *Interpreter's Dictionary of the Bible* Supplementary Volume (Nashville: Abingdon Press, 1976).

2. This is true, as we saw, notwithstanding his accent on human election "before the creation." Of great importance for his understanding of human salvation, it is a relatively singular theme in his thought as a whole. Contrast the systematic exploitation of the doctrine in Barth's thought.

3. Like Origen, Teilhard takes pains to stress that he believes in the resurrection of the body; but, although he can show that he does this in a way that is more convincing than Origen's, his final word is not all that compelling, particularly when compared to the balanced treatment of the subject we find in Augustine.

4. G. W. H. Lampe, "The New Testament Doctrine of *ktisis*," *Scottish Journal of Theology* 17:4 (December 1964): 449–62.

5. G. Ernest Wright, *God Who Acts: Biblical Theology as Recital* (Chicago: Alec R. Allenson, 1952).

6. Gerhard von Rad, "The Theological Problem of the Old Testament Doctrine of Creation," *The Problem of the Hexateuch and Other Essays*, trans. E. W. Trueman Dicken (New York: McGraw-Hill, 1966), 131–43.

7. Rudolf Bultmann, *Jesus Christ and Mythology* (New York: Charles Scribner's Sons, 1958).

8. Lampe, "New Testament Doctrine," 449.

9. Ibid.

10. Ibid., 430.

11. Ibid., 452.

12. Ibid., 450.

13. Ibid., 452.

14. Ibid.

15. Ibid., 453.

16. Ibid.

17. Ibid., 454.

18. Ibid., 455.

19. Ibid.

20. Ibid., 455f.

21. Ibid., 456f.

22. Ibid., 459.

23. Ibid.

24. Ibid., 456.

25. Wright, *God Who Acts*, 42.

26. Ibid., 26.

27. Ibid., 46.

28. Ibid., 43.

29. Bultmann believes that Christianity and Gnosticism stand together in their removal of God and humanity from—what for him is—the fateful web of nature, but that Gnosticism does not break away from the propensity to ontologize (that is, it uses naturalistic categories) God and humanity. See his *Primitive Christianity in Its Contemporary Setting*, trans. R. H. Fuller (New York: Meridian Books, 1956): "The New Testament understands human existence as a historical existence. The Gnostics on the other hand, attribute everything to fate, and therefore they understand human existence in the categories of natural being" (194). "The discovery of the absolute distinction between humanity and its objective environment, the discovery made in the experience of the blows of fate, is nullified when that distinction is interpreted in ontological terms, as can be seen by the use of the phrase 'being saved by nature'" (202).

30. Bultmann, *Primitive Christianity*, 20.

CHAPTER 10

1. This schematization, it virtually goes without saying, will not permit us to touch on every disputed exegetical question pertaining to the biblical theology of nature. In particular, we will not be able to give any attention to the much-discussed question concerning the Old Testament understanding of human dominion over the earth. Champions of the critical ecological wisdom and their fellow travelers have made much of the—alleged—Old Testament understanding of humanity's "domination" of the earth. Some have suggested, with varying degrees of historical sophistication, that the Old Testament theology of dominion lies behind the environmental crisis in our century: "domination," in their eyes, has become exploitation. But this topic, and others like it, must remain a secondary exegetical consideration here. Our concern is deeper: with underlying theological motifs and their influence, which, as a matter of fact will fundamentally shape the results of our interpretation of individual exegetical questions. (Those who wish to pursue the particular question about the meaning of human dominion over nature in the Old Testament, may consult the following studies, each of which moves the discussion beyond the influence of the spiritual motif in significant ways: James Barr, "Man and Nature: The Ecological Controversy and the Old Testament," in *Ecology and Religion in History*, ed. David and Eileen Spring [New York: Harper & Row, 1974], 61f., originally published in the *Bulletin of the John Rylands Library* 55:1 [Autumn 1972]: 9–32; Bernard W. Anderson, "Human Dominion Over Nature," *Biblical Studies in Contemporary Thought*, Trinity College Biblical Institute [Somerville, Mass.: Green & Hadden, 1957].)

2. Gerhard von Rad, "The Promised Land and Yahweh's Land in the Hexateuch," *The Problem of the Hexateuch and Other Essays*, trans. E. W. Trueman Dicken (New York: McGraw-Hill, 1966), 79–93.

3. Walter Brueggemann, *The Land: Place as Gift, Promise, and Challenge in Biblical Faith*, Overtures to Biblical Theology (Philadelphia: Fortress Press, 1977), 6.

4. Ibid.

5. Ibid., 3.

6. Ibid., 48.

7. Ibid., 49.

8. Ibid., 51.

9. Claus Westermann, *Blessing: In the Bible and the Life of the Church*, Overtures to Biblical Theology, trans. Keith Crim (Philadelphia: Fortress Press, 1978).

10. Ibid., 4.

11. Ibid., 6.

12. Ibid., 48ff.

13. Johannes Pedersen, *Israel, Its Life and Its Culture*, Vols. 1–2 (London: G. Cumberledge, Oxford University Press, 1953), 170, 458, 459, 474.

14. Walther Zimmerli, *The Old Testament and the World*, trans. John J. Sullivan (London: SPCK, 1976), 7.

15. Gerhard von Rad, "The Theological Problem of the Old Testament Doctrine of Creation," *Problem of the Hexateuch*, 131.

16. But see the critique of James Barr, *Old and New in Interpretation: A Study of Two Testaments* (New York: Harper & Row, 1966), 75f. Barr points out that "there is no doubt that [von Rad's] fixation of 'faith,' 'salvation,' 'confession' and even 'Yahwistic' is to a large extent theological, in the sense that it depends on models of understanding which cannot be tested and approved against the Old Testament itself directly." He argues further that von Rad's demonstration that doctrine of creation is not "independent" means very little, since that question is raised, as it were, in the abstract and does not emerge from his dealing with the intentionality of the Old Testament texts themselves.

17. Cf. Walther Zimmerli, *Old Testament Theology in Outline*, trans. David E. Green (Atlanta: John Knox Press, 1978), 23: "it is quite clear that the Old Testament, however much it thinks of Yahweh as majestic and free, knows this God from the very outset as the God who wants to involve himself with Israel. In the Old Testament we never come across any attempt to inquire into the nature of Yahweh *per se*."

18. Quoted by G. Ernest Wright, *The Old Testament and Theology* (New York: Harper & Row, 1969), 97. Cf. also John Bright, *The Kingdom of God: The Biblical Concept and Its Meaning for the Church* (Nashville: Abingdon Press, 1953); and Rudolf Schnackenburg, *God's Rule and Kingdom*, trans. John Murray (New York: Herder & Herder, 1963).

19. Von Rad, *Problem of the Hexateuch*, 142: ". . . in genuinely Yahwistic belief the doctrine of creation never attained to the stature of a relevant, independent doctrine . . . [it was] invariably related and subordinated to soteriological considerations."

20. George M. Landes, "Creation and Liberation," *Union Seminary Quarterly Review* 33:2 (Winter 1978): 80. Cf. Helmer Ringgren, *Israelite Religion*, trans. David E. Green (Philadelphia: Fortress Press, 1966), 104ff.

21. Landes, "Creation and Liberation," 80.

22. Cf. Hans Heinrich Schmid, "Schöpfung, Gerechtigkeit und Heil: Schöpfungstheologie als Gesamthorizont biblischer Theologie," *Zeitschrift für Theologie und Kirche* 70 (1973): 1–19.

23. Cf. Otto Eissfeldt, "El and Yahweh," *Journal of Semitic Studies* 1 (1956): 36: ". . .

in its beginning, the concept of Yahweh as Creator of the world and king of the gods had already taken shape in the period before Israel became a state." Cf. also Walther Eichrodt, *Theology of the Old Testament*, Vol. 2, trans. I. A. Baker (Philadelphia: Westminster Press, 1967), 230f.: "Certainly it is possible to point to the fact that Babylonian creation myths and the Egyptian contemplation of nature supplied Israelite thought with varied material—possibly through the mediation of Canaanite festivals and cultic hymns—and stimulated it in many ways. But it should not be forgotten, that the most influential assumptions supporting the subjection of the whole natural order to the mighty authority of a divine Lord were attached in the religion of ancient Israel to the covenant God, who not only led the people in war, but also granted them Canaan as the land of inheritance, and thus was naturally worshipped as the giver of all the blessings of nature and everything else that went with the fuller life of civilization." Cf. further the balanced estimate of Frank M. Cross, Jr., *Canaanite Myth and Hebrew Epic: Essays in the History of the Religion of Israel* (Cambridge: Harvard University Press, 1973), 143f.:

> Study of the mythic pattern of Bronze Age Canaan and the history of traditions of the episode at the Reed Sea in Israel's literature reveal a dialectic in the evolution of Israelite religion and religious institutions. Israel's religion in its beginning stood in a clear line of continuity with the mythopoeic patterns of West Semitic, especially Canaanite myth. Yet its religion did emerge from the old matrix, and its institutions were transformed by the impact of formative historical events and their interpretation by elements of what we may call Proto-Israel which came together in the days of Moses and in the era of the Conquest. . . . The reenactment of primordial events of cosmogonic myth gave way to festivals reenacting epic events in Israel's past, thus renewing her life as a historical community. . . . It will not do to describe the process as a progressive historicizing of myth. Even in Hegel's dialectic, the movement from the natural to the historical was complex, and the modern historian presumably permits no metaphysical principle to motivate the movement from natural to historical consciousness. The Canaanite mythic pattern is not the core of Israel's epic of Exodus and Conquest. On the other hand, it is equally unsatisfactory to posit a radical break between Israel's mythological and cultic past and the historical cultus of the [twelve tribe] league. The power of the mythic pattern was enormous. The Song of the Sea reveals this power as mythological themes shape its mode of presenting epic memories. It is proper to speak of this counterforce as the tendency to mythologize historical episodes to reveal their transcendent meaning. The history of the Exodus-Conquest theme illustrates this dialectic well.

24. Arthur Weiser, *The Psalms: A Commentary*, trans. Herbert Harwell (Philadelphia: Westminster Press, 1962), 255ff.

25. In some respects, standing within the context of the classical Christian theological tradition in the West is not always the best vantage point from which to view the faith of ancient Israel. Thought concerning God as Creator and Redeemer is one of these

instances. In his study of classical Christian thought about creation, Leo Scheffczyk, *Creation and Providence*, trans. Richard Strachan (New York: Herder & Herder, 1970), has documented how in the early Christian centuries the theology of creation (the First Article of the Creed) began to be separated from the theology of redemption (the Second Article). Later in the tradition, moreover, the theology of creation became something of an independent undertaking, which was related closely to various metaphysical speculations about nature and the world in general. It is no wonder, then, that thought about God the Creator in the Old Testament has been something of a puzzle to modern students of the Scriptures. Apart from Genesis 1, they have found nothing that appears to them to be a "doctrine of creation," as that expression came to be understood in Western theology. This is a point where John Reumann's otherwise illuminating study, *Creation and New Creation: The Past, the Present, and Future of God's Creative Activity* (Minneapolis: Augsburg Publishing House, 1973), needs some correction; by raising the question whether creation is superior to redemption or vice versa, he is really asking a question that is appropriate for modern Christian thought, but which is anachronistic in the context of Hebraic faith. This point is all the more applicable to von Rad's essay on the Old Testament doctrine of creation, "The Theological Problem." See n. 15 above. On the unity of creation and redemption in the Old and New Testaments, and the integrity of each in the greater scheme of things according to biblical thought, see the thoughtful discussion by Edward Schillebeeckx, *Christ: The Experience of Jesus as Lord*, trans. John Bowden (New York: Crossroad Publishing Company, 1983), 515–53.

26. Psalm 136 gives us a good glimpse of the richness and the fluidity of this kind of celebration of Yahweh's lordship. It is predicated on the experience of his mercy or his steadfast love (*hsd*). This is the Yahweh of Israel's most ancient memories. But that God was already known then as a God of power and wisdom as well. The psalmist therefore needs only to focus his vision more fully on all those facets of the ancient God of Israel. First he gives thanks to the God of gods and Lord of lords (vv. 1–3). Then he celebrates Yahweh's wondrous power and understanding in nature (vv. 4–9). Next he praises Yahweh for the deliverance from Egypt and for leading the people to the land of promise (vv. 10–22). Finally he concludes by praising the God who rescues people from their foes and who feeds all the creatures of the earth (vv. 23–26). The psalmist is not concerned to distinguish God the Creator and God the Redeemer, surely not to consider "which is more important." He is, however, concerned to celebrate the lordship of Yahweh, to praise his Lord's help in time of trouble, his Lord's wonderful power throughout the whole creation, and his Lord's care for all creatures.

Likewise for the prophecies of 2 Isaiah. Although this exilic prophet focuses virtually all of his attention on the people's situation in exile and the proclamation of hope for their future, he also does not really distinguish between God the Creator and God the Redeemer. So much is this the case that a recent book-length study of this prophet, by Carroll Stuhlmueller, bore the title *Creative Redemption in Deutero-Isaiah* (Rome: Biblical Institute Press, 1970).

27. Cf. Claus Westermann, *Genesis 1—11: A Commentary*, trans. John J. Scullion (Minneapolis: Augsburg Publishing House, 1984), pp. 175–76:

It is not possible to regard Gen. 1 directly and without reservation as the beginning of salvation history or even as its preparation. The reason why this chapter is at the beginning of the Bible is so that all God's subsequent actions—his dealings with humankind, the history of his people, the election and covenant—may be seen against the broader canvas of his work in creation. . . .

The Old Testament has something of its very own to say about the creator and creation; this must be left intact, and must not be seen merely in relation to salvation history. . . .

The simple fact that the first page of the Bible speaks about heavens and earth, the sun, moon, and stars, about plants and trees, about birds, fish, and animals, is a certain sign that the God whom we acknowledge as the Father of Jesus Christ is concerned with all these creatures, not merely with humans. A God who is understood only as the God of humankind is no longer the God of the Bible.

28. Cf. S. R. Driver, *The Book of Genesis*, 2d ed. (London: Methuen & Co., 1904), 5: "It [the notion of God creating by his word] is an indication not only of the ease with which He accomplished His work, and of His omnipotence, but also of the fact that he works consciously and deliberately. Things do not emanate from him unconsciously, nor are they produced by a mere act of thought, as in some pantheistic systems, but by an act of *will*, of which the concrete word is the outward expression. Each stage of the creation is the realization of a deliberately formed purpose, the 'word' being the mediating principle of creation, the means or agency through which his will takes effect."

29. Schillebeeckx, *Christ: The Experience of Jesus as Lord*, 202.

30. At this point, as at others, Alfred North Whitehead's oft-cited judgment that the biblical-classical tradition understands faith in God as faith in an "oriental despot" needs radical revision.

31. The theme of wisdom became, of course, the subject of a large literature, continuous with the Priestly writer and Psalm 104, yet moving, as a whole, in its own independent direction. For one summary of this trend in Old Testament theology, see Harvey H. Guthrie, Jr., *Theology as Thanksgiving: From Israel's Psalms to the Church's Eucharist* (New York: Seabury Press, 1981), chap. 4.

32. Cf. Eichrodt, *Theology of the Old Testament*, Vol. 2, pp. 113, 155f.

33. Driver, *Book of Genesis*, 5. So also Gerhard von Rad, *Genesis*, trans. John H. Marks (Philadelphia: Westminster Press, 1972), 50.

34. For a comprehensive study of the rise and meaning of the apocalyptic literature, see Paul Hanson, *The Dawn of Apocalyptic: The Historical and Sociological Roots of Jewish Apocalyptic Eschatology*, revised ed. (Philadelphia: Fortress Press, 1975).

35. Ernst Käsemann, "The Beginnings of Christian Theology," *New Testament Questions of Today*, trans. W. J. Montague (Philadelphia: Fortress Press, 1969), 82–108.

36. Cf. Amos Wilder's careful statement, after a thorough review of the scholarly discussion of Jesus' eschatological expectation, in *Eschatology and Ethics in the Teaching of Jesus*, revised ed. (New York: Harper & Row, 1950), 50: "Jesus felt himself part of,

and a witness to, a great redemption-transaction being effected by God in his generation. This he proclaimed in both prophetic-messianic and apocalyptic terms. That is, he
could use terms drawn from the older messianism, like the allusion to the thrones of
David, or from the new apocalyptic, like the references to the Son of Man. The main
point is that he saw a world-process underway and moving toward its climax, and called
upon men to recognize it and commit themselves to it. All this he saw and presented in
terms of Israel first of all. His proclamation was both by word and by deed of healing
and exorcism. All this evidences the arriving eschaton. Its outcome he saw as the Kingdom of God or the life of the age to come." On the "parables of growth" in particular,
see N. A. Dahl, "The Parables of Growth," *Studia Theologica* 5:2 (1951): 132–66.

37. Edward Schillebeeckx, *Jesus: An Experiment in Christology*, trans. Hubert Hoskins
(New York: Crossroads Publishing Company, 1981).

38. William Manson, in *Eschatology: Scottish Journal of Theology Occasional Papers*, No.
2 (London: Oliver & Boyd, 1963), 11, 15, 8.

39. See, for example, James H. Cone, *A Black Theology of Liberation* (Philadelphia:
J. B. Lippincott Company, 1970), chap. 6.

40. J. Christiaan Beker, *Paul the Apostle: The Triumph of God in Life and Thought*
(Philadelphia: Fortress Press, 1980).

41. Commentators sometimes note the similarity between texts such as Romans
11:36 and "Stoic formulae." It may well be the case that there was a borrowing going on
here, at some point in the development of the earliest tradition (perhaps mediated
through Hellenistic Judaism), much as there was a certain borrowing of Canaanite imagery going on in ancient Israel's monarchical and post-monarchical epochs. But it is
another matter to discount these formulae as if they meant nothing, given their apparent Stoic origins, as the Bultmann school tends to do. As if the Apostle were not trying
to say something when he quoted them! As if he were so rhetorically pedestrian as to
tuck "throw-away quotes" into his discourse, as some modern preachers have been
known to do, meaning nothing in particular by them, only intending a kind of rhetori-
cal halo effect!

42. Schillebeeckx, *Christ: The Experience of Jesus as Lord*, 241.

43. Ibid., 182.

44. Ibid., 184. See also C. H. Talbert, "The Myth of a Descending-Ascending Redeemer in Mediterranean Antiquity," *New Testament Studies* 22 (1976), 418–40.

45. This discussion has been reviewed (through 1973) by John Reumann, *Creation
and New Creation*, 42–57.

46. This hymn, in its original form, was one of a number of early Christian hymns—
Phil. 2:6–11 was another—which apparently had a common origin in Hellenistic
Christianity, yet with Jewish roots (ibid., 44f.). These hymns celebrate the resurrected
Christ's present lordship and show a diminished interest in what for Paul was always a
key point, the resurrection to come. But these hymns are not products, it appears, of a
gnostic climate. Their roots, rather, are best traced to the world of Jewish wisdom speculation. (So Eduard Lohse, *Colossians and Philemon*, Hermeneia—A Critical and Histor-

ical Commentary on the Bible, trans. William R. Poehlmann and Robert J. Karris, ed. Helmut Koester [Philadelphia: Fortress Press, 1971], 46, 50; and F. W. Beare, "Colossians," *Interpreter's Bible* [Nashville: Abingdon Press, 1955].) Which means, as should be clear from a prima facie reading of the Colossians pericope, that we have to do here with an affirmative "creation theology," not a negative gnostic denial of the created order.

In this context, the Pauline redactor apparently sought to qualify the original creation-hymn with more normative Pauline themes. He specified (see the underlines in the text) that Christ's body is not the world, as the original hymn probably took it to be, but the church. Likewise, he took pains to explain how God "reconciled all things" and "made peace" through Christ: it was "by means of the blood of the Cross." To see Christ's body as the church and the cross as a key revelation of God for this world brought the hymn much more into the orbit of Pauline theology than it was before.

The question is, however, what are the implications of this redaction? Here one group of scholars, largely from the school of Bultmann, although not exclusively, stress the *contrast* between the theology of the hymnic source and the theology of the Pauline author. Thus Eduard Lohse comments that the Pauline author's additions "arrest for all attempts to utilize the hymn for the purpose of a natural or cosmic theology" (60).

But did the Pauline author mean to deny Christ as lord of the whole creation? If that were the case, then he might *not* have quoted the hymn; or he might have said that Christ is *not* the cosmic lord in so many words. Later, indeed, he refers to Christ as "head of all rule and authority" (2:10). So presumably the content of the whole hymn, the first strophe on creation, as well as the second on redemption, was on his mind. Likewise, we can well imagine that he knew of Paul's identification of Christ with the Creator in 1 Cor. 8:6, or, at least, of that aspect of Paul's theology, and did not want to deny that.

John Gibbs has instructively observed in this connection that evidence is lacking that the Pauline author would have us believe that the first part of the edited hymn must have its meaning solely in terms of the second part, "unless a theological presupposition that Pauline theology was only soteriological counts as evidence" ("Pauline Cosmic Christology and the Ecological Crisis," *Journal of Biblical Literature* 90 [1971]: 471). Lohse himself allows that "the hymn emphasizes the universal significance of the Christ-event by exhibiting its cosmic dimensions and speaking of salvation for the whole world, including the whole creation" (60f.). This is the same Lohse who also holds that the edited hymn cannot be properly employed in discussions of contemporary cosmic Christology! Is not the latter point protesting a little too much? Is he not more dependent on his—Bultmannian—presuppositions and less on his exegesis than he might be aware?

It seems much more to the biblical point, therefore, to maintain that there is a certain *critical continuity* between the original hymn and the Pauline theology of Colossians. Whereas the hymn in its original form collapses what for Paul was an apocalyptic distance between Christ the first fruits and the future general resurrection (on this see

Beker, *Paul the Apostle*, 181 et passim), the Pauline author of Colossians seeks to reemphasize Paul's "eschatological reservation" (Käsemann) by highlighting the church and its mission, and the reality of the cross as a sign of Christian existence before the final consummation. But the Pauline author surely also means to take seriously the cosmic role of Christ, as Paul himself had already done in 1 Cor. 8:6.

It is as if we were to read an essay on the American frontier: "He spent the rest of his days walking in the foothills of the Rockies. Often he would visit with his friends in town." If it were discovered that the second sentence were an editorial addition, would that mean that the editor was denying that the man spent a lot of time walking in the foothills of the Rockies? No, it would mean that the editor also wanted to draw attention to the fact that the man had a gregarious bent as well, that his life was lived both in solitude with nature and with the company of friends. This is the kind of critical continuity that seems to obtain in the case of the redaction of the original hymn in Col. 1:15ff.

Once the framework of critical continuity is established, however, as the base line for our interpretation, we must not neglect the fact that that continuity is indeed critical! At this point we can be instructed by a comment Bultmann makes in his *Theology of the New Testament*, Vol. 1, trans. Kendrick Grobel (London: SCM Press, 1955), 181f., referring to the New Testament's interest in the cosmic character of Christ's work. "But," he says, "the question now is whether this cosmic occurrence is to be understood as only a sublime process of nature which takes place bypassing, so to say, my conduct, my responsibility, my decisions—a process which has me at its mercy for better or for worse."

47. Beare, "Colossians."

48. Ibid. Cf. also his comment: the verb "hold together" is a perfect, "expressing the state of the universe as an ordered system."

49. Henry Chadwick, "Ephesians," *Peake's Commentary on the Bible*, ed. Matthew Black and H. H. Rowley (London: Thomas Nelson, 1962), 859a.

50. Schillebeeckx, *Christ: The Experience of Jesus as Lord*, 203.

51. Ibid.

52. Ibid., 202.

53. Ibid.

54. Thus Athanasius writes that the Word, while incarnate in Jesus, was still "present in all things by its own power, giving order to all things, and overall and in all, revealing his own providence, and giving life to each thing and all things, quickening the whole universe." Cited by Payne, *The Holy Fire: The Stories of the Fathers of the Eastern Church* (New York: Harper & Row, 1957), 71.

55. Hans Conzelman, *The Theology of St. Luke*, trans. Geoffrey Buswell (New York: Harper & Row, 1960).

56. Regarding 2 Peter, see Ernst Käsemann, *Essays on New Testament Themes* (Philadelphia: Fortress Press, 1982), chap. 8.

57. Beker, *Paul the Apostle*, 162.

58. Conzelman, *Theology of St. Luke*, especially 136. On Mark and Matthew, see Karl

Paul Donfried, *The Dynamic Word: New Testament Insights for Contemporary Christians* (San Francisco: Harper & Row, 1982), chaps. 4 and 5.

59. Beker, *Paul the Apostle*, 33.

60. Ibid., 364.

61. Cf. Donfried, *Dynamic Word*, chaps. 7 and 8, who describes this "trajectory," drawing especially on the major commentary on John by Raymond Brown.

62. Beker, *Paul the Apostle*, 156.

63. Ibid.

64. Ibid.

65. Schillebeeckx, *Christ: The Experience of Jesus as Lord*, 326.

66. Ibid., 307.

67. Ibid., 314.

68. Ibid.

69. Ibid., 321f.

70. Ibid., 322.

71. Ibid., 326.

72. Ibid.

73. Ibid.

74. Ernst Käsemann, *The Testament of Jesus: A Study of the Gospel of John in Light of Chapter 17*, trans. Gerhard Krodel (Philadelphia: Fortress Press, 1968), 64.

75. Ibid., 36.

76. Cf. ibid., 59: "There is no indication in John that love for one's brother would also include love toward one's neighbor, as demanded in the other books of the New Testament. On the contrary, John here sets forth an unmistakable restriction such as we also know from the Qumran community."

77. Ibid., 61.

78. Ibid., 60.

79. Ibid., 64.

80. Ibid., 65.

81. Ibid., 66.

82. Ibid., 62.

83. Ibid., 63.

84. This comes to expression especially in Bultmann's great work, *The Gospel of John: A Commentary*, trans. G. R. Beasley-Murray (Philadelphia: Westminster Press, 1975).

85. Schillebeeckx, *Christ: The Experience of Jesus as Lord*, 285.

86. Ibid., 239.

87. Ibid., 275.

88. In putting the question this way, it should be clear, the point is that we must decide which motif is to offer us the primary hermeneutical context for our biblical interpretation in this respect. The point is not that we must somehow choose between, say, Paul and John, as if only one or the other could legitimately claim the allegiance of faith in our day. Further, that some hermeneutical decision such as this *will* be made in any case seems clear. The history of interpretation of the biblical theology of nature in this

century surely shows that such a choice was in fact made: the great majority of biblical interpreters took the spiritual motif for granted as their primary interpretive context (see the discussion above in chapter ten, part two). The plea of this study here is that we should be self-conscious about making this choice and understand what the exegetical and constructive-theological stakes are.

INDEX

Marcion, 32, 233 n.65
Markus, R. A., 231 n.44, 232 n.60, 234
  nn.10, 11
Marx, Karl, 137, 160
Maximus the Confessor, 36
Mazzeo, Joseph A., 245 nn. 21–24, 30,
  31
Metaphor of ascent, 16, 17–23, 34–35,
  44, 46, 51, 56, 59, 61, 63, 72–73,
  76, 88, 94, 101, 103, 105, 121, 122,
  145, 151, 153, 158, 159, 169, 170,
  176–83, 189, 195–96, 211, 215
Metaphor of fecundity, 16, 17–23,
  39–41, 44, 46, 56, 59, 72–73, 76,
  88, 94, 101, 110, 130, 145, 151,
  158, 159, 169, 176–83, 189,
  195–96, 199, 203, 205, 207, 208,
  210, 215
Metaphor of migration to a good land, 16,
  23–25, 38–41, 51, 56, 59, 72–73,
  76, 104, 131, 145, 151, 158, 159,
  169, 176–83, 189, 196, 203, 207,
  208, 210, 215
Metaphors and motifs. See Motifs
Miles, Margaret, 63, 67, 68, 237 nn.45,
  46; 238 nn.64, 68; 239 n.73
Miller, Perry, 227 n.28
Milton, John, 20, 134, 227 n.23
Miracles, according to: Augustine, 63;
  Luther, 130; Thomas Aquinas, 89–90
Models, theological, 257. See also Motifs
Moltmann, Jürgen, 257 n.83
Monden, Louis, 237 n.45, 242 n.49
Mooney, Christopher, 254 n.50, 255
  n.63, 256 n.64
Motifs, 9–10; ecological, 9–10, 25–29,
  43, 44, 56, 60, 72–73, 118–20, 122,
  128, 141, 142, 146, 169, 171, 182,
  189, 195–96, 203, 210, 215, 216,
  217; spiritual, 9–10, 25–29, 52–53,
  60, 120, 127, 138, 140, 141–42,
  145, 155, 164–69, 171, 176,
  182, 189, 195–96, 211, 215,
  216–17, 218; and metaphors, 14–17,
  25–29; and models, 15, 227 n.10
Mumford, Lewis, 78, 135, 240 n.8, 249
  n.51

Nature:
  alienation from, 7, 8, 47–48, 209; ac-
    cording to Origen, 49–53; and the
    early Middle Ages, 77–78. See also
    Gnostics/Gnosticism

Beauties of: according to Augustine,
  61–62, 66–67; Luther, 130;
  Calvin, 128–29
Definition of, 11–12, 222–23
  nn.37–43
Dominion over (human), according to:
  Augustine, 69–70; Barth, 154;
  Bultmann, 139; Calvin, 126–27;
  Irenaeus, 44; Thomas Aquinas,
  91–92; Teilhard, cf. 164, 257 n.82;
  biblical view, 259 n.1; modern secular view, 137, 249 n.54, 251 n.79
Fall of. See Cosmic fall
Future of. See Eschatology
God and, according to: Augustine,
  61–67; Barth, 154; Bonaventure,
  98–100, 101–2; Francis, 108–9;
  Irenaeus, 38–40; Luther and Calvin,
  128–30; New Testament, 200–
  207; Old Testament, 190–92,
  196–99; Origen, 49–51; Teilhard,
  163–64
History of, 62–64. See also Eschatology
Humanity and, according to: Augustine, 69–70; Barth, 154; Francis,
  108–17; Irenaeus, 37–43; Luther
  and Calvin, 130; Origen, 52;
  Teilhard, 161–64; Thomas
  Aquinas, 90–92. See also Human
  body; Nature, dominion over
  (human)
Theology of. See Theology, ecological
Travail of. See Theology, ecological
Newton, Isaac, 133, 136
Nicolson, Marjorie Hope, 227 n.13, 247
  n.9
Nietzsche, Friedrich, 136
Nygren, Anders, 228 n.9

O'Connor, Regina, 256 n.64
Olivers, Thomas, 27, 228 n.30
Origen, 21, 28, 31–54, 55, 56, 59, 65,
  68, 69, 71–73, 75, 77, 78, 83, 84,
  85, 88, 89, 93, 95, 98, 101, 118,
  127, 142, 153, 157, 165, 169, 177,
  178, 179, 181, 188, 216, 229 n.6,
  233–34 nn.69–86, 235 n.20, 240
  n.88, 258 n.3
O'Toole, J., 236 n.40, 237 n.44

Pagels, Elaine, 229 n.7
Pannenberg, Wolfhart, 228 nn.1, 4; 257
  n.83